# Poetry, Pictures, and Popular Publishing

# Poetry, Pictures, and Popular Publishing

*The Illustrated Gift Book and Victorian Visual Culture 1855–1875*

Lorraine Janzen Kooistra

Ohio University Press
Athens

Ohio University Press, Athens, Ohio 45701
www.ohioswallow.com


Printed in the United States of America
Ohio University Press books are printed on acid-free paper ∞ ™

First paperback printing 2022
Paperback ISBN: 978-0-8214-2522-0

*Library of Congress Cataloging-in-Publication Data*

Janzen Kooistra, Lorraine, 1953–
Poetry, pictures, and popular publishing : the illustrated gift book and Victorian visual culture, 1855–1875 / Lorraine Janzen Kooistra.
p. cm.
ncludes bibliographical references and index.
ISBN 978-0-8214-1964-9 (acid-free paper)
1. Gift books—Publishing—Great Britain—History—19th century. 2. Illustration of books, Victorian—Great Britain. 3. English poetry—Illustrations. 4. Publishers and publishing—Great Britain—History—19th century. 5. Art and literature—Great Britain—History—19th century. 6. Books and reading—Great Britain—History—19th century. I. Title.
AY13.A2J36 2011
002.0941'09034—dc22

2011009680

*For Alison, my most Uncommon Reader*

# Contents

# Illustrations

# Acknowledgments

My first grateful thanks go to the women readers who made this book possible.

One of my early memories is of my (virtually Victorian) grandmother Helene listening to my aunt read aloud to her while she embroidered in the quiet afternoons when their housework was done. From the time I could sit up, reading and looking at pictures was a favorite activity with my mother, Irma; now that she can no longer sit or read, we continue to enjoy the Victorian poetry she so often recited. My daughter, Alison, has always shared my delight in pictures, words, and paratextual matter. Her enthusiasm and support for this project were a daily inspiration, and my work has benefited throughout from her keen engagement with its ideas and her remarkable editorial eye. This book is dedicated to her.

Although signed with a single name, this book is very much a work of corporate authorship, with many contributing individuals and institutions. While I cannot name all those to whom I am indebted, I do wish to highlight those who made this project both possible and pleasurable. My first thanks go to David Sanders, former director of Ohio University Press, for his encouragement over the years it took to bring my manuscript from conception to acceptance. I would also like to thank Nancy Basmajian and Sally Bennett for their careful copyediting and Gillian Berchowitz and her staff for their attention to the paratextual details so important to this book's visual/verbal argument. I am enormously grateful to my anonymous readers, whose insights into my nascent arguments and suggestions for improvement were invaluable as I revised the manuscript for publication. Any errors or missed opportunities are, of course, entirely my own responsibility.

I would also like to single out some fellow Victorianists for special thanks. Although I suspect he will no longer recall this, Antony H. Harrison inspired the first formulation of this project. Linda K. Hughes graciously critiqued an early draft of my chapter on the Dalziel gift books and the periodical press. Robin de Beaumont, Paul Goldman, Jan Marsh, Roger Peattie, and Leonard Roberts responded to queries and provided helpful information at various stages of my research. I shall always be grateful to Leslie Howsam for her ongoing interest in my work and her sage counsel. I am also indebted to the research assistants who have contributed to various stages of my work: Constance Crompton, Jennifer Douwes, Abigail Godfrey, Alison Kooistra, and Kathryn Schweishelm.

Dependent as it is on archival sources, this book owes its building blocks to several libraries in Canada and England. I wish to acknowledge the wonderful resource of Pre-Raphaelite literature and Victorian illustrated books contained in the Roger and Marlene Peattie Collection, Queen Elizabeth II Archives and Special Collections, at Memorial University in Newfoundland. I am grateful to the Peatties for the generous sharing of information they provided during my visit. I am also indebted to the Tennyson Research Centre in Lincoln and its director, Grace Timmins, who assisted me so ably during my stay and subsequently answered my numerous queries with good grace. I made repeated trips to the Dalziel Brothers Collection in the Department of Prints and Drawings at the British Museum, and to the Routledge and Kegan Paul Archive, housed in University College London's Special Collections; my thanks to the various staff members who assisted me at these institutions is heartfelt. Much formative work was done at the Ruari McLean Collection of Victorian Book Design and Colour Printing, in the Robertson Davies Library at Massey College, Toronto, and I would like to thank Marie Korey and her staff for their informative assistance.

The research for this book was made possible by the generous funding of the Social Sciences and Humanities Research Council of Canada. An internal grant from Ryerson University's Faculty of Arts and the dean's additional support for a research assistant were also crucial to the successful completion of this project. The timely administrative leaves I received, first from Dr. Andrew Dean, dean of arts and science at Nipissing University, and then from Dr. Carla Cassidy, dean of arts at Ryerson University, enabled me to travel to archives and to dedicate uninterrupted time to the business of writing; I cannot thank them enough for this support. I am also grateful to Dean Cassidy and the Department of English at Ryerson for generously providing additional funding to assist in the preparation of the manuscript for publication.

Conceived, researched, and written during a period of intensive administrative commitments at two different institutions, this book has been a long time in the making. I will always be grateful to my colleagues at Nipissing and Ryerson for their interest and support, as well as to the students whose questions and ideas stimulated my thinking about illustrated books. I would also like to thank the Victorianists at various conferences over the years who have listened to my developing ideas and provided incisive critique, informed suggestions, and collegial encouragement. Parts of chapters 2 and 5 appeared in altered forms in the *Journal of Pre-Raphaelite Studies* (Fall 2005) and *Victorian Poetry* (Spring 2007).

I have saved my last thanks for the men in my life: to Jak, for providing tech support and comic relief, and to John, for everything.

# Introduction

## *Poetry, Pictures, and Popular Publishing*

> "I sing," says the modern Bard, "speaking to the eye alone, by the help of type-founders, papermakers, compositors, ink balls, folding, and stitching."
>
> *Anglo-American*[1]

Taken from an 1847 review of Eliza Cook's poems, the epigraph points to a nineteenth-century recognition of poetry's materiality in print culture. Far from functioning as a uniquely inspired transcendent voice, the "modern Bard" operated within an industrialized publishing industry that—as the magazine's title suggests—had a transatlantic, if not global, reach. Poetry's "author-function" encompassed "type-founders, papermakers, compositors," and all the other workers who built books out of texts and brought them to the reading public.[2] The sensuous address of modern poetry, this critic observes, is principally to the eye.

This recognition of poetry's visuality underscores two critically important points I take up in this study. The first is that at the moment the text becomes embodied form and enters the material world, the "eye" of the reader replaces the "I" of the poet, affirming the book's human uses and social destinations. The second is that, as a material object addressed to the eye, the book occupies a significant position in visual culture: it is an optical instrument for viewing, representing, and forming the world.[3] While this may be true for the book in general, it has special bearing on the gift books of illustrated poetry that proliferated in Britain between 1855 and 1875.

The illustrated book participates in the nineteenth-century process of elevating the image and the reader and detaching the author from the work. As I hope to demonstrate, the role of the periodical press is critically important to this process. This study traces the complex interconnections between the periodical press and the gift books of the "golden age" of wood-engraved illustration, known as "the sixties" and encompassing the decades between 1855 and 1875.[4] As an annual publication whose bindings often branded it as part of a publisher's uniform series, the Christmas book of poetry and pictures was itself a form of serial. Moreover, its reception and audience were constructed through the increasingly sophisticated advertising and marketing mechanisms of the periodical press. Magazines and newspapers in the second half of the century sponsored an extensive reviewing apparatus dedicated variously to "Illustrated Gift Books" (*Illustrated London News* [hereafter abbreviated as *ILN*]), "Christmas Books" (*Saturday Review* [hereafter abbreviated as *SR*]), and "Christmas Gift-Books" (*Athenaeum*) in the weeks leading up to the end of the year. Extended notices, complete with poetic extracts and sample pictures, appeared in illustrated Christmas supplements. These reviews, advertisements, and supplements schooled their readers in a form of bibliographic consumption designed to mark a season organized around the activities of selling, buying, giving, and reading.

The principal criterion for a Christmas book was not seasonal content but rather the material features of ornamental binding and wood-engraved illustration. In brilliant reds, blues, and greens picked out with gilt, the packaging of these books announced their exchange value as gifts to be presented and then displayed: aesthetic objects combining instruction, entertainment, decoration, cultivation, and conspicuous consumption. These ornate illustrated works collectively reviewed as "Christmas books" included a wide variety of subjects; their only common feature might be identified as "pictureability." As the reviews indicate, illustrated gift books typically included works of travel and adventures in exotic lands; books of popular science displaying the beauties of seaweeds, shells, and flowers; religious books; fine-art books; poetry; children's literature; and short fiction.[5]

Among this heap of books piled high on the booksellers' tables each Christmas, volumes of illustrated verses predominated—not because they outweighed the other genres in size of print run or proportion of the market, but because more was at stake in their production and reception. Reviewers gave poetic gift books pride of place in their columns and frequently characterized the ideal

Christmas book as a volume of pictures and poems; in one way or another, all engaged with the way material packaging affected poetry's place in Victorian culture. Some critics saw this ornamental object as a literally closed book, not designed or used for reading at all: a mere "furniture book" for vulgar display that, by its very nature, degraded the poetry associated with it.[6] Others, more confident in the gift book's openness to readers, celebrated its association of poems and images, seeing mass production as a means of disseminating the elite arts of poetry and pictures to an audience in need of cultivation. In this respect, the technologies of the age of mechanical reproduction play a crucial role in the story of this middlebrow artifact, connecting the "high art" of painting and exhibition culture with the mass art of wood engraving and print culture.

In what sense were poetic gift books a form of popular publishing? Although mass-produced, they were clearly not produced for the masses, if we equate the working classes with this undifferentiated term. Nor were they a mass art in terms of the reach and size of their readership in the way that, for example, many illustrated periodicals of the time were. Gift books typically came out in print runs in the thousands rather than the tens of thousands, constituted less than 5 percent of titles published at midcentury,[7] and were aimed at the broad middle classes, who represented about 20 to 25 percent of Britain's population.[8] Produced in the industrialized economy of Victorian print culture and priced at twenty-one shillings—roughly the equivalent of a maidservant's annual salary (Hibbert, *ILN*, 20)—the Christmas gift book appears far removed from any notion of the popular in the sense of a folk culture made by and for the people (although, as I demonstrate in chapter 4, it does have some complex connections with both oral traditions and chapbooks). Drawing on Raymond Williams's *Keywords*, I understand the gift book as a popular form in the sense of a cultural product that "deliberately sets out to win favour" (237). I also recognize that its hostile critics viewed it in the derogatory sense of inferior work, as in "popular literature." For the gift book's proponents, however, the special meaning of *popular* that emerged in the nineteenth century—"presenting knowledge in generally accessible ways"—is certainly relevant (237). As I hope to demonstrate, poetic gift books were a "popular" form of "high" art—that is, mass-produced, accessible forms of the elite arts of pictures and poetry, packaged for a middle-class audience eager for cultivation.

In distinguishing painting (high/fine/elite/unique) and illustration (popular/applied/decorative/mass-produced) and in conceptualizing poetry as the acme of literary production, I invoke traditional categories to clarify what is at stake in the gift book's categorical challenge. However, throughout this study I also employ the less value-laden and more carefully theorized terms used by

Pierre Bourdieu: restricted and large-scale cultural production. *Restricted cultural production* refers to the creation of supposedly noncommercial "art *as art* . . . for a public of producers of cultural goods"—the educated intellectuals and creative elites ("Market," 1232). Opposed to this is middlebrow culture, defined as "the product of the system of large-scale cultural production" (1242). Explicitly market-driven and focused on maximum profits, *large-scale cultural production* is "organized with a view to the production of cultural goods for non-producers of cultural goods, 'the public at large'" (1234). Bourdieu shows how the two fields have unequal symbolic and material values, and how symbolic cultural capital accrues to those with "cultural competence"—that is, the learned ability to appreciate restricted cultural goods (1244). Because this ability is classed and (to a lesser extent) gendered, it is also a status indicator. Connoisseurship of art and poetry thus becomes a means of upward mobility through the display of refinement and cultivation. These desires and tensions, too, are embedded in the illustrated gift book, as a product of large-scale cultural production that carries with it some of the symbolic value of restricted cultural production.

This book offers a case study in what D. F. McKenzie calls "the sociology of texts," an approach to book history that takes into account both the materiality of the works it investigates and their social and cultural functions. Taking as its object a largely forgotten material artifact of middlebrow culture, it proposes that the poetic gift book's brittle and crumbling pages offer new ways of seeing and understanding the high Victorian period. A hybrid form, the poetic gift book linked the elite arts of poetry and pictures with a mode of popular publishing unabashedly commercial. Its raison d'être was its ornate bibliographic form, which connected it to the scopic regimes of spectacle, visual art, material culture, and social status. Made and marketed as a gift to mark a ritual occasion, it connected the commercial world to the domestic home, even as it constructed and interpellated subjects marked by class, gender, and nation. Its recipient was usually a woman, and it lived with her in the space central to Victorian middle-class domesticity: the drawing room. Here, as Thorstein Veblen observed in his *Theory of the Leisure Class* (1899), both recipient and object were on display as material evidence of the household's level of income and cultivation (83–86). But here, too, readers had the opportunity to turn the book's creamy pages—to look at its black-and-white pictures by contemporary British artists and to read its printed poems by national poets. Mass-produced by the Victorian culture industry, the poetic gift book was a standardized form whose ideological and disciplinary manipulation of consumers cannot be ignored. However, I do not wish to lose sight of the fact that it was also a domestic object embedded in the daily lives of women and accessible to their creative work as readers and users.[9]

Historians of the book and reading recognize that "all reading takes place in context" (Colclough, "Readers," 52). Gift books did not fit in masculine pockets or travel between city and suburbs on commuter trains. Their large quarto size and ornately tooled and gilded bindings marked their exhibit value for face-up display on the surface of a table. Gift books were designed for the drawing room, the physical and spiritual center of the Victorian home that functioned as "the status indicator, the mark of gentility, the room from where the woman governed her domain" (Flanders, *Victorian House,* 131). As Thad Logan's detailed *Victorian Parlour* has shown, the parlor or drawing room in the middle-class home was a privileged, feminized cultural space "in which material things simultaneously asserted and concealed a relation to the marketplace" (xiii).[10] If the drawing room was the center of the middle-class home, the center of the drawing room was the circular table with its display of books (2).

It is in this complex material context of domesticity and display that we can begin to understand the aesthetic and ideological features of the poetic gift book as a middlebrow art form. In its ornate architecture, the book symbolically represented the middle-class home itself, and its most cherished values, while also marking boundaries of inside and outside, public and private, female and male, individual and community, nation and world. As I hope to demonstrate, these ornamental books displayed in middle-class homes constitute a crucially important site for our understanding of poetry's *place*—I use the word in all its senses—in nineteenth-century culture.

In reading the book as an expressive form, then, I am not as concerned with inter-art analogies and comparative structures relating image to text as I am with the various ways in which pictures and poems on the printed page build readers and meanings. Gérard Genette has written about the significance of paratextual matter—which he defines as "a heterogeneous group of practices and discourses"—in making texts *present* in the world and available to readers as historicized, material objects (*Paratexts,* 1–2). This study follows Genette's methodology in its examination of both internal elements that present the text materially (for example, bindings, title pages, prefaces, tables of contents, and the like) and external elements that interact with, and constitute, the text in the public sphere (for example, interviews, reviews, publishers' advertisements, catalogs, contracts, letters, and so on) (5). It also takes up as one of its principal points of consideration the "immense continent" of paratextual significance Genette identifies but does not examine: "that of *illustration*" (406).

The multiple roles played by illustration in nineteenth-century print culture do indeed constitute an immense continent. Even while I focus on the poetic gift books produced during the golden age of illustration, I am aware of the enormous variety of wood-engraved images in the periodical press: war journalism by "special artists," scientific drawings and diagrams, rural scenes, fashion plates, zoological specimens, exotic topography, images of train wrecks, caricatures of contemporary life, documentary records of destitution, illustrations for serial fiction and other forms of literature—the list seems endless.

Similarly, if we move from the volume of poetry and pictures promoted as the ideal Christmas present to other illustrated books produced during this period, we immediately enter another enormous terrain. Even if we set aside school and travel books, we are still left with the Victorian novels that Robert Patten, John Harvey, David Skilton, J. Hillis Miller, and others have written about so insightfully; the works of popular science to which Bernard Lightman and Ann Shteir have opened our eyes; and the huge field of children's books explored by many astute scholars, including Richard Dalby, F. J. Harvey Darton, Percy Muir, and Perry Nodelman. Furthermore, the illustrated gift book of the 1860s is positioned between the "Romantic book" surveyed by John Buchanan-Brown and the decorated belles lettres produced at the fin de siècle discussed by Nicholas Frankel, Simon Houfe, and John Russell Taylor, as well as many others. Much as I want to situate the poetic gift book historically and materially as an integral part of visual culture in the third quarter of the nineteenth century, I am well aware that even if I could travel this vast continent comprehensively, my ability to map it remains limited.

In establishing the limits of my synchronic study, I have found it helpful to reimagine Genette's enormous land mass as a vast body of water. Inspired by Lytton Strachey's historiography, I shall be purposely selective as I "row out over that great ocean of material, and lower down into it, here and there, a little bucket, which will bring up to the light of day some characteristic specimen, from those far depths, to be examined with a careful curiosity" (*Eminent Victorians,* vii). In the following chapters, I examine the material form and physical features of selected Christmas gift books produced between 1855 and 1875, attentive to the ways in which their pages bring readers and relationships (social, cultural, ideological, and economic) to the fore. Each chapter presents historicized case studies of individual texts, relating them to specific elements of Victorian visual culture as it overlaps with publishing history. To recognize the contributions of different makers, each chapter also highlights a different aspect of the production process: chapter 1 provides an overview of gift-book commissioning, printing, marketing, and reception, while chapter 2 focuses on illustrators, chapter 3 on engravers, chapter 4 on poets and readers, and chapter 5 on Tennyson and his relationships with his illustrators (especially his female illustrators) and publishers.

Chapter 1, "Reading the Christmas Gift Book," establishes the contexts out of which the illustrated poetic gift book emerged. I distinguish the poetic gift book of the 1860s from the earlier Victorian annuals in terms of its material form, mode of production, and implications for the history of authorship, publishing, and reading. My genealogy begins with James Burns's *Poems and Pictures: A Collection of Ballads, Songs, and Other Poems* (1846), regarded by Victorian critics as "the very first of the Christmas Books of which illustrations were planned with an artistic aim" (*SR,* Dec. 31, 1859, 818). Citing contemporary reviews, I show how the well-bound book combining poetry and artistic illustrations became a standardized object of Christmas gift exchange, directed principally at women, and caught up with notions of British identity and cultural capital.

The gift book moved poetry into popular publishing through its complex associations with visual culture. A hybrid form, the book of wood-engraved pictures and poetry was connected to the graphic vernacular of the periodical press while also asserting some of the elite values of art from the fields of restricted production. In the nineteenth century's age of mechanical reproduction, the gift book's principal technology, wood engraving, facilitated a new modular art form simultaneously unique and multiple. I examine in detail just what this technology meant in terms of bringing a book through the press and connecting it to readers. This chapter also establishes the theoretical and methodological frameworks I use in my analysis of the poetic gift book as an expressive form. A product of corporate authorship, its composited text interpellates a mobile modern reader who is also a producer capable of authorizing uses and meanings.

Chapter 2, "The Moxon Tennyson, Pre-Raphaelite Art, and Victorian Visual Culture," recognizes the important contribution that Pre-Raphaelite artists made to the art of the sixties book and its meanings in both the private reading experience and the public sphere. As is well known, the Pre-Raphaelites were literary artists and poets whose short-lived journal, *The Germ* (1850), announced their combined commitment to "Art and Poetry."[11] Three of the founding members—John Everett Millais, William Holman Hunt, and Dante Gabriel Rossetti—revolutionized the art of illustration by taking their woodblock designs as seriously as their easel paintings. Their pictures for the Moxon Tennyson of 1857 launched the new style of illustration the sixties became known for.

Well known as it is, however, the Moxon Tennyson needs to be examined more thoroughly as a material object in the historical context of its publication and reception. Significantly, the Moxon Tennyson came out in the same month that the first national exhibition, "Art Treasures of the United Kingdom," was held in Manchester. Consequently, its wood-engraved illustrations were immediately caught up in contemporary discourses about art, national culture, and tradition. This chapter explores the complex relationships instituted between the illustrated gift book and the fine art of painting through a synchronic investigation of visual discourses and practices in the formative year of 1857.

In chapter 3, "The Dalziel Brothers' Fine Art Book and the Mass Production of Culture," the focus switches from artists to engravers and from the discursive practices of the field of restricted cultural production to those of large-scale cultural production. In this chapter, I examine the formidable role played by the engraving firm of the Dalziel brothers in the production and reception of Christmas gift books. The Dalziel family of artists and engravers dominated the second half of the nineteenth-century book and periodical trade. They provided cuts for important newspapers and magazines, including the *Illustrated London News*, *Once a Week*, the *Cornhill*, *Good Words*, and *Punch*, and engraved many of the images that have come to be most associated with this period, from Tenniel's illustrations for Lewis Carroll's *Alice* books to the zoological and botanical images in Reverend J. G. Wood's *Illustrated Natural History* series to the Moxon Tennyson and other gift books. They trained both illustrators and engravers and helped establish the careers of many of the period's book artists, including Frederick Walker and Arthur Boyd Houghton. Significantly, they also supported and promoted women writers, featuring the work of women in books produced for domestic consumption.

As we shall see, the Fine Art Books produced by the Dalziels at their Camden Press became, in many ways, synonymous with the Christmas gift book of poems and pictures. Effectively, the Dalziel Fine Art Book was a new form of serial publication, produced specifically for an annual event and caught up in cultural practices associated with the season. This chapter situates the Dalziel gift book in relation to the illustrated poetry published in the periodical press and to print culture's discursive production of Christmas as the British festival of the home. It examines two particular types of Christmas book: the poetic anthology of standard or popular authors illustrated by the original work of contemporary artists; and the gallery of pictures by a popular artist accompanied by the ekphrastic poetry of commissioned authors. Seeking to demonstrate the importance of illustrated poetry to daily middle-class life in the third quarter of the nineteenth century, this chapter investigates how the poems and pictures of the Christmas gift book both expressed and shaped middle-class concepts of childhood, femininity, home, and family, inscribing ideologies of gender, nation, and class in its gilt-edged pages.

In chapter 4, "Second-Rate Poets for Second-Rate Readers," I turn to the questions of value raised by Christmas books produced by women poets for a principally female audience. This chapter also explores the transatlantic reach of popular poetry and the Christmas gift book as an object of exchange, situating works by Eliza Cook, Adelaide Anne Procter, and Jean Ingelow within the periodical culture and reading constituencies of Britain and the United States. As in chapter 3, I position the production and reception of these gift books within the emergent feminist discourses of the 1860s. Because Cook, Procter, and (to a lesser extent) Ingelow were all involved in the women's movement, gift-book editions of their poetry offer particularly compelling sites in which to explore the form's uneasy dialogue between conservative and progressive values and ideologies. Moreover, as each of these women poets had large followings on both sides of the Atlantic, the physical features of their illustrated editions provide an opportunity to analyze how the "popular" is constituted within daily life and to ask how poetry takes up its traditional role of instruction and delight in works by women for women.

Chapter 5, "Poet and Publishers: Tennyson and the Image," examines the numerous illustrated editions of Tennyson's work that proliferated in the 1860s, when his peak popularity as a poet coincided with the craze for Christmas gift books. The emphasis here is twofold. First, I examine the author-publisher relationship and show how even a poet with the laureate's muscle was no match for the publishing industry's agenda for extending readerships and increasing purchases in the nineteenth-century age of the image. Here I consider the image both in its metaphoric sense, as the poet's "brand" or identity within celebrity culture, and in its material sense, as a visual picture. Tennyson's well-known dislike of illustrated editions did not prevent him from being a partner in, and profiting from, the production of illustrated editions with various publishers between 1857 and 1875. Citing some illustrated editions of his work by women artists and independent publishers, I also suggest that Tennyson's objections had more to do with issues of authorial agency and control than with the actual practice of picturing his poetry. Indeed, I find that Tennyson and his publishers learned a great deal to their profit from the work of women artists.

My second emphasis in this chapter is the importance of various nineteenth-century technologies to the production and reception of illustrated gift books. In particular, I analyze the significance of a variety of photographic processes and discourses to gift-book editions of Tennyson's poetry, from *Enoch Arden* (1866) to the Cabinet Edition of his *Poetical Works* (1874–75), the last of his books to be illustrated in a new edition by his own publisher and with his consent. Indeed, the Cabinet Edition, published serially in inexpensive volumes for the working classes, is the only one of Tennyson's editions to have been illustrated at his instigation. Evidently, by this late date, the association of images and poetry in popular culture was incontrovertible even for the laureate: the target audience of "the people" thus made the inclusion of illustrations desirable for the man who had become known as "the People's Poet." The fact that Tennyson shared this appellation with Eliza Cook, as he did the material form of the poetic gift book and its associations with middlebrow culture, popular readerships, and women, may well have contributed to the so-called reaction against Tennyson that emerged at the end of the 1860s (Mazzeno, *Tennyson,* 20).

The coda, "Poems and Pictures in the Modern Age," examines why the sixties Christmas book lost its central place in Victorian culture and explores its legacies for literary and publishing history. By the early 1870s, the illustrated gift book had virtually played itself out as a popular form combining pictures and poetry. Artistic innovation in the textual interaction of picture and word began to be redirected to the burgeoning field of juvenile publishing. Replacing verses with fairy tales and wood-engraved images with pictures reproduced from the three-color process, the new Christmas gift books inculcated the practice of collecting in a generation of child readers. Meanwhile, the most popular poetic gift books of the golden age—Willmott's *Poets of the Nineteenth Century,* for instance, or Mackay's *Thousand and One Gems of English Poetry*—continued to appear each Christmas season in a variety of versions: as new editions or reprints, as recycled pictures with new texts, and as cannibalized parts of previous works. But new poetic gift books with original wood-engraved illustrations all but disappeared from the adult market. By the fin de siècle, process reproduction had replaced wood engraving so effectively that the Dalziels, together with other engravers, were forced to close shop. With the new technologies, new art forms emerged, along with new ways of combining poetry and pictures and new types of books for another generation of buyers and readers.

# one

# Reading the Christmas Gift Book

> The approach of Christmas shows itself on our Library Table in every fantasy of gold and colour—covering every sort of poetry and illustration with binding worthy of the literary and pictorial artist.
>
> *Athenaeum*[1]

In 1846, a new form of gift book appeared on the Christmas market when James Burns published *Poems and Pictures: A Collection of Ballads, Songs, and Other Poems Illustrated by English Artists.*[2] The title is instructive. Like the contemporary *Illustrated London News*, launched only four years earlier, Burns's anthology foregrounds the relative equality of pen and pencil, verbal art and visual art.[3] Presented by the publisher simply as "A Collection of Ballads, Songs, and Other Poems," the poetry appears to be drawn from a rich cultural storehouse without the mediation of author or editor. If the literary contents represent a shared inheritance of ballads, songs, and poems, the pictures derive value from their connection to contemporary ways of making national art: they are "by English artists."

When we open the green and gilt ornamental covers, we notice a similar balancing of verbal and visual arts, with a wood-engraved frontispiece followed by a decorative title page. Every subsequent page of text sets the poetic letterpress within wood-engraved borders or beside ornamented margins. Intermittently, the verses appear with a wood-engraved illustration that takes up at least half the textual page. The image is typically set at the head or tail of the poem and represents scenes and figures from the poetic text. While the book as a whole presents the graphic ornaments as integral units of the printed page, its bibliographic apparatus draws special attention to the figural illustrations. Two tables of contents separate verbal and visual items into distinct lists. At the same time, the contents pages connect the differentiated lists semantically through the shared subjects and graphically through the woodcut borders and decorations present on each textual page.

Like the title's pairing of *Poems and Pictures,* the separate contents tables announce the relative parity of verbal and visual subjects in the book while also constructing a reader interested in both pictures and words. Organized alphabetically by "subject" (that is, title) with no apparent classification of period, style, genre, or theme, the poetic contents represent a wide range of popular poetry, with verses taken from the periodical press, church liturgy, and authors' collections (fig. 1.1). Beside each subject/title, another column

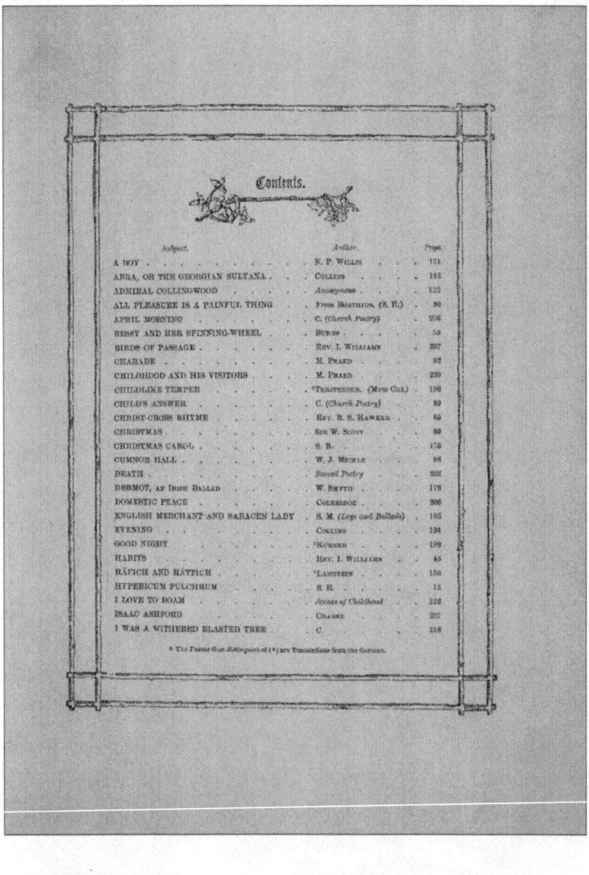

Contents.

| Subject. | Author. | Page |
|---|---|---|
| A BOY | N. P. WILLIS | 131 |
| ABRA, OR THE GEORGIAN SULTANA | COLLINS | 143 |
| ADMIRAL COLLINGWOOD | *Anonymous* | 133 |
| ALL PLEASURE IS A PAINFUL THING | From BOETHIUS. (S. R.) | 80 |
| APRIL MORNING | C. (*Church Poetry*) | 238 |
| BESSY AND HER SPINNING-WHEEL | BURNS | 59 |
| BIRDS OF PASSAGE | REV. I. WILLIAMS | 207 |
| CHARADE | M. PRAED | 92 |
| CHILDHOOD AND HIS VISITORS | M. PRAED | 230 |
| CHILDLIKE TEMPER | *TERSTEGEN. (Miss Cox) | 196 |
| CHILD'S ANSWER | C. (*Church Poetry*) | 89 |
| CHRIST-CROSS RHYME | REV. R. S. HAWKER | 65 |
| CHRISTMAS | SIR W. SCOTT | 90 |
| CHRISTMAS CAROL | S. R. | 175 |
| CUMNOR HALL | W. J. MICKLE | 98 |
| DEATH | *Sacred Poetry* | 222 |
| DERMOT, AN IRISH BALLAD | W. SMYTH | 178 |
| DOMESTIC PEACE | COLERIDGE | 206 |
| ENGLISH MERCHANT AND SARACEN LADY | S. M. (*Lays and Ballads*) | 105 |
| EVENING | COLLINS | 194 |
| GOOD NIGHT | *KÖRNER | 199 |
| HABITS | REV. I. WILLIAMS | 45 |
| HÄFICH AND HÄTPICH | *LANGBEIN | 158 |
| HYPERICUM PULCHRUM | S. R. | 13 |
| I LOVE TO ROAM | *Scenes of Childhood* | 222 |
| ISAAC ASHFORD | CRABBE | 227 |
| I WAS A WITHERED BLASTED TREE | C. | 218 |

* The Poems thus distinguished (*) are Translations from the German.

Figure 1.1
Contents page, *Poems and Pictures* (Sampson Low, 1860). *The Thomas Fisher Rare Book Library, University of Toronto.*

identifies the author's name. Because the subjects appear alphabetically, works by individual poets are not grouped together but are instead distributed throughout the contents.

When we turn to the illustrative contents, an alternative organizational structure for the book presents itself (fig. 1.2). Unlike the verses, the artistic contents are listed sequentially, in the order each subject appears in the book. Parallel columns indicate the number of illustrations associated with the subject/ title and identify two authors for each picture: the artist who designed the drawing and the engraver who cut the woodblock. To identify the author who composed the subject as a poetic text, one would need to turn back to the verbal contents page. Because the poet is not listed as the originator of the subject that the artist draws and the engraver cuts, the book accords neither priority nor superiority to the poetry. In the composite art of the illustrated gift book, the authority of the author gives way to the imperative of the book's material and social systems of making and using.

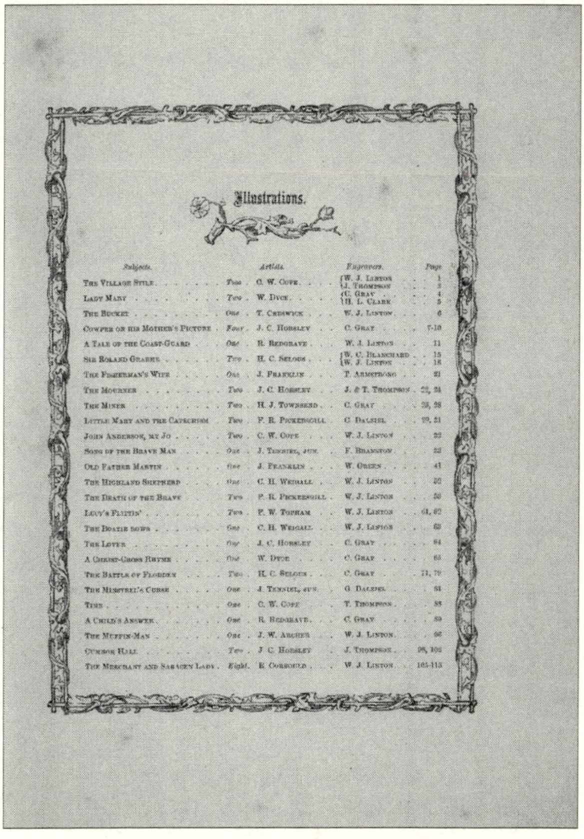

Illustrations.

| Subjects. | | Artists. | Engravers. | Page |
|---|---|---|---|---|
| The Village Stile | Two | C. W. Cope | W. J. Linton<br>J. Thompson | 1<br>3 |
| Lady Mary | Two | W. Dyce | C. Gray<br>H. L. Clark | 4<br>5 |
| The Bucket | One | T. Creswick | W. J. Linton | 6 |
| Cowper on his Mother's Picture | Four | J. C. Horsley | C. Gray | 7-10 |
| A Tale of the Coast-Guard | One | R. Redgrave | W. J. Linton | 11 |
| Sir Roland Graeme | Two | H. C. Selous | W. C. Blanchard<br>W. J. Linton | 15<br>18 |
| The Fisherman's Wife | One | J. Franklin | T. Armstrong | 21 |
| The Mourner | Two | J. C. Horsley | J. & T. Thompson | 23, 24 |
| The Miner | Two | H. J. Townsend | C. Gray | 35, 38 |
| Little Mary and the Catechism | Two | F. R. Pickersgill | G. Dalziel | 29, 31 |
| John Anderson, my Jo | Two | C. W. Cope | W. J. Linton | 32 |
| Song of the Brave Man | One | J. Tenniel, jun. | F. Branston | 33 |
| Old Father Martin | One | J. Franklin | W. Green | 41 |
| The Highland Shepherd | One | C. H. Weigall | W. J. Linton | 52 |
| The Death of the Brave | Two | F. R. Pickersgill | W. J. Linton | 58 |
| Lucy's Flittin' | Two | F. W. Topham | W. J. Linton | 61, 62 |
| The Boatie rows | One | C. H. Weigall | W. J. Linton | 63 |
| The Lover | One | J. C. Horsley | C. Gray | 64 |
| A Christ-Cross Rhyme | One | W. Dyce | C. Gray | 65 |
| The Battle of Flodden | Two | H. C. Selous | C. Gray | 71, 79 |
| The Minstrel's Curse | One | J. Tenniel, jun. | G. Dalziel | 84 |
| Time | One | C. W. Cope | T. Thompson | 88 |
| A Child's Answer | One | R. Redgrave | C. Gray | 89 |
| The Muffin-Man | One | J. W. Archer | W. J. Linton | 96 |
| Cumnor Hall | Two | J. C. Horsley | J. Thompson | 98, 102 |
| The Merchant and Saracen Lady | Eight | E. Corbould | W. J. Linton | 105-113 |

Figure 1.2
Illustrations page for *Poems and Pictures* (Sampson Low, 1860). *The Thomas Fisher Rare Book Library, University of Toronto.*

These distinct methods of organizing literary and artistic contents acknowledge not only the book's multiple makers but also its mobile users: readers are able to enter its pages at various points for a variety of purposes. Using the alphabetic guide of subjects, a reader could locate poems connected with Christmas or childhood, or search out a favorite title such as "King Arthur's Last Tournament," by Sir Walter Scott. If the reader is keen about particular poets, the author list could be searched for their names. Browsing the author column, a reader could also decide to read poems by women (this would not take long) or focus on the anonymous verses taken from *Church Poetry* (this would take considerably more time, especially if the reader then decided to move on to all the poetry by "Reverend" poets, including Isaac Williams and Henry Alford).

Alternatively, a reader could begin with the pictorial contents and choose to read only the fifty-one poems accompanied by pictures. A reader might even elect to skip the poetry entirely and concentrate solely on the illustrations, one day choosing to look at all the pictures by Clarkson Stanfield and another, perhaps, comparing the engravings made by W. J. Linton to those made by G. Dalziel or T. Armstrong.

The architecture of *Poems and Pictures* built its readers into its gilt-edged pages, tacitly giving them a degree of authority not accorded to any single individual on cover or title page. Associated with a publisher rather than either author or editor, Burns's *Poems and Pictures* asserts, in its title, contents, and material form, that the gift book is a cultural commodity, mass-produced through the technologies of the publishing industry and its divisions of labor for a mobile reader keen to select her own collection of poems and pictures.

The combination of literary and pictorial content had proved to be a winning one in the popular annuals published for Christmas markets from the 1820s to the 1850s. However, with the emergence of wood engraving in the 1840s as an efficient and affordable method of reproducing images, the bibliographic format and contents of the annuals began to look old-fashioned. *Poems and Pictures* established the new vehicular form for the illustrated gift book this study addresses. As John Buchanan-Brown demonstrates persuasively in *Early Victorian Illustrated Books*, the steel-engraved annuals had become "an outworn tradition" when Burns's *Poems and Pictures* emerged "to establish the new pattern of Christmas gift book, one of the most important genres for the Sixties' illustrators" (134–35). Because both the early Victorian annuals and the characteristic sixties publications were Christmas gift books encasing poetry and pictures in ornamental covers, it is worth taking a moment to consider what distinguishes them.

The new style of gift book combined poetry by standard or popular authors with original wood-engraved illustrations conceived and produced specifically for mass reproduction. Each picture in the new style of gift book was uniquely designed for the printed page and appeared in the familiar vernacular of wood engraving, the graphic language of the illustrated press. In contrast, each picture in the older style of gift book, the annual, was not uniquely designed for the book in which it appeared. Rather, it was a copy of a preexisting artwork owned by a wealthy collector or institution. These large, steel-engraved reproductions of existing academy paintings—picturesque landscapes and ruins, portraits of fashionable ladies, and sentimental genre paintings—were not illustrations. Instead, they were illustrated by literature composed in response to them. In addition to these ekphrastic works, the linguistic contents of annuals also contained a miscellany of other writings, both poetry and prose.

Paula Feldman notes the significance of the annuals in allowing "ordinary people to own high quality reproductions of significant works of art" (*Keepsake*, 7). If annuals gave access to fine art in the form of reproduced paintings, the wood-engraved poetic gift book permitted ownership of an original artwork that straddled the borders of "high" art and mass production. As I argue in greater depth below, the new gift books of the sixties allowed ordinary people to own copies of prints for which no originals existed. The wood-engraved art of the gift book was not a shadowy, tonal reproduction of a unique easel painting, reduced to accommodate codex form. On the contrary, it was an exact-size graphic art expressed in black, inked lines on white paper. The wood-engraved illustration was a book art designed by a living British artist for the express purpose of being printed in relief with letterpress, using the most advanced technologies of the age. Combining hand and machine, art and craft, the wood-engraved image was, in fact, a popular art form unique to the age of nineteenth-century reproduction.

## Picturing Poetry in "Cuts"

The significance of the illustrated poetic gift book as a popular publishing phenomenon linked to contemporary visual culture must be understood in the context of its modes of production. When the wood-engraving industry emerged in the 1830s and 1840s as the principal method of mass-producing images, a new artistic form was made possible because the reproductive technology allowed the picture to be set up and printed with the type.[4] Because the engraver's woodblock and the compositor's leads used the same relief process, they could be printed together with a steam-powered press on ordinary paper, thus reducing costs and enabling large print runs. This common printing process also permitted a new proximity of picture and word on the page and a visual similarity in inked effect, as typography and design could, theoretically at least, be of similar weight. The method was pioneered by Thomas Bewick, who altered forever the rough linear woodcut of past centuries by using the end-grain of boxwood (or other similarly hard wood) instead of the side-grain of a softer fruitwood. The hardness of the end-grain permitted the use of a finer and more delicate graver and the nuanced representation of light and shade. Earlier woodcut artists of the popular chapbooks and broadsides treated the plank as a white space on which black lines were cut with a knife. Bewick revolutionized the art of relief engraving by treating the block as "a black void out of which the subject appears in a varying range of grey tones with pure white for the lightest parts."[5]

Bewick developed his method in the early nineteenth century, but its commercial possibilities were not fully realized until the technologies of mass production and demands of increased literacy revived the wood-engraving industry in the 1830s and 1840s. The launch of Charles Knight's *Penny Magazine* in 1832 and, a decade later, the first illustrated weekly, the *Illustrated London News*, revolutionized print culture and the reading experience of the popular audience. These mass-produced periodicals and the books that followed them, however, could not achieve the requisite production levels by following Bewick's artisanal methods. Bewick drew his design on the wood, cut the block himself, and oversaw the printing process in his own shop. In contrast, the wood-engraved pictures in the periodicals and books of the second half of the nineteenth century were produced in an industrialized economy characterized by the division of labor.

The pressing deadlines of a periodical required that "large cuts" be divided into separate woodblocks and given to different engravers, the whole being reunited at press time. Although engravers typically worked alone on a single illustration in book projects, this did not necessarily lead to increased unity in the final product. The practice of using a variety of artists and engravers—including engravers from different firms—for the same volume often resulted in a variety of styles and skills. A gift book such as Edward Moxon's 1857 illustrated edition of Tennyson's *Poems* (discussed in chapter 2), for example, was the work of multiple artists and craftspeople, each aware only of their own labor and ignorant of the whole—an assembly-line approach that made mass cultural production possible and the products accessible but had a deleterious effect on overall design and artistic unity.

This mode of production resulted in books whose repetitive sameness and montage character might be seen as analogous to the mass-media products of the twentieth-century culture industry critiqued by Max Horkheimer and

Theodor Adorno. Certainly, the standardized effects of the Victorian culture industry's methods were not lost on nineteenth-century observers. However, the Christmas book also evoked some national pride in Britain's industrial power. Indeed, the Christmas book represented a recognizable British brand. As one contemporary reviewer noted, "Christmas books are made, not written. . . . It is no discredit to a Christmas book that it is manufactured, got up to order—size, price, and contents being determined by the state of the market. . . . They are just as recognized, and perhaps as legitimate, a branch of national industry as Paris bronzes or Birmingham buttons. And as in one case, so in the other, every rank of the skilled workman finds his employment in the manufacture of this literature of the magazine and periodical and Christmas book sort" (*SR,* Nov. 24, 1866, 653).

Although there are a few exceptions—William Allingham, for instance, proposed the illustrated edition of *The Music Master* to Routledge—the typical gift book was not the tangible outcome of an artist's or author's inspiration but instead was a commodity conceived in the office of a publisher or engraver. As we shall see in chapter 3, if the publisher or engraver were preparing an anthology, he might also act as editor, choosing and arranging the poetical selections himself or commissioning poets to write on a set theme. The poetic contents might also be focused on the writings of a particular author: for example, on the collected works of a popular living poet such as Jean Ingelow (discussed in chapter 4) or on a single narrative poem by Tennyson, such as *Enoch Arden* or *The Princess* (discussed in chapter 5). In these cases, the publisher would determine when the writer's popularity was sufficient to command the kind of sales that would offset the expenses of illustration and calculate the number of images, the size of the print run, and the time of release. Generally, this process began in winter or spring for an expected publication date between October and December for the Christmas sales season.[6]

The publisher would then set about commissioning the necessary artist(s) and engraver(s); sometimes, the publisher would subcontract an engraving firm to supervise all arrangements relating to the book's illustrative contents. Once the artists had been confirmed, they typically had a free hand in selecting their own pictorial subjects. Where necessary, the publisher would also supply the artist with copy text. As I discuss in chapter 5, Moxon appears to have provided Daniel Maclise with the most recent edition of *The Princess* when he gave Maclise the commission, just as Strahan provided Arthur Hughes with Tennyson's lyrics for *The Window.* Occasionally, as we shall see in chapter 3, an engraving company such as the Dalziels' might take on responsibility for the entire contents and produce gift books that were artist- rather than author-focused. In such cases, the Dalziels would commission an artist (for example, Myles Birket Foster or Arthur Boyd Houghton) to produce a set number of pictures on a particular theme, then commission a poet or poets to write a page of verse to accompany each full-page plate. In such cases, the Dalziels supplied the poets with proofs of the prints so they could carry out their commissions.

Working in his own studio, the artist would cover the end of the boxwood in Chinese white, creating a smooth, blank surface on which he then drew his design in reverse. Dante Gabriel Rossetti was so unfamiliar with the reproductive process that he neglected to reverse his first design on wood and had to redraw "The Maids of Elfen-Mere" for William Allingham's *Music Master* painstakingly on a new block (Rossetti, *Correspondence*, 1:388) (fig. 1.3). Because the end pieces of boxwood were small—generally no more than about three inches by five inches—the drawing required extremely fine work by the artist and the engravers. In the early 1860s, new technological developments enabled the photographic transfer of the artist's design to the woodblock. As I discuss in more detail in chapter 5, this innovation allowed the artist to draw direct rather than in reverse and to produce his composition on paper in a larger scale, as it could be reduced when transferred. Before this new technology was harnessed to the wood-engraving process, the artist's original drawing was lost when the engraver cut the penciled lines. In an effort to preserve a record of the design, artists sometimes photographed the block before giving it to the engraver, but apart from their preliminary studies, there was no "original."[7] Thus the wood-engraved image was simultaneously unique and multiple.

Another innovation of the sixties was the new requirement of facsimile engraving. Prior to about 1855, wood engravers were not expected to cut each line drawn by the artist but rather to interpret the composition for reproduction. The illustrators of the sixties, however, demanded facsimile engraving (Houfe, *Dictionary*, 109). Engravers used magnifying glasses and extremely fine cutting tools to reproduce the artist's drawing as an exact copy of the original, rather than a translation of it. Although a printed wood engraving could never actually be an exact duplicate of a line drawing, some reproductions did come very close to realizing the artist's design. This desired outcome, however, required more than simply the engraver's skill: it also depended on the artist's ability to adjust aesthetic technique to technological requirements. Facsimile engraving could only be achieved when the designing artist had a working knowledge of the reproduction process and a willingness to collaborate with other artistic workers and the technology they used. The Dalziels described Rossetti's drawing on wood for "The Maids of Elfen-Mere" (fig. 1.3) as "a remarkable example of the artist being altogether unacquainted with the necessary requirements in

Figure 1.3 Dante Gabriel Rossetti, "The Maids of Elfen-Mere," in William Allingham, *The Music Master* (Routledge, 1855), 202. *The Thomas Fisher Rare Book Library, University of Toronto.*

making a drawing on wood for the engraver's purposes." Rossetti, the brothers complained, "made use of wash, pencil, coloured chalk, and pen and ink, producing a very nice effect, but the engraved reproduction of this many tinted drawing, reduced to the stern realities of black and white by printers' ink, failed to satisfy him" (Dalziel and Dalziel, *Record,* 86). For his part, Rossetti disowned the illustration, maintaining that it "used to be by me till it became the exclusive work of Dalziel who cut it" and wishing that "Dalziel had the credit as well as the authorship" (*Correspondence,* 2:50).

In fact, as we have seen, the gift books of the period did credit engravers as well as artists on the signed images as well as the title and contents pages. The modes of production of the 1860s gift book challenged the ideology of individual genius and the myth of sole authorship by acknowledging many of the hands involved in making the work. This recognition was appropriate, as the process of facsimile engraving required extensive collaboration between artist and engraver before the book went to press. When the engravers finished cutting the block, they would pull a proof on India paper and return this to the artist for comment and revision. Using Chinese white and adding notations as required, the artist would make corrections, often very detailed, and return the corrected proofs to the engravers.[8] Sometimes, if the engravers were also acting as publishers, they might ask the artist to change a detail of the composition. The Dalziels, for instance, asked Ford Madox Brown to add a slashed sleeve to the main figure's dress in his "Prisoner of Chillon" design for *The Poets of the Nineteenth Century* (see fig. 3.3) so that the composition would have a more medieval look (Hueffer, *Brown,* 122).

On rare occasions, the artist might discover an error in cutting after the book had gone to press. In such cases, a plug would be inserted and the block recut to achieve the necessary modifications. Such a correction was undertaken for the second edition of Christina Rossetti's *Goblin Market and Other Poems,* as the mistake in cutting the woman's (missing) jawline in Dante Gabriel's title-page vignette was not caught before publication of the first edition (Fredeman, "Woodman," 16). Sometimes, though not always, the publisher would include preliminary pulls of the engravings when he sent the poet proofs of the textual pages prior to publication. Yet while the latter were for the poet's correction, the former were generally only for his information. As Kegan Paul reminded Alfred Tennyson, "illustrations could hardly 'be considered other than a publisher's question'" (Hagen, *Tennyson,* 140).

Once the engravers had made the final corrections, a metal facsimile of the woodblock, called an electrotype, would usually be made. This facsimile of a facsimile permitted the mechanical reproduction of multiple copies without wear on the woodblock, which would remain as the master.[9] The printers would then set up each page of the book by combining the electrotyped block (where necessary) with the composited type (which might itself be preserved in electro- or stereotype). In some rare cases, as with the Moxon Tennyson, for instance, the usual steam cylinder machine press was not considered adequate for the fineness of the engraving and the quality of the book desired. In such rare instances, the pages that included illustrations would be printed separately on a handpress. All ten thousand copies of the first edition of the Moxon Tennyson were prepared in this way (Dalziel and Dalziel, *Record,* 82–83).

The division of labor required to mass produce a gift book brought with it many significant results for the history of authorship, reading, and publishing. Dispersed among poets, artists, publishers, and engravers, the gift book's author-function was a corporate entity. Within this corporate authorship, however, there were some evident hierarchies. Despite the fact that the work of engravers was acknowledged in the book itself, facsimile engraving had the effect of elevating artist-designers for their intellectual, creative work, while relegating engravers to the role of skilled craftspeople.[10] This distinction in turn contributed to the extraordinarily high status of nineteenth-century book artists, who were not only paid royally for their designs but were also given the social standing of painters, with entrée into the best circles and even the recognition of knighthoods (graphic artists John Gilbert and John Tenniel, for example, were each knighted). Such status put illustrators on par with authors in the literary field and illustration on par with painting in the visual field, blurring the boundaries between fine and applied art—or, in Pierre Bourdieu's terms, restricted and large-scale cultural production. But it also divided the book and its contents.

The artist who designed the illustration did not engrave it. Nor—except in rare cases—did the artist choose the paper and typographic font, plan the page layout, or design the cover that encased the whole. These tasks were performed by other hands and minds. With few exceptions, gift books of the period had no guiding artistic intelligence to bring all elements into concert: they were not a "literature by design" in the limited sense of individual authorship. Rather, gift books were products of the Victorian culture industry: their standardized formats were developed to maximize profits and minimize risks for the publisher. They were commodities with very specific designs on consumers. But gift books were also, to adapt Jerome J. McGann's general comment to this specific application, "graphical and bibliographical ventures by authors, artists, publishers, and their collaborating agents," with many-layered meanings imbricated in their physical features ("Literature," 11).

 In this description of the process of bringing the illustrated gift book from publisher's conception to printed page, there is one noticeably absent or silent partner: the author. Poetry was a requisite element in the popular Christmas book of the sixties, but the poet was considered more or less superfluous to the process of production. Once the poet produced the copy, his or her work was, in effect, finished. Only on rare occasions did publishers consult poets about details relating to the pictorial content, and only rarely did poets take an active part in the process, as William Allingham did with *The Music Master* and Christina Rossetti did with her poetry collections.[11] For the most part, poets were content to wait until the book was published before they saw the pictures that would accompany their poems and influence their readers. Those who wanted to exercise their authority over the collaborating artist could be thwarted by the exigencies of the production process. When Tennyson, for example, asked a willing Arthur Hughes to show him the drawings for *Enoch Arden* before they went to the engravers, the publisher's tight schedule and need to bring out the book before Christmas made this prepublication dialogue impossible (Roberts, *Hughes,* 256).

The gift book that was characteristic of the 1860s did not arise from the collaborative partnerships we think of in relation to the illustrated fiction of Dickens, Trollope, Thackeray, or Carroll, in which the author worked closely with the artist.[12] Although the gift book paired poems and pictures, the most significant partnership was not between poet and artist but rather between the work and its users. As Nicholas Frankel astutely observes, the illustrated edition is part "of a larger, ongoing process in which the poem becomes detached from the domain of its author" and power and authority come to "reside in the new printing processes or with the reader" ("Beardsley," 288).

## The Illustrated Book as a Hybrid Form

The starting place for understanding the illustrated gift book as an object in Victorian visual culture lies in the materiality of its wood-engraved pictures and their complex relationships with both the elite art of painting and the vernacular expressions of the popular press. In *Reading Popular Prints, 1790–1870,* Brian Maidment makes the important observation that wood engraving in the illustrated press had a divided history and, in consequence, a dual register. On the one hand, as the ubiquitous graphic medium for portraying the newsworthy and topical, it was the pictorial method that readers recognized for representations of contemporary life. In this context, its purpose was to document, describe, and explain "with accuracy and precision" in an apparently naturalistic way. On the other hand, as Maidment points out, "wood engraving also belonged to deep-rooted traditions of non-naturalistic representation" through the woodcut's centuries-old association with broadside songs and ballads, penny fiction, tracts, and chapbooks. Maidment concludes that the wood engraving carried with it both the vernacular register of popular woodcuts, with their evocation of fantasy or sensation and, at the same time, the press's documentary language of social realism (145–47).

This dual register of naturalistic/nonnaturalistic representation clearly impacts on the meanings available to historical readers of illustrated gift books. However, complicating this connection to popular prints and their graphic vernacular is the language of fine art that the gift book's wood-engraved illustrations also referenced. Unlike many earlier illustrators—for example, George Cruikshank, who engraved chapbooks and lottery tickets before becoming a leading book artist of the 1830s (Houfe, *Dictionary*, 273)—the illustrators of the sixties typically worked both in easel painting for exhibition and sale and in black and white for books and magazines. Pre-Raphaelite artists in particular treated book illustrations with the same seriousness as their paintings. Whether drawing on wood or painting on canvas, the Pre-Raphaelites drew from live models and actual places and objects, researched their subjects, and prepared preliminary studies.

Both publishers and the reading public, including reviewers, recognized that the Christmas gift book of poetry and pictures had a foot in the fine art camp. Indeed, as we shall see in chapter 3, the Dalziel brothers named their illustrated series "Fine Art Books." For its part, the periodical press reviewed poetic gift books in columns variously dedicated to "Fine Art," "Illustrated Books," and "Christmas Gift Books," underscoring in their headers the blurred categories of art and commerce that these works occupied. Furthermore, the artistic and cultural value of the images was such that booksellers and owners from the nineteenth century to the present have removed the wood-engraved pictures to sell or exhibit as standalone prints. There is also an entire critical history of analyzing the illustrations of the sixties as individual artworks, rather than as graphic material belonging to the printed book and the technologies of mass reproduction.[13]

The significance of this historical crossover between fine and mass-produced art deserves special consideration and some adjustment of Walter Benjamin's well-known discussion of the "aura" lost from original artwork in the age of mechanical reproduction. Far from being separated in time and space from a distant original with auratic presence, wood-engraved illustrations existed simultaneously and paradoxically as originals and multiples. Each printed picture was immediately present in the book it inhabited and was always available to its reader. Like the printed poem, the authenticity of the picture was guaranteed not by an absent, handmade original but rather by the authoritative apparatus of the book itself, including its cover, title page, table of contents, and, of course, images, initialed by artist and engraver. Instead of "the presence of the original" (Benjamin, "Work," 64) functioning as the prerequisite to authenticity, print culture and its multiple makers—publishers, engravers, printers, artists, poets, reviewers, and readers—authenticated the art of the book as well as its contents, values (in all senses of the word), and purposes. However drawn "from nature" it might have been, the wood-engraved illustration did not, in the first instance, represent the world, but the poem. It lived in its own environment, the printed book. And the book belonged to readers.

Mid-nineteenth-century technologies of reproduction and distribution ensured that the wood-engraved artwork traveled to its own place, usually the middle-class drawing-room table, located at the very center of the Victorian household's domestic and social life. Unlike an original artwork reproduced by mechanical processes, the wood-engraved image did not "meet the beholder halfway" by leaving its original locale and traveling to private space (Benjamin, "Work," 65). On the contrary, lacking an originary presence and unique locale, the wood-engraved image's book-bound destinations preempted origins, and it lived at home with the middle-class family as a domestic object combining utility and ornament. From this culturally central location, the illustrated gift book emphasized, in Benjamin's terms, its "exhibition value" as a work of art whose purpose was both aesthetic and ideological (68). Though perhaps not politically revolutionary in the way Benjamin envisions, it marks a significant moment in the development of mass art (63).[14] As a consumer object specifically made and marketed as a gift to be given at Christmas or New Year's, the illustrated book carried something of the "ritual function" Benjamin considers coincident with the unique artwork's imbrication in "the fabric of tradition" (67). Indeed, its connections to the traditions of national art were among its distinguishing features. At the same time, the illustrated gift book was a mass art produced without the constraints of singularity in time and space to which a unique artwork is subject. As a ritual object, the gift book had material features that expressed a conservative desire for preserving and celebrating Victorian domestic and national values and traditions. At the same time, its technological innovations were embedded in, and constitutive of, its immediate contemporary culture and the everyday lives, desires, and identities of its subjects.

The hybrid nature of the illustrated gift book establishes several theoretical positions that ground the methodology of this study. First, the illustrated gift book brought the putative "fine arts" of poetry and original pictures—Bourdieu's "field of restricted production"—into "the field of large-scale cultural production," or middlebrow culture. Whereas art from the restricted field is made by cultural makers (artists) for other cultural makers (artists, critics, intellectuals, and the like) who establish the criteria of aesthetic value, art in the field of mass production is made for nonproducers, meeting the market criteria of supply and demand (Bourdieu, "Market," 1234). Because works of art from the field of restricted production hold symbolic value, an individual's social status can be elevated through the demonstration of a socially approved and legitimated "cultivated taste" (1238–39). Furthermore, as Bourdieu outlines elsewhere, "the socially recognized hierarchy of the arts"—which, in the nineteenth century, placed poetry at the top of the verbal arts and painting at the top of the visual arts—"corresponds [to] a social hierarchy of the consumers" ("Introduction," 323). In the 1860s, we can map this as follows: poetry and painting for the elites, and penny dreadfuls with sensational woodcuts for the masses. In this schema, original wood-engraved illustrations by highly regarded British artists occupy a dynamic middle ground between the "high" art of painting and the anonymous popular art of woodcuts in broadsides and chapbooks.

In drawing on Bourdieu's studies as part of my theoretical framework, I contend that the illustrated gift book of the 1860s challenged the artistic and social hierarchies sketched above. In the form of a commercialized mass art, the gift book made available the poetry of laureates who represented the highest echelon of state-sanctioned art—for example, Southey, Wordsworth, and Tennyson—and the visual art of some of the nation's most esteemed artists, including those legitimated by the Royal Academy—for example, John Everett Millais, who became president of this prestigious institution.

Recognizing the artistic work of those who designed book art by drawing on the woodblock, Millais believed that the best of the book illustrators "were entitled to rank with the best exponents of oil and watercolour" and hoped eventually to open academy membership to them (*Life*, 1:358–59). Although this honor was never bestowed, illustrators in the second half of the nineteenth century nevertheless enjoyed greater artistic and social recognition than at any time before or since. The Victorians' high regard for book artists corresponds to the prestige of gift books in the golden age of illustration. Coinciding with a period of great social mobility when the broad middle classes were seeking increased cultural and political status, the rise of the illustrated book in the artistic hierarchy paralleled its owner's hope for social advancement. Prominently displayed on the drawing-room table, the poetic gift book represented a middle-class aspiration to acquire cultural currency in the nation's poetry and art—or, at least, the desire to display a luxury good that attested to the owner's taste, cultivation, and disposable income.

## Constructing Christmas Custom(s)

In illustrated papers and periodicals, the mass audience developed its expectation of a pictured page and a visual/verbal reading practice. Poetry and pictures became part of readers' everyday lives, as newspapers and periodicals regularly printed poems, both with and without illustrations.[15] This exposure to accessible and inexpensive illustrated material in the ephemera of print culture created a reader expectation that publishers capitalized on by developing a new style of wood-engraved gift book.[16] The speed with which the new gift book emerged after the rise of the illustrated press is instructive. In 1842, the *Illustrated London News* announced the marriage of "Art, 'a very fair and jeweled bride,' to the Press" with its launch of the first illustrated weekly (quoted in Sinnema, *Dynamics,* 16). In 1846, as we have seen, James Burns published *Poems and Pictures,* setting the pattern for a new form of illustrated gift book. In 1850, David Bogue followed with *Christmas with the Poets: A Collection of Songs, Carols, and Descriptive Verses, Relating to the Festival of Christmas, from the Anglo-Norman Period to the Present Time,* embellished with fifty-three illustrations after Myles Birket Foster's designs. By the sixties, illustrated collections and anthologies of poetry had begun to flood the Christmas market. Keenly aware of different audiences and income levels, publishers produced books, as one reviewer observed, "to suit" every person and every place from "the cotton lord's drawing-room . . . [to] the lady's maid's drawer" (*SR,* Nov. 24, 1866, 653).

The title of Bogue's anthology draws attention to another important connection between the periodical press and the gift book: both participated vigorously in the discursive production of the Victorian Christmas. Charles Dickens's series of illustrated Christmas books in the 1840s and the illustrated Christmas supplements in various periodicals worked to define a secular festival that was distinctively British. Characterized by nostalgia for a simpler rural past and an associated celebration of childhood and home, along with expectations of benevolence and the practices of gift giving, caroling, feasting, and celebrating around a joyous domestic hearth, the Victorian Christmas was both symptom and effect of what it meant to be British. As Mark Connelly, Tara Moore, and others have shown, the making and marketing of traditions for a domestic festival identified with the values and character of the British nation were largely an effect of the popular press. This "invention of tradition" was especially prominent in the pages of the *Illustrated London News.*[17] In its articles, engravings, illustrated poetry, and reviews of gift books, the *Illustrated London News* connected the celebration of Christmas with domestic and national values and identities.[18]

The sixties gift book became the period's standardized object of Christmas exchange. "The most noticeable mark of Christmas," as the *Saturday Review* critic observed in 1857, "is the universal exchange of books . . . and being—or thinking we are—a very good people, the run is upon good books" (Dec. 19, 1857, 557–58). "Good books" were repositories of cultural value as well as ideological instruments for schooling readers in "the home affections pourtrayed by the poets," as announced by the title of one of the period's popular anthologies (edited by Charles Mackay). Commodified in gift book form, the idea of home and its affective values became associated with poetry by highly regarded national poets (for example, Tennyson's "Oriana" and Elizabeth Barrett Browning's "Dead Rose") and with artwork by "eminent artists" in the form of one hundred wood-engraved illustrations.

In its review of *The Home Affections* in late autumn of 1857, the *Athenaeum* highlighted the book's merit as a material object suitable for drawing-room display: "The approach of Christmas shows itself on our Library Table in every fantasy of gold and colour,—covering every sort of poetry and illustration with binding worthy of the literary and pictorial artist" (1359). "Every sort of poetry and illustration" could serve the fantasy of "home" as constructed through the unifying discourse of the British Christmas and its annual exchange of books. Reflecting, reinforcing, and shaping middle-class ideologies of home and nation, the Christmas gift book became, as the *Saturday Review* solemnly announced in 1863, "a British institution" (Dec. 5, 1863, 738).

In the age of wood-engraved reproduction, Christmas customs became Christmas custom for a nation of shopkeepers and consumers. Thanks to carefully managed marketing that included lengthy seasonal reviews and prominent advertising lists of "books suitable for presents" in the periodical press, as well as glowing visual displays in windows decked out for the holidays, the illustrated gift book became a standard token of Christmas exchange in the sixties. "A present is not thought to be right," the *Saturday Review* claimed, "unless it affects the useful as well as the ornamental" (Dec. 5, 1863, 738). A decorative object containing poetry and pictures capable of conveying instruction and delight without bringing a blush to the cheek of any young person in the drawing room, the poetic gift book's respectability confirmed its appeal. The Victorian middle classes embraced the illustrated book as their present of choice because the gift book's cultural capital as a symbolic good was closely associated with notions of national identity. As a material object, the illustrated book represented the excellence of English manufacturing. As a symbolic object, it functioned as a repository of national greatness in art and literature, offering access to cultural capital and social status. And as a domestic object, it was embedded in, and helped shape, ideologies and identities based on gender, class, ethnicity, age, and nation.

This brings me to a second theoretical position grounding my study. Following Michel de Certeau, I conceptualize the illustrated gift book as part of a "practice of everyday life" for its middle-class consumers. Here the question is, how did these "users who are not its makers" manipulate the poetic and pictorial texts and make the book their own? (de Certeau, *Practice,* xiii). As I indicate above in my reading of the tables of contents for *Poems and Pictures,* I am as interested in the book's uses as I am in its symbolic value—that is, in its ritual and personal functions as well as its exhibition and political functions. The historical record tells us that one important use for these books was as a Christmas or New Year's gift, most often a present given by a man to a woman (fiancée, wife, daughter, granddaughter, sister, and so on). Connecting the gift book's material form to its domestic destination and assumed feminine recipient, Margaret Oliphant's review of the illustrated edition of Longfellow's *Evangeline* in 1857 alerts us to some of the ideological and ritualistic freight bound up in Christmas gift books. Remarking that "[y]oung readers, and more especially women, will always like *Evangeline,*" Oliphant advises "all uncles, grandpapas, and brothers willing to do pleasure to the young ladies of their respective households, to make large provision of this most maidenly and pretty volume, which would not come at all amiss either, as a love-token of a more special kind" ("Picture-Books," 311–12). As Oliphant's language suggests, the book itself—described here as a "maidenly and pretty volume"—is not simply destined for a female user; it also symbolically represents her in its physical features and domestic habitus.

Produced and marketed for women—though only occasionally, as this study shows, involving female workers in its production—the gift book is intensely gender-marked. I explore the significance of this intended female audience in each of the following chapters. At this point, I simply want to note that the gift book's function as a present to a female reader involves it and its users in human social relationships of power and authority, as well as in the networks of exchange that determined daily life in both domestic and national contexts.

One of the most fundamental aspects of consumption in a society organized by print culture, as de Certeau reminds us, is reading itself (*Practice,* 167–68). Displayed on the drawing-room table, the center of family life and the locus for receiving visitors, the poetic gift book served multiple purposes. The gift book simultaneously functioned as status symbol, home furnishing, ritualized exchange object, poetic reader, and portable gallery. Visitors could browse its contents while waiting for a member of the family to appear to receive them; children could be entertained by its black-and-white images. In some cases, children might even use the black outlines to extemporize a coloring book of their own making; this practice of what de Certeau calls "making do" (xvi) is evident in some of the Victorian illustrated books left to posterity. Family members could read the poetry out loud in a group or silently to themselves. The pictures, too, could be viewed with another person as an aid to conversation or studied alone. Both reading the poetry and looking at the pictures could be sustained or intermittent, lengthy or short, singular or repetitive. As the earlier discussion of *Poems and Pictures* makes clear, the illustrated gift book encouraged and enticed multiple users and various ways of reading and looking. Readers, as de Certeau claims, are never passive. Rather, they are "unrecognized producers, poets of their own acts" of reading (xxii, xviii).

I want, then, to foreground readers and reading as much as I do authors, artists, and other producers in this study of illustrated gift books. At the same time, I am fully aware that I cannot access the actual daily practices of ordinary readers. The recorded histories of reading that remain to us are largely composed of reviews by professional critics in the periodical press and of the letters and memoirs of writers, publishers, engravers, and artists. However, a third theoretical proposition provides another means of access to nineteenth-century readers. This theoretical position asserts that the book itself is an expressive form and that readers are, as Pierre Macherey observes, "made by what makes the book" (*Theory*, 70). The materiality of a book—"its every particle," Macherey reminds us—"*manifests*, uncovers, what it cannot say" (84). Alternatively, as Jerome J. McGann puts it, "Various readers and audiences are hidden in our texts, and the traces of their multiple presence are scripted at the most material levels" (*Textual Condition*, 10).

## The Gift Book as Expressive Form

It follows, then, that close scrutiny of the material forms of the poetic gift book—its bibliographic, iconic, and linguistic features—will bring readers, uses, and functions into view. Here I am indebted to theories of the book as socially constructed and historically contingent, particularly the work of D. F. McKenzie, Jerome J. McGann, and George Bornstein. My methodology assumes that a gift book of poetry is a "version" of poetic text that is socially rather than authorially sanctioned. As Bornstein observes, "[a] theory of versions tends to shift our conception of the artwork itself from product to process" and to move authority from the author "in favor of an authority more dispersed among those who actually bring the text to its published form—the author, certainly, but also any collaborators, scribes, editors, designers, printers, or others involved in the process of primary production and dissemination" (*Palimpsest*, 3, 4). One of the questions guiding this study asks what it means to make a book of poetry and pictures for middle-class women—what difference does this make to the book's matter, and what does it mean for us as its inheritors?

In numerous case studies, McGann has shown that between about 1820 and 1930, "artists and writers gradually developed a new and extraordinarily sophisticated understanding of the expressive character of physical text" (*Rossetti*, 82). While not the outcome of a single controlling designer, the illustrated gift book is, nevertheless, an expressive form that has much to tell us about poetry, pictures, and reading in the third quarter of the nineteenth century. This study seeks to examine the expressive character of the sixties gift book by focusing on the materiality of the book: its poetic texts, iconic images, and graphic ornaments, as well as its paper, typography, binding, and layout. Because gift books combine poetry—which is itself an iconic form on the printed page—and in-text pictures, "the very disposition of space itself," as McKenzie reminds us, has "an expressive function in conveying meaning" to which I shall be attentive (*Bibliography*, 17).

As a form of mass art, the gift book was conceived not as a creative expression by individual artists but rather as a commercial venture by entrepreneurs—publishers such as James Burns, David Bogue, and Edward Moxon, and engravers and printers such as Henry Vizetelly and the Dalziel brothers. They marshaled the talents of numerous workers—artists, poets, editors, engravers, printers, and binders—to create books that would sell. I stress this not to denigrate the expressiveness of these works but to emphasize their significance as what Nicholas Frankel calls "a corporate event" (*Wilde*, 158). As Frankel does in his analysis of Wilde's decorated books, I read the poetic gift book "in terms of production rather than inspiration" (158), eschewing artistic hierarchies to concentrate on how the printed page and the bound book speak to, and reify, their readers. With a play on W. J. T. Mitchell's description of the "composite art" of William Blake, who uniquely combined the functions of artist, designer, poet, engraver, publisher, and bookseller in one person, I have termed the illustrated poetic gift book a *composited* art—a three-dimensional work assembled in engraving firms, print shops, and binderies, rather than an abstract text composed in the ethereal space of artistic inspiration. I read it not to discover authorial intentions but to historicize and interpret the textual production of meanings and readers in a significant, but almost forgotten, nineteenth-century artifact.

As a composited work, the illustrated gift book is a modular art form that has much to tell us about nineteenth-century print culture and its discursive production of subjectivities, identities, and values. In *Graphic Design: A Critical Guide*, Johanna Drucker and Emily McVarish remind us that the composited page requires letters, graphic ornaments, and images that "fit together physically and visually in various combinations" (80). At an economic and practical level, the modular art form of the gift book suggested that, just as alphabetic metal type could be broken down and reset to compose a different poet's verses, so too could the electroplated image be removed from one material site and reused in another. *Poems and Pictures* once again offers an instructive example. First published by Burns in 1846, it was reissued by Sampson Low in 1860 for the Christmas market, when it was hailed as the unrivaled originator that had set "the example of all succeeding Christmas books" in literary and artistic content, typography, and binding. "It seems," commented the *Saturday Review* critic, "that Christmas books, like the art of printing, acquired perfection at the first experiment" (Dec. 31, 1859, 818).

As a reprint of the original by a different publisher, this version of *Poems and Pictures* assumes newly historicized meanings, including those of generic originator and artistic standard for the whole class of sixties gift books. But even this ideal Christmas book had no status as a unified whole in the usual sense of a work of art; its modular parts could be broken into new units and redirected to new audiences to maximize profits. In 1865, Cassell, Petter, and Galpin (publishers of the Doré Bible) acquired the electroplates for *Poems and Pictures* and set to work recycling and repackaging its contents in a variety of smaller versions: *Favourite Poems by Gifted Bards; Jewels Gathered from Painter and Poet: A Selection of Poems, Songs, and Ballads;* and *Beauties of Poetry and Gems of Art*. The target audience is evident in the publisher's pricing system. Whereas the Sampson Low reprint of *Pictures and Poems* sold at the established gift-book price of twenty-one shillings, or one guinea, the smaller offshoots were available for seven shillings and sixpence each. At roughly one-third the regular price and, at eighty to eighty-two pages, approximately one-third the size of the original volume, these "favourites," "jewels," "beauties," and "gems" put luxury goods within reach of those members of the lower middle classes who had discretionary income to expend on a tasteful present during the season of gift giving. Publishers understood that, just as the type could be broken down and redistributed, so too could the modular form of the book be broken down and redistributed into different social demographics, effectively constructing new readers with each new version.

As William St. Clair's quantitative research shows, there is a direct correlation between the material format of the book and the class of its readers. During the nineteenth century, "[p]oetry was moving socially and materially downward, reducing from quarto to octavo and then to duodecimo," while the novel, in contrast, "was moving upwards from duodecimo to octavo" (*Reading Nation*, 176). The lavish ornamental bindings and quarto format of the poetic gift book signaled the preciousness of the object as a luxury item and the importance of pictures and poetry to a middle-class audience seeking cultural cultivation. Although advertisements claimed that the guinea gift book was "within the reach of all," the price tag definitively establishes a classed readership. With the head of the family's average real annual income being about twenty pounds in 1855 (Hibbert, *ILN*, 129), the average person would not have had the surplus wealth to purchase an item that cost one-twentieth of the household's yearly intake. Moreover, even the commodity's designation as a "guinea gift book" denotes its status as a luxury good accessible only to well-heeled purchasers with surplus money and leisure time. While there were twenty shillings in the pound, there were twenty-one shillings in the guinea. Just as payment in guineas rather than pounds was an indication of class status (S. Mitchell, *Daily Life*, 29–30), so too did marking prices in guineas indicate a restricted class of consumers capable of purchasing artistic objects to decorate their drawing rooms and provide cultivated entertainment in leisure hours.

Both the material format and the institutionalized pricing system designated the poetic gift book as a work directed at the broad middle classes—that is, those households with annual incomes between £300 and £800—professionals, merchants, bankers, industrialists, well-to-do farmers, shopkeepers, and clerks whose female family members did not work for pay (S. Mitchell, *Daily Life*, 19–21, 32–38). For those in the lower segment of the middle classes, finding the money for such an expensive item, even for a gift, could have been prohibitive. However, even within the twenty-year period that I cover in this book, the falling cost of living and correlative increase in real income meant that a pound could go considerably farther in 1875 than it could in 1855. In addition, publishers routinely offered books at discounted prices. The Routledge catalog shows that books listed at the publisher's price of a guinea, such as R. A. Willmott's *Poets of the Nineteenth Century*, for example, were offered at the wholesale price of fifteen shillings, while those listed at ten shillings and sixpence, such as Moxon's illustrated edition of Tennyson's *Princess*, were discounted to seven shillings and sixpence.[19] A lower-middle-class family who wished to own a book of pictures and poetry to display on their central table, then, had high-quality books available to them at prices closer to what they might be able to afford as a present, especially toward the end of the 1860s. It also seems likely that families with limited incomes might have awaited the publication of the smaller, less expensive spin-offs of the guinea gift books, such as *Jewels Gathered from Painter and Poet*.

The modularity of the gift book resulted in significant material effects in the everyday lives of readers. Constructing its pictorial and poetic contents from illustrated newspapers and magazines as well as from other books, the gift book was inherently intertextual and interpictorial, constantly citing other images and texts. Moreover, the placement and size of the image conditioned the display of poetic verses on the printed page, effectively disrupting the continuous form of stanzaic units and disrupting both the poem's iconicity and the reader's experience of it. Poetry itself, of course, is a visual object within print culture, signaling its identity *as* poetry by the graphic arrangement of black line and interval, or white space. The wood-engraved image similarly creates iconic shapes through black lines and white space. As we shall see, the modular art of the gift book cuts into the printed page to assert the visuality of poetry, the legibility of pictures, and the mobility of the modern reader. A "bimodal" work of art, the Christmas gift book moved poetry and pictures into the heart of middlebrow Victorian life.[20]

two

# The Moxon Tennyson, Pre-Raphaelite Art, and Victorian Visual Culture

Surely one painting a year, shown in London and then shut up, is not result enough for such a mine of invention and miraculous power of reproduction as you possess. This is the age of printing and a countless public, and the pictorial artist may and ought to aim at exercising a wider immediate influence.

*William Allingham*[1]

"So Mr. Montgomery's *Oxford*, by the help of some pretty illustrations, has contrived to prolong its miserable existence to a second edition!" (Hallam, "Characteristics," 1190).[2] The first sentence of Arthur Henry Hallam's famous review of Tennyson's *Poems, Chiefly Lyrical* (1830) has long passed without comment, but its presence and placement in the essay are both critical to his argument and instructive to our understanding of poetry's place in nineteenth-century visual culture. If the book, as Herbert Tucker observes, "had become a multimedia event" by the time of the first Reform Bill ("Literal," 164), Hallam's review registers an early protest against this encroachment of pictorial visuality into the domain of the typographic word.

Hallam's opening invective against the popular illustrated editions of the 1830s frames his subsequent argument for a modern poetry that expresses itself in the "picturesque" ("Characteristics," 1192, 1196). In an implicitly antipictorialist move against the picturesque images that one might find in Montgomery's *Oxford,* Hallam appropriates the visual term *picturesque* here to emphasize poetic imagery's capacity to conjure pictures in the reader's mind. I shall return later to the material combination of poetry and picturesque engravings in nineteenth-century illustrated books. At this stage, I merely wish to recognize that, in his opposition of poetry with pictures to picturesque poetry, Hallam aligns the first with mass appeal and the machinations of marketing and the second with a poetic genius accessible only to a limited readership capable of the "requisite exertion" (1193).

Hallam's valuing of metaphor over matter constitutes an apologia for verbal over visual culture, high over popular art. He identifies the linguistic appeal of poetry as a cultivated taste belonging to an educated elite willing to expend intellectual energy on the attainment of "the author's point of vision" (1193). The common reader, he insinuates, lacks both discriminating taste and imaginative effort and "wants to peruse his author in a luxurious passiveness" (1193). Both the luxury and the passivity of such a reading experience, Hallam's critique implies, are materially formulated in illustrated books such as Montgomery's *Oxford,* where the point of vision is realized for the reader by means of steel-engraved views.

Hallam's review demarcates with both precision and prescience the dilemma Tennyson faced at the height of his popularity as poet laureate, which happened to coincide with the golden age of illustration. How could he retain what Hallam extolled as the "rare and exclusive privilege" of his artistic "mission" (1192) when the market determined how his poetry would be produced, distributed, and received? Edward Moxon's new edition of Tennyson's early *Poems* as an illustrated gift book in 1857 highlights the complexities of the shift to a predominantly visual culture, a shift already evident in the early nineteenth century.[3] In its very material existence within the bindings of a midcentury gift book, poetry became middlebrow—a commodity for mass consumption, an object within Victorian material culture. When the poet descended from his isolated Palace of Art into the social world of publishers and readers, he found that he was not weaving his verses in "a cottage in a vale" but rather producing them in the factories of cultural industry, where the division of labor increasingly detached the author from his verses.

Between the first Reform Bill and the second, the mass production of poetry with pictures became a popular publishing phenomenon, with the works of national authors from Shakespeare to Tennyson visualized for the printed page by some of the period's foremost artists. A significant player in creating a middle-class audience for poetry with pictures was Edward Moxon, Tennyson's publisher for almost forty years. From the inception of his firm in 1830, Moxon developed a niche market as a publisher of poets and illustrated editions.[4] At the same time that he was bringing out Tennyson's *Poems, Chiefly Lyrical* and publishing Hallam's review in his *Englishman's Magazine,* Moxon was also making his mark as the preeminent publisher of high-class art and poetry with his edition of Samuel Rogers's *Italy,* illustrated with 128 steel-engraved vignettes after J. M. W. Turner and Thomas Stothard. Printed on a separate leaf inserted into the text, and protected by a tissue-paper guard, each small, centered vignette featured picturesque Italian landscapes. Later editions of the collected *Poems* (1834) moved the vignettes directly onto the printed page with the verses.

The integration of image and text through the placement of scenic vignettes at the head or end of a poem is characteristic of Romantic book design, as John Buchanan-Brown has shown in his study of illustrated books between 1820 and 1860. This preference for head- and tail-pieces remained a feature of British pictured poetry, but the new gift book of the sixties increasingly moved away from vignettes, whose blurred edges fade into the page, in favor of more formal demarcations of pictorial subjects through the use of circular, arched, and rectilinear frames (*Early Books,* 279). While the distant view of the vignette manipulates the reader to take in the poem from a detached seeing position, the framed close-up of human figures emphasizes the subjectivity of perception and interpretation. Moxon's illustrated edition of Tennyson's *Poems* in 1857 is a remarkable cultural object precisely because of the legible tensions between the Romantic tradition of vignettes and the dramatically new illustrative approach of the Pre-Raphaelite artists. The traditional illustrators presented their pictorial subjects as picturesque "views" akin to those that eighteenth- and early nineteenth-century tourists might seek in a Claude glass. In contrast, the Pre-Raphaelite illustrators signaled their modernity by presenting their subjects as objective correlatives for the poem in the form of "personified emotion" (D. G. Rossetti, *Correspondence,* 4:450).[5] And just as each illustrative method proposed a different relation to the poem, the book, and the world, so too did each construct a different reader for Tennyson's *Poems.*

As a material art object, the illustrated *Poems* participated in contemporary debates about visual and verbal culture, the possibilities of pictured poetry, and the relative authority of the book's various makers and readers. Published in May 1857, its release coincided with the opening of the Art Treasures of the United Kingdom Exhibition in Manchester, which marked a new middle-class involvement with visual art. The Art Treasures Exhibition and its multiple print-culture spin-offs also heightened public interest in both Pre-Raphaelite art and the technology of wood engraving as objects of national pride. Thus, although Moxon's initial publication of Tennyson's illustrated *Poems* was neither a commercial nor a critical success, within a very few years its Pre-Raphaelite engravings had come to represent a touchstone for artistic illustration. Reissued by Routledge as one of its guinea gift books, the volume became a reliable Christmas seller throughout the sixties and a critically important book for the printing revival at the fin de siècle. This chapter focuses on the production and reception of the Moxon Tennyson and seeks to locate its contemporary values and meanings in the context of Victorian visual culture. If its contents were a mishmash collection of the good, bad, and indifferent in art, this merely made the Moxon Tennyson, as the *Saturday Review* observed, "like an Academy Exhibition" (June 27, 1857, 601). A "bundle of splendid incongruities,"[6] the illustrated *Poems* put original art by living British illustrators, and poetry by the nation's most acclaimed poet, into the form of a miniaturized portable gallery and library for the middle-class home.

## The Making of the Moxon Tennyson

As a publisher always interested in extending his poets' shelf lives "with the help of some pretty illustrations," Moxon first broached the subject of an illustrated edition with Tennyson in 1849. After the new two-volume edition of *Poems* had reached a fifth edition, Moxon proposed to reissue the collection as a modest version of his elaborate editions of Samuel Rogers's poetry, "in one volume octavo illustrated by 30 vignettes engraved on steel." This proposal came to nothing, possibly because of Tennyson's objections.[7] The new decade brought the publication of *In Memoriam*, the dignity of the laureateship, and new national prominence. It also witnessed the definitive shift from steel to wood engraving and the development of the new gift-book industry.

In February 1854, after his successful Christmas publication of Keats's poetry with 120 wood engravings after designs by the antiquarian George Scharf, Moxon renewed his proposal for an illustrated edition.[8] This time, he proposed that Tennyson's *Poems, Chiefly Lyrical* (1830) be added to the two-volume *Poems* (1842) to form a single illustrated collection. Given the popularity of gift books at the time, Moxon felt sure that an illustrated edition of the early poetry would secure a second market and establish new readers for future Tennyson volumes. Certain of success, the usually cautious publisher guaranteed Tennyson a fee of £2,000 for the illustrated *Poems,* which he hoped to recuperate despite the extraordinary cost of paying both artists and engravers for their labor, which more than doubled his overall expenses.[9]

As was typical of gift books at the time, the plan was to invite several well-known artists to select about six subjects each and draw their designs on the woodblock for engraving. Moxon drew up a preliminary list of established illustrators, all Royal Academicians. Tennyson, initially cooperative in the project, seems to have suggested John Everett Millais and possibly Daniel Maclise; the former successfully proposed his young Pre-Raphaelite colleagues William Holman Hunt and Dante Gabriel Rossetti.[10] In May 1854, Tennyson traveled to London to meet Moxon; together, they called on Thomas Creswick, William Mulready, John Horsley, and John Everett Millais to secure their participation and confirm their selection of poems (A. Tennyson, *Letters,* 2:89). Publisher and poet were unable to see Hunt, who was painting in Jerusalem, but the artist sent word of his eagerness to contribute. Moxon seems to have contacted Rossetti and Maclise on his own; as we shall see in chapter 5, he contracted with the latter for an illustrated edition of *The Princess* at the same time.

The record also indicates that the poet endorsed the invitation of a novice woman artist, Elizabeth Siddall, to the project. According to Dante Gabriel Rossetti, their Pre-Raphaelite colleague Thomas Woolner interested the Tennysons in Siddall's artwork in March 1855, telling them she had produced a number of designs based on the early *Poems* that Ruskin had greatly admired. Although Emily apparently wrote Moxon to say that she would willingly pay the artist fees if the publisher could see his way to including Siddall among the illustrators, no contract was forthcoming.[11] For his part, Rossetti believed that the volume should have been illustrated exclusively by Pre-Raphaelite artists. "The right names," he declared, "would have been Millais, Hunt, Madox Brown, Hughes, a certain lady [i.e., Siddall] & myself. No others" (*Correspondence,* 2:7). While partisan, Rossetti's comment also underscores his abiding interest in a coherent approach to book design, which he was to develop later in his own works with such sophistication.[12] An edition of Tennyson's *Poems* exclusively by Pre-Raphaelite artists using a common approach to illustration would have integrated the book's visual style and pictorial hermeneutics.

Although Emily Tennyson's proposal that Siddall be included among the illustrators came to nothing, it does indicate the influence of the Pre-Raphaelites on the edition from the moment of their inclusion in the project. The record shows that Moxon had in mind an edition with illustrations by established Royal Academicians, but his control over the artistic contents was disrupted when Millais and his inexperienced but assertive Pre-Raphaelite colleagues joined the group of makers. From this point on, the edition may be fairly called, as Richard Stein does, "The Pre-Raphaelite Tennyson," with Millais, Hunt, and Rossetti considered joint authors in the book. Their participation changed the physical appearance, publication process, and significance to cultural history of the illustrated *Poems*. Millais eventually produced eighteen illustrations rather than the six Moxon proposed—almost three times as many as any other single artist and a third of the book's total of fifty-four. In addition to ensuring the collaboration of Hunt, who produced seven illustrations, and Rossetti, whose five designs represent 50 percent of his entire published oeuvre, Millais also recommended the services of the Dalziel brothers to Moxon. The engraving firm supervised the preparation and printing of the illustrations and acted as the publisher's liaison with the artists (Dalziel and Dalziel, *Record*, 82). In short, the Pre-Raphaelites dominated the production of the Moxon Tennyson just as they subsequently dominated its reception.

The book had been three long years in the making when Moxon finally issued the illustrated *Poems*. Owing to delays with preparing the pictures for reproduction, the gift book missed not just one but three Christmas markets, coming out in May 1857 rather than December 1856, 1855, or—as Moxon had fondly imagined—1854. Moreover, it spectacularly failed to generate the sales on publication that Moxon had counted on to offset his costs. Priced at thirty-one shillings and sixpence, the book was too expensive for middle-class book buyers accustomed to the guinea gift book. The price placed the edition halfway between the old and the new, just as its pictorial contents did. In the 1830s, Moxon's upmarket editions of Rogers's poetry with engraved vignettes sold to a select audience for forty-two shillings; in contrast, the new Christmas gift book was usually priced at twenty-one shillings and aimed at a broader range of buyers. The clashing pictorial styles may also have given potential purchasers pause. According to Hunt, "Those who liked the work of artists long established in favour felt that the pages on which our designs appeared destroyed the attractiveness of the volume, and the few who approved of our inventions would not give the price for the publication, because there was so large a proportion of the contributions of a kind which they did not value" (*Pre-Raphaelitism*, 2:75).

Hunt's retrospective assessment of the effect of the clashing pictorial styles on sales, however, needs some adjustment. Although the book was not well received in the first instance, it soon became a desirable object in many middle-class homes. When Moxon sold the remaindered sheets to Routledge in autumn 1858, he had moved only 2,210 copies of the original print run of ten thousand. Routledge reduced the price to a guinea and promoted the illustrated *Poems* as a gift book in his Christmas sales catalogs and advertisements. By 1863, Routledge had sold all remaining copies and contracted with Tennyson to bring out a new impression of a further five thousand copies; in 1869, the firm wanted to print another five thousand copies.[13] With about fifteen thousand copies in circulation during the sixties, the illustrated *Poems* was clearly something of a popular success. Moreover, within a few years it had already become a touchstone in critical essays and reviews referencing illustrated gift books. Significantly, there was a concurrent change in the appreciation of its images. While early reviews were mixed, they showed a preference for the traditional artists' work. After the Art Treasures Exhibition of 1857, however, the Pre-Raphaelite images quickly became the most valued visual aspect of the book. A barometer for the change in illustrative styles and tastes that characterized the sixties, the Moxon Tennyson also marks the moment that the sister arts of pictures and poetry shifted direction in popular publishing.

## Pre-Raphaelite Illustration and the Sister Arts

In the nineteenth century's emerging culture of the image, Victorian thought was steeped in the sister arts tradition. Following the Horatian maxim *ut pictura poesis* ("as a picture, so also a poem"), popular criticism considered that the fine arts were, as Walter Pater complained in *The Renaissance,* "but translations into different languages of one and the same fixed quantity of imaginative thought" (107). The notion that the excellences in poetry and pictures were analogous is ubiquitous in reviews of both art and literature. Throughout the period, storytelling pictures and painterly poems were the most admired; poets were celebrated for their word painting and painters for their poetry. In Hallam's early praise of Tennyson's picturesque poetry, for instance, he emphasized, as did many subsequent critics, the poet's "clearly painted" images. Tennyson's poems presented "a perfect gallery of pictures," and he had the ability to lay "the scene . . . before us" in "a complete picture" ("Characteristics," 1198–99). In keeping with the contemporary understanding of the sister arts, Hallam's conflation of poetry and pictures was not limited to Tennyson's metaphoric painting by means of vivid imagery. He also considered the comparable effect of sound in poetry (tones) to coloring in painting (tints), taking the Horatian maxim to its logical limits and connecting his criticism to Simonides' proposition that as poetry was a speaking picture, so painting was mute poesy ("Characteristics," 2000).[14]

John Ruskin, the foremost art critic of the day, similarly insisted that one should not oppose pictures and poetry but conflate them, insofar as all good art is poetry, whether in colors or words.[15] Privately, he wrote to Tennyson after the publication of the illustrated *Poems* to say that good pictures "are always another poem" rather than subservient "illustrations" (H. Tennyson, *Memoir,* 1:420). Ruskin's theoretical position is similar to that of many practitioners, including poet-painter Dante Gabriel Rossetti, who observed, "My own belief is that I am a poet (within the limit of my powers) primarily, and that it is my poetic tendencies that chiefly give value to my pictures" (*Correspondence*, 4:449). By using *poetry* as a term that encompasses the visual arts, Ruskin and Rossetti imply the legibility of all visual marks and objects as expressive signs capable of being read. It follows, then, that there is also a poetics of the book as an expressive form. The Moxon Tennyson represents the most concerted effort in the art of the book by Pre-Raphaelitism's founding members: John Everett Millais, Dante Gabriel Rossetti, and William Holman Hunt.

With their dual commitment to "art and literature," as announced on the title page of their short-lived illustrated journal, *The Germ* (1850), the Pre-Raphaelites were strong proponents of the sister-arts tradition and significant contributors to its popular dissemination through their paintings, illustrations, poems, and decorative objects. Although *The Germ* had a small circulation and did not survive beyond four monthly numbers, it continued to exercise its influence on nineteenth-century art and visual culture through to the fin de siècle. Moreover, the Pre-Raphaelites brought art and poetry together as the mainstay of the periodical, featuring an original etching connected to the lead poem of each issue. *The Germ* modeled the collaborative artistic practice of verbal-visual interaction that the Pre-Raphaelites had established with the founding of the Brotherhood in 1848. This practice continued in later phases of the movement through such activities as the decoration of the Oxford Union (1857), the work of the Firm (Morris, Marshall, Faulkner and Co., 1861–75), Christina and Dante Gabriel Rossetti's image/text collaborations in her first two collections of poetry (1862 and 1866), and, at the fin de siècle, William Morris's establishment of the Kelmscott Press. In both their decorative commercial work and their paintings, the Pre-Raphaelite artists and their associates visualized literary subjects taken from biblical scripture, Shakespearean drama, medieval literature, Arthurian legend, and the poetry of Keats and Tennyson. Constantly bringing the fields of visual and verbal art into dialogue, they wrote poems on pictures—both as ekphrastic abstractions of material paintings and as physical inscriptions on the canvases and frames of their paintings. However, their various modes of commingling visual and poetic art were not what raised the ire of critics in the 1850s. Rather, it was their artistic style that provoked controversy in the columns of the periodical press and brought Pre-Raphaelite art to public attention.

Upsetting contemporary aesthetic discourse with an approach that combined "truth to nature" with an emulation of the artistic practice of Raphael and his antecedents, the Pre-Raphaelites had a revolutionary effect on contemporary art. With brilliantly colored canvases featuring large figures set in intensely detailed landscapes or interiors, Pre-Raphaelite painting troubled the hierarchies established by Renaissance perspective and the viewing position it had formulated. As Elizabeth Prettejohn's work has shown, Pre-Raphaelite pictures "reconfigure traditional spatial relationships" because they "do not ordinarily present a regularly measured progression from the foreground through to the distance; equivalent distances on the canvas do not translate logically into equivalent distances in the putative 'real' space" (*Art*, 188). This bringing of foreground and distance into contiguity has two significant results. First, Prettejohn suggests, the "elision of the middleground" indicates "a gap in the logic of 'truth-to-nature'" (188). Second, just as no representation can encompass the entire truth of a worldly event or literary story, so too no single viewing position can be established from which the viewer is manipulated to view the scene. Pre-Raphaelite "pictures do not prescribe a hierarchy of viewing patterns that might finalise the interpretative process"; instead these artworks encourage "close looking" and ongoing imaginative engagement with the image (259).

The elision of the middle ground in Pre-Raphaelite paintings also has important implications for their book art. Indeed, going beyond the Pre-Raphaelite concern with bringing the sister arts of pictures and poetry into dialogic relationship, the Pre-Raphaelites' visualization style is admirably suited to book illustration. From a design perspective, the flat plane of the printed page is better suited to a two-dimensional decorative style than it is to the three-dimensional style of perspectival painting. This graphic approach also recognizes, complements, and comments on the iconic values of typographic letters and lines of poetic verses, bringing the Pre-Raphaelites' artistic interest in patternings and repetitions into their approach to pictured poetry. The Pre-Raphaelite insistence on "close looking" in their paintings translates to "close reading" in the codex form, where the image is printed on the page with letterpress and read along with it. An art designed for readers in domestic space, book illustration combines utility and ornament, bringing the aesthetic object into everyday use.

Of all the sister-arts relationships, illustration is the one that has the closest and most immediate interaction and integration with the printed word and the daily life of the ordinary person. As literary painters, decorative artists, and poets committed to experimenting formally with the sister arts, the Pre-Raphaelites brought a theory and a practice to the art of the book that proposed a radical new direction for art and poetry in the modern world. Rather than opposing the fields of restricted and large-scale cultural production, the individual hand of the artist and the machinery of mass production, the Pre-Raphaelites sought to bring them closer together and to acknowledge the social practices and uses of art. Flawed as it is, the Moxon Tennyson represents their most sustained and comprehensive project in realizing visual art on the printed page for the enhanced experience of quotidian middle-class users.

Writing in praise of the Pre-Raphaelite style at the end of the Victorian period, book artist Laurence Housman called attention to the Moxon Tennyson's introduction of a *readerly* approach to the illustration of poetry: "[T]he main difference between their work and that of the others was that the Pre-Raphaelites had something to say very pertinent to the subject in hand, the rest nothing—nothing, that is to say, to show that they had any sense that they were illustrating not nature but literature" (*Houghton,* 13). As Housman explains, "the illustrations of the pre-Raphaelites were personal and intellectual readings of the poems to which they belonged, not merely echoes in line of the words of the text" (13). Effectively, the Pre-Raphaelite illustrators combined the roles of author and reader, thereby making visible the modern reading experience as bricolage, a creative ordering that puts into play a range of possible responses.[16] Their designs materialized a bold poetics of reading, making a spectacle of the art of interpretation and asserting the reader's right to make meanings. To apply de Certeau's theory to Pre-Raphaelite practice, the illustrations of Hunt, Millais, and Rossetti—especially Rossetti—did not take up Tennyson's position but rather invented in Tennyson's poems "something different from what they 'intended'" (*Practice,* 169). In so doing, they upset the cultural hierarchy of writer/producer and reader/receiver by making visible the autonomy and creativity of readers as makers.

The effect of the Pre-Raphaelite interpretive designs on the book's immediate audience was threefold: they challenged the authority of the poet and emphasized the social and collaborative dimensions of art production; they demonstrated the autonomy of readers' imaginations and showed how poems exist in historically specific reading experiences; and they claimed the book as a vehicular form for art in the age of mass production.

## Picturing Poetry and the Material Book

By 1857, a whole generation of readers had grown up reading Tennyson's early verses. For these readers, the *Saturday Review* critic suggested, the affront of the illustrated edition constituted a visual assault that went beyond the interpretation of individual poems to strike at the very meaning of the book as a physical object imbricated with social meaning. Comparing the shock value of the illustrated edition to that prompted by the bronzed, bearded, and unrecognizable faces of friends returning from the Crimea, the writer continued: "Our intimacy with a book is equally dependent on its physiognomy maintaining the old familiar type. We have carried Tennyson in duodecimo in our hand or our portmanteau for year after year. We have learnt him by heart, by the eye as much as by the ear—the size of page and print, the position of each line and each thought upon the page, has been lastingly impressed upon the retina of our memory" (June 27, 1857, 601).

The critic assumes an intimacy with, and ownership of, Tennyson's poetry, his authoritative "we" clearly delimited by the masculine perspective of an educated cultural producer. This reader's reaction reminds us that Tennyson's *Poems* interpellated different readers and meanings in its "gorgeous regeneration" in "the royallest of octavos, with a sumptuous satin margin to set off the print, and a fringe of pictorial illustrations to accompany the words" (June 27, 1857, 601).

The change in format from plain duodecimo to ornate royal octavo is class- and gender-marked. The duodecimo travels in the pocket of the moving man of the public sphere; the royal octavo sits in the private sphere with women and juvenile members of the middle-class family. From this critic's viewpoint, visual culture and popular publishing have moved poetry out of its preserved precinct of restricted appreciation, vulgarizing it through the trappings of mass production and middle-class consumerism: "As long, however, as there are drawing-room tables to be laden with ornamental books—as long as there are persons to give presents, and persons to receive them—so long may we assume that the supply of such works will be regulated in accordance with the demand, and that the works themselves will form in turn a large material for eulogy from such enthusiastic admirers, and jealous inquiry from such colder critics, as may chance to stand around the tables aforesaid" (*SR*, June 27, 1857, 601). The illustrated book's "enthusiastic admirers" are implicitly women, the persons whose role it is "to receive" such books for display on their drawing-room tables. The "colder critics" are the men of the family, who may, occasionally, "chance to stand around the tables aforesaid" but whose principal role in this structured economy is to be "the persons to give presents."

When the Moxon Tennyson was reissued for the Christmas market as a Routledge guinea gift book in 1858, the critic for *Fraser's Magazine* took up the charge against "the illustrated book, which for the last two or three years has been overrunning the tables of every boudoir and drawing-room in the kingdom, and which now apparently occupies a regular and most active department of art manufacture" ("Furniture Books," 98). Sarcastically calling "for the intervention of the literary police" to put a stop to "the degradation of a great poet's text by a host of flashy woodcuts," this critic particularly abhorred the increasingly dominant role of the image in poetic texts. Rather than being "*plates,* modest ancillaries to the text, thrown in for the delectation of the 'polite reader,'" as in the days of the annual, the presumptuous illustrations in the new gift books of the sixties vied with the verses on the page for the reader's attention, as wood-engraving technology allowed images to "thrust themselves into the body of the text" (99). Significantly, this critic linked this predominance of the image on the printed page to the encroachments of visual culture: "The eye is unhappily too much fed nowadays, to the prejudice of our nobler faculties. Museums and Crystal Palaces pamper us with sights which used to be achieved with effort, and seen at long intervals. We have so much to see, that we have no leisure to muse on what we see" (102). The critic's conclusions situate illustrated poetry squarely within mass visual culture, connecting it to the emerging dominance of the image in the realm of popular entertainment. From this perspective, the gift book's threat was that it was moving the fine arts of poetry and pictures into the arena of mass-cultural production, cheapening both by the democracy of access and the vulgarity of reified vision.

Despite these critical protests, the conditions of the marketplace and the economics of publishing at midcentury made an illustrated edition of Tennyson's *Poems* inevitable. As the *Art Journal*'s critic commented in his review of July 1857, the laureate's fame made it "only reasonable to expect, according to the fashion of the day, an illustrated edition of at least some of his poems; and we now have a very beautiful volume, issued by Mr. Moxon, of the early poems . . . adorned with a large number of woodcuts from drawings by some of our most distinguished artists" (231). While the *Art Journal*'s mandate was to celebrate and disseminate the nation's art to the wide middle-class audience it sought to educate, its position on the wood-engraved pictures by the three Pre-Raphaelite artists was equivocal. Although acknowledging apt similarity in style, the *Art Journal*'s critic maintained that book art ought to presuppose the superiority of the verbal over the visual: "The peculiarity of Tennyson's style of writing, imaginative and highly-coloured, but frequently open to the charge of affectation, was perhaps, in some degree, a justifiable reason for enlisting the services of the Pre-Raffaelite [*sic*] school of artists in the work of illustration" (231). However, the reviewer went on to criticize, rather than praise, this stylistic fitness: "The quaintness of thought and expression that is found in the verse, need not necessarily be followed by quaintness of pictorial design" (231). Illustrations, in this critic's view and that of many others, should be modest and subservient pictorial companions to the printed word.

The debate over the relationship between poem and picture, the printed page, and the reader was materialized in the Moxon Tennyson itself in the contrasting pictorial styles of the younger group of artists (Rossetti, Millais, and

Hunt) and the older group (Mulready, Creswick, Stanfield, Horsley, and Maclise). In both artistic style and interpretive praxis, the three Pre-Raphaelites and five Academicians approached the illustration of Tennyson's poetry in startlingly different ways. For the most part, the older school of illustrators provided traditional vignettes: picturesque scenes of landscapes and ruins that ornamented the page but did not detract attention from the poetic lines or presume to comment on them. Moxon had selected the traditional artists both for their prestige value as members of the Royal Academy and for their separate strengths: Maclise specialized in history paintings, Mulready in genre, Creswick in landscapes, Horsley in domestic scenes, and Stanfield in seascapes and landscapes.[17] Their contributions were such stock elements of their standard repertoire that a despairing Rossetti knew in advance exactly what they would be. "What do you think?" he wrote to Allingham in January 1855, having just completed his block for *The Music Master* and turned to his work for the Moxon edition; "Stanfield is to do *Break, break*, because there is a sea in it, and *Ulysses*, too, because there are ships" (*Correspondence*, 2:7).

Rossetti's disappointment is merited. Stanfield's illustration for "Ulysses" is such a generic marine scene that it could, without damage, equally adorn just about any poem by any poet of any period that mentions the sea, especially if it alludes to either abandoning ship in a storm or embarking in rough weather (fig. 2.1). Because there are no such references in "Ulysses," the vignette's relationship to the monologue by the eponymous adventurer—who had "become a name / For always roaming with a hungry heart" and determines, in the course of his address to his people, "to seek a newer world"—is tenuous (265–66).[18] One cannot single out, among the indistinct figures in the boat, which of these sailors might be Ulysses. What is interesting for our purposes is that the lack of alignment between Stanfield's vignette and Tennyson's poem occasioned neither authorial nor critical protest, whereas any perceived discrepancy between the Pre-Raphaelite illustrations and Tennyson's text assuredly did. The *Art Journal*, for example, actually praised Stanfield's "Ulysses" for its "picturesque and truthful character," while critiquing Rossetti's "Sir Galahad" for being "without the slightest reference to any descriptive line in the poem it professes to illustrate" (231).

The critic's praise of Stanfield's "Ulysses" as a "truthful" illustration, when it makes no more—in fact, considerably less—reference to its accompanying poem than does Rossetti's "Galahad," highlights the degree to which perception is informed by learned visual codes and conventions. Stanfield and his colleagues produced illustrations in a familiar language, one whose well-worn graphic lines had been familiar companions to the illustrated book of verses at least since Turner's engraved vignettes for Rogers's *Italy* in 1830. The conventional

ULYSSES.

It little profits that an idle king,
By this still hearth, among these barren crags,
Match'd with an aged wife, I mete and dole
Unequal laws unto a savage race,
That hoard, and sleep, and feed, and know not me.
I cannot rest from travel: I will drink
Life to the lees: all times I have enjoy'd
Greatly, have suffer'd greatly, both with those

Figure 2.1 Clarkson Stanfield, "Ulysses," in Alfred Tennyson, *Poems*, 2nd ed. (Moxon, 1859), 264.

vignette establishes a viewing position for the reader that assumes a distant and objective view of the pictorial—and, by extension, poetic—subject. From a distance, the vignette implies, it is not details but overall effect that matters, not particularized human emotions but generalized affective scenes. Moreover, because the vignette's use of perspective establishes a singular viewing position, the pictured scene puts the reader in the place of the artist, who stands in the place of the poet. In this sense, the blurred lines of the vignette also imply the homogenization of different points of view. The convention dictates that, just as the pictured scene fades into the printed page, so too does the reader's personality fade into the author's during the reading experience.

In Sophie Thomas's astute study of "the Romantic textualization of the image," she shows how the visual paradigm of the picturesque brought the standards of art to bear on "views" of the natural world (*Romanticism*, 7). Emphasizing effects of light and shade, the introduction of unusual features such as ruins, and rough textures represented in broad strokes, the discourse of the picturesque shaped the ways in which scenery was seen in the early nineteenth century (9). Although the discourse of the picturesque in this period is too large a subject to canvas here, its predominant technology of vision, the Claude glass, is relevant to book illustration and the relationship it proposes to the poem and the world. A convex tinted mirror, the Claude glass was used by artists and tourists to reflect a scene in such a way that gradations in light and shade emerged clearly, with the result that the reflected landscape appeared in the form of a Claude painting (S. Thomas, *Romanticism*, 10). The rounded shapes of the scenic vignettes that embellished popular books of poetry in the early nineteenth century presented readers with the image of the poetic scene as one might see it through a Claude glass. In effect, readers were positioned as landscape tourists seeking extractable "views" of the poem. This approach to illustrating poetry suggests that the poem is not a text to be read so much as a scene to be imagined. To apply Hallam's words to a new context, the vignettes are pictorial aids assisting readers to attain "the author's point of vision" ("Characteristics," 1193). The artist-reader's vignette objectifies Hallam's injunction "*to start from the same point*" as the poet by providing a place to stand and look at a subject (1193).

In contrast, the Pre-Raphaelite artists approached "the author's point of vision" as something to respect rather than to represent. What interested them most was the imaginative and intellectual challenge of re-creating poetic subject matter in their own graphic material. This entailed objectifying their reading of the poem, rather than representing the supposed scene of its writing. Following Dante Gabriel Rossetti's lead, and with varying degrees of intensity, the Pre-Raphaelite artists sought Tennysonian subjects in which one could, as Rossetti famously put it, "allegorize on one's own hook on the subject of the poem" without destroying the author's idea, the reader's pleasure, or the book's aesthetic value (*Correspondence*, 2:7). Rossetti's articulation of the ideal relationship between poetry and pictures also gives us insight into another striking feature of Pre-Raphaelite illustration. Unlike the fuzzy-edged scenic vignettes of the traditional illustrators, the Pre-Raphaelite pictures tended to be marked off from the textual page with the use of a framing device; to incorporate a wealth of symbolic detail; and to feature a large, central figure or figures in a dramatic and defining moment.

This preference for large central figures pictured at a moment of great intensity is a crucial aspect of the innovative Pre-Raphaelite approach to art and poetry. As he explained in a famous letter to Thomas Gordon Hake, Rossetti sought, in his poetry as he did in his painting, "to deal . . . chiefly with personified emotions" rather than with so-called word-painting that merely realized a scene (*Correspondence,* 4:450). Rossetti's approach to poetry and painting also extended to illustrative practice. Here, the artist designed the foregrounded figure or figures and the details of the symbolic setting as a visual means of embodying the particularity of the poem's affective experience. This was a graphic version of T. S. Eliot's "objective correlative" in poetic art. In his well-known essay on *Hamlet,* Eliot wrote, "The only way of expressing emotion in the form of art is by finding an 'objective correlative'; in other words, a set of objects, a situation, a chain of events which shall be the formula of that *particular* emotion; such that when the external facts, which must terminate in sensory experience, are given, the emotion is immediately evoked" (100). The Pre-Raphaelites' artistic practice shows their understanding of the theoretical concept that Eliot later articulated. As illustrators, they expressed poetic emotion in the form of intensely realized objective correlatives. Personifying a poem's emotions in this objectified way was, according to Rossetti, to "embody [the work's] ideas" (*Correspondence,* 1:363). "Inevitably," as Elizabeth K. Helsinger observes in her acute analysis of Rossetti's art of the book, "to embody its ideas is also to interpret them" (*Poetry,* 183).

As embodied interpretations of Tennyson's poetic texts, Pre-Raphaelite illustrations were designed to belong to the material book and the social world of readers. Signaling their legibility as iconic and semantic statements distinct from the stanzaic blocks of verse, they demarcated their separate textual space on the printed page with the use of rectilinear borders. Already in this first, and only major, collaborative book work, the Pre-Raphaelite designers understood what William Morris later identified as the essential qualities of "book-pictures" (*Ideal Book,* 56). As works of art in themselves, Morris explained, "Their two main merits are first their decorative and next their story-telling quality" (56). Although the Moxon Tennyson fell far short of the ideal unity that Morris espoused for the book as an expressive form, the individual "book-pictures" of the Pre-Raphaelites realized the qualities Morris articulated. With remarkable clarity, their illustrations combined the decorative patterning of planar art designed for the printed page with the narrative intensity of emotion distilled into a particularized human situation and an associated set of objects or things. This combination of qualities is what made their illustrations embodied "acts of *attention*" requiring similar acts of attention from the reader.[19]

A Pre-Raphaelite illustration of "Ulysses" would no doubt have included a sea, and perhaps even a ship, as part of the background, but its principal purpose would have been the realization of "personified emotion" in the foregrounded representation of the eponymous hero. Like Millais' "Mariana," Hunt's "Oriana," and Rossetti's "Lady of Shalott," but unlike any of the traditional artists' illustrations, this figure would have been drawn "from nature" through the use of a live model and multiple preliminary studies. The final position and placement of the figure, and the highly realized objects, architecture, and landscape of the entire scene, would all be symbolic details of a concentrated interpretation of the poem as a whole. Unlike Stanfield's actual vignette for "Ulysses," this imagined illustration by a Pre-Raphaelite artist would use a rectilinear border to emphasize the picture's separation from the poem and highlight its status as a distinct text to be read. It would require a reader with visual/verbal literacy, one capable of reading the picture both on its own and in relation to the verses whose theme it "allegorized." As Julia Thomas comments, "The aim of such an illustration is not to illuminate the poem in the sense of clarifying it, but to add to the range of its possible meanings" (*Pictorial Victorians,* 60). On the illustrated pages of the Moxon Tennyson, the subject of debate between the two schools of artists becomes the interpretive possibilities historically available to readers.

This stylistic and interpretive argument is also carried on between the traditional illustrators and the Pre-Raphaelites through their selections of poetic subjects. While the Academicians illustrated lyrical poetry as frequently as they did narrative, Hunt and Rossetti absolutely avoided the lyric. Alone of the Pre-Raphaelites, Millais included illustrations to three lyric poems among his eighteen pictorial contributions. One of these, "St. Agnes' Eve," combines a headpiece by Millais with a tailpiece by Stanfield (figs. 2.2 and 2.3). Over the space of three pages, a fascinating dialogue on the relation of pictures to poetry and possible approaches to illustrating lyrics emerges. Tennyson's poem is composed of three numbered stanzas, each twelve lines in length with six alternating rhymes in common meter. Spoken in the voice of a nun who hopes, according to the medieval tradition, to see her future mate on St. Agnes's Eve—no mere mortal, but "the Heavenly Bridegroom" himself—the poem is an atmospheric mood piece in which the chill setting of the winter night becomes an objective correlative for the nun's emotional and psychological state of purity, innocence, faith, and hope:

ST. AGNES' EVE.

I.

Deep on the convent-roof the snows
Are sparkling to the moon:
My breath to heaven like vapour goes:
May my soul follow soon!

Figure 2.2 John Everett Millais, "St. Agnes' Eve," in Alfred Tennyson, *Poems*, 2nd ed. (Moxon, 1859), 309.

Deep on the convent-roof the snows
Are sparkling to the moon:
My breath to heaven like vapour goes:
May my soul follow soon!
The shadows of the convent-towers
Slant down the snowy sward,
Still creeping with the creeping hours
That lead me to my Lord:
Make Thou my spirit pure and clear
As are the frosty skies,
Or this first snowdrop of the year
That in my bosom lies.

(309–10)

ST. AGNES' EVE. 311

The sabbaths of Eternity,
One sabbath deep and wide—
A light upon the shining sea—
The Bridegroom with his bride!

Figure 2.3 Clarkson Stanfield, "St. Agnes' Eve," in Alfred Tennyson, *Poems,* 2nd ed. (Moxon, 1859), 311.

The addition of Millais' headpiece and Stanfield's tailpiece to Tennyson's "St. Agnes' Eve" impinges on the page layout, causing the first and last stanzas to be divided into chunks of four and eight lines. The initial visual effect of the illustrative matter is therefore physical and spatial. The pictorial headpiece occupies half the textual page, leaving room only for the first four lines of the poem to be printed below the horizontal line of its bottom edge; the consequent severance of these lines from their stanza alters the reader's experience of the poem's first numbered movement (fig. 2.2). Similarly, the coherence of the final stanza's apocalyptic description of the nun's imagined union with the Bridegroom is disrupted by the page turn after line eight and the consequent isolation of the poem's last four lines above the tailpiece:

> The sabbaths of Eternity,
>     One sabbath deep and wide—
> A light upon the shining sea—
>     The Bridegroom with his bride!
>
> (311)

By altering the typographical display of the words on the page, the pictures change the reader's linguistic, iconic, and semantic experience of the verses. In addition, the distinct pictorial styles of the two artists introduce alternative imaginative spaces for the poem and propose different relations to the reader. Stanfield's tailpiece concludes the nun's euphoric vision of eternal union with Christ with the familiar rudiments of gothic convention (fig. 2.3). The vignette depicts a tiny figure praying before a shrine on a cliff; in the background, a full moon illuminates the convent on the hill. The picturesque scene evokes the romantic atmosphere found in the pictorial tradition of the early nineteenth-century illustrated book. Indeed, the picture would have been an apt accompaniment to the poem in its first appearance in the illustrated annual *The Keepsake* (1837). Sketchy in both graphic style and pictorial detail, Stanfield's tailpiece functions as an atmospheric textual decoration anchoring the poem in its scenic effect rather than its psychological affect.

In contrast, Millais' introductory headpiece to the poem takes the reader inside for a close-up consideration of the nun's state of mind (fig. 2.2). Far from disappearing into the textual page in the blurred edges of a vignette, the framed picture presents itself as a black square on the page, an interior space into which the viewer is invited before entering the speaker's subjective display of her own interiority. Visually dominant, the picture takes more than its share of the page and even claims some of the principal verbal matter for itself. Between image and text, the name of the subject asserts itself in capitals, "ST. AGNES' EVE," operating simultaneously as poetic title and pictorial caption. The page layout splits the reader's attention between the reading of the picture and the reading of the verses and encourages a back-and-forth engagement between them. Positioned at the top of the poem, the image functions as a lens through which the lyric speaker's meditation is mediated.

In one way, Millais' approach to the business of illustrating lyrical poetry is similar to Stanfield's: neither artist attempted to illustrate individual lines. But unlike Stanfield, Millais set out to encapsulate, in pictorial form, an overall reading of the speaker and her hope. To do this adequately, he combined visual details taken from the poem with his own pictorial imagery. As a graphic representation of the threshold experience the poem explores, Millais invented a liminal setting for the young sister: the winding stair of a round tower whose window opens out to a wintry night scene. Although Millais depicts important details from Tennyson's verses—the nun's vaporous breath on the frosty air, the snow on the rooftops, her white gown and candle—his illustration's main purpose is to capture the personified emotion of the whole. In this way, Millais proposed a modern approach to the illustration of lyric poetry, one that focuses on speaker, symbolic detail, and atmosphere.

MARIANA.

"Mariana in the moated grange."—*Measure for Measure.*

I.

WITH blackest moss the flower-plots
Were thickly crusted, one and all:
The rusted nails fell from the knots
That held the peach to the garden-wall.

Figure 2.4 John Everett Millais, "Mariana," in Alfred Tennyson, *Poems*, 2nd ed. (Moxon, 1859), 7.

Millais used the same method in his illustration for "Mariana" (fig. 2.4). Here he depicts Mariana cast down on a window bench, her face turned away from the casement, whose view—were she to look at it—would only confirm the cause of her despair: "He cometh not" (8, 9). In the positioning of the central figure and the claustrophobic enclosure of the room's walls, which seem to be pressing in from all sides, the illustration becomes an objective correlative for the emotions expressed in the poem. Whereas Tennyson equates the speaker's charged emotional situation with the dreary stasis of the villa's exterior landscape, however, Millais uses the defeated gesture of the human figure in the confines of interior space. As he did for "St. Agnes' Eve," Millais here proposed an approach to the illustration of lyric poetry that conveys the emotional tenor of the speaker and her situation through figure positioning and symbolic setting. His method of personifying emotion was

CLARIBEL.

A MELODY.

I.

Where Claribel low-lieth
The breezes pause and die,
Letting the rose-leaves fall:
But the solemn oak-tree sigheth,

B

Figure 2.5 Thomas Creswick, "Claribel," in Alfred Tennyson, *Poems*, 2nd ed. (Moxon, 1859), 1.

so successful that the "Mariana" image later became, as David Skilton has shown, part of the stock graphic vocabulary for representing despair in the illustrated periodicals that emerged after the Moxon Tennyson ("Centrality," n.p.). In 1857, however, this illustrative approach was innovative.

Because the Moxon Tennyson opens with a vignette by Thomas Creswick and closes with one by Clarkson Stanfield, the reading experience of the volume as a whole is framed by the approach proposed for lyrical poetry by these traditional illustrators. Creswick's opening vignette for "Claribel" depicts a reedy stream in the foreground, a graveyard and tree in the middle ground, and a church and moon in the background (fig. 2.5). These pictorial details are very similar to those that Creswick provides for "A Dirge" (47) and "Move Eastward, Happy Earth" (371), just as his illustrations for "Ode to Memory" (25) and

"Farewell" (347) present nearly identical bucolic scenes of streams and trees. In its architectural structure, then, the illustrated *Poems* implicitly constructs lyric poetry as a picturesque "view" shared by poet, artist, and reader.

As the pictorial introduction to the volume as a whole, Creswick's illustration for "Claribel" establishes a "long view" of the subject and implies an objective observer/reader who, standing back from the scene rather than engaging with it, feels a general emotion. The picture's placement also necessarily disrupts the typographic display of the verses, and hence the reader's experience of them. The lyric moves from a generalized first stanza emphasizing an undifferentiated "melody" to a particularized second stanza that dilates upon temporal changes ringing a variety of distinct sounds at evening, noon, and midnight. The large headpiece vignette forces the poem down the page and results in a division of the first stanza into two parts. To complete the thought initiated by "But the solemn oak-tree sigheth . . ." (1), the reader must turn the page. This typographical dislocation disturbs both the intellectual and the aural effect of the poem. Moreover, the musical devices by which the poem creates its atmospheric effects seem supplanted by the image, which establishes the mood at the outset. Sight elbows out sound as the dominant sense.

Implicitly making a final claim for the power of the poetic voice over the printed image, the last lyric in the Moxon Tennyson is "Poet's Song," an unillustrated poem that imagines the modern poet as an Orpheus whose musical chanting charms the natural world (375).[20] The book's vehicular form, however, contests this celebration of poetry's aural power, a challenge reinscribed in the printed effect of the penultimate lyric, "Break, break, break" (373–74). As the final image in the book, Stanfield's illustration asserts the trace of the artist's invisible hand in the shaping of modern poetry in print culture (fig. 2.6). His headpiece for "Break, break, break" divides the four-stanza poem over recto and verso, necessitating a page turn that formally breaks the poetic wish "that my tongue could utter / The thoughts that arise in me" from its subsequent expression over the remaining twelve lines (373–74). Representing waves crashing on a shore where a small boy and girl huddle near a fishing boat hauled up under a cliff, the vignette combines with the first quatrain to imply the inadequacy of verbal language. Only after the page turn do the poetic lines complete the initial thought and establish the nostalgia for a lost past that the picturesque scene evokes at the outset. At this point, retrospectively, the inadequacy of the image is made manifest. The pictured scene appears trite and sentimental next to Tennyson's cumulative building up of longing and loss through the repetitive patternings of vowel sounds, rhymes, and metrical rhythms, and the sustained musical meditation on that which cannot be seen or touched.

Break, break, break,
  On thy cold gray stones, O Sea!
And I would that my tongue could utter
  The thoughts that arise in me.

Figure 2.6 Clarkson Stanfield, "Break, break, break," in Alfred Tennyson, *Poems*, 2nd ed. (Moxon, 1859), 373.

Recognizing the difficulty of adequately illustrating the affective and subjective experience of lyric poetry, the Pre-Raphaelite artists favored narrative verse, which gave them greater scope, according to D. G. Rossetti, for allegorizing on the poetic subject without detriment to the poet's leading idea (*Correspondence*, 2:7). In a way similar to illustrated fiction, narrative poetry allowed artists to realize characters in dramatic situations. Unlike fiction, however, narrative poetry also required the artist to find a way to encapsulate the poem *as* a poem rather than as a story. This was an intellectual and imaginative challenge that the Pre-Raphaelite artists took up with relish. Moreover, given the prevalence of female characters in Tennyson's early poems, focusing on his narrative poetry also gave them the opportunity to represent in black-and-white illustrations, as they did in their paintings, large female figures in highly realized symbolic scenes.[21] Hunt, for example, depicted Oriana, the Lady of Shalott, Godiva, and the Beggar Maid at moments of intense emotion. Like Rossetti, who also drew the Lady of Shalott, as well as Mariana in the South, St. Cecily, the weeping queens of Arthurian legend, and Sir Galahad, Hunt favored Tennyson's medieval poetry, though he was also attracted to the orientalism of "Recollections of the Arabian Nights."

Millais, in contrast, was as comfortable with the medieval narratives of Tennyson's "Dream of Fair Women," "Lord of Burleigh," "The Daydream," and "The Sisters" as he was with the contemporary narratives of "The Miller's Daughter," "Dora," "Edward Gray," and "Locksley Hall"; significantly, he was later to become an inspired illustrator of novels.[22] Millais also experimented with different stylistic approaches, using a dark and detailed composition set within a frame for the medieval illustrations and a light, linear, unframed drawing for the contemporary ones. The length of the narrative poems also occasioned some new page layouts, presumably established by the Dalziel brothers, who oversaw the printing. Rather than appearing exclusively at the head or the end of a poem, as in the shorter works, the illustrations for the narrative pieces were occasionally embedded partway through, thus introducing another visual interruption into the continuity of the reading experience.

To embody event-filled stories of multiple characters in scenes that shift temporally and spatially, an illustration for narrative poetry requires an intensity of interpretive conception and a concentrated distillation of the whole. One approach the Pre-Raphaelites took to narrative poetry was to convey distinct critical moments in paired pictures.[23] Hunt designed two pictures for "The Ballad of Oriana," for example: a headpiece that shows the lovers parting as the knight leaves for battle (fig. 2.7); and a tailpiece depicting their final earthly separation, with Oriana stretched out on her tomb (fig. 2.8). The framing pictures work well

THE BALLAD OF ORIANA.

I.

My heart is wasted with my woe,
Oriana.
There is no rest for me below,
Oriana.
When the long dun wolds are ribb'd with snow,
And loud the Norland whirlwinds blow,
Oriana,
Alone I wander to and fro,
Oriana.

Figure 2.7 William Holman Hunt, "The Ballad of Oriana," in Alfred Tennyson, *Poems,* 2nd ed. (Moxon, 1859), 51.

THE BALLAD OF ORIANA. 55

XI.

When Norland winds pipe down the sea,
Oriana,
I walk, I dare not think of thee,
Oriana.
Thou liest beneath the greenwood tree,
I dare not die and come to thee,
Oriana.
I hear the roaring of the sea,
Oriana.

Figure 2.8 William Holman Hunt, "The Ballad of Oriana," in Alfred Tennyson, *Poems*, 2nd ed. (Moxon, 1859), 55.

with the page layout of the poem, which comprises eleven stanzas, each nine lines in length, stretched out over five pages. The headpiece illustration is positioned above the entire first stanza and the tailpiece below the entire last stanza, thus allowing a more coherent reading experience than the disrupted stanzas found in "St. Agnes' Eve" and "Claribel."

Hunt designed the two pictures as companion pieces commenting on each other as well as on the verses. Using an identical linear rule to set off each picture from the letterpress, Hunt created a separate pictorial narrative using repeating motifs and common features. In the first image, Oriana places her foot inside her lover's bow to help him tighten its string. In reaching toward the knight, her hand appears ready to pluck an arrow from his quiver. This gesture connects to the final scene, where the knight's "bitter arrow" pierces Oriana's bosom (53). In both images, the knight's restless need for constant movement is depicted symbolically by a form of transportation in the far right: in the first picture, his horse appears to be calling him to battle, while in the last, a boat awaits him in the harbor. The hope of union is conveyed in the headpiece by the lush and fertile growth around Oriana, who sits on a gushing well. The tailpiece shows the negation of that hope through the bleakness of a treeless landscape, with a mortuary bier in the extreme foreground, and the sea and barren mountains in the distance. In drafting his compositions, Hunt made full use of the possibilities of the tiny 3¼ × 3¾-inch woodblock, turning it lengthwise to depict the two vertical figures of the headpiece and sideways to convey the horizontal funerary scene of the tailpiece.

In layout and design, the art and poetry presented by "The Ballad of Oriana" in the Moxon Tennyson suggest what the Victorian gift book might have achieved as a modern multimedia art form, given the cooperation of artists, poets, publishers, engravers, and printers. Rossetti considered Hunt's illustrations for "Oriana" and "The Lady of Shalott" to be "masterpieces" in book art (*Correspondence*, 2:146). His enthusiasm for the latter did not extend to giving up his own design for "The Lady of Shalott," however. Had he done so, Hunt might have been able to bring a coherent pictorial narrative to "The Lady of Shalott" as he did for "The Ballad of Oriana" and "The Recollections of the Arabian Nights." Instead, Rossetti insisted on sharing the "Lady of Shalott" subject with Hunt, who eventually agreed that Rossetti could illustrate the ending while he retained the leading picture at the head of the poem (Hunt, *Pre-Raphaelitism*, 2:74).

As a result, the poem was accompanied by two distinct interpretations of the narrative and its characters, literally presenting different Ladies of Shalott. The massively conceived sensuous figure of Hunt's Lady, with her wild hair and sultry look (fig. 2.9), stands in stark contrast to the delicate form and spiritual

THE LADY OF SHALOTT.

PART I.

I.

On either side the river lie
Long fields of barley and of rye,
That clothe the wold and meet the sky;
And thro' the field the road runs by
To many-tower'd Camelot;

Figure 2.9 William Holman Hunt, "The Lady of Shalott," in Alfred Tennyson, *Poems,* 2nd ed. (Moxon, 1859), 67.

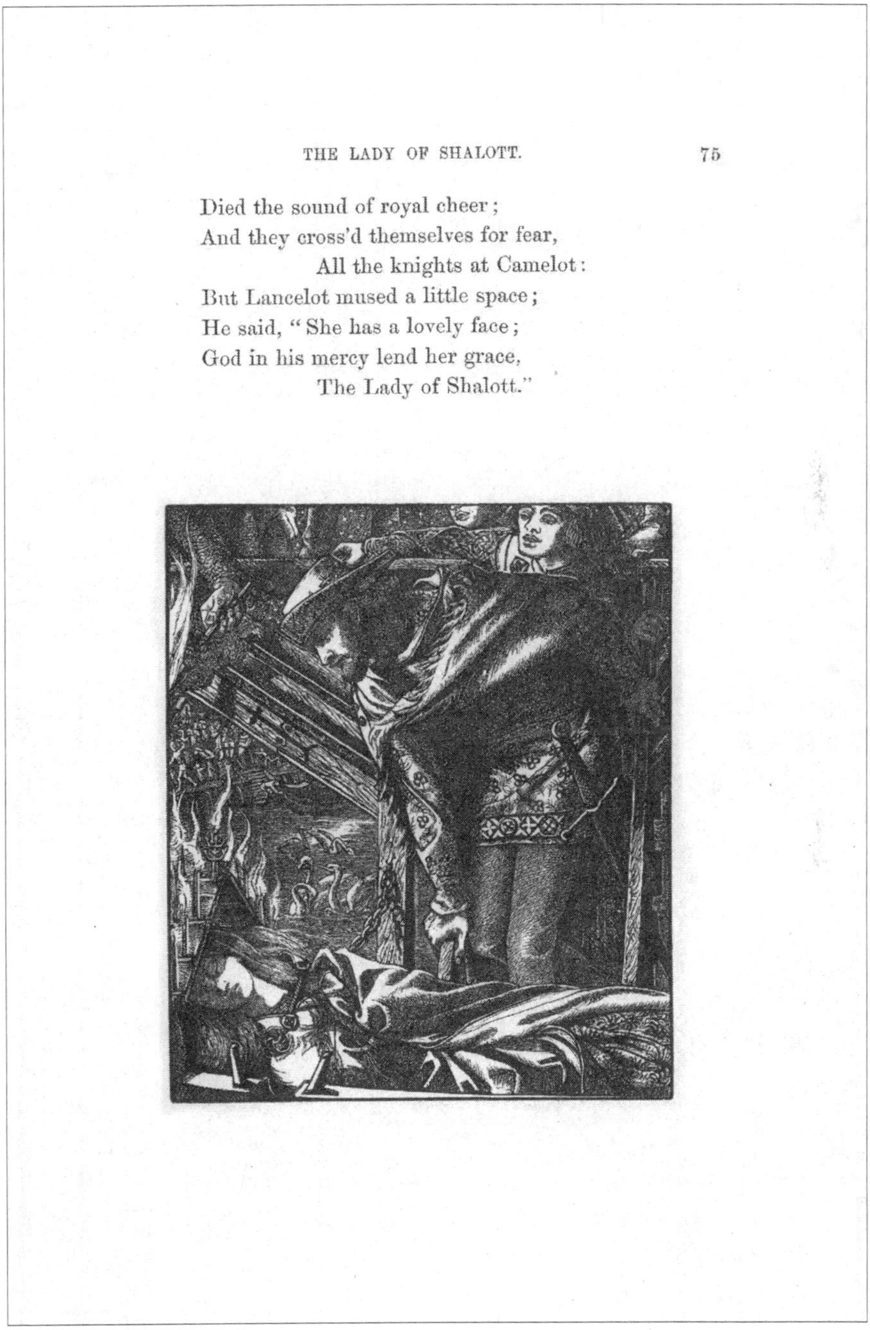

THE LADY OF SHALOTT. 75

Died the sound of royal cheer;
And they cross'd themselves for fear,
All the knights at Camelot:
But Lancelot mused a little space;
He said, "She has a lovely face;
God in his mercy lend her grace,
The Lady of Shalott."

Figure 2.10 Dante Gabriel Rossetti, "The Lady of Shalott," in Alfred Tennyson, *Poems*, 2nd ed. (Moxon, 1859), 75.

 mien of Rossetti's corpse (fig. 2.10). Similarly, the distant glimpse of Sir Lancelot through the window in Hunt's illustration depicts a much more traditionally conceived medieval knight than Rossetti's intense young man in a tunic, cloak, and unusual headgear. The distinct approaches display different readings of Tennyson's imagined Arthurian narrative, one viewing it as a story of temptation, fall, and punishment, and the other removing it from the world of cause and effect, action and consequence, into the romantic realm of wonder and mystery. Both very powerful images, the two illustrations manifest the ability of the reader to take possession of the poem, while at the same time underscoring the impossibility of achieving hermeneutic mastery in the act of interpretation. The compressed spaces gesture toward a "whole" that cannot be seen, and thus they imply an array of other possible seeing positions.

In its multiple ambiguous details that simultaneously demand and defy reading, Rossetti's composition for "The Lady of Shalott" allegorizes the acts of seeing and interpreting (fig. 2.10). Crowded into the extreme foreground of the picture, with her face toward the viewer but dark with shadows, the dead body of the Lady of Shalott lies in a shallow boat illuminated by candles. Immediately behind her, pale in the twilight, swim five white swans, an iconographic detail reminding the viewer that the lady has died, like the legendary swan, in the act of "singing her last song." Rossetti captures the tumult of the town as "Knight and burgher, lord and dame" come "out upon the wharfs" to "read her name" on the boat and to wonder "Who is this? And what is here?" (74). In the triangle formed by the bridge's beam, a crowd of witnesses rush to the scene; on the bridge itself, Rossetti inserts a confusion of partial figures, some holding torches to light their view of the corpse. The effect ironically heightens the unintelligibility of illumination: despite all these candles and torches, the assembled witnesses do not really know the meaning of what they are seeing.

The principal figure of this composition is the unwitting Lancelot, who stands on the steps that join bridge and wharf to get the closest look possible at this wonder, his figure strained with the tense fascination of complete absorption. The details in the picture, however, emphasize the inscrutability of the Lady's face and story, the impossibility of reading this text in any complete or masterful sense. The picture positions readers of the *poem* of "The Lady of Shalott" in an ironic relationship to this image of Lancelot as reader of the *body* of the Lady of Shalott. Knowing, as Lancelot cannot, his role in the Lady's death, and aware of the mysterious curse that resulted in the corpse's arrival at Camelot, readers are also confronted with the incommensurability of the work of art—whether poem or picture.

## Pre-Raphaelite Art in Visual Culture

Just as he had been the early champion of Pre-Raphaelite painting, praising it for its truth to nature, John Ruskin was one of the first to value the Pre-Raphaelites' approach to illustration in the Moxon Tennyson. In an appendix to his *Elements of Drawing*, published only a month after the illustrated *Poems*, Ruskin publicly extolled the virtues of closely studying the volume's "woodcuts from drawings by Rossetti and other chief Pre-Raphaelite masters" (224). Privately, he congratulated the unenthusiastic Tennyson on the illustrated edition: "[T]hese woodcuts will be of much use in making people think and puzzle a little; art was getting quite a matter of form in book-illustrations, and it does not so much matter whether any given vignette is right or not, as whether it contains thought or not" (H. Tennyson, *Memoir*, 1:420).[24] Believing, according to William Holman Hunt's testimony, that "an illustrator ought never to add anything to what he finds in the text" (*Pre-Raphaelitism*, 2:95), Tennyson could not concur with Ruskin's view of the function of illustration. Unlike the poet, however, Ruskin was indifferent to whether the images were "right" as interpretations. And although he valued what Housman later described as the Pre-Raphaelites' "personal and intellectual readings of the poems to which they belonged" (*Houghton*, 13), Ruskin's primary concern with gift books such as the Moxon Tennyson was social rather than hermeneutic.

Many contemporary critics, Ruskin among them, recognized the potential educational value of encasing high-quality art and poetry between the gift book's attractive covers. Writing for *Blackwood's* in 1857, Margaret Oliphant, for instance, posited that "there are few things more likely to cultivate the taste of the mass of ordinary people than pretty books" ("Picture-Books," 310). With more specific educational purpose, Ruskin urged viewers to study the Pre-Raphaelite illustrations in the Moxon Tennyson closely: "[T]hey are full of instruction," he asserted, in the qualities that make authentic art (*Elements*, 224). Although they might offend the uninitiated at first, the Pre-Raphaelite designs are certain, Ruskin insists, to teach the difference between "spurious work, in which sentiment, action, and style are borrowed or artificial" and "genuine work, which is intense in feeling" (224).

While Ruskin supported the individual Pre-Raphaelite illustrations as artistic renderings "with which no other modern work can bear the least comparison" (224), he was less keen on the aesthetic and social results of mechanical reproduction. He protested, for example, that the artistic merit of the Pre-Raphaelite drawings "was terribly spoiled in the cutting, and generally the best part, the expression of feature, *entirely* lost" because of the wood-engraving process (224). In a later essay, "The Cestus of Aglaia," published in the *Art Journal* in 1865–66 when the gift-book craze was at its height, Ruskin raised concerns about the popular publishing of pictures and poetry. While conceding the educational value that good illustration in affordable books could play in familiarizing the general public with the standards of fine art, Ruskin mistrusted "this increased power of obtaining examples of art for private possession, at an almost nominal price" ("Cestus," 137). His anxiety was occasioned by two concerns with illustrated poetry, the first to do with the relations between visual and verbal culture, the second with the erosion of social collectivity in the new ethos of individual consumption.

Ruskin's first concern with illustrated poetry was that it divided the reader's attention between picture and word. He saw this divided attention as symptomatic of the emerging visual culture in which the word's dominance was becoming unsettled, and constant sensuous stimulation led consumers "restlessly to demand new subjects of interest" (137). Ruskin's second concern was that the distribution of illustrated books into middle-class homes prevented Victorians, "satisfied with the multiplication of minor art in our possession," from appreciating the cultural and social value available "in great public works." "The more we have of books," he warned, "and cabinet pictures, and cabinet ornaments, and other such domestic objects of art, the less capable we shall become of understanding or enjoying the lofty character of work noble in scale, and intended for public service" (137). To put the danger he apprehended in crass terms, Daniel Maclise's illustrations for "Morte d'Arthur" in the Moxon Tennyson might become a miniaturized, individually owned substitute for collective appreciation of his large frescoes depicting scenes of national importance in the Houses of Parliament. The popularization of symbolic goods brought about by the emerging visual culture in this age of mechanical reproduction thus challenged not only the sway of the verbal but also the social value of national, public art.

The social value of national art was, however, in ascendance in this age of museums and Crystal Palaces. Indeed, May 1857, the moment of the Moxon Tennyson's appearance, marked a watershed in Victorian visual culture. In this month, the Art Treasures of the United Kingdom Exhibition opened in Manchester, showing British paintings from the collections of cotton lords to people of all classes, including workers from the local mills (Macleod, *Art,* 102). Like the Great Exhibition of 1851, the Art Treasures of the United Kingdom Exhibition combined aesthetic, educative, and commercial goals, fostering national pride and a sense of collective ownership. In all, nearly 1.5 million people visited the exhibit during its six-month run; others experienced it vicariously in the pages of the *Art Journal,* which reproduced some of the works and published columns on the various galleries (H. Morris, *Hand,* 110), or in the printed guides, catalogs, commentaries, periodical essays, and so forth that the exhibition generated. According to Diane Sachko Macleod, the moment that English art and contemporary painters became "treasures" possessed and accessible by the nation "unequivocally announced the middle class's intervention in the cultural sphere" (*Art*, 74).[25] It also marked the moment that the British art of wood-engraved illustrations by contemporary artists like the Pre-Raphaelites, encased in books of poetry by national poets, became particularly valued and desirable commodities. Significantly, the *Art Journal*'s July 1857 issue contained not only essays on the Art Treasures Exhibition but also a review of the illustrated *Poems*, thus associating the latter with the nation's art.

Tennyson went to see the pictures shortly after the publication of *Poems*, and most of his illustrators both toured the exhibition and had their works displayed in it. William Holman Hunt, for example, showed *The Awakening Conscience*, *The Hireling Shepherd*, *Two Gentlemen of Verona*, and *Claudio and Isabella*. After he had been to the exhibition himself, Hunt wrote Ford Madox Brown to say that "any artist who missed it would certainly regret the fact for the rest of his life" (Hueffer, *Brown*, 145). Brown went and subsequently declared his enthusiasm for the Pre-Raphaelite work on view: "Hunt, in fact, made the exhibition." He also observed that he found "the music . . . jolly" but believed that "the waiters tried very hard to cheat" (155).

Brown's diary entry reminds us just how much of an event the Art Treasures Exhibition was, combining cultural education with multiple sensuous pleasures in a way that had broad appeal for Victorians. The Crystal Palace, which moved to its permanent location in Sydenham in 1854 and attracted two million visitors a year for the next thirty years (Leith, *Delmotte's Crystal Palace*, 7), had demonstrated the effectiveness of combining commercial, "cultural, educational and recreational agendas" in the metropolis (Greenhalgh, "Art," 278). The Art Treasures Exhibition showed that a temporary art exhibit in a provincial industrial center could not only attract a steady stream of visitors but also support a burgeoning cultural industry in printed catalogs, guides, commentaries, walking tours, maps, menus, and musical programs. Significantly, virtually all these printed spin-offs were illustrated with wood engravings of some kind. Indeed, wood engraving is associated with the exhibition at every level of its communication with visitors, from diagrams to art objects. On multiple levels, the Manchester exhibition implied that the graphic language of everyday life could not only represent but also be high art.

The art of wood engraving was accorded its own distinct section of the Manchester exhibition and given particular emphasis as a national treasure by numerous commentators. According to the official *Supplemental Catalogue*, the

Galleries of Engraving at the exhibition offered the general public, for "the first time in the history of the art of Engraving . . . a complete chronological series of prints from the commencement of the art up to the present time" (Bradbury and Evans, *Supplemental Catalogue,* 23). Various guides to the exhibition also highlighted the wood engravings on display. For example, the guide prepared by Dr. Waagen, which John Murray and W. H. Smith copublished as a companion to the official catalog, specifically drew attention to wood-engraving technology and popular culture: "This species of engraving, probably invented about the beginning of the 15th century, is highly important, because the cheapness of the material, and the great number of impressions which can be produced from the same block, fit it to spread art among all the classes of society" (*Walk,* 71). In its reprint of notices previously published in the *Manchester Guardian,* Bradbury and Evans's *Handbook to the Water Colours, Drawings, and Engravings in the Art Treasures Exhibition* similarly stressed the significance of the wood-engraving collection: "All visitors to Manchester who have opportunity or desire to make systematic study of the treasures of the Exhibition should devote careful attention to that unequalled series of engravings, which, more than any other department of this collection, deserves to be called 'complete'" (47). The *Handbook* implies that an ordinary visitor could "master" the history and art of wood engraving by a thorough study of the exhibition's only historically complete national collection.

The *Handbook* also connects national art treasures to the poetic gift book, drawing particular attention to engravings by the Dalziel brothers, "the worthy continuators of British reputation" (65). As artists, draftsmen, engravers, teachers, and printers of the Fine Art Books series and as commissioners and collectors of paintings, the Dalziels represented the culmination of the British tradition in the modern age of wood-engraved reproduction. Because the Dalziel firm had a hand in almost every important gift book of the period, including the Moxon Tennyson, the appearance of "A Selection of Woodcuts" owned by Edward Dalziel in the Art Treasures Exhibition established a connection between wood engraving, national art, and the printed book.[26] Situating the period's most popular form of reproduction within the nation's art historical tradition and treasures, the exhibition educated a public of consumers. If the boundaries between fine art and popular culture were as fluid as the exhibition implied, then the illustrated book could be viewed as a portable art gallery for the middlebrow collector willing to invest a guinea in national art.

*John Cassell's Art Treasures Exhibition* provides another link between the exhibition's educational function, wood engraving, and the common reader (fig. 2.11). As the title announces, the Manchester exhibition had been claimed for the world of print culture by an enterprising publisher. Recognizing that

Figure 2.11 Illustration for *John Cassell's Art Treasures Exhibition: Engravings of the Principal Masterpieces* (W. Kent, 1858), 1. *Toronto Reference Library.*

 the technologies of wood engraving and mass production could override the exhibition's unique occurrence in time and place, Cassell published annotated reproductions of the masterpieces on view at Manchester. Published in monthly numbers starting in June 1857, the whole was gathered into volume form the following year. At this point, the publisher deemed it appropriate to say a word about purpose:

> The Art Treasures Palace at Manchester, of the year 1857, which now exists only in the memory of those who enjoyed the privilege of inspecting the unrivalled collection of private paintings assembled within its walls, was, from the very nature of the undertaking, of an ephemeral character. . . . Fearing, therefore, that the taste for art which this Exhibition had widely engendered in the public mind might—like a tender child, which requires the care of a fond nursing mother—perish for want of encouragement, JOHN CASSELL determined to keep alive, if possible, not only the memory of the Manchester Art Treasures Exhibition, but also that craving for Art Education which it had fostered, by the reproduction in wood, in the highest style of art, the most famous *chefs-d'oeuvre* exhibited at Manchester, and also of the best paintings by the chief masters of the various schools, wherever they are preserved, either in private collections or public galleries. (Cassell, *Art Treasures,* vii)

Cassell's elaborate and somewhat patronizing prose establishes Art (rather than, as usual, Nature) in a maternal role, with the public as the child requiring nurturing, and the publisher as midwife (or perhaps wet nurse) to a nation of middle-class art lovers. The book, the publisher claimed, was "*sui generis,*" offering art history "in a clear and popular style" and "purposely written in language intelligible to all readers, professional or otherwise." Art education for ordinary people was the dominant goal: "[T]he unprofessional reader, for whom the work is more especially designed, will, by the study of *JOHN CASSELL'S ART TREASURES EXHIBITION,* have his mind enlarged, his intellect improved, his stock of general knowledge widely increased, and a taste for art awakened if it was dormant in him, and created if it was non-existent" (vii–viii).

Like the "clear and popular style" of the text, the wood-engraved reproductions of the paintings presented an intelligible art language to the "unprofessional reader" targeted by the publisher. Among the "Engravings of the Principal Masterpieces of the English, Dutch, Flemish, French, and German Schools" announced in his subtitle, Cassell included reproductions of three paintings by Millais: *Autumn Leaves* (fig. 2.12), *The Proscribed Royalist,* and *The Order of Release.* Cassell described *Autumn Leaves* as "perhaps one of the greatest triumphs hitherto achieved by any disciple of the pre-Raphaelite school" (47). The linear

Figure 2.12 W. J. Linton's engraving of J. E. Millais' *Autumn Leaves* for *John Cassell's Art Treasures Exhibition: Engravings of the Principal Masterpieces* (W. Kent, 1858), 48. *Toronto Reference Library.*

effects of wood engraving, however, were not well suited to representing the tonal and color-based effects of an oil painting, even when W. J. Linton, an expert engraver, was responsible for the cutting. Linton's engraved reproduction of Millais' *Autumn Leaves* for *Cassell's Art Treasures Exhibition* results in a flattened picture plane, inexpressive faces, and very material-looking smoke rising from the piled leaves. Given the difficulty of reproducing tonal art with linear engraving and the overall poor quality of the printing in Cassell's book, the 260 wood engravings of oil paintings may have had the unintended effect of diminishing the status of painting rather than elevating the reader's aesthetic appreciation. Moreover, because the illustrated advertisements at the back of the book—depicting the virtues of Sydenham Trousers and nickel-plated Cruet Frames—are presented with the common materiality of engraved lines, black ink, and white paper, fine art and commercial objects appear here within the same visual range and artistic value.

If Cassell's goal was to preserve a taste for art in those earnest middle-class readers who had been to the exhibition and to inculcate it in those who had not, Manchester publisher John Heywood's *Peep at the Pictures; or, A Catalogue of the Principal Objects of Attraction in the Manchester Art Treasures Exhibition, with Biographical Notices of the Painters, Ancient and Modern, and a Ground Plan of the Building* aimed "to tempt the sons of toil from the beer-house to gaze on the master-pieces of art" (14). Directed at a working-class audience assumed to be unfamiliar with fine art, the book's title, *A Peep at the Pictures,* deliberately situated the exhibition within the context of popular culture by referencing the visual entertainment of the peep show. Priced at a modest penny and available at bookstalls at the exhibition and in railway stations, the slim volume of 36 pages (the official catalog was a hefty 232 pages) offered an accessible introduction to the nation's painting and the poetry that inspired it. Its popularity may be gauged by its multiple editions: *A Peep at the Pictures* sold tens of thousands of copies.

*A Peep at the Pictures* was not a catalog but a primer in art and poetry, focusing on those pictures whose subjects "seem most likely to interest the working classes" (1). The annotations to the selected paintings provide history lessons, commentary, and quotation and spur the reader to gain further education in the nation's poets, available to all at Manchester's Free Library.[27] For example, Heywood accompanies Sir Joshua Reynolds's *Puck* with a citation of the "merry wanderer of the night" speech from Shakespeare's *Midsummer Night's Dream.* Concluding the extended quotation with "So wrote the poet, and thus painted the painter" (15–16), *A Peep at the Pictures* seems designed as an *ut pictura poesis* introduction for the masses. In fact, poet and painter are never far from each other in this workingman's guide. Asserting the Victorian love of narrative art—"We like a picture that tells a story" (24)—Heywood finds great scope for commentary in the Pre-Raphaelite paintings, which are disproportionately and preferentially represented in *A Peep at the Pictures.* Sometimes he simply provides the literary reference, as in the note attached to Hunt's *Two Gentlemen of Verona:* "This picture is taken from a play of Shakspere [*sic*]" (25). Often, he encourages the reader to turn to the textual source as a guide to interpreting the visual scene, as in this commentary for Hunt's *Claudio and Isabella:* "A scene from Shakspere's 'Measure for Measure.' The face of Isabella is wonderful for its mixed expression of surprise, affection, and horror. You must read the play to understand it" (26).

If Heywood's commentary condescends to his working-class audience, his treatment of art and poetry is more reverential. Not all print culture ephemera that remain as our twenty-first century guides to the long-vanished Art Treasures Exhibition are so respectful of either Pre-Raphaelite painting or poetry. Perhaps the most entertaining of these cultural curiosities is that by Tennyson Longfellow Smith, of Cripplegate, who wrote the satiric *Poems Inspired by Certain Pictures at the Art Treasures Exhibition, Manchester.* Dedicated, "with Profound Admiration and Awe, to That Greatest of Modern Poets, Philosophers, Artists, Art-Critics, and Authors, the Immortal Ruskin," Smith's verses are an exercise in humorous ekphrasis, targeting both the upstart Pre-Raphaelites and their uncultivated, exhibition-going public. The verses accompany eight caricatures of Pre-Raphaelite paintings, including the popular *Autumn Leaves,* here reduced to linear ridicule (fig. 2.13). The work is further mocked in parodic scholarly notes purportedly by the Hon. Botibol Bareacres, who glosses the engraving's legibility thus: "The explanation of the sad tale symbolized in this painting is, however, no less made clear to us by the eyes of the industrious domestic and of the sweet and innocent little prattler to the right, who sees nothing more before her—like many an uneducated child of longer growth—than a heap of dirty damp leaves." Smith's collection concludes with a "Pre-Raffaelite Chorus," to be sung to the melody of "The One-Horse Chaise." As ventriloquized by Smith, the Pre-Raphaelites' message is "That High Art in Great Britain has at last been brought to birth":

> So, you see, we must be right; and having put you in a fright,
> Go, burn your stupid ancient daubs, and come to us to school;
> Then perhaps you may, some day, find out the proper way
> To look on Art and nature, and cease to be a fool.
>
> (n.p.)

Figure 2.13 Caricature of J. E. Millais' *Autumn Leaves* in Tennyson Longfellow Smith, *Poems Inspired by Certain Pictures at the Art Treasures Exhibition, Manchester* (Manchester, 1857), n.p.

Smith was not alone in his ridiculing of the Pre-Raphaelites' dedication to following nature for stylistic method and going to books for artistic inspiration. Nevertheless, the impact of the Pre-Raphaelites' dedication to linking art and poetry was widely seen as positive. According to the enthusiastic Cassell, "though the success of the school still trembles in the balance, all admit that the movement has effected a beneficial reform among artists" (*Art Treasures*, 43)—and, many other writers implied, among the masses who were introduced to national art and literature by the Pre-Raphaelites' work. However varied the reception, the display of Pre-Raphaelite works at the Art Treasures Exhibition, coupled with their energetic reproduction, discussion, and dissemination in print culture, brought this group of artists to new national prominence and appreciation in the summer that the Moxon Tennyson was published. The *Manchester Guardian* provides insight into this sudden popularization of the Pre-Raphaelites' engagement with the sister arts. In a series of essays published in the newspaper and subsequently printed by Bradbury and Evans—who were also the printers of the Moxon Tennyson—as *A Handbook to the Gallery of British Paintings in the Art Treasures Exhibition*, the *Manchester Guardian* championed the Pre-Raphaelite school. Declaring Hunt's *Claudio and Isabella* "far and away the most impressive work (the greatest, we mean, in that quality, which takes most hold on the mind,—Expression) in the whole of this English Gallery," the critic emphasized that its merit lay in its profound combination of art and poetry:

> We would earnestly beg of any visitor to this Exhibition who has been used to hear the pre-Raphaelites ridiculed, to give some minutes' quiet attention to this picture,—to read it awhile, and then say if it does not speak its meaning marvellously and touchingly, through the painter's embodiment of the poet's thought. When a painter can so interpret a poet, our objection to subjects from play or poem vanishes at once. He justifies his choice of subject by making us feel what the poet's conception was meant to convey. (Bradbury and Evans, *Gallery*, 97)

The writer begins the article by raising the obvious question of the fitness of the locale for an exhibition of this magnitude and import: why should Manchester, "land of industry and cotton spinners," host the nation's first great public art show? His answer is that, in the modern and increasingly democratic nineteenth century, labor alone cannot satisfy: as "books grow daily cheaper and more accessible" and "public reading-rooms, popular lectures and schools of design" increase, "culture spreads among all classes." A critical component of this cultural diffusion is an increased taste for, and acquisition of, works of art by the upper middle classes, who could afford to invest in the cultural capital displayed at the exhibition. With an element of self-congratulation, the critic claims that the middle-class preference for "modern pictures" is "a wholesome fact" bringing credit to the nation as a whole (4, 14).[28] Exposing the working and broad middle classes to the best in visual art is also flagged as a national good, likely to lead to the desire to make beautiful objects part of everyday life. "As society grows more cultivated," the writer avers, "it demands more and more as much beauty in things of daily use as can be infused into them" (4–5). One sign of this greater cultivation was an increased middle-class demand for objects that combined utility and beauty. Wood-engraved illustrated books such as the Moxon Tennyson placed the beauties of national art and poetry in the everyday life of ordinary Victorians. Selecting and displaying such art objects could testify to the owner's discerning taste, as well as to a cultural knowledge about contemporary art trends. In 1857, knowing who the Pre-Raphaelite artists were and what kind of work they made in various media—oil and watercolor painting, etching, sketching, drawing on the woodblock, and illustrative design—was definitely evidence of cultural currency.

While the Art Treasures Exhibition was attracting visitors to Manchester in the summer of 1857, the small but also important Russell Place Exhibit was taking place in London. The first show dedicated exclusively to Pre-Raphaelite art, this exhibition organized by Ford Madox Brown is particularly important for its treatment of book illustration as a fine art. The exhibit made a bold public statement about the artistic value of original drawings designed specifically for reproduction with printed text. Viewers could inspect not only drawings and studies for illustration but also photographs of some of the "Designs on Wood for Tennyson's Poems" by William Holman Hunt and Dante Gabriel Rossetti.[29] Because the actual designs on the block disappeared in the cutting, the photographs recorded the artists' drawings on wood prior to engraving. Thus, the emerging technology of photography documented the artists' drawings and guaranteed authenticity. Reversing the usual procedure, the Pre-Raphaelites used the means of mechanical reproduction itself to provide an auratic trace and testify to the artist's handwork. Paradoxically, the indexical function of the photograph and the ritual function of the exhibit bore witness to an artwork that was not itself present and existed only in multiple copies in the illustrated book, the Moxon Tennyson.

This synchronic study of the illustrated edition of Tennyson's *Poems*' moment of publication shows how deeply involved the work was in the discourses of contemporary visual culture and its associated ephemera, from exhibitions, catalogs, and guides, to photographic prints, carved woodblocks, and wood-engraved reproductions. Periodical notices in reviews of literature and art confirmed the work's hybridity. The *Art Journal,* for example, reviewed the illustrated edition in its July 1857 issue along with Ruskin's *Elements of Drawing* and the Art Treasures Exhibition at Manchester. As Laurel Brake observes, "The links of art criticism in the period with a number of upmarket publishing genres such as the travel guide, scholarship, and art 'news,' and with distinct reading communities—such as connoisseur/collectors, contemporary artists, and the middle-class spectator/consumer, results in a *hybridity* in illustrated texts" (*Print,* 203). To Brake's list of genres I would add the volumes of high-quality poetry and pictures published by Edward Moxon, of which the illustrated edition of Tennyson's *Poems* is a particularly resonant example. A work of mass production designed for middle-class consumers, it was also shot through with the discourses and values of "high" art and poetry. As the century wore on, its primary audience became a specialized group of contemporary artists, collectors, and connoisseurs; new editions narrowed the pictorial contents to include only the engraved work of the Pre-Raphaelites.

Writing at the height of the fin de siècle's revival of fine printing and book design, Gleeson White observed that decorative illustrators considered Moxon's edition of Tennyson to be "the genesis of the modern movement" in illustration (*English Illustration,* 105).[30] Although the Moxon edition included fifty-four wood-engraved illustrations by eight artists, White refers only to the pictures by the three Pre-Raphaelites: John Everett Millais, William Holman Hunt, and Dante Gabriel Rossetti. From his forty-year distance, White offers the following perspective on the book as a whole:

> Except for these few drawings, it differs in no respect from the average "quarto poets" before and after. The same "toned" paper, the same vignetted pictures, appear; the proportions of the type-page are merely that in ordinary use; the size and shape of the illustrations was left apparently to pure chance. Therefore, in place of talking of the volume with bated breath as a masterpiece, it would be wiser to regard it as one of the excellent publications of the period, that by the fortuitous inclusion of a few drawings, quite out of touch with the rest, has acquired a reputation, which considered as a complete book, it does not deserve. (105)

Critics from White's day to this have taken his admonition to heart and largely refrained from discussing the Moxon Tennyson "as a complete book." In an effort to identify the unique characteristics the Pre-Raphaelites brought to illustrating poetry, and to understand the importance of the Moxon Tennyson in relation to the period's "quarto poets" and their audience, I have attempted, in this chapter, to recover the Moxon Tennyson as a material object in its immediate visual culture. Despite poor book design and the disunity of its artistic contents, the Moxon Tennyson was made in 1857 as a work to be read and looked at, and it continued to circulate as a gift book throughout the sixties. Moreover, as the following chapters show, the "failed" illustrated edition of Tennyson's *Poems* had a significant impact on the history of Victorian publishing, authorship, and readership.

# three

## The Dalziel Brothers' Fine Art Book and the Mass Production of Culture

Nothing can surpass the cleverness of our own school of Dalziel.

*John Ruskin*[1]

"Of late years," the *Saturday Review* critic wrote in one of the paper's Christmas Book columns in 1863, "it seems to have been held that the whole mind of England was so passionately devoted to the English poets that no selection of them could come amiss" (Dec. 5, 1863, 738). With his reference to the evident enthusiasm for national poetry displayed by "the whole mind of England," the reviewer indicates the commercial success of the poetic gift book, as well as its ideological shaping of collective notions of culture and nation. His opening gesture—"it seems to have been held"—balances this homogenization of the reading population with a parallel erasure of the specific agencies involved in the book's production.

Both readers and makers were, of course, varied and specific, and both were built into the bibliographic, iconic, and linguistic codes of gift books and their external paratexts in the public sphere of the popular press.[2] These were not the cheap editions of standard poets produced throughout the nineteenth century for working-class readers, which rarely acquired the dignity of periodical notice and review.[3] Rather, they were anthologies and collections in quarto or octavo format, lavishly illustrated with wood-engraved pictures, and priced for a middle-class audience. Encased in ornamental covers and advertised as

Christmas presents, these gift books united poetry and pictures in one tasteful package for middlebrow consumption and cultivation. They were, as the title of the Dalziel brothers' series suggests, produced by their makers and received by their purchasers as "Fine Art Books."

The reviewer's offhand comment on this historic instance of poetry's central place in popular publishing bears investigating. How did the "quarto poets" become tantamount to a sure sell in the Christmas book trade? William St. Clair has mapped the presence of "old canon" poets in a large reading constituency throughout the nineteenth century and shown how, as the Romantic poets came out of copyright in the 1850s and 1860s, their works began to be included in the standard collections of English poets (*Reading*, 127–28).[4] St. Clair has also shown the importance of pictures in these editions of out-of-copyright poets, noting that illustrations "were an intrinsic part of the book's design" and that "illustrated versions seem to have been by far the more popular" vehicular form for poetry (134). These standard poetic works, then, could be bought fairly inexpensively. New work by living poets, in contrast, remained relatively expensive for the ordinary consumer. However, verses by contemporary poets, from the anonymous reader-turned-writer to the laureate himself, were readily available in newspapers and magazines.

This chapter argues that the popular appeal of the poetic gift book was largely established in the periodical press, which fostered an expectation that poetry and pictures belonged together. Laurel Brake has shown that the "spheres of the serial and the book" were interrelated and interdependent in the nineteenth century (*Print in Transition*, 3).[5] The contingent relationships between serial and volume publication are also evident in the publication of poetry; indeed, the Dalziels seized on this crucial interconnectedness in their Fine Art Gift Books.[6] I begin, then, with the mass production of poetry in the periodical press before considering how both standard and contemporary verses moved to gift-book form in the popular market.

In tracing poetry's place in popular culture, our journey is signposted by pictures at every step along the way. At the outset, it is worth remembering that one of the illustrations of Tennyson's "Lady of Shalott" at the Russell Place Exhibit came from the hand of Elizabeth Siddall. Siddall apparently discovered the poet when she unwrapped a pound of butter protected by a page of the periodical press that happened to contain one of his verses (Marsh, *Sisterhood*, 22). The anecdote suggests the materiality of poetry's domestic reach in the age of mechanical reproduction, greater literacy, and an increased desire for cultivation. It also reminds us of de Certeau's insight that readers are also "poets of their own acts" of reading, recombining the elements of the written text with "artisan-like inventiveness" (*Practice*, xviii).

## Poetry in the Periodical Press

The illustrated periodical press that emerged in the 1840s circulated image and text, including poetry and pictures, to a mass audience of readers from every walk of life. Because of advances in the mechanized making of paper, the steam-powered press, stereotype printing, and the technology of wood engraving, as well as reductions in the so-called knowledge taxes and the improvements in access to information that came with the building of the railways, illustrated periodicals and magazines became profitable for publishers and affordable for buyers. By the end of the century, thanks to highly developed marketing and distribution systems, the illustrated periodical "had become an integral part of people's cultural experience at every level of Victorian society" (Anderson, "Illustration," 128–29, 130). Moreover, books and serials were connected at every level of the publishing process. A type of serial publication in themselves, the new gift books of the 1860s show how the earlier annuals were reimagined and reconfigured after the emergence of the wood-engraved periodical established new reader expectations for the combination of pictures and poetry.

Viewed by contemporaries as a sign of their culture's modernity, the significance and reach of the illustrated press in nineteenth-century print culture are on par with computer developments in our own digital age. Although Victorian critics could not foresee how that prototype of the modern computer, the Babbage calculator,[7] would eventually develop into the present system for preserving our cultural inheritance while creating and disseminating popular culture, they were certainly cognizant of the historic significance of their own periodical press and the Christmas serials it sponsored:

> The amount of skilled labour and intelligence which is engaged in the production of magazine literature is the phenomenon of our times. . . . The whole range and level of writing and drawing, including a thick deep stratum of verse and story and illustration, has been elevated, and has attained a very respectable elevation indeed. Week after week, month after month, Christmas after Christmas, we get our literature reeled off with the regularity, neatness, and precision of a machine. The Babbage calculator, which was never completed, is fairly distanced by the literary and artistic machine which employs so many hands, and is daily turning out so vast a mass of industrial production of stories, articles, reviews, and sketches. (*SR,* Dec. 8, 1866, 717)

The founding editors of the *Wellesley Index to Victorian Periodicals,* that invaluable resource for students of the popular press in the nineteenth century, chose not to include this "thick deep stratum of verse" in their monumental work.[8] As a result, we have overlooked, as Linda K. Hughes reminds us in "What the *Wellesley Index* Left Out: Why Poetry Matters to Periodical Studies," the critical importance of original poetry to periodical editors and readers (91). We also need to explore more thoroughly the crucial connection between the production of illustrated poetry in the serial press's daily papers, weekly magazines, and monthlies, and the establishment of the Christmas gift-book industry in the second half of the century.

Hughes's groundbreaking study identifies some of the central functions of poetry in Victorian periodicals. Far from being used as "filler"—as she rightly points out, "prose is so much better for the purpose" ("*Wellesley*," 103)—poetry played an important role in defining editorial policy, reputation, and readership. "Serious poetry," Hughes shows, "was a 'value-added' feature" sought by editors targeting educated readers or wishing "to enhance the symbolic capital of their enterprise" by soliciting work from "celebrity" poets (94). Original poetry by Matthew Arnold, Charlotte Brontë, Elizabeth Barrett Browning, and Alfred Tennyson, for example, appeared in the *Cornhill Magazine* in 1860, its first year of production (94). Unlike *Macmillan's Magazine* or the *Fortnightly Review*, which also featured original poetry, the *Cornhill* was an illustrated magazine. The wood-engraved illustrations after designs by prominent artists added extra cultural value.

The Dalziels recall that "[w]hen the *Cornhill Magazine*, in 1859, was first advertised for publication at the price of one shilling, with Thackeray as editor, the announcement fell like a bomb in the midst of the magazine publishers—Blackwood, Fraser, Colburn, Bentley and others—for nothing of this description had even been so much as dreamt of before at a less price than the orthodox half-crown" (*Record*, 132). At publisher George Smith's invitation, the Dalziels took on the engraving of the full-page plate or two proposed for each monthly number (134). At the time that Smith, "perhaps the ablest and most imaginative of the Victorian publishers," conceived of his affordable illustrated magazine, combining the information of a general review with the entertainment of first-class literature, the competition was limited (Houghton, *Wellesley*, 321). But with the repeal of the paper tax and the ready availability of writers, artists, engravers, and printers in the golden age of wood-engraved illustration, magazines disseminating the sister arts to every class of reader proliferated. Poetry and pictures were combined in *Once a Week*, the *Shilling Magazine, Good Words,* the *Graphic,* and the *Argosy,* to name only a handful of the illustrated magazines that emerged in the sixties.

In *Good Words,* a sixpenny monthly launched by Alexander Strahan in the same year as the more upscale *Cornhill,* illustrated poems were particularly plentiful. Unlike the single plate or two featured in the *Cornhill*, the numerous illustrations in *Good Words* were always inset as part of the printed page. Large, half- or three-quarter-page wood engravings cut by the Dalziels accompanied verses with such affective titles as "Love," "A Cloister Legend," "The Deformed Child," "The Lone One," "The Little Girl's Lament," and "God's Singer."[9]

Produced by some of the leading artists of the day—including Edward Burne-Jones, William Holman Hunt, Arthur Boyd Houghton, Arthur Hughes, John Everett Millais, George Pinwell, Frederick Sandys, and Frederick Walker—the illustrations democratized art while adding, in Strahan's words, to popular literature's "own attractiveness and heightening its proper delights" (quoted in Srebrnik, *Strahan,* 39). With so many Pre-Raphaelite artists and associates contributing, it comes as no surprise that periodical publications continued the approach to illustrating poetry that was inaugurated in the Moxon Tennyson: the bold black-and-white designs demanded to be read with the same attentiveness as the poetic lines. Signed by both artist and engraver, the pictures represented the nation's best in black-and-white art as well as the height of its modern technological capacity. In contrast, periodical poetry was frequently anonymous or pseudonymous. Sometimes, however, the poetic contents also included signed verses by popular contemporary poets such as Isa Craig, Sydney Dobell, Austin Dobson, Dora Greenwell, Jean Ingelow, George Massey, George MacDonald, Alexander Smith, and Alfred Tennyson. Both poetry and pictures, then, belonged to the present moment and were made for the modern reader. The proliferation of illustrated periodicals made poetry and pictures an expected part of quotidian domestic experience.

With a circulation of between 80,000 and 130,000 per issue,[10] *Good Words* testifies to poetry's place in the lives of ordinary people. The periodical's index and layout highlight this cultural importance of poetry and pictures for a mass audience. The table of contents for each volume lists its poetic and illustrative contents separately from the general index, which itemizes its prose contents alphabetically, with no distinctions of category among serial fiction, travel writing, or essays on natural history, politics, and religion. The pride of place taken by poetry and pictures, however, is balanced by the frequent anonymity of the poets. Significantly, some of these unknown poets derive from the periodical's own readership, suggesting that the poetry in *Good Words* served a different purpose than it did in the *Cornhill.* Whereas, in its first year, at least, the *Cornhill* sought to elevate its cultural profile by including select poetry by acclaimed writers, *Good Words* presented an inclusive array of poetic contents from the pens of writers ranging from the laureate to the laborer.

In *Good Words,* poetry's value lay in its ability to connect readers through morally elevating and emotionally affecting expressions of common human experiences. The wood-engraved illustrations by some of the period's best-known artists worked to enhance the reader's experience of the beauty and sentiment of the verses. Significantly, poems by writers identified only by initials or occupation were given the same illustrative treatment as those by well-known writers. "The Mother and the Angel," by "A Railway Surfaceman," for instance, is accompanied by a three-quarter-page, highly detailed diptych by Arthur Hughes. Frederick Walker provided a large illustration for "Out among the Wild-Flowers," by "A Police Constable," while J. D. Watson illustrated "Some Verses Written by a Working Man for the Children to Sing at an Anniversary Meeting in Hertfordshire." William Holman Hunt illustrated "Go and Come," by a frequent contributor to *Good Words* who signed simply as "D***." John Everett Millais dedicated the same interpretive attention to a poem by the popular Jean Ingelow as he did for verses by the unknown "R.B.R." Similarly, Arthur Boyd Houghton illustrated Adelaide Procter's "True or False?" (fig. 3.1), Alfred Tennyson's "The Victim," and the unknown R.M.'s "My Treasure" with equivalent care.[11] This equitable pictorial attention to verses, whether composed by ordinary readers or by well-known poets, highlights the cultural value that poetry had in everyday life.

The centrality of poetry in *Good Words* was further enhanced by the visual layout, which typically centered the illustration on the first page of the poem, with the verses arranged in disrupted double columns of type below the cut (and sometimes above as well). Readers required a mobile visual/verbal literacy, as the reading experience was presented through, and mediated by, a pictorial lens. But every poem was also a visual object in its own right, as typographic display in magazines and newspapers always signaled an immediately evident poetic code to a reader's roving eye. Even in periodicals published as letterpress only, unaccompanied by wood-engraved illustrations, poetry added visual value. Linda K. Hughes offers the interesting example of the *London Journal*, noting that "[f]rom March to November 1857 virtually every poem in the [paper] was positioned at the heart of each page, a spatial trope of poetry's association with the heart as well as a material means of highlighting poems into significance" in domestic life ("*Wellesley*," 103).

The surprising centrality of poetry in periodicals targeted at the common reader leads Hughes to speculate that the sentimental or religious poetry so often found in the Victorian popular press "helped adjudicate what also defined the periodical: its modernity" ("*Wellesley*," 99). She suggests that "the periodical's jumble of deracinated, ephemeral information drawn from multiple sources and abruptly juxtaposed, yet also poured into pre-existing, usually predictable structures (leaders and middles, financial and foreign news, the arts and sport, serial

Norman Macleod, D.D.] TRUE OR FALSE? 721

TRUE OR FALSE?

So you think you love me, do ou ?
Well, it may be so;
But there are many ways of lo ving
I have learnt to know.

Many ways, and but one true way,
Which is very rare;
And the counterfeits look brightest,
Though they will not wear.

III—46

Figure 3.1 Arthur Boyd Houghton, illustration for Adelaide A. Procter, "True or False?" *Good Words* 3 (1862): 721.

novels and gossip), was a textual counterpart to the experience of the modern city as defined by Raymond Williams: a paradoxical 'coexistence of variation and apparent randomness with what had in the end to be seen as a determining system'" (99). Within the random yet determining textual system of the Victorian press, poetry represented "traditional cultural and literary ideals such as wholeness, harmony, and communal virtue" and therefore "mediate[d] the miscellaneousness and ephemerality of the periodical itself" (99).

Illustrations in the periodical press also mediated the ephemeral nature of passing events and topical opinions recorded on disposable paper. With a more immediate representational connection to the world of experience than that produced through the arbitrary codes of alphabet and typography, pictures provided another kind of reassuring grounding for readers. Even when the images themselves represented figures, landscapes, or objects that readers had never seen—perhaps never *could* see in this world—their recognizable shapes suggested a material presence, a familiar visuality connected to the world in which they lived. Until late into the century, every image in the periodical press was reproduced by the technology of wood engraving—a splendid miscellany, including daily events in the metropolis, nation, and empire; war journalism depicting scenes from the Crimean War or the Indian Mutiny; illustrations for literature of various kinds; diagrams, charts, maps, and pictures for scientific and geographic essays; satiric "cuts" and caricatures; and advertisements for everything from soap and patent medicines to ladies' fashions and men's haberdashery. The ubiquity of wood engraving in the period has dulled our sensitivity to the way this technology shaped not simply a mode of representation but also, crucially, a way of seeing and understanding for generations of Victorians. The common materiality of wood engraving brought the world, and its representations in pictures and print, into recognizable view and tactile apprehension.

Dominating the wood-engraving industry for fifty years was the family firm of the Dalziel brothers. Headed by George and Edward, the engraving company also included John, Thomas, and—the lone sister among the brothers—Margaret, as well as assorted nephews and the trained artisans of their atelier.[12] The contribution of the Dalziel firm to Victorian visual culture and popular publishing cannot be overstated. Week after week and month after month, the Dalziel brothers cut wood engravings featured on the pages of periodicals as varied as the *Illustrated London News*, *Punch*, the *Cornhill Magazine*, *Good Words*, and *Good Words for the Young*. At the school attached to their engraving studio, the Dalziel brothers taught some of the most important illustrators of the period, including Fred Walker, J. W. North, and George Pinwell (Engen, *Dictionary*, 62). As publishers in their own right at their Camden Press, they were able to promote artists whose work they admired, such as John Everett Millais, Arthur Boyd Houghton, and Myles Birket Foster. From 1850 onward, they were involved in a lucrative relationship with George Routledge, who published many of the Dalziel gift books under his imprimatur, promoting them in his Christmas catalogs for decades.

As Graham Reynolds comments in his foreword to a reprint of the Dalziel brothers' memoir, *The Brothers Dalziel: A Record of Fifty Years' Work*, the family firm pioneered "a new method of publication, whereby the engraver acted as publisher, selecting both the subject of the book and the artists who were to design the cuts" (n.p.). Silently assuming the role of editor, the Dalziels sometimes chose and arranged the poetic selections or commissioned poets to write on a determined subject. Occasionally, one of the brothers would contribute an original poem or picture from his own pen or pencil. The Dalziel method resulted in close associations among poetry, picture, wood engraving, and printing and established significant social and material networks of production. In effect, the firm combined the functions of author, artist, engraver, printer, and publisher, in a commercial or corporate version of William Blake's artisanal practice. The firm's manufacturing model also connected its standardized formats to the mass productions of the culture industry. Canny entrepreneurs, the Dalziel brothers were well aware that entering the publishing business allowed them to establish a marketing niche for the "Dalziel Gift Book"—a title, as a reviewer noted in 1866, suggesting "that the 'brothers Dalziel' get up every year a Christmas annual, of which the successive volumes have something more than a family likeness" (*SR*, Dec. 1, 1866, 684).

With their standardized format, the Dalziels established a crucial continuum in popular publishing, from the early steel-engraved annuals to the wood-engraved illustrated poetry found in the periodical press to the Christmas gift books of the sixties. Like the earlier annuals, the Dalziel Fine Art Book offered a seasonal Christmas gift combining literary and pictorial contents in ornamental covers. But unlike the annuals, and in keeping with the popular market generated by illustrated periodicals, the pictures were original wood engravings made expressly for the printed page by some of the best artists of the day. Furthermore—in contrast to the miscellaneous writings of both the annuals and the magazines—the gift book focused exclusively on poetry, selected for its national, moral, and affective values.

### The Brothers Dalziel and the Christmas Gift Book

As publishers like Alexander Macmillan recognized, "People who want to read poetry generally buy it" (Graves, *Life*, 196). The crucial business issue then became targeting the audience who wanted to read, and therefore own, poetry. The Dalziel brothers' genius lay in seeing that the periodical press had established a popular market for poetry and that these new readers would become buyers if a volume of verse could be made to carry sufficient symbolic and material value to make ownership desirable.

In 1857, the Dalziel brothers "set up a small printing office" to print their own Fine Art Books at the Camden Press, a publishing business affiliated with their wood-engraving firm that dominated the market for "high-class art work" for forty years (Dalziel and Dalziel, *Record*, 352). These gift books produced annually for Christmas were affordable to middle-class shoppers willing to lay out fifteen shillings (the wholesale price advertised in the Routledge catalogs) in a display of seasonal munificence that paid dividends in cultural capital. Solidly reposing on the book tables of drawing rooms throughout the nation, the Dalziel Fine Art Book represented the householder's investment and participation in the nation's art and industry. Through the mass production and marketing strategies of the period's largest and most influential engraving firm, fine arts from the field of restricted production—poetry and visual art—became domesticated, miniaturized, and portable.

Prior to their emergence as publishers of Christmas gift books, the Dalziels were involved in producing volumes of illustrated poetry originating from other firms. In 1852, they engraved John Gilbert's illustrations for a deluxe edition of Charles Mackay's fantastic poem *The Salamandrine* for Ingram and Cook. This journeywork brought them into contact with one of the period's most prolific and popular black-and-white illustrators and ultimately led them into their career-long association with George Routledge. "Following 'The Salamandrine,'" the Dalziels recalled, "began the most important works of our lives, and it was through the enterprise of Messrs. Routledge and Warne that we were enabled to produce so long a list of 'Fine Art Books,' some of them on commission, and many others entirely on our own responsibility" (*Record*, 70).[13] The commissions they received were wide ranging and transatlantic and included such prestigious firms as Longmans, Blackwood's, and Smith, Elder, and Co. in England and Appleton and Roberts Brothers in the United States (70). As we have seen, the Dalziel brothers also received a significant commission from Edward Moxon when the publisher hired them to look after the artistic contents of the illustrated edition of Tennyson's *Poems* (82).

Distinct from their various commissions for book and magazine publishers was the Dalziels' own line of Fine Art Books, which they published under the Routledge imprint. This arrangement allowed the Dalziels a free rein in the conception, production, and printing of each book's literary and artistic contents, while leaving the business of promotion, distribution, and sales to Routledge.

The brothers recognized the potential of the popular market for illustrated poetry after working with Routledge and Warne on an edition of *The Poetical Works of H. W. Longfellow* (1856), profusely illustrated by John Gilbert. The Dalziels received one thousand pounds for the pictures—a sum that was to include the cost of both Gilbert's designs and the firm's engraving. Routledge's investment in illustration and packaging proved well worth the outlay. The illustrated Longfellow "created a sensation" when first published and continued to be a favorite on both sides of the Atlantic for years to come (Dalziel and Dalziel, *Record*, 30, 31). One of the few poets to command consistent mass sales throughout the century—Richard Altick notes that Routledge and Warne "together sold over 1,126,900 copies of Longfellow's various volumes" (*Reader*, 387)—Longfellow was also, like Tennyson, supremely pictureable, with his narrative poems and highly realized characters. Why, then, did the illustrated Tennyson, published a year later, fail to generate similar sales, while the illustrated Longfellow succeeded? After all, the Longfellow volume was, artistically speaking, a very ordinary affair, while the Tennyson edition, as the Dalziels well knew, stood "out as a landmark in the history of book illustration," thanks to the "extreme beauty" of the Pre-Raphaelite designs (Dalziel and Dalziel, *Record*, 83).

From the respective success and failure of these commissions, the Dalziels learned two critically important things about the niche market they wished to target in their Fine Art Book series. First, middle-class consumers had a price threshold above which they were reluctant to venture. Second, sales of illustrated poetry were dependent on the Christmas season, when generous buyers were willing to pay extra for a luxury good to give as a present. The difference could be finely calculated in the half measures of pounds and years: the illustrated Longfellow came out before Christmas and was priced at 21s. (or a guinea); the illustrated Tennyson was released in May, at £1 11s. 6d. (or a guinea and a half). The guinea gift book was the new annual that publishers could depend on for substantial sales at Christmas.

Of course, even twenty-one shillings was a considerable sum for families with modest middle-class incomes. However, the Victorian practice of underselling—that is, offering books at a discount below the advertised price—meant that the Dalziel guinea gift book was, in fact, regularly sold for fifteen shillings, a "wholesale" price Routledge advertised in his catalogs. Moreover, the 1860s saw a significant rise in disposable income in middle-class families. Richard Altick calculates that prior to 1850, potential customers for poetry books were limited to some 27,000 families with an annual income of £400 or more.[14] Between 1850 and 1880, the number of families with an annual income between £150 and £400 more than doubled, while the average family income of lower-middle class families rose to about £100. The family's buying power also rose considerably during this time. As a result of falling prices, the real income of the average family rose by about 75 percent, giving the middle classes additional spending money. By the 1860s, in Altick's famous formulation, "[t]he three great requisites of a mass reading public—literacy, leisure, and a little pocket-money—became the possession of more and more people" (*Reader*, 306).

Regardless of the buyer's purchasing power, or whether he paid twenty-one or fifteen shillings, an illustrated book of poetry in ornate covers was a luxury good, not a necessity. It made a far greater demand on the pocket than did the average book of newly published poetry then available, which was usually priced at five shillings.[15] The pragmatic middle classes who worked hard for their pounds, shillings, and pence required a solid rationale for their purchases. Publishers discovered that people would buy into what Thorstein Veblen names "accredited canons of consumption" (*Theory*, 116) by investing in the nation's artists and poets packaged in decorative covers for the purposes of presentation and display. The optimum time of release for such books were the weeks leading up to Christmas and the New Year. As Simon Eliot's research demonstrates, "the size and importance of the Christmas season (October–December) grew dramatically in the period from 1850 to 1890" for the book trade in general ("Trends," 34); for illustrated poetry, it was virtually the only season. With carefully managed marketing that included lengthy seasonal reviews and prominent advertising lists of "books suitable for presents" in the periodical press, as well as glowing visual displays in windows decked out for the holidays, gift books combining pictures and poetry became a standard Christmas present of the 1860s.

The book may be considered one of the first commercial commodities to be associated with the Christmas season; it is a transatlantic success story of enormous scale. Stephen Nissenbaum has shown how Christmas became established in the nineteenth-century United States as a domestic holiday centering on children and the home, with "books on the cutting edge of a commercial Christmas, making up more than half of the earliest items advertised as Christmas gifts" in American periodicals (*Battle*, 140). The tradition of giving books at Christmas is recorded in young people's fiction of the period, with the March girls receiving personal copies of *Pilgrim's Progress* in variant bindings in Louisa May Alcott's *Little Women* and Laura receiving a book of Tennyson's poems in Laura Ingalls Wilder's *Little Town on the Prairie*. These Christmas presents may have been produced by American publishers, but they may also have been British imports distributed by American firms. As the *Fraser's* critic remarked in 1859, "American bibliomaniacs love good binding, and for that they must be beholden in a great measure to English workmen" ("Furniture Books," 96).

The bookbinding industry made a critically important contribution to the gift book's material appeal. Writing for *Blackwood's* in 1857, Margaret Oliphant declared, "Our wealth, our luxury, and our generous habit of present-making, have resuscitated the half-forgotten art of binding books" ("Picture-Books," 310). Oliphant's capitalist discourse of supply and demand assumes an authentic popular desire for gift books and a ready-made public waiting for them to appear. In fact, however, publishers carefully built up this market. Oliphant tacitly admits this in a subsequent review, when she acknowledges "the allure" of material objects and connects the "art of manufacture" to a commercialized production of consumer desire:

> The book-sellers' windows glow splendid with colours more than green and scarlet. Christmas wakes a melodious crowd of storytellers, and gentle professors of the kindred art [of illustration]. . . . Books did not rain down out of all the clouds in the firmament of old, when *we* had our holidays; and as for the miracles of paste-board and gilt paper, the glories of Russia leather and *papier maché*, which allure every passer-by into the prevalent mania for Christmas gifts, such delights had not appeared within our horizon. Certainly, if the art of giving presents has not wonderfully extended of past years, the arts of manufacturing the same have immensely multiplied. ("Christmas," 106–7)

Oliphant's reviews connect conspicuous consumption with the commodification of literature and demonstrate some of the ideological work performed by the gift book as a standardized product of the culture industry. Testifying to its disciplinary force, Oliphant associates the commodity with domestic virtues and national values. "It is pleasant to go along the brightened streets," she writes, "to see the dainty contrivances everywhere about, and to note what stores of home gratification, what tender mementoes, and treasures of youth, to be gratefully remembered in darker days, are lighting up into a common exhilaration the everyday craft of buying and selling" ("Christmas," 107). The drawing-room books that contain these "stores of home gratification" are also, Oliphant notes in another review, "memorials of the season in which we sober British people, whether we call our feast the Christmas or the New Year, take our most thorough and honest holiday; and of all the affection, neighbourship, and kindness which reach their spring-tide" in the darkest days of the year ("Picture-Books," 318).

As one of the season's most aggressively marketed commodities, the gift book tapped into the dominant idea that "Christmas and Englishness were . . . indistinguishable and the values of the one were those of the other" (Connelly, *Christmas*, 4). These cultural values constellated around a domestic vision celebrating the centrality of home and childhood; a bucolic vision celebrating rural landscape and a nonindustrialized economy; and a national vision celebrating British moral, physical, intellectual, artistic, and industrial superiority.

As both material object and social practice, the gift book represented the British to themselves and others, confirming and constructing dominant ideological values. When the *Saturday Review* critic proclaimed that "[t]he Christmas Book is a British institution," he connected it to what we now see as the characteristics associated with Victorian middle-class respectability. Noting that "[l]ike all other British institutions, it has grown into general use no one knows exactly how," the reviewer suggested that "[i]ts rise may be pronounced to be coeval with that curious development of the modern mind which affects the useful and the practical and the earnest. To give mere luxuries and carnal material enjoyments is thought to argue a low moral standard both in the giver and [the] receiver. A present is not thought to be right unless it affects the useful as well as the ornamental" (Dec. 5, 1863, 738). In multiple ways, the gift book institutionalized networks of association and relations of authority and power. Although the *Saturday Review* might question why "this beautiful access [*sic*] of all the home virtues ought always to take the form of giving books away" (Dec. 15, 1866, 743), the magazine nevertheless contributed aggressively to the book-buying Christmas mania in its reviews and advertisements.

Other papers also participated in this promotion of the Christmas book as the ideal present. The *Illustrated London News,* for instance, wholeheartedly supported the tradition of Christmas book giving, "there being no more elegant and convenient form yet devised for a token of friendship or family affection" (Dec. 15, 1866, 582). Victorians embraced the illustrated book as their Christmas present of choice because the gift book's cultural capital as a symbolic good was closely associated with notions of national identity. As a material object, illustrated poetry in decorative covers represented the excellence of British manufacturing and commercial power, as well as its wealth. As a symbolic object, it functioned as a token of affection, cementing familial and social ties; as a repository of greatness in art and literature, it reinforced national unity; and as an item of conspicuous consumption, it attested to the individual owner's cultivation, taste, and surplus income.

The launching of the Dalziel Fine Art Book series in 1857 was coincident with the *Saturday Review*'s recognition that "[a]s poetry is thought to be popular, most of the Christmas books are in the poetical line" (Dec. 19, 1857, 558). The Brothers Dalziel contributed to this seasonal demand by producing Fine Art Books of two principal kinds: poetic anthologies that gave prominence to the verses and included wood-engraved illustrations; and artists' galleries that gave prominence to the pictures and included ekphrastic poetry. Both types were commissioned by the wood-engraving firm on topics calculated to appeal to middle-class consumers because of their association with notions of national and/or domestic identity.

## Illustrated Poetry Anthologies

Published in the inaugural year of the Camden Press, the Dalziels' *Poets of the Nineteenth Century* (edited by Willmott) often shares pride of place with the Moxon Tennyson in terms of its importance to illustration, but it is perhaps even more significant in terms of book history. In contrast to the Tennyson collection, *The Poets of the Nineteenth Century* was an immediate commercial and critical success and had a large, ongoing readership for decades. In its first year of publication, an initial issue of five thousand and a second of three thousand sold; the following year, another three thousand copies sold, and the volume was reissued for Christmas in 1865, 1868, 1878, and 1885 (Haass, "Victorian Poetry," 55). Concentrating their energies on producing the volume's pictures, the Dalziels hired the Reverend Robert Aris Willmott to edit the poetic contents.[16] Willmott selected poetry from "a period of about eighty-five years," from 1771 to 1856, thus combining the work of canonical poets such as Cowper, Coleridge, Wordsworth, Byron, and Keats with contemporaries such as Barrett Browning, Hemans, Tennyson, Browning, and Allingham. Drawing on the connections they had made from their various commissions, including the Moxon Tennyson, the Dalziels hired eighteen prominent artists to produce the one hundred illustrations. The work's four hundred pages were edged with gold and enclosed in a decorative cloth cover with a gilt-stamped design.

"This is a gorgeous book," declared the *Athenaeum*, "bound in blue and gold,—latticed with gilding, and all a-bloom with the colour of the sky" (Nov. 8, 1856, 1364).[17] The reviewer's comments suggested that there was something both intrinsically natural and exquisitely well made about the gift book—attributes particularly appealing to middle-class consumers. The value of the material object, as a luxury good, was also evident in its "cream-coloured paper, thick, glossy, and soft," making the book as a whole "altogether a wonder and a delight" (1364). Here was something substantial, worthy of purchase—not a flimsy and ephemeral production of the periodical press but an object of permanent value to be displayed with pride and perused at leisure.

Like most of the Dalziel Fine Art Books, *The Poets of the Nineteenth Century* offers a selection of poetry calculated to appeal to middle-class readers. Unlike many of their later gift books, however, the principle of selection here is not subject or theme but rather the historical and national categories that consecrate canons and confer cultural value. Despite its claim to be representative of a century that was only a few years past its midpoint, *The Poets of the Nineteenth Century* could not hope to be encyclopedic. As Willmott acknowledged in his preface, "a great Constituency can only be represented by a few Members" (viii). In his selection of this constituency, Willmott had, the *Athenaeum* recognized, "a catholic taste not usual in poetical partizans [*sic*]" (Nov. 8, 1856, 1365). For his part, Willmott advises that his editorial approach was informed by his own reading preferences, determined by his personal connections to living poets (for example, Mary Russell Mitford, Lisle Bowles, James Montgomery, and Robert Southey); his strong support of "the tuneful Sisterhood" of women writers; and his predilection for religious, patriotic, and sentimental verses (*Poets*, vi). In fact, his selections are strikingly similar to the kinds of poems found in the pages of illustrated periodicals such as *Good Words* and *Once a Week* and would therefore have been familiar to ordinary readers in general style and subject if not specific authorship. While Margaret Oliphant, writing for *Blackwood's*, might complain that the poetic contents "are very well worn and familiar—the stock examples, which suggest themselves at once to every one moderately well-read in poetry" ("Picture-Books," 315), she seems to have missed the point that *The Poets of the Nineteenth Century* was aimed at the popular readership, not the traditional audience of those "moderately well-read in poetry." *The Poets of the Nineteenth Century* sought to capture readers of periodical poetry by giving them verses familiar in style from an accredited national store.

Natalie Houston reminds us that "[a]nthologies produce literary history and aesthetic conditioning not simply through their contents, which have generally been the focus of academic study, but also in their material design, which determines how readers relate contextual information to literary texts" ("Anthologies," 366). In the making of this particular canon of nineteenth-century poets, Willmott had to work within the parameters of the Dalziel Fine Art Book, including its specific physical features, multiple makers, and planned four-to-one ratio of poetry and pictures. Willmott's selections were necessarily governed by considerations of space—he omitted Wordsworth's "Tintern Abbey," for example, "from want of room" (*Poets*, vii).

The problem of space constraints is shared by all anthologists, but Willmott's selections were further complicated by the need to find poetry that artists could illustrate. Willmott noted, with regret, that he could not include "the most striking effort of Southey's imagination, the agony of Kailyal at her father's flight," as it "was ill-adapted for pictorial use" (vii). Like the poetry selected by editor Samuel Lucas for publication in *Once a Week*, the verses chosen by Willmott for *Poets* had to be pictureable. And by identifying poems adaptable "for pictorial use," as his example from Southey's Oriental epic, *The Curse of Kehama,* suggests, the editor had to consider not only the visual quality of a poem—that is, its potential for pictorial representation—but also whether that potential image was an appropriate representation in a book intended for a wife, daughter, niece, or friend. Like Lucas, Willmott appears to have kept his audience in mind by deliberately avoiding sensational verses likely to inspire sensational pictures (L. Hughes, "Inventing," 65). The gift book, like the illustrated magazine, was intended for use and display in intergenerational family space. Its verbal and visual contents ought not, in the words of Dickens's immortal Podsnap, "bring a blush to the cheek of the young person." Readers are made by what makes the book, but the book is also made by its reading subjects as they are constructed by a dominant culture's disciplinary forces.

Willmott's omission of Southey's poem and other potential selections on the basis of their visual and moral qualities was offset by his deliberate choice of certain verses for their pictureability. These selections, too, show the informing influence of illustrated periodicals on the making of *The Poets of the Nineteenth Century.* "Love," for instance, the only verses by S. T. Coleridge that Willmott included in the anthology, is a romantic poem of courtship and fantasy whose quatrains would not have been out of place in *Once a Week* or *Good Words.* Willmott observed, "The fame of Coleridge . . . will not suffer loss by resting on Genevieve, who has caught a new grace from the hand of Millais" (*Poets,* vii) (fig. 3.2). Like the pictured poetry in periodicals, that in *The Poets of the Nineteenth Century* emphasized the close integration and mutual elucidation of verbal and visual texts. Moreover, the wood-engraved illustrations after the designs of living artists added a contemporary graphic notation to the verses of dead poets, bringing their words into the present and adding—in Willmott's words—"new grace."

The one hundred pictures had a particular appeal for the middle-class purchaser, partly because they came in a language—wood engraving—that the ordinary person knew and understood. As Willmott acknowledged in his preface, "the tasteful skill of the Brothers Dalziel" was critically important in translating "the grace and beauty of the pencil . . . into the popular language of their own Art" (v). In addition to adding beauty and pictorial appeal to the book of verse, the wood-engraved illustrations also provided a miniaturized and domesticated "picture-gallery" for the private pleasure and connoisseurship of ordinary consumers (v).

*The Poets of the Nineteenth Century* brought the work of artists whose paintings were exhibited that year in the Art Treasures of the United Kingdom Exhibition in Manchester—artists such as John Everett Millais, Ford Madox Brown,

COLERIDGE.

LOVE.

All thoughts, all passions, all delights,
Whatever stirs this mortal frame,

137 T

Figure 3.2 John Everett Millais, illustration for S. T. Coleridge, "Love," in *The Poets of the Nineteenth Century*, 3rd ed. (Routledge, 1858), 137.

Arthur Hughes, and Myles Birket Foster—into middle-class drawing rooms. In her review, Margaret Oliphant recognized the added cultural value of having England's national painters illustrate selections from accredited poets, offering her opinion that "most people will look first at the two designs of Millais, the art-hero of the day—the first of which illustrates Byron's *Dream,* and the second *Genevieve* [*sic*]."[18] While she was less enthusiastic about the results, Oliphant dutifully drew readers' attention to the fact that "[a] lesser member of the pre-Raphaelite brotherhood also contributes to this book" ("Picture-Books," 315, 316). This was Ford Madox Brown, the organizer of the Russell Place Exhibit and painter of *The Hayfield* and *Christ Washing Peter's Feet,* which were on view that summer in Manchester. In keeping with Pre-Raphaelite practice, Brown approached his illustration for Byron's "Prisoner of Chillon" (fig. 3.3) with the same artistic standards as he did painting, spending days in the morgue making studies of the gradual transformation that takes place in the human body in the process of decay (Hueffer, *Brown,* 118–20).

While readers might find the drawing gruesome, or disagree, as Oliphant did, with Brown's interpretation of Byron's characters, none could deny that, in workmanship, the drawing was a mini-masterpiece. Moreover, if figure drawings from life (or, in this case, dead) models were not to the taste of the book owner, he or she could turn the pages, as Oliphant did, to the "exquisite bits of landscape" ("Picture-Books," 316) from the hands of Myles Birket Foster (fig. 3.4). Commenting that "his works have become a marvel of truth, poetry and skill," the *Athenaeum* singled Foster out as "pre-eminent" among the illustrators (Nov. 8, 1856, 1365). In terms of spatial allotments and architecture, Foster's representation of the English landscape is central to the book's visual appeal. Foster's work takes pride of place on the first page of *The Poets of the Nineteenth Century* and appears frequently throughout the volume—seventeen times to Millais' two and Brown's one. As both a celebrated landscape artist and "one of the most prolific and popular illustrators of the day" (Muir, *Victorian,* 135), Foster represented one of the book's principal attractions, from a marketing point of view. But the Dalziels' canny selection of what the Routledge advertisements termed "the most celebrated Artists" ensured that there would be something for all tastes in the book's picture gallery (*SR,* Dec. 6, 1856, 715). With contributions from artists with the popularity of Foster and the avant-garde appeal of the Pre-Raphaelites, the Dalziels' Fine Art Book offered the middle-class consumer a miniature Manchester exhibition of black-and-white designs by painters hailed as national treasures, adding a significant value-added factor to the poetic selections.

But even these at length grew cold.
Our voices took a dreary tone,
An echo of the dungeon stone,
  A grating sound—not full and free,

111

Figure 3.3 Ford Madox Brown, illustration for George Gordon, Lord Byron, "The Prisoner of Chillon," in *The Poets of the Nineteenth Century*, 3rd ed. (Routledge, 1858), 111.

BEATTIE.

THE POET IN YOUTH.

Lo! where the stripling, wrapt in wonder, roves
Beneath the precipice o'erhung with pine,

1 B

Figure 3.4 Myles Birket Foster, illustration for James Beattie, "The Poet in Youth," in *The Poets of the Nineteenth Century*, 3rd ed. (Routledge, 1858), 1.

In preparing the anthology for publication, the Dalziels were very much in charge of the artistic contents, aligning appropriate artists with individual poems and making specific recommendations for pictorial details. Brown recorded in his diary that one of the brothers called at his studio in March 1856, apparently on a recommendation from Dante Gabriel Rossetti, who did not contribute to *The Poets of the Nineteenth Century* but seems to have been involved behind the scenes. Brown wrote tersely, "Wants me to do him a *Prisoner of Chillon* on wood. I will this evening"—meaning, of course, that he would begin the preliminary sketches that evening. The actual drawing on the wood took many days of effort (Hueffer, *Brown*, 118). On seeing Brown's design the next month, the Dalziels requested that he amend it to include a "slashed sleeve on the arm of the prisoner, to give him a more mediaeval look." Brown recorded that he obligingly "worked at the block in consequence, but I think harmed it" (122). When the Dalziels sent him the India-ink proof of their engraving, Brown spent seven hours correcting its details (130). For this the Dalziels paid him the handsome sum of eight pounds (122)—significantly more than the typical two-guinea fee provided for the deadline-induced magazine illustration and a signal that they considered the work, as did Brown, in the category of art (Buckler, "*Once a Week*," 937).[19]

"The Prisoner of Chillon" was Brown's first book illustration in an entire published oeuvre that consists of a mere nine drawings on wood. His valuation of the illustration is evident in both the labor he devoted to it and his inclusion of a pen-and-ink study for the drawing in the Russell Place Exhibit. It may have been there, or in the cream-colored pages of *The Poets of the Nineteenth Century*, that art collector Thomas Plint (who purchased Brown's *Christ Washing Peter's Feet* for £200) saw Brown's "Prisoner." Plint subsequently commissioned Brown to produce the illustration as a watercolor for him (Hueffer, *Brown*, 146, 156). Thus, the unique painting was technically a copy of a work that originally existed as a multiple.

This brief history of versions reminds us again of the complicated relationships between illustration and painting, popular and high art. The black-and-white engraving as it appeared in *The Poets of the Nineteenth Century* was the original artistic conception, designed for inclusion in the printed pages of a bound book as a companion to a well-known poem. Brown did not need to look up his Byron when the Dalziels commissioned him to illustrate "The Prisoner of Chillon"; the poem was familiar to him, as it was to most men of his generation and class. For others less versed in poetry, who might be reading Byron's "Prisoner of Chillon" for the first time in the Dalziel Fine Art Book, Brown's arresting illustration must have had a considerable impact.

Brown's illustration does not appear in the usual headpiece location. Instead, like the yawning grave this engraving represents, it suddenly cuts into the verses on the third of thirteen printed pages (fig. 3.3). A long narrative poem, Byron's "The Prisoner of Chillon" relates the gothic tale of three brothers cast by a tyrant into the dungeon of his castle. The eldest, who survives the ordeal, narrates the horror of seeing first one brother, then the other, die before his eyes, their remains buried in shallow graves close to his fettered feet. Brown's "cut" physically severs the narrative, separating the narrator's story of imprisonment from his tale of his brothers' deaths. In so doing, it participates in the reader's experience of the narrative, proleptically shaping the anticipation of events while also evoking an affective range of horror and grief.[20]

If the illustration thus foreshortens the reader's view of the ending, this perspective is also formalized in the design itself. Brown's design focuses on the decomposing corpse, which the jailors are cutting from its chains preparatory to depositing it in a shallow grave. A single shaft of light divides the scene in a dramatic diagonal descending from the upper right, illuminating the dreadful details of the dungeon. Its beams connect the protesting elder brother who survives and the stunned youngest, whose death will soon follow. Two jailors and a gravedigger are positioned to form a triangle around the brothers' bodies.

In the dimness of the background, we can just make out the head jailer in his robes of office smoking his pipe in the doorway, perhaps to counteract the smell of decomposing flesh. He appears unconcerned and detached from the scene. In contrast, the undertaker, who has dug the grave, seems to enjoy his work: a grim smile hovers on his face as he rests his shovel and prepares to pull the corpse into the pit by its hair. Only the muscular turnkey at left, cutting the chains no longer needed to hold the lifeless body, seems interested in the responses of the grieving prisoners. He turns his head toward the oldest brother, who, with his arms held up to the shaft of light, strains in grief toward his dead sibling. The younger brother, already losing his grip on life, appears listless and confused. Like the three jailors, the three brothers each presents a different response to the experience of death, graphically portraying the variety of responses available to the horrific story relayed in Byron's poem and Brown's picture.

Taste in art, as in all things, is various, and an anthology such as *The Poets of the Nineteenth Century* benefited from a range of poetic modes as well as artistic styles, meeting the needs of a wide range of readers. In this variety and plenitude, the gift book also took its cue from the pages of illustrated periodicals. The success of Willmott's anthology was evident in its steady sales over the next decade. Subsequent anthologies produced by the Dalziels for their Fine Art Book series capitalized on the success of the form they had established with this early venture. Some of these selected the poetry of standard authors based on a theme, such as Christian faith. This was the subject of Willmott's next edited anthology for the Dalziels, *English Sacred Poetry of the Sixteenth, Seventeenth, Eighteenth, and Nineteenth Centuries* (1862).

Occasionally, as we shall see in the next chapter, the Dalziels speculated in an illustrated collection by a single contemporary author, such as Eliza Cook or Jean Ingelow. These initiatives sought to capitalize on the popular readership for "the tuneful Sisterhood" established by the periodical press and reinforced in *The Poets of the Nineteenth Century*. But the typical Dalziel Fine Art Book made pictures and poetry viable for the popular market by focusing specifically on domestic thematics, as in *Home Affections Pourtrayed by the Poets* (1858; edited by Charles Mackay), *Home Thoughts and Home Scenes* (1865), and *Ballad Stories of the Affections* (1869).[21] Later, they often based their anthologies on the slenderest of alliterative associations: *Golden Thoughts from Golden Fountains* (1867), *Rhyme and Reason* (1869), *Picture Poesies* (1874), and *Sunlight of Song* (1874). The vagueness of these later titles indicates that, by the late 1860s and early 1870s, the Dalziels had begun to recycle illustrations from their vast stock of wood engravings, recombining them with different pieces of poetry, and encasing them in new bindings adorned with new titles. In the early days of their enterprise, however, the pictures and poetry were purpose-made or specially chosen for each new Christmas season's Fine Art Book.

## Artists' Galleries and Ekphrastic Poetry

As we have seen, the typical gift book of the period presented, in a style similar to that of contemporary magazines, a miscellany of different artistic styles, combining the landscape illustrations of an artist such as Myles Birket Foster or Harrison Weir with the bold figure designs of a Pre-Raphaelite illustrator such as John Millais or Ford Madox Brown. Such a miscellany marred the overall aesthetic unity of books from the Moxon Tennyson to Willmott's editions of *The Poets of the Nineteenth Century* and *English Sacred Poetry*.

While book design remained an underdeveloped aspect of the 1860s book trade, some of the Dalziel Fine Art Books did achieve a degree of visual unity by commissioning a set of pictures from a single artist. Once they had engraved the artist's pictures, the Dalziels would set about hiring poets to compose a page of verse for each plate. Apparently unaware that the double-page opening is the visual unit of the book for the reader, the Dalziels conceived each page separately, printing pictures and poems only on the rectos of each leaf. The layout alternated full-page picture with single-page poem, thereby emphatically dividing the visual and the verbal contents. This method resulted in books whose principal purpose was to serve as a gallery of a given artist's compositions, with the poetic contents representing the additional feature, rather than the images. Just as the *Illustrated London News* was the first periodical to make a practice of subordinating text to image in the 1840s (Altick, *Reader*, 344), the Dalziel Fine Art Book was the first of the sixties books to foreground the picture as the vehicle of meaning, with the verses designed as accompanying letterpress made to fit the measurements of a specific textual space.[22]

A direct outcome of this form of Dalziel Fine Art Book was the development of a new kind of ekphrastic poetry for the gift-book market. In some ways, this was a throwback to the method of the earlier Christmas annuals, whose steel-engraved plates were "written up" by commissioned authors. The pictures in the Dalziel series, however, were not reproductions of celebrated paintings but original art produced specifically for the wood-engraved environment of the printed book on a theme determined by the enterprising publisher. Moreover, unlike the companion literature of the annuals, the new ekphrastic verses tended not to reference the picture, verbalize its story, address the image, or otherwise "write up" the pictorial contents in the longstanding tradition of poetry and painting. Rather, they drew on ekphrastic strategies established in the illustrated press of the time. As described by Peter Sinnema, the ekphrastic methodology of the *Illustrated London News,* for example, comprehended language's ability to speak about a world presented by a picture and lived in by a reader (*Dynamics,* 31).

In the Dalziel Fine Art Books, poets followed D. G. Rossetti's illustrative example and "allegorize[d] on [their] own hook[s] on the subject of the [picture]," (*Correspondence,* 2:7). Their verses' chief function was to elaborate musically the affective and moral values of the topic at hand. Sinnema notes that one of the most significant aspects of the image/text relationship in the popular press was "its capacity to construct versions of the world gratifying to a particular audience" (*Dynamics,* 31, 30). In their themed Christmas books, the Dalziels built worlds of pictures and poetry their readers could step into, presenting images of domestic or national ideals that corresponded with those in the documentary pages of the popular press.

Among the significant productions of this sort, two stand out: *Home Thoughts and Home Scenes in Original Poems and Pictures* (with the former supplied by selected women poets and the latter by Arthur Boyd Houghton) and *Birket Foster's Pictures of English Landscape, with Pictures in Words by Tom Taylor.* In contrast to anthologies such as *The Poets of the Nineteenth Century* and *English Sacred Poetry,* these books emphasized the modern by combining the original work of living writers and artists in a manner akin to the popular press. Unlike the inset images found in either the illustrated press or the anthologies, however, these Dalziel Fine Art Books offered a picture book of full-page engravings, alternating with full-page poems. The format of these quartos was designed for browsing and viewing. They were books for occasional encounters rather than prolonged study.

Each of these elegant quartos *presents* itself as a present. *Pictures of English Landscape* was encased in an ornamental binding designed by Owen Jones; *Home Thoughts* was bound in similarly resplendent covers by John Leighton. "As to gorgeous binding and illustrations," the *Saturday Review* acknowledged, "they are of the essence of the thing defined. A certain sumptuousness and splendour is asked for at Christmas" (Dec. 17, 1859, 744). Christmas books, Margaret Oliphant recognized, were the outcome of "a sumptuous craft, belonging to an age of luxury" ("Christmas," 108). Their value as material objects could therefore outweigh their literary merit. *Fraser's Magazine* called them "furniture books," recognizing that one of their principal functions was drawing-room display in bindings selected to accord with home décor (99) while meeting the requirements of respectable social space.

The Dalziel brothers commissioned Myles Birket Foster to produce a series of "pictures, which were to be the best and most perfect work he could do, . . . [and] to be thoroughly representative subjects of rustic English scenery" (Dalziel and Dalziel, *Record,* 139). In making this commission, they knew exactly the kind of scenes he would supply, as they had engraved "hundreds of his drawings" over the years (139). As we have seen, the Dalziels had previously included Foster among the artists hired to illustrate *The Poets of the Nineteenth Century.* The following year, they sought his contributions for their edition of *Wordsworth's Poems,* as well as for Charles Mackay's anthology, *Home Affections Pourtrayed by the Poets.* Prior to *Pictures of English Landscape,* the Dalziels had commissioned Foster as the sole illustrator for *Odes and Sonnets* (1859). Foster had also been involved in Christmas gift books with other publishers, starting with his first illustrated book in 1847, Thomas Miller's *Country Year Book.* In this initial venture, Foster established his artistic territory of rustic country scenery and negligible human figures, which remained "his stock in trade," as Edward Hodnett remarks, "for the rest of his career" (*Five Centuries,* 120). Foster secured his fame with a very popular edition of Longfellow's *Evangeline* in 1850, in which his landscapes combined with action scenes by John Gilbert to great effect (Hodnett, *Five Centuries,* 120). He also contributed to two extremely popular Christmas gift books, Burns's *Poems and Pictures* (1846) and Bogue's *Christmas with the Poets* (1851). Indeed, illustrations by Myles Birket Foster played a significant role in constructing the meanings and values associated with the British Christmas tradition in both gift books and periodicals.

A prolific contributor to the *Illustrated London News,* Foster disseminated his images of bucolic Britain to a mass readership; the vision gained authority from its ubiquity and familiarity in the documentary newspaper. The regular appearance of his rustic representations in the *ILN*'s Christmas supplements further reinforced their association with Christmas and national identity. Throughout the 1850s, Foster provided "his most characteristic works" for these Christmas supplements (Lewis, *Foster,* 14), an annual publication that Mark Connelly deems instrumental in the construction of "many of the essential nineteenth-century concepts of Christmas," particularly the belief that Christmas "was the festival of the home and that the home was a deep-rooted English cultural expression" (*Christmas,* 11). Similarly, Peter Sinnema traces the *ILN*'s "identification of Englishness with the 'authentic' celebration of Christmas" by situating this authenticity in the domestic hearth and the rural countryside and forming a collective national identity out of assumed middle-class values (*Dynamics,* 111).

Some of Foster's engravings would have been particularly prized by the *ILN*'s mass audience and no doubt subsequently formed decorative scenes in many modest homes, after he became the first artist to be reproduced in color in the *ILN*'s Christmas supplement of 1857 (Houfe, *Dictionary,* 308). Although other artists, such as John Gilbert, John Leech, and Kenny Meadows, drew comic or convivial scenes for these special numbers, "it was generally reserved," according to the artist's biographer, "to Birket Foster to supply those scenes which appealed to the poetic feelings of the festive season" (Lewis, *Foster,* 14). The "poetic feelings of the festive season" may be easily inferred from some of the titles for Foster's works: "The First Fall of Snow"; "Christmas—The Cottage Door"; and "Christmas Eve—The Cottager's Return from Market" sufficiently indicate the genre's connection between an imagined pastoral landscape and home as the center of the nation, uniting and sustaining labor and leisure.

An active publisher of pictures and poetry for the common reader, the *Illustrated London News* always accompanied Foster's Christmas image with a poem set into the same page. "Christmas Eve—The Cottager's Return from Market," for example, is accompanied by a two-stanza lyric by "S.C.," whose concluding lines encapsulate the poetic feelings of Foster's depiction of the festive season:

> Glad Christmas comes, and every hearth
>     Makes room to give him welcome now;
> E'en Want will dry its tears in mirth,
>     And crown him with a holly bough.
> Each house is swept the day before,
>     And windows stuck with evergreens;

The snow is besom'd from the door,
And comfort crowns the cottage scenes.

(Foster, 720)

Emphasizing the universality of joyous experience in the standardized decoration of "every hearth," the verses construct a personified image of "glad Christmas" that unifies English subjects, irrespective of class, gender, or location. Through a process of aestheticization and homogenization, poem and picture work together to erase actual experiences of hunger, cold, sickness, and discomfort in substandard rural housing. By a similar process of mystification, this visual/verbal product of an industrialized urban print culture redirects attention from its actual origins by celebrating and instituting an imagined nonindustrial, artisanal, and rural ideal. Contemplating the serene snowdrifts crowning happy cottage scenes, the reader is reassured that shared values remained constant in a fractured industrialized world.

When the Dalziels commissioned Foster to produce a series of pictures on the theme of the English rustic landscape, they were banking on his appeal to an audience established in the *Illustrated London News*. For these readers, the name of Myles Birket Foster was "a household word," and pictures by him were tantamount to a sure sell on the Christmas market. Indeed, Foster was something of a cultural icon in the age of mechanical reproduction: an artist who seemed to belong to ordinary people rather than the elite academy. In 1890, when the *Art Journal* dedicated its annual Christmas number for the first time to "an English artist from outside the ranks of the members of the Royal Academy," the magazine justified its selection of Foster by his indisputable popularity and significance in sixties mass culture:

> Had one of the now fashionable plebiscites been held amongst Englishmen all the world over, during any year of that period, the name of Birket Foster would have been found very near the head of the list of artists; for not only to the present but to the past generation his name has been for years a household word, and no living artist can be cited who has afforded greater pleasure to a larger *clientèle*, or who has done more to educate the masses to a love of all that is healthy and all that is beautiful in that phase of Art which appeals to his countrymen more than any other, namely, English landscape. (Huish, *Foster*, 1)

On receiving a set of proofs of Foster's drawings for *Pictures of English Landscape*, Ruskin hinted to the Dalziels that they might go beyond the merely "charming" to "educate the public taste as well as meet it." However, he also acknowledged that the engravings were "superb specimens of the kind of

Landscape which you have rendered deservedly popular" (Dalziel and Dalziel, *Record*, 154). To be popular, according to Ruskin, meant to respond to mass culture's demand, not to educate it. While *Birket Foster's Pictures of English Landscape* is generally acknowledged to be his best and most typical work, critics from his day to our own have also recognized its "popularity" in the sense of a lesser form of art designed to meet with favor. As the *Saturday Review* critic complained in his column on Christmas books in 1862, "Mr. Birket Foster must have drawn almost all the commons and groves in England; and the price of boxwood must have risen from the incessant and annual calls made upon it by the manufactory of the Brothers Dalziel" (Dec. 13, 1862, 721). Nonetheless, the reviewer conceded that "Mr. Foster's drawings, most elaborately cut on wood . . . , reproduce pleasantly the quiet and familiar landscapes of the south of England. Old mills, rustic cottages, and boys fishing in a pond, are always suggestive subjects; and if they are not the highest, yet are of the pleasantest art" (722). Pleasant rather than high art, *Birket Foster's Pictures of English Landscape* appealed to middle-class buyers by its brand-name marketing of a popular artist. At the same time, the multiplied mechanical reproductions of Foster's idyllic and nostalgic images helped construct national subjects whose sense of self was associated with a unifying love of countryside and home life.



The poetry accompanying Foster's pictures offered equally pleasant reading in an ekphrastic methodology calculated to appeal to a popular readership. Aware that Foster's audience associated his images with poetry, the Dalziels decided that the book would "have a page of verse, either descriptive of or in sympathy with each picture, so that it might possess literary as well as pictorial interest" (Dalziel and Dalziel, *Record*, 142). In addition to his *ILN* work, Foster's book illustrations were predominantly of poems, lending credence to Jan Reynolds's description of him as "England's most popular illustrator of poetry" (*Foster*, 51). The Dalziels were also acutely aware that although Foster had illustrated most of the foremost poets of the day, his work had never been combined with Tennyson's (Lewis, *Foster*, 15).[23] Through the mediation of Millais, they therefore hoped to entice Tennyson to "write up" Foster's pictures, no doubt considering that the coupling of the poet laureate with England's best-known landscape artist would make the gift book a highly prized object of symbolic cultural capital and national pride, particularly because this was to be Foster's final foray in book illustration.[24] When Tennyson said it was impossible for him to produce poetry to order in this way, the Dalziels turned to journalist Tom Taylor and his wife, Laura, who dutifully wrote thirty pages of verse to accompany the thirty full-page pictures.[25] According to the Dalziels, "the book was fully appreciated by the British Public" and unanimously praised by the press, selling so steadily throughout the next decade that in 1881 the Dalziels published an Edition de Luxe (Dalziel and Dalziel, *Record,* 142, 154).

Although Taylor claimed in his preface that these were "the first serious original poems to which I have attached my name," he was well known as a poet in the illustrated pages of *Once a Week*. As Linda K. Hughes has shown, Taylor frequently contributed free translations of Breton verses to this magazine, later publishing the collection as *Ballads and Songs of Brittany* (1865) ("Inventing," 43–46). This verbal translation work (from Breton into English) was perhaps a help to him as he sought an apt poetic language for his linguistic translation of Foster's pictures. In any case, Taylor's efforts at harmonious poetic response were reasonably well received. The *Athenaeum* noted that he kept "himself strictly to like themes; and while pleasantly accompanying the painter with words that have almost always a musical ring in them—constantly a point, and here and there a dash of humour,—he does not wander from home, nor quit the green lanes, heaths, farm-yards, pools or sea-shores of the English land" (Nov. 22, 1862, 666). With praise for "a fidelity which, if prosaic, is always agreeable" (666), the reviewer recognized in Taylor's "word painting" a distinct ekphrastic genre within the Christmas gift book format.

Taylor (whose principal work to date, other than his *Once a Week* verses, had been as an essayist for the periodical press) approached his task with a businesslike style, asking the Dalziels for £100 for his thirty poems. As he pointed out, this would be "putting the work at 'Once a Week' terms" (Dalziel and Dalziel, *Record,* 144), bringing the kind of poetry and the payment for it into clear alignment. *Once a Week* paid its poets a guinea a column. Noting that "the verses were usually made the subjects for the major illustrations" in *Once a Week,* William E. Buckler supposed that "from time to time . . . poems were actually chosen for the magazine according to their adaptability to the artist's pencil" ("*Once a Week,*" 937, 934, 933).[26] Taylor's approach to the business of writing gift-book poetry is very much in keeping with the methodologies of the illustrated press.

While the illustrations in *Once a Week* included plenty of bucolic images and rural idylls, the large cuts generally favored figure drawings over picturesque scenery. The generic landscapes in *Birket Foster's Pictures of English Landscape,* in contrast, celebrated the representative rather than the singular, implying shared and generalized values and experiences rather than individual passions or desires. Foster's exclusive focus on the bucolic in *Pictures of English Landscape* reinforced a nostalgia for an imaginary rural simplicity in an age of urbanization and industrialization and was of a piece with the kinds of Christmas engravings the public associated with him in the *Illustrated London News.* Foster's "At the Cottage Door," for example, is similar in tone and ideology if not in season and composition to his "Christmas Eve—The Cottager's Return from Market" for the Christmas supplement in 1855.

The ideological formations constituted by the picture and poem titled "At the Cottage Door" in *Pictures of English Landscape* are instructive. The image depicts a secluded cottage with a maiden in a clean white apron contentedly sewing as a bird sings in a cage hanging from the grapevine above her head (fig. 3.5). The signs and tools of her constant labor—broom, hoe, bucket, beehive,

Figure 3.5 Myles Birket Foster, "At the Cottage Door," in *Birket Foster's Pictures of English Landscape* (Routledge, 1862), 19.

cabbage patch, mending—are arranged as aesthetic elements in the composition, just as the morning-glory and grapevines artfully cover the irregularities of the timbered cottage. Behind her, the open door marks a black hole we cannot penetrate, a peasant life we cannot see. As viewers, we do not enter Foster's cottages or even stand on their thresholds. Rather, we always view them from a distance, as part of a picturesque and pleasant scene. From this vantage point, we do not belong to the scene, with its smells and other uncomfortable sensations; it belongs to us, as an aesthetic view.

A turn of the page, and the position shifts. Although the picture denies us entry to the interior of the cottage, the poem provides easy access to the imagined interiority of the rural subject, the cottager herself. Seeking a way to vocalize the mute idyll, Taylor takes advantage of the only human figure in Foster's landscape. An act of ventriloquism makes the scene speak in the voice of the maiden. Picture and poem thus locate the reader in two places at once: the distant knoll or garden gate from which the scene is pictured, and the chair by the cottage door, where the maiden sits, sews, and sings. In this sense, as W. J. T. Mitchell observes, "Ekphrasis is stationed between two 'othernesses,' and two forms of (apparently) impossible translation and exchange: (1) the conversion of the visual representation into a verbal representation, either by description or ventriloquism; (2) the reconversion of the verbal representation back into the visual object in the reception of the reader" (*Picture Theory*, 164).

Taylor's page of verse for "At the Cottage Door" rings the changes on an idealized domestic scene in which women, the working poor, and even flora and fauna know and accept their place in the great scheme of things:

> Sing out, my thrush, for all thy cage;
>     I too am caged like thee,
> But narrow bounds, I dare engage,
>     Will never sadden me.
>
> . . . . . . . . . . . . . . . . . . . . . . . . . . . . . . .
>
> The vine that climbs above our heads,
>     The wilder shoots it throws,
> The thinner is the shade it spreads,
>     The sourer grapes it grows.
> So sing, my thrush, a happy thrall,
>     And I will sing with thee,
> For narrow bounds are best for all,
>     And home's enough for me.

Not high art, but pleasant art, *Birket Foster's Pictures of English Landscape with Pictures in Words by Tom Taylor* reinforced, and helped shape, a middle-class understanding of England that was deeply "connected with a bucolic vision" (Connelly, *Christmas,* 4). As Mark Connelly remarks, "The very forces that were rapidly changing the landscape—industrialization, urbanization, the canals and railways—added a greater emphasis to the significance of the soil and the 'roots' of the people" (*Christmas,* 4). As a Christmas gift book, *Pictures of English Landscape* provided the reassurance of tradition in the form of poetry and pictures that celebrated a vision central to national identity. Another Dalziel Fine Art Book in the artist gallery genre, *Home Thoughts and Home Scenes in Original Poems and Pictures,* changed the focus from rural cottages to bourgeois interiors but also addressed a theme crucial to the nation's concept of itself, at Christmas and throughout the year. "Home meant a great deal to the Victorians," Connelly reminds us. "It was the instrument of civilization, duty and obedience. . . . Home, sweet home, was therefore a celebrated institution: Christmas was its perfect expression" (11).

The gift book's generic focus on the domestic was a function of its audience as well as its season. As contemporary reviewers generally agreed, "The publishers of Christmas books aim[ed] very reasonably at a domestic circulation"; hence, "unquestionable propriety" in content was of the essence (*SR,* Dec. 19, 1857, 558). The primary recipients of these illustrated quartos were women, who typically received them from husbands and fathers. The gift book's prominent display in middle-class drawing rooms ensured that the pages would be frequently turned by children as well as visitors. As one of the rooms of the Victorian middle-class house that permitted both intergenerational familial activity and the reception of guests, the drawing room with its central book table was an important cultural site for the construction and reinforcement of values and identities. Uniting form and content, the gift book's elegant architecture put a miniaturized home into the hands of its domestic audience, who had the pleasure of viewing idealized images of themselves in its beautiful pages.

When the Dalziel brothers issued *Home Thoughts and Home Scenes in Original Poems and Pictures,* their Fine Art Book for 1865, reviewers immediately recognized its mixed, intergenerational readership within the family home. The *Daily News* declared it to be "[a] work which will be doated [*sic*] over by ladies and which will even be tenderly regarded by those of the male sex who have an amiable fondness for children." *Notes and Queries* was enraptured by the book's potential for entertaining the children themselves: "Oh! How many little critics will turn over with delight the thirty-five pictures which Mr. Houghton has designed for them! Pictures which will, if possible, add to the reputation of the Brothers Dalziel, and it would be hard to give them higher praise."[27]

Like *Birket Foster's Pictures of English Landscape, Home Thoughts and Home Scenes* originated as neither literary expression nor artistic inspiration. Rather, it was a commercial speculation instigated by the Dalziel brothers, following their successful formula of commissioning a sequence of pictures from an artist, then hiring poets to write a page of verses for each image.[28] Once again, the Dalziels did not take Christmas itself as their subject but instead focused on the themes associated with it, a canny move that increased the book's daily-use value. Whereas both books capitalized on an interest in the innocent, the sequestered, and the domestic, the artistic subject matter of *Home Thoughts and Home Scenes* focused on figures rather than landscape—in particular, the figures of beautiful mothers and cherubic children. With *Home Thoughts and Home Scenes,* we see the Dalziel Fine Art Book targeted very specifically at a domestic market. More than simply a token of conspicuous consumption in an age of luxury or a symbol of cultural status represented by the possession of poetry and pictures, the Christmas gift book also performed an ideological function, as it "glorified an almost heroic domesticity" (Maxwell, *Victorian,* 390). The book's idealization of the middle-class home's occupants and activities involved it in contemporary debates of the popular press, where notions of gender and class were undergoing interrogation, challenge, and shifting construction.

The Dalziel brothers' marketing strategies aimed directly at a domestic audience. They chose the artist, Arthur Boyd Houghton, to produce thirty-five pictures of "child life" for the book's "home scenes" because of some particularly charming illustrations of the middle-class family he had recently done for *Good Words* using his wife and children as models (see fig. 3.1).[29] Their selection of seven women writers to provide the "home thoughts" for Houghton's "home scenes" is slightly more complicated. As we saw in *The Poets of the Nineteenth Century,* the Dalziels were supporters of the "tuneful Sisterhood." Indeed, they promoted women's poetry almost as vigorously as they did the works of up-and-coming draftsmen. At one level, then, their decision to commission exclusively women poets signals their intention to make *Home Thoughts and Home Scenes* as desirable for its poetic contents as it was for its pictorial contents.

This was as much a business as an aesthetic decision. The Dalziels selected women who had considerable stature with the popular readership and whose names were likely to draw customers. Their advertisements proudly announced *Home Thoughts and Home Scenes* as "[t]hirty-five original poems by eminent authors, and thirty-five pictures by A. B. Houghton, Engraved by the Brothers Dalziel." The title page of the published volume enumerates the "eminent authors": Jean Ingelow, Dora Greenwell, "Mrs. Tom Taylor, the Hon. Mrs. Norton," Amelia R. Edwards, Jennett Humphreys, and "the Author of *John Halifax, Gentleman*."[30] Unlike Myles Birket Foster, Arthur Boyd Houghton was not a household name and did not carry significant celebrity appeal at the time, whereas some of the authors' names would have been very familiar to readers of the illustrated press. Poems by Jean Ingelow, Dora Greenwell, and "the Author of *John Halifax, Gentleman*" (Dinah Mulock) were frequently to be found—often in illustrated form—in the pages of *Good Words* and *Once a Week*. The poetry of Mrs. Norton had established a following in the earlier annuals and was also available in volume form, with *The Lady of la Garaye* published as recently as 1862. The remaining three women would not have had similar name recognition or poetic value, simply because they were either relatively unknown as writers, as was the case with Jennett Humphreys and Laura Taylor (who had assisted her husband by contributing two poems for *Birket Foster's Pictures of English Landscape*), or unknown as a poet, as was the case with Amelia Edwards, a novelist, Egyptologist, and travel writer for the periodical press.

The Dalziels' selection of the women poets was as informed by prevalent notions of middle-class gender roles as it was by their admiration of either the poetic gifts or the popular appeal of these women. Clearly, the Dalziels selected women to compose "home thoughts" to accompany Houghton's "home scenes" because they believed children and the domestic to be a special feminine preserve. This essentialist assumption was undeterred by the irony of facts. None of the women invited to write poems for *Home Thoughts and Home Scenes* had, at the time, written children's verse; most were single, independent wage-earners; and several had published on women's rights.

The Dalziels' gender bias resulted in a book that simultaneously idealized and critiqued the very domesticity that the gift-book genre represented. Significantly, the critical response to the book's producers also divided along gender lines: reviewers ascribed the true representations of domesticity to Houghton and the false images of child life to the women writers. Although contemporary critics (mostly male) could see nothing in Houghton's designs but the "natural and beautiful,"[31] the women's poetry appeared affected and morbid. In a review of *Home Thoughts and Home Scenes*, the *Athenaeum* protested against the poets' "affectation," which the critic claimed was occasioned by the women's "revulsion against that ultra-domesticity of feeling" of a poet such as Eliza Cook.[32] Further cause for their failure to construct childhood as the critic knew it was ascribed to the marital status and consequently meaningless lives of these "spinster-bards," who lacked "experience on the subject" (Nov. 26, 1864, 712–13).

The reviewer's misogynistic sneer, directed at women whose lives were made meaningful by the publication of their writing rather than by raising children or ministering to husbands, is illuminated by historical context. When we turn the pages of 1860s periodicals, we witness a vigorous debate on women's issues leading up to the failed attempt at female enfranchisement in 1867 and revisions to the laws relative to married women's property the following decade (Hamilton, *Cobbe,* 15; Brake, *Print in Transition,* 96–110). The "spinster-bards" of the reviewer's phrase were the "redundant women" of contemporary idiom. Some were active participants in agitating to improve the conditions for women's lives and work. Dora Greenwell urged the extension of educated women's work in "Our Single Women" in the *North British Review* in 1862 and later campaigned for women's suffrage, as did Amelia Edwards. Dinah Mulock published *A Woman's Thoughts about Women* in 1858, which made a plea for more meaningful lives for women in teaching, art, music, and writing; the Honorable Mrs. Norton, after her notorious separation and divorce, engaged in the pamphlet wars that influenced the Infant Custody Act of 1839 and the Matrimonial Causes (Divorce) Act of 1857 (Shattock, *Oxford Guide,* 317–18).

Houghton's ostensible celebration of domesticity likewise requires closer scrutiny. While contemporary reviewers praised his pictures for their truthful representation of children—"he does not make them always beautiful, nor even always good" (*Athenaeum,* Nov. 26, 1864, 712)—in our day, his work has been viewed as a bourgeois realism tinged with the fantastic. Paul Hogarth, for example, sees Houghton's designs as representing a domestic vision that accorded with Victorian readers' imagined ideals of childhood and home, suggesting that in *Home Thoughts and Home Scenes* Houghton "created an extraordinary universe of rosy-cheeked children, of long-haired beautiful women, of impulsive youth and venerable old age, in settings so various and idyllic as to make it all a never-never land, threatened by the reality of the outside world" (*Houghton,* 11). Reviewers who universally admired Houghton's domestic scenes for their truthfulness and charm thus provide a historical touchstone for the ideological freight of home, family, and idealized domesticity in the 1860s. The appeal of *Home Thoughts and Home Scenes* lay in its remarkable ability to provide bourgeois readers with comfortingly beautiful images of the private world of women and children, images that reinforced a nation's notion of the domestic source of its public strength.

The imaginative power of this heroic domesticity extended well into the twentieth century, when Forrest Reid continued to argue for the truth of Houghton's "home scenes": "the charm of childhood could hardly be expressed with more understanding and less sophistication: the pouting lips, the modeling of the sturdy limbs, the lovely drawing of the hair—all are as true as they are beautiful" (*Illustrators,* 187). What we see, however, is conditioned by the cultural lenses through which we look. At the end of the twentieth century, Paul Goldman drew attention to the disruptive elements in Houghton's Edenic imagery, which had been overlooked for over a century. Calling "his images of children . . . some of the most dark and disturbing of any book, not just in British, but in all illustration," Goldman suggests that Houghton's pictures "hint at a real unease at the centre of the Victorian psyche, and although ostensibly about children, the work itself is definitely a far more complex and disturbing volume than the innocent title might suggest" (*Victorian Illustration,* 126). Goldman is also alone of all the critics in his insistence that *Home Thoughts and Home Scenes* is more than merely a gallery of Houghton plates, reminding us that "the poetry, all by leading women poets such as Jean Ingelow and Dora Greenwell, is also overdue for revaluation" (128). His reminder is timely. Art critics and literary scholars alike have yet to examine fully the complex, mutually constitutive relations of illustrative designs and Victorian women's poetry in their bibliographic format and material context.[33] In the discussion below (and more extensively in chapter 4), I examine the poetry of Victorian women writers in the forms in which it reached its contemporary readership.

Although panning most of the women's verses, the *Athenaeum* did recognize particular poetic merit in poems by "Miss Ingelow and Miss Greenwell," which, its reviewer claimed, "by the beauty of their thoughts or constructions redeem the common error of their class" (Nov. 26, 1864, 712). In examining how domesticity and childhood are simultaneously celebrated and troubled in *Home Thoughts and Home Scenes,* it is informative to read the two poems singled out by the *Athenaeum* as among the handful of "healthy" poetic contributions ("The Music of Childhood" and "A Child's Garden" [713]) in the context of two not so distinguished ("Toy-Music" and "Noah's Ark"). To demonstrate the domestic tensions built into the pages of this gift book, I read the poems in relation to each other, to their accompanying images, and to the volume as a whole.

Both picture and poem for "A Child's Garden" and "The Music of Childhood" situate the child in the natural world rather than the domestic interior. The poets' representations appear to celebrate a Wordsworthian vision of childhood innocence and beauty. Informed by the Victorian language of flowers and her own emblematic style, Greenwell's lyric is organized by the poetic structure of the list and grammatical structure of the command, and it has the unmistakable music of poetry, if not of childhood:

Seek in the hill, and seek in the vale
    For foxglove, and broom, and heather;

Seek in the woods for the primrose pale,
Seek for the hyacinths, dim and frail,
And plant them all close together.
Flowers that are bold, and flowers that are shy;
The drooping bell, and the starry eye
That looks bright in the cloudiest weather.
And fling in all seeds that twine and that trail,
To bind them safe together;
Then plant the sunflower and lily tall,
Tulip and crown imperial;
With a blossomed rose for the heart of June
Set in the midst of all, and say
A charm to make them come up as soon
As the mustard and cress that were sown last May,
And all be in bloom together!
Emblem of youth's warm heart, thick sown
With blooms that need fear no weather;
With wingèd dreams, and hopes half-blown,
With flowers that love to bloom alone,
And flowers that bloom together!

("A Child's Garden," 22)

Houghton's image for "A Child's Garden" (fig. 3.6) depicts a group of four young children digging up wildflowers. This potentially destructive activity is domesticated by the verbal text. First, the shared title, "A Child's Garden," implies that the fragile blooms will be transplanted for nurturing at home. Second, Greenwell's poem describes this imagined domestic plot more than it does the wild hillside actually depicted in the plate. The incantatory rhythms and imperative voice are addressed to the children, who are imagined as the carefree gardeners of a fertile Edenic space where flowers "need fear no weather." Simultaneously, the verses emblematize the children as the wildflowers they pick; like the flowers, the children will be domesticated through a process of cultivation in a sheltered spot. The final lines, with their allusion to "wingèd dreams, and hopes half-blown," introduce into this picture of Eden the possibility of discord, difference, and departure. Furthermore, in her recognition of "flowers that love to bloom alone," Greenwell hints that this sheltered growth may not satisfy all. In this final emphasis on singularity, she asks us to reconsider the title and to ask, which particular child's garden are we attending to in "A Child's Garden"?

Figure 3.6 Arthur Boyd Houghton, "A Child's Garden," in *Home Thoughts and Home Scenes* (Routledge, 1868), 22.

Greenwell's hint asks the viewer to look again at the pictured scene of innocent pleasure. This alternating reading of picture and poem is, in fact, a particular feature of the verbal/visual literacy conditioned by nineteenth-century print culture. As Linda K. Hughes reminds us, in the illustrated pages of the popular press, "the image changes (by contextualizing) the text, but the text also conditions what is seeable in the image" ("Inventing," 46). Returning to Houghton's image for "A Child's Garden," we now notice that one child remains on the margins of the self-absorbed group. The viewer can see only the back of this child as she or he (the distance of the figure and the androgyny of the clothing confound identification) marches away from the gathered siblings, holding a gardening implement like a man-at-arms. The children in the foreground take no notice of their isolated member, a recurring feature in Houghton's pictures. Indeed, the motif of the child excluded from the charmed family circle repeats so frequently in *Home Thoughts and Home Scenes* as to call attention to the impossibility of perfect domestic harmony as well as to the darker side of childhood experience.

In the plate that immediately follows "A Child's Garden," for example, Houghton depicts a grandmother holding an infant on her lap, both completely absorbed in a small toy's special properties (fig. 3.7). In the shadows behind granny's voluminous skirts, we can glimpse another child with his back turned to the central pair, whom the pictorial light illuminates with the splendor of a St. Ann and child. In the foreground, Houghton deploys a motif of violence repeated throughout his pictorial series, undermining any easy or untroubled association of childhood with carefree innocence. Although not observed by the caregiver, this child is intent on closing a pair of scissors on the baby's plump and inviting calves. Jennett Humphreys's accompanying poem, "Toy-Music," does not observe either the marginalized child or the threat of the weapon in her celebration of the central figures. In drawing religious meaning from this elderly Madonna and babe, the familiar cultural icon is so luminous as to blind the writer (and perhaps other readers) to the elements that work against the self-satisfied serenity of this domestic scene:

> Well! What can Age do better?
> Grandma moves the toy, and Grandson listens!
> Yet is she her nursling's debtor,
> Tho' his eye glistens.
> Say! See you not my theme?
> —Children teach us hope and sweet endurance!
> Prove to us this Life a dream!
> Oh, blest assurance!
>
> ("Toy-Music," 23)

As in another of Greenwell's contributions, "Noah's Ark," Humphreys's didactic poem reads childhood activities as emblematic of future spiritual hope and the promise of life everlasting. To "allegorize on its own hook," this emblematic form of ekphrasis requires the erasure of any disturbing elements the picture

Figure 3.7 Arthur Boyd Houghton, "Toy-Music," in *Home Thoughts and Home Scenes* (Routledge, 1868), 23.

might record. In "Noah's Ark," Houghton and Greenwell take distinct approaches to the theme named by the shared title. Houghton depicts three plump, well-dressed, and pampered children in a well-stocked middle-class nursery (fig. 3.8). Two of them are intent upon the game at hand, but one—the nonparticipating outsider—rests his head on the seat of a chair through whose back he has just plunged a knife. Ignoring both separation and violence, Greenwell draws on

Figure 3.8 Arthur Boyd Houghton, "Noah's Ark," in *Home Thoughts and Home Scenes* (Routledge, 1868), 2.

the representation of "childish play" as an emblem "Of a Coming Day" promised by the Peaceable Kingdom (2).

Together, picture and poem seem to imply a divergence of values, one focused on religious hope and spiritual gain, the other on the immediacy of the acquisitive present. In the context of the Christmas season's orgy of spending, the poem has the comforting effect of removing these self-absorbed middle-class children from the capitalist economy that supports and justifies their play by interpolating them into a transcendental and transhistorical schema. But Houghton's gratuitous suggestion of violence undermines the future paradise Greenwell wants to read into this picture. Easy to miss but impossible to forget once noticed, the blade sharply reminds us not only of the impossibility of perfect children in an eternally harmonious home but also of the cut-throat capitalism on which the luxury, peace, and security of this scene depend.

The "Noah's Ark" pairing of poem and picture immediately follows "The Music of Childhood," by Jean Ingelow. In pride of place as the first in the volume, the location of Ingelow's verses attests to her poetic star power at this time, the title possibly making a gracious allusion to her much-recognized musicality.[34] Here, her lyricism is a concentrated, melodious expression of memory and loss carried out in cascades of falling rhythms and rhymes. Ingelow writes in the retrospective voice of a mature, first-person narrator who combines nostalgia for a lost innocence with knowledge of the inexorable march of time and change. The poem opens with a lament that finds the lyric speaker's present experience out of joint with springtime:

> When I hear the waters fretting,
> When I see the chestnut letting
> All her lovely blossom falter down, I think, "Alas the day!"
> Once, with magical sweet singing,
> Blackbirds set the woodland ringing
> That awakes no more while April hours wear themselves away.
>
> ("The Music of Childhood," 1)

Recalling the childhood days when "fair hope lay smiling"—days "when we talked of joy and splendour / That the years unborn would render"—Ingelow's speaker concludes that this hope is unrealized: "no fairer days have we to hope for, little girl and boy." With their direct address to an audience, the final lines imply a scene in which a mother or caregiver is reading to her children from *Home Thoughts and Home Scenes.* Read in dialogue with Houghton's accompanying picture, this view of the world is not a happy one.

Like his design for "Noah's Ark," and like many of his other designs for *Home Thoughts and Home Scenes,* Houghton's illustration for "The Music of Childhood" is claustrophobic in its compression of figures and pictorial details within the picture frame (fig. 3.9). Completely enclosed by the large fan-like leaves of the surrounding chestnut trees, the two children and their pets are barely distinguishable from their natural surroundings. Lying with his head on

Figure 3.9 Arthur Boyd Houghton, "The Music of Childhood," in *Home Thoughts and Home Scenes* (Routledge, 1868), 1.

the grass, a young boy watches his older sister tickle their kitten's whiskers with a tuft of long grasses; behind him, a little dog seems ready to leap into the circle and claim his share of attention. The cuts of the Dalziels' engraving blend the children and animals with each other and the natural environment, producing a harmonious vision of unity. This idyllic scene is at odds with the tenor of Ingelow's poem, which sets out to separate human experience from that of flora and fauna and to insist on their occupation of a linear, rather than cyclical, temporal progression. Ingelow's "Music of Childhood" introduces the suggestion of sound and temporality to Houghton's silent, frozen image, animating it with the breath of loss. Like the picture she "writes up," childhood, Ingelow suggests, is a carefully crafted composition, a story we tell to connect our lives with the songs of birds and the sound of waters, an image of hope and joy and pleasure that our adult selves know "no more while April hours wear themselves away" (1).

*Home Thoughts and Home Scenes* makes a direct appeal to the daily life of middle-class families divided by age and gender into private and public spaces, each with their special activities. This connection between the book's bibliographic format and its audience was recognized by an American reviewer who wrote, "'Home Thoughts and Home Scenes' are busy with the play of childhood; the volume is, indeed, a child's book,—just such a book, in fact, as a mother may open to her boy sitting on her knee, the one reading snatches of the poetry, the other looking the while at the enticing illustrations" (*Living Age*, Dec. 24, 1864, 660). In their advertisement for *Home Thoughts and Home Scenes*, the Dalziels expressed confidence that "the theme chosen was certain to excite wide and general interest";[35] the book's positive reception on both sides of the Atlantic suggests that they knew their market. They followed up the next year with a Fine Art Book that took a slightly different approach to the domestic. Rather than child life, the Dalziels took daily life as their theme and produced "a collection of Poems and Pictures representing every-day scenes, occurrences, and incidents in various phases of existence."[36]

Published in an ornate binding intended to be uniform with *Birket Foster's Pictures of English Landscape* and *Home Thoughts and Home Scenes, A Round of Days Described in Original Poems by Some of Our Most Celebrated Poets and in Pictures by Eminent Artists* (1866) represents a final modification of the Dalziels' series of Fine Art Books. In bibliographic format, poetic, and pictorial contents, *A Round of Days* combines the anthology style of *The Poets of the Nineteenth Century* with the picture-book approach of *Pictures of English Landscape* or *Home Thoughts and Home Scenes.* However, its contents offer neither the canonical tradition of *The Poets of the Nineteenth Century* nor the star appeal of a themed pictorial series by Myles Birket Foster. In their explanatory preface, the Dalziel brothers hint that they may have exhausted their themes: "No attempt at a classification of subjects has been made; for as the occurrences in real life often come unexpectedly, the grave and the gay jostling each other, so in this 'ROUND OF DAYS' the Poems have been promiscuously inserted—scenes of various and, perhaps, of opposite kinds following close together, as they do in the alternate cloud and sunshine of men's actual experience" (n.p.).

To this hodgepodge of topics, the Dalziels added a various methodology. "In some cases," they explained, "The Artist has illustrated the Author's Poem; in others, the Authors have shown themselves willing to portray in words the ideas conveyed in the Artists' original Designs" (n.p.). In fact, this disparate methodology was driven more by business considerations than artistic innovation and experimentation. It gave the pragmatic Dalziels great flexibility in selecting pictures and poems and enabled them to recycle images that were then on hand. The Dalziels had previously commissioned black-and-white artist Fred Walker to produce a series of drawings on the theme "English rustic pictures" for a gift book intended as a companion to Myles Birket Foster's. When Walker's series failed to be completed in time for Christmas production, the Dalziels appropriated the eight finished designs for *A Round of Days.* The ever-ready Tom Taylor wrote a page of verse to accompany Walker's "Broken Victuals" (Muir, *Victorian,* 141–42), and Jennett Humphreys, Amelia B. Edwards, and Mrs. Norton again wrote poems to accompany other premade pictures.

To round out the volume and add to its consumer appeal, the Dalziels also solicited poetry from some of the best contemporary writers, which they then either illustrated themselves or paired with artwork they had on hand. For example, the Dalziels included two excellent contributions by Christina Rossetti in *A Round of Days:* "An English Drawing-Room," illustrated with what appears to be a recycled picture by A. B. Houghton (5–6); and the lovely lyric "By the Sea," which Thomas Dalziel ornamented with a pleasant but uninspired medallion-framed illustration (68) (fig. 3.10). Letterpress and picture of "By the Sea" were printed from a plate that was islanded in the middle of a larger textual page. The blankness of the verso and the smallness of the print relative to page size and margins do not invite pleasure in the reading experience, suggesting that this book may have had another primary purpose. Its desirability for the middle-class collector *manqué* is spelled out in its luxurious trappings and in the title page's recommendation of "original poems by some of our most celebrated poets" and "pictures by eminent artists." With *A Round of Days,* we begin to move away from illustrated anthologies for reading and poetic artist galleries for browsing, toward a book built more for the collector than the reader/viewer.

The appeal of *A Round of Days* lay in its symbolic weight as a cultural object that bespoke the owner's cultivation and knowledge of contemporary art and poetry, a fact played up in the reviews. As the *Saturday Review*'s Christmas columnist noted, "the contributions are original, and . . . own fashionable and distinguished parentage[;] . . . the printing is magnificently executed, and the volume is one *de luxe*" (Dec. 2, 1865, 711). The *Illustrated London News* echoed this appraisal: "If beautiful typography and exquisite binding can do aught to

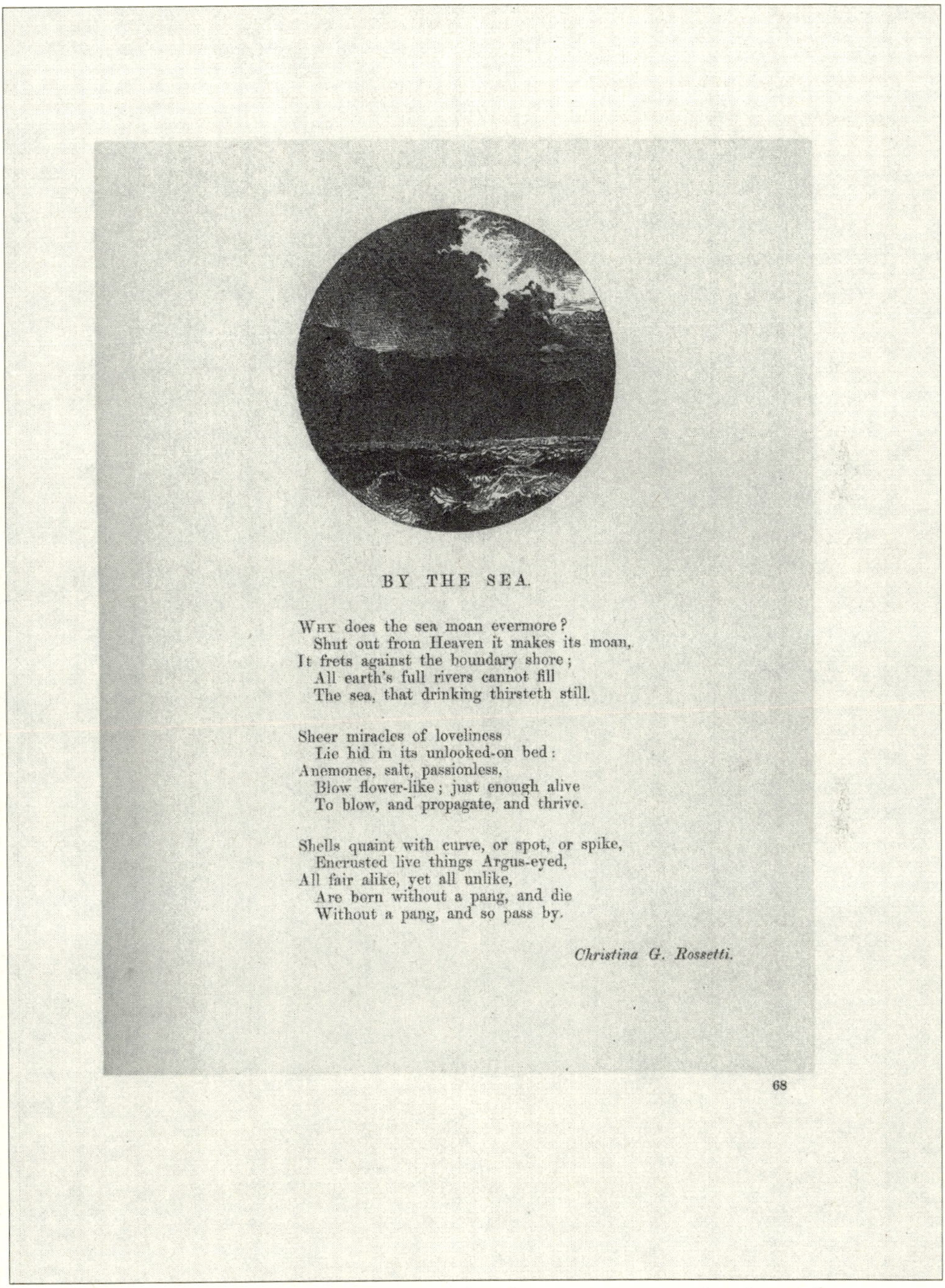

BY THE SEA.

WHY does the sea moan evermore?
Shut out from Heaven it makes its moan,
It frets against the boundary shore;
All earth's full rivers cannot fill
The sea, that drinking thirsteth still.

Sheer miracles of loveliness
Lie hid in its unlooked-on bed:
Anemones, salt, passionless,
Blow flower-like; just enough alive
To blow, and propagate, and thrive.

Shells quaint with curve, or spot, or spike,
Encrusted live things Argus-eyed,
All fair alike, yet all unlike,
Are born without a pang, and die
Without a pang, and so pass by.

*Christina G. Rossetti.*

68

Figure 3.10 Thomas Dalziel, illustration for Christina G. Rossetti, "By the Sea," in *A Round of Days* (Routledge, 1866), 68.

 increase the charm of the literary and artistic gems contained in the volume, such aids are not wanting . . . the Brothers Dalziel have produced a book overflowing with beauties—the whole blended and harmonized by refined taste" (Dec. 23, 1865, 608).

*A Round of Days* testifies to a genre whose heyday was, after an intense decade of production, rapidly drawing to a close. Subsequent Dalziel Fine Art Books tended to repeat and recycle what had previously proved popular, rather than to develop new bibliographic approaches or introduce new poets and artists. By the 1870s, most Christmas gift books were either reprints of volumes with established readerships, like *The Poets of the Nineteenth Century* and *English Sacred Poetry*, or recycled poems and pictures under the pretense of new titles and themes. The poems and illustrations for *Picture Poesies* (the Dalziel offering for 1874), for example, had appeared in earlier Fine Art Books: *A Round of Days* (1866) and *Wayside Posies* (1867; edited by Robert Buchanan). Although one reviewer suggested that "[t]he fact of both works being out of print certainly justifies, as the publishers say, the present issue" (*SR*, Dec. 12, 1874, 777), another reading of the situation seems equally justified. With both *A Round of Days* and *Wayside Posies* out of print by 1874 and the "new" Dalziel gift book simply a remix in new bindings with an alliterative title, the poetic gift book as an innovative multimedia form may have played itself out, for both makers and readers.

# four

# Second-Rate Poets for Second-Rate Readers

Her card or motto might be "Poetry at Home."

*Anglo-American, review of Eliza Cook's poetry*[1]

While publishers and engravers might speculate annually on a domestic theme calculated to appeal to buyers shopping for a Christmas present, anthologies were only one form of the poetic gift book. A living poet who had achieved strong sales might also be given the signal honor of an illustrated collection. The Moxon Tennyson is the best known of these today, but the palm for illustrated collections and mass readerships in the sixties goes to a trio of women poets: Eliza Cook, Adelaide Anne Procter, and Jean Ingelow. The *Saturday Review* categorized them as second-rate poets for second-rate readers (Dec. 16, 1865, 765), but Lucy Larcom, writing for *Arthur's Home Magazine*, noted that many so-called second-rate poets "have become a heart and home blessing to thousands" in what she was careful to call "the verse-reading world" ("Procter," 379, 380). Larcom was championing the cultural education of readers by popular verses, claiming that "they teach the mass readership to cultivate taste" (379). Larcom was speaking from a position of knowledge, as she was one of those "second-rate readers" of poetry who developed not only literary taste but also a life of letters, leaving her manual job as an industrial worker in the textile mill in Lowell, Massachusetts, to become a journalist, poet, and life writer.[2]

The transformative power of reading witnessed in Larcom's personal story is also a theme common to the publications of the women poets this chapter investigates. The effect their poetry had on readers around the English-speaking world, but especially in Britain and the United States, is less easily mapped. Ordinary readers with busy working lives do not often leave records of their reading experiences, while those who did are not easy to locate. Fortunately, these popular poets were reviewed by diverse transatlantic representatives of the periodical press, from the *Ohio Farmer* to *Godey's Lady's Book*, from the *United States Magazine and Democratic Review* to the *Merchants' Magazine*, from the *Athenaeum* to the *Weekly Dispatch*. Their poetry was set to music and sung, celebrated at literary evenings, and recited at public performances. Their deaths were acknowledged by newspapers around the world, which frequently noted that they had once been household words. These records and the material witness of the printed pages in their books, once read by thousands but now seldom considered in their nineteenth-century physical forms, testify to a poetry that was very much at the heart of a transatlantic popular culture in the 1860s.

In Bourdieu's terms, Cook, Procter, and Ingelow wrote not for other producers in the realm of restricted production but rather for consumers of large-scale cultural production, "the public at large" ("Market," 1234). Whereas the latter is market-driven, the former establishes its own criteria for value, assessment, and consecration as literature—that is, "pure" poetry rather than verse (1238). The mass readership clearly found the verses of Cook, Procter, and Ingelow worthy, purchasing their books in the tens of thousands, often from very limited discretionary income. Contemporary critics, however, provided mixed reviews, with negative assessments predominating from the end of the nineteenth century to the present day. Reading these women's verses in their contemporary visual-verbal vehicular forms allows us to reconnect with the poets and their readers by locating them within a popular culture and a materiality that made their "poetry at home."

Despite their aesthetic, ideological, and religious differences, the three poets had many similarities. Born within seven years of each other, Cook, Procter, and Ingelow also ceased publishing new books of poetry in the same decade. By 1864, Eliza Cook had passed the high point of her career and published her last collection, *New Echoes and Other Poems;* her remaining years were spent in failing health, and apart from some poems in the *Weekly Dispatch* and a collection of aphorisms, she ceased publishing (Shattock, *Oxford Guide*, 115–16). In the same year, Adelaide Procter's poetic career came to an end with her early death. Her popularity only increased, however, and a decade later the demand for her verses remained higher than for any poet other than Tennyson (Shattock,

*Oxford Guide*, 348). Jean Ingelow achieved her popularity later than the other two women. The publication of her first collection in 1863 secured her reputation: *Poems* went into thirty editions (Peters, *Ingelow*, 64). Despite the enormous popularity of her narrative poetry, however, Ingelow had effectively stopped writing verse by the end of the 1860s, focusing instead on the fictional forms of children's stories and adult novels.

In each woman writer's case, the popular press was critically important in establishing and maintaining her poetic reputation and audience. After publishing *Lays of a Wild Harp* at age seventeen, Cook sent some of her poems to the *Weekly Dispatch*, a radical Sunday paper for the working classes with the largest metropolitan circulation at the time (Law and Lawrence, n.p.). The editor published the poem that made her name and fame, "The Old Arm-Chair," and eventually hired Cook, at an annual salary of £200, to be a regular contributor (*Atlanta Constitution*, 2). Throughout the 1840s, when its circulation of 60,000 was three times higher than its closest competitor (Law and Lawrence, n.p.), the *Weekly Dispatch* printed her verses for a large and admiring audience. In 1847, *Reynolds's Miscellany*, another popular weekly, placed Cook in the illustrious company of Lady Blessington and the Honorable Mrs. Norton in its featured woodcut, identifying the working-class, self-made Cook as "*par excellence* our national poetess" (233).

Cook capitalized on her poetic fame by venturing into periodical publishing on her own in 1849 with *Eliza Cook's Journal*, a radical weekly aimed at the working and lower middle classes (Gleadle, *Early Feminists*, 43–44).[3] As proprietor and editor, Cook supplied both poetry and essays to the popular *Journal*, which enjoyed a circulation of 50,000 to 60,000—greater than that of Dickens's *Household Words*, whose regular issues averaged sales of 40,000 during its best years (Altick, *Reader*, 394). Although Cook's degenerating health forced her to cease publishing the *Journal* in 1854, her writings in it continued to reach readers throughout the century. Responding to popular demand in 1860, Routledge published, in London and New York, *Jottings from My Journal* as part of its Cheap Literature Series. Back issues of the *Journal* also abounded. In 1897, a journalist reported that "the typical village reading room" contained, among its score or so of devotional books, odd volumes of *Chambers' Journal*, a few Waverley novels, *Uncle Tom's Cabin*, Beeton's *Dictionary of Geography*, and "five or six volumes of *Eliza Cook's Journal*" (Altick, *Reader*, 226n34). This would no doubt have pleased the publisher-author. As she wrote in her initial preface, Cook sought, in her magazine, "to give [her] feeble aid to the gigantic struggle for intellectual elevation," particularly that of women and workers ("Word," 1).

Active in Chartist causes, Cook was associated with radical Unitarian feminism (Gleadle, *Early Feminists*, 43–44). In her examination of nineteenth-century feminist publishing, Pauline Nestor notes that *Eliza Cook's Journal* celebrated domestic, national, and rural virtues while taking up many of the issues—the plight of single women, the need for improved access to education and employment for women, the emigration of women, and the legal rights of women—that the early feminist movement would organize itself around. Yet, as Nestor observes, Eliza Cook "did so with a curious blend of radicalism and conservatism," claiming, for example, the right to work but disparaging female suffrage ("New Departure," 94). Although she acknowledges the progressive elements of Cook's politics, Johanna M. Smith also shows the extent to which the *Journal* reinforced Victorian ideals of domestic femininity ("Textual Encounters," 58). This mixed political stance was one Cook shared with Procter and Ingelow; judging by their wide readership, it was a position that struck a chord with many.

Adelaide Procter first found her mass readership in the more middlebrow but still socially conscious *Household Words,* edited by Charles Dickens. Her reputation developed after 1854, when she abandoned her initial anonymity and allowed her poems to appear with her signature.[4] Often featured as the only poetic component of Dickens's popular Christmas numbers, which sometimes sold as many as 250,000 copies, Procter's narrative poetry became immensely popular (Gregory, *Life,* 199). When *Household Words* folded in 1858, Procter published the first series of *Legends and Lyrics,* principally made up of her periodical pieces. While she continued to publish in Dickens's new periodical, *All the Year Round*—where he lampooned her as "Belinda Bates," a philanthropic young woman "obsessed to absurdity with 'everything that is Woman's with a capital W'" (quoted in Gregory, *Life,* 171)—she also began to appear in the newly launched *English Woman's Journal* (*EWJ*) (Gregory, *Life,* 230). An offshoot of the feminist Langham Place circle, with which Procter was deeply involved, the *EWJ* promoted the employment of women and put theory into practice by becoming the first periodical to be typeset by female compositors at Emily Faithfull's Victoria Press (Nestor, "New Departure," 94, 97). Jan Marsh suggests that the *EWJ* was also something of a "house journal" for the Portfolio Society, a group of mostly female middle-class artists and writers who shared creative work on set themes.[5]

Both Procter and Jean Ingelow were members of the Portfolio Society; both, too, were published, reviewed, and promoted in the *English Woman's Journal* and, like Cook, supported some of the feminist causes. When Louisa May Alcott provided copy about her visit to Ingelow's home in London for the *Independent* in 1866, she noted that, led by Frances Power Cobbe, the assembled company was "talking earnestly and gravely on the suffrage question, which just then absorbed the circle in which I found myself" ("Glimpses," 1). Ingelow's first biographer, however, was at pains to insist that Ingelow should not be tarred with the feminist brush, claiming that the poet "resolutely shrank from supporting the women's movement" (Anon., *Recollections,* 120). Nevertheless, Ingelow wrote poetry in defiance of her mother's evangelical prohibition; rented a room across the street from the family home so that she could write without domestic interruption; supported herself with her pen; and recognized the advantages of her spinsterhood to her career, candidly admitting, "If I had married, I should *not* have written books" (Anon., *Recollections,* 126).[6] And she was associated, through the Portfolio Society and the *English Woman's Journal,* with the most prominent feminists of the period.

In addition to the *EWJ,* which had a small readership, Ingelow also published in other periodicals with larger circulation, including Alexander Strahan's *Good Words.* Indeed, she had tested the periodical waters well before bringing out her first collection of *Poems* to immediate acclaim. As the critic of the *Valley Farmer* (of St. Louis) observed in 1864, hailing her as a "true singer" with great promise, Ingelow's poetry was familiar to readers of the popular press: "Some papers have published so much of her poetry, that they have almost printed her entire" (252–53). Sandwiched, in this two-column format, between an article on the proper care of cool cellars and one on the abomination of "DIRT" in an unkempt household, this review in an American agricultural paper bears witness to the reach of Ingelow's poetry and the range of her readership. In this setting and for this audience, the criticism that the "management" of her poems could be better takes on local resonance: "Each poem is not a building, deliberate, inspired, everything in its place—all with a view to force and beauty" (253). Not content with superficial beauty, this critic knew that in all enduring works, form should follow function. Popular readers could be astutely critical as well as appreciative of the poet's craft.

What was it about their verses that generated such large, diverse, and appreciative audiences for Cook, Procter, and Ingelow? Although individually distinct in style, their poetry tended to be narrative in nature, direct in expression, musical in appeal, and affective or sentimental in content, dilating on losses familiar to all: the disappearance of rural and other Edenic states of bliss and innocence, such as childhood; the death of family members, friends, and lovers; and the erosion of time and hope. They also celebrated the resilience of the human spirit; the various joys of domestic work and social life; the love of everyday objects and animals; and the beauty of nature. From a variety of nonestablishment perspectives—Cook was a Unitarian, Procter a Catholic, and Ingelow an evangelical—they expressed faith in an afterlife of rest after labor. They wrote, with sympathy and knowledge, a poetry for the everyday. Musing about the differences between the kind of poetry that appeals to an "elite" readership and that which appeals to the masses, the *Catholic World* suggested, in

1866, that "[s]uch an appreciation must arise . . . from the touching of universal emotions; from a true correspondence with those thoughts and feelings which are the heritage of the race under its most general conditions, or which have become the common property of a people in all its various grades of culture" (839). From the perspective of an elite reader such as Andrew Lang, however, such "true correspondence" with the thoughts and feelings of the masses is precisely what made "'popular poets,' . . . not really poets at all, but [versifiers] who express blameless emotions in easy verse, who give to the general reader ideas which are, or easily might be, his own, in language rather better than that in which he could clothe them" ("Ingelow," 246).

Although the poems of Eliza Cook, Adelaide Anne Procter, and Jean Ingelow undoubtedly expressed emotional material in easy verse, they also offered inspiring messages by, about, and for women that connected with contemporary feminist and social justice agendas. Moreover, these women poets were able to reach their wide audiences partly because of their ability to combine aspects of traditional oral culture's songs, ballads, hymns, legends, and folklore with contemporary visual culture in the age of mass reproduction. They excelled at using the considerable power of the popular press to present their verses and were deft at selecting appropriate venues for both periodical and book publication. Appearing in the dialogic format of nineteenth-century newspapers and journals, their poetry became a contextualized feature of their readers' everyday lives, associated with the topical concerns, leaders, advertisements, and pictures of the popular press.[7] Their enormous popularity among "the people" of metropole, country, colony, and republic enabled their publishers to expand their market upward into the more affluent middle classes. In the 1860s, Cook, Procter, and Ingelow were each awarded what the *Saturday Review* named "those honours which have hitherto been for the most part reserved for the registered stars of higher magnitude" than these modest "poetesses": an illustrated gift-book edition of their verses (Dec. 1, 1866, 684). This honor was bestowed on second-rate poets and readers alike, as it enabled the latter (at least those with discretionary spending money) to possess, as a luxury item, much-loved, familiar verses, with the added beauty of the author's engraved portrait and artistic wood engravings, all encased in a sober but decorative binding that could, with dignity and respect, be placed on the parlor table with the family Bible.

## Eliza Cook (1818–1889): Singer for the Millions

In an essay in her *Journal* entitled "People Who Do Not Like Poetry," Eliza Cook defines poetry as an attitude toward and approach to life that is not necessarily tied to an appreciation of metrical feet. People who do not like poetry, she claims, "are totally ignorant that Poetry is identified and incorporated in the primitive elements of all that makes God visible and man glorious; they know not that poetry is co-existent with a flourishing state and a great people; they know not that it is poetic instinct which prompts a Washington to free his country, and calls the tear of repentance into the felon's eye, as he wakes from a dream of green fields and his mother" (*Jottings*, 170).



For Cook, as for Raymond Williams, culture—which Cook glosses here as poetry—is not only "a body of intellectual and imaginative work" but "also and essentially a whole way of life" (*Culture*, 312). Just as Williams claims revolutionary activity takes the shape of cultural as well as political activity, rooted in the idea of "active mutual responsibility" and common advancement (317), so too does Cook connect the "poetic instinct" to the desire for democracy. In both her *Journal* and her poetry, Cook inscribes a fervor for social justice and a passion for egalitarian politics into her belief in education's transformational capacity of "leveling up."[8] Furthermore, as Solveig Robinson notes, Cook expressed this politics in her commitment to making her writing accessible to readers in content, expression, and cost, striving to produce both her poetry and her *Journal* in a price range affordable to the working classes ("Haymakers," 232). From 1850 on, she began to reprint previously published poems in her *Journal*, so that subscribers could own the verses she had published prior to its launch (Johnston, "Cook," n.p.). Her poetry and her *Journal*, then, participated in the same politics and spoke to and for a common readership.

In 1859, when her *Journal* had been out of print for five years, Cook brought out a collected edition of her four volumes of poetry, writing in her preface, "I have long had an earnest desire to present my writings to the public in a form and at a price that would place them within the reach of 'the many,' and on the prompting of this desire I have foregone propositions for an expensive work; feeling that I shall derive much greater pleasure from seeing my poems widely circulated, than from an increase of pecuniary benefit" (*Poetical Works*, n.p.). The "expensive work" to which Cook alludes here is the illustrated edition to be published as a Christmas book the following year, *Poems: Selected and Edited by the Author* (1861).[9] Cook negotiated with Routledge for the two editions at the same time, insisting that the cheaper volume come out first and that it also be illustrated. In their agreement, Routledge was to "have the use without charge of eight of the twelve plates now belonging to Miss Eliza Cook and used in the said . . . edition [*Poetical Works* (1859)]."[10] These illustrations came from an 1844 publication of Cook's poetry. Because she owned the plates, she was able to persuade Routledge to take the unusual step of inserting the separately printed images, newly engraved by the Dalziels, in the cheap edition. Although she was not able to include illustrations in her own *Journal,* Cook seems to have believed in visual/verbal literacy and considered images to be an essential part of the contemporary reading experience.

For the following Christmas season, Routledge published an ornate quarto of Cook's verses, embellished with wood engravings after designs by John Gilbert, J. Wolf, H. Weir, J. D. Watson, and others in the Dalziel stable of illustrators. Priced at twenty-one shillings—four times more than the cheap edition—the gift book was not a complete collection of her works but rather a selection aimed at a broad middle-class audience. Cook agreed to select poems from her previous collection and to add some new verses, while Routledge committed to providing original, "first-rate wood engravings."[11] Ultimately, the book contained over two hundred poems and some eighty-one illustrations, printed directly with the letterpress on high-quality paper with ample margins.

Despite the care that had been devoted to its visual and verbal contents, the edition was not a commercial success. As a guinea gift book, it was beyond the price range of most of Cook's usual readers, while the more affluent middle-class audience did not seem as attracted to the work as the publisher had anticipated. Although Routledge issued Cook's *Poems* in a print run of four thousand for the Christmas season of 1860/61, the gift book sold slowly, and in the spring of 1862 the publisher renegotiated terms with Cook. Under the original agreement, Cook was to receive two shillings, or roughly 10 percent, on every copy sold. Under the new agreement, Cook sold her rights for £255, and Routledge undertook not to print any more copies once the stock had been exhausted. Meanwhile, the publisher continued to pay Cook a royalty of six pence per copy sold of the cheap edition, over and above the £75 paid out on the day of publication of the first impression.

Unlike the costly *Poems,* the inexpensive *Poetical Works* was a popular favorite and steady seller. Issued in an initial print run of three thousand in 1859, the cheap edition with the eight illustrations sold rapidly, and Routledge brought out new impressions of two thousand each Christmas season throughout the following decade.[12] At a time when the usual first printing of a volume of poetry was between five hundred and one thousand copies (Gray, "Macaulay," 79), Routledge's faith in Cook's selling power is evident in the size of these print runs.

At 564 pages, all edges gilt, with gilt decoration on the blue cloth binding, an engraved portrait of the author, and eight inserted illustrations, *Eliza Cook's Poetical Works* was a good buy for five shillings. When the early volumes collected there were first published, the frontispiece portrait had been a welcome addition; critics regularly drew attention to this value-added feature (fig. 4.1). As

Figure 4.1 Frontispiece portrait of Eliza Cook, in *Eliza Cook's Poetical Works* (1859) (Routledge, Warne and Routledge, 1862).

an engraving made from a photograph, the frontispiece presented Eliza Cook in the familiar carte-de-visite format, grounding the poet in the everyday lives of her readers. Invariably accompanied by a facsimile of the poet's signature, the frontispiece portrait added a personal touch to verses that often drew from an autobiographical store of childhood memories.

The portrait served to make the poet a familiar face and a welcome domestic presence, notwithstanding the "masculine character" of her features and costume, which, declared the *Eclectic Magazine*, apparently by way of praise, "her writings do not belie" (430).[13] The reviewer for the *Anglo-American* conveys something of the enthusiasm with which readers met Eliza Cook's face, as well as the general inclination to benefit from Cook's imaginative and intellectual work: "[W]hile thousands are receiving with delight, and treasuring with care, the excellent engraving which makes her at home in their dwellings, I would stimulate them to make her at home also in their minds and memories, and to read her works not only for the enjoyment of particular songs and passages, but so as to realize the intellectual and moral companionship of the writer, and understand and appreciate her character" (342).

Although the portrait engraving was reused in the gift-book edition, the eight full-page illustrations Cook supplied for the cheap collection were not, as they were neither the right size for the large quarto nor the appropriate style for a high-quality edition. Two cuts in the cheap edition are views of ships at sea; three center on young children playing variously in a barn (fig. 4.2), at home, and by a stream; two focus on key moments in adult life, that is, old age and courtship; and one presents a quiet woodland scene. Taken from a book published in the 1840s, the set of images participates in the visual culture boom of the decade in which illustrated periodicals met a mass readership for the first time. By 1859, the mass readership had become accustomed to reading image and text in paired or proximate relationships. In giving the plates to Routledge for reproduction "without charge," Cook likely sought to ensure that the cheap edition included the pleasure of the imaged scene with the written word. No doubt she was aware, as her critics were, of the ways in which the modern book compensated for print culture's displacement of the oral tradition, in which "[t]he song and the singer were one," as the *Anglo-American* reviewer wrote. "For the charm thus lost, we must make up, as we can, in other ways. The painter's and the graver's art does something; the reader must do the rest" (343).

In the gift-book edition published in the following year, *Poems: Selected and Edited by the Author*, Cook's selections, arrangements, and additions show her self-reflexively engaging with the visual/verbal culture common to all readers of the day. She signals her book's theme on the title page, with an excerpt taken from a manuscript poem:

> Give me the magic wand whose wondrous might
> Evokes from mingled hues undying light;
> Give me the secret Spirit-Life that throngs
> The brain with Pictures, and the voice with Songs.

Figure 4.2 Anon., "Dobbin," full-page illustration inserted to face page 44 in *Eliza Cook's Poetical Works* (1859) (Routledge, Warne and Routledge, 1862).

The invocation applies equally to poet and reader. Just as the poet needs inspiration to infuse her book with poetry's stock-in-trade, imagery and music, so too does the reader require a responsive imagination to "Pictures" and "Songs." This fugitive piece from an unpublished manuscript enacts the book's strategy of connecting the private and individual with the public and collective. For the pages that follow, Cook wrote and selected poems that celebrate the power of reading that, she implies, has the force of a "magic wand" in its capacity to transform experience.

The selection opens with a prefatory poem written expressly for the edition, "To My Readers," subtitled "New Lines on an Old Subject" (vii–viii).[14] The subtitle's reference to "new lines" playfully puns both on the lines of poetry that follow and on the engraved lines of the illustrative headpiece positioned above (fig. 4.3). It may also allude to the "good strong line" that the speaker longed for in childhood, to "hang the uncle three times over" for his cruelty to the Babes in the Wood. Recalling her early reading of an illustrated chapbook, and her particular absorption in the popular folk tale "The Babes in the Wood," Cook deliberately connects the effect that picture and story had on her imagination with the hoped-for effect of her illustrated collection on its readers. Acknowledging that the picture in the chapbook was "crude and rough," she insists that it provided an aid to the imagination and a schooling in empathy: "That bit of Ideal made fearfully real / The story of cruelty, murder, and death." Her speaker explains:

> 'Twas the "picture" I felt made my young heart melt
> Into the direst sorrow of all;
> As my love was stirred for each dear, little bird,
> Wrapping the Babes in an emerald pall.
>
> 'Twas the "picture" that caught my most pitying thought;
> 'Twas the "picture" that told of a sad, true thing;
> 'Twas the "picture" that shone with a charm of its own
> Like the gem that enriches a Memory ring.
>
> Oh! May kind ones look into this fair book,
> And deem its "pictures" as precious and good,
> As I, when believing, and weeping, and grieving,
> Did that of "The Babes in the Blackberry Wood."
>
> ("To My Readers," viii)

The poem claims that visual images have the power to make a story "fearfully real" in a way that words alone cannot. As the speaker's recorded memory makes clear, the image is an inextricable part of the reading process. Itself a text to be read, and one that impresses the mind with its visual stamp, the picture's meaning is also contextualized through its dialogic relation to a verbal partner. "That 'picture' gave the 'unmade grave' / In the desolate wood—I can see it now— / With an extra gloom on the foreground bloom," the speaker claims, underscoring

TO MY READERS.

NEW LINES ON AN OLD SUBJECT.

Long years ago, ere an earnest woe
  Had lessened a dimple, or dimm'd a glance;
I sat with a book in the chimney nook,
  Sighing o'er Infancy's sweet Romance.

I loved to look in that hard-worn book,
  For it always left me in mournful mood;
And my cheeks turned pale o'er the well-known tale,
  So simple and sad, of "The Babes in the Wood."

With rage and grief I read each leaf,
  Though knowing by rote what each leaf would discover,
Longing to twine a good strong line,
  And hang the uncle three times over.

Oh! uncles then seemed terrible men,
  And lucky it was I had none of my own;
For I saw them at night in visions of fright,
  With daggers, and poison, and hearts of stone.

Each page I read bowed down my head,
  With a darker brow, and a heavier sigh,
Till of hope bereft, the Babes were left,
  Weeping and hungry, to starve and die.

Figure 4.3 John Gilbert, headpiece for "To My Readers: New Lines on an Old Subject," in Eliza Cook, *Poems: Selected and Edited by the Author* (Routledge, 1861), vii.

 the link between image and text by providing a direct quotation of the story's remembered words. At the same time that she links image and text, chapbook tradition and contemporary illustrated book, Cook also connects the oral tradition of the past to the poetry of the present, uniting all in a common popular culture. Writing in a modified ballad quatrain, with end rhymes linking the second and fourth lines, Cook extends the musicality and mnemonic power of her poem with internal rhymes for the first and third lines. In this way, "New Lines on an Old Subject" engages with and meditates on the various elements of popular culture, from ballads and songs in oral traditions to woodcut illustrations and fairy tales in chapbooks to modern poetry in illustrated books, newspapers, and magazines.[15]

John Gilbert's headpiece illustration introduces Cook's collection, both literally, by its position on the prefatory page, and figuratively, by its pictorial allusion to her well-known "The Old Arm-Chair," which appears soon after in the book's early pages. The small design for "To My Readers" draws us to a modest hearth, where a young girl—apparently meant to represent the young Eliza—sits reading a book. Beside her is a piece of domestic furniture that, in its immediate bibliographic context, speaks volumes: an empty wing chair. The visual detail is indexical, simultaneously pointing to Cook's poetic lines on the subject, the traumatic effect of the mother's death that the empty chair represents, and even, perhaps, the reader's personal memories associated with a particular reading experience of the poem. On viewing the prefatory picture, the reader might even be able, before turning to "The Old Arm-Chair" itself, to recall its words, as Cook's verses were often memorized and recited. If so, the remembered lines—"'Tis past, 'tis past, but I gaze on it now / With quivering breath and throbbing brow" (17)—would infuse both picture and prefatory poem with additional layers of times past and present, as well as with a deepened sense of shared experience. The empty armchair of Gilbert's picture is both quotational and performative, enacting "new lines on an old subject" by making the absent presence of the mother "fearfully real" to the reader.

Although the Dalziels employed a total of eleven artists for this Fine Art Gift Book, John Gilbert designed well over half of the illustrations, contributing fifty-one of the eighty-one pictures in all. This artist's visual predominance results in several textual effects. Just as his headpiece is the first printed image the reader confronts (after the frontispiece portrait), and establishes some of the collection's critical tropes, so too does his tailpiece close the book, effectively assigning the lyre and the laurel wreath to both Thomas Hood (whom the attached poem eulogizes) and Eliza Cook, who was frequently compared to her admired predecessor (fig. 4.4). Between these two visual signposts, Gilbert constructs a pictorial narrative that responds to Cook's verses by connecting them to her

"POOR HOOD!"

"Poor Hood!" for whom a people wreathes
The heart-born flowers that never die;
"Poor Hood!" for whom a requiem breathes
In every human Toil-wrung sigh.

Let the Horse-tamer's bed be known
By the rich mausoleum-shrine;
Give the bold Quack his charnel-throne,—
Their works were worthier far than thine.

And let thy soul serenely sleep,
While pilgrims stand as I have stood,
To worship at a nameless heap,
And sadly, fondly, say, "Poor Hood!"

London:—R. Clay, Printer, Bread Street Hill.

Figure 4.4 John Gilbert, tailpiece for "Poor Hood," in Eliza Cook, *Poems: Selected and Edited by the Author* (Routledge, 1861), 408.

autobiography and by reinforcing her celebration of reading in ordinary life. His familiar style also links Cook's verses to the everyday by its graphic allusion to the popular press. If Cook was one of its most popular singers, John Gilbert, as Mason Jackson reminds us, "stands out pre-eminently [as] the great popular illustrator of the Victorian era" (quoted in Buchanan-Brown, *Early Books*, 169).

As one of "the new class of professional illustrator" who emerged with the rise of the illustrated press, Gilbert created images that were ubiquitous, appearing in the *Graphic*, the *Leisure Hour*, the *London Journal*, *London Society*, *Once a Week*, and *Punch*, as well as in the *Illustrated London News* (*ILN*), where he was a principal contributor. Even if the *Times* obituary was guilty of some exaggeration with its claim that Gilbert contributed thirty thousand illustrations to the *ILN*, proprietor Henry Vizetelly is on record as saying that without Gilbert the paper would not have been able to meet its required twenty to thirty engravings per number (Buchanan-Brown, *Early Books*, 168–69). Gilbert was also a prolific book artist, frequently contributing to gift books illustrated by many hands, such as Cook's *Poems* and Willmott's *Poets of the Nineteenth Century*. He also produced immensely popular single-artist volumes, such as the illustrated *Longfellow* and his three-volume masterpiece, known as the *Gilbert Shakespeare*, published in parts by Routledge from 1858 to 1861 (Suriano, *Pre-Raphaelite Illustrators*, 24). Although John Gilbert may not have had the aesthetic and interpretive approach to book illustration of a Dante Gabriel Rossetti or a Frederick Sandys, he did, as Buchanan-Brown suggests, have "a style to match the taste of the 1860s" (*Early Books*, 171).

Gilbert's series of pictures for Eliza Cook's *Poems* celebrates domestic dailiness and the sanctified maternal with a sentiment that matches Cook's own. In his illustration for Cook's most popular poem, "The Old Arm-Chair" (16–17) (fig. 4.5), Gilbert visualizes the second of the four stanzas while capturing the poem's overall emotional message, that "a sacred thing is that old arm-chair":

> In Childhood's hour I linger'd near
> The hallow'd seat with listening ear;
> And gentle words that mother would give;
> To fit me to die, and teach me to live.
> She told me shame would never betide,
> With truth for my creed and God for my guide;
> She taught me to lisp my earliest prayer;
> As I knelt beside that old arm-chair.
>
> ("The Old Arm-Chair," 17)

Using the visual technique of interpictoriality,[16] Gilbert brings the symbol of the armchair forward to the reader's view several times in *Poems*. The vacant wing chair in the headpiece to the prefatory poem (fig 4.3) is later occupied by the mother in the picture that accompanies "The Old Arm-Chair" (fig. 4.5) and appears again in "Lines Written at Midnight, in the Anticipation of a Dreaded

THE OLD ARM-CHAIR.

I LOVE it, I love it; and who shall dare
To chide me for loving that old arm-chair?
I've treasured it long as a sainted prize;
I've bedew'd it with tears, and embalm'd it with sighs.
'Tis bound by a thousand bands to my heart;
Not a tie will break, not a link will start.
Would ye learn the spell?—a mother sat there;
And a sacred thing is that old arm-chair.

16

Figure 4.5 John Gilbert, headpiece for "The Old Arm-Chair," in Eliza Cook, *Poems: Selected and Edited by the Author* (Routledge, 1861), 16.

Bereavement" (109). Gilbert's pictured scene for "The Old Arm-Chair" speaks to the idealized image of the maternal represented in so many Victorian documents, with a young, beautiful, tender mother enthroned in a comfortable chair in well-dressed leisure, absorbed in her beautiful child rather than the book that lies open on her lap. Like most fantasies, this image mystifies the actual labor involved in child-rearing and household responsibility, especially for a woman such as Eliza Cook's mother. Mother of eleven children and wife of an urban artisan, she likely bore little resemblance to this Victorian Madonna. Gilbert's picture works iconically to inscribe an ideology of universally sanctified motherhood across class lines, and indexically to connect these verses of loss with the personal life of the poet.

Gilbert's illustration also works intratextually with the trope of reading that is introduced in the prefatory poem and picture and developed throughout the visual-verbal collection. As defined by Garrett Stewart in his fascinating examination of the pictured reading scene in *The Look of Reading: Book, Painting, Text,* an intratext is a text that falls "within the four walls ('intramural,' as it were) of the framed view" (15). In his historical survey of the trope, from illuminated manuscript to contemporary painting and graphic art, Stewart locates the nineteenth century as the moment in which "the painted scene of reading has reached its apogee in the portrayal of literate interiority as the very sign of the human in an age of industrial distraction" (7). Even more ubiquitous than the painted scene of reading in the nineteenth century is the graphical scene of reading. A miniaturized meta-book within printed reading material, this scene must be read along with the letterpress it accompanies, even though its tiny pages cannot, themselves, be read. The scenes of reading in Gilbert's pictorial series work with Cook's verses to assert not only a literate interiority in the face of increasing urbanization and industrialization but also a literate human connectedness and common national culture.

While the mother's book lies open and unread on her lap in "The Old Arm-Chair," it reappears in her hand in the headpiece to "Old Story Books," one of Cook's many verses celebrating reading (fig. 4.6). Unlike the headpiece to "To My Readers" that introduces the trope, where Gilbert squares off the scene as if it were a proscenium stage presented to an audience, the large vignette for "Old Story Books" fades into the textual page. As viewers, we seem to be positioned around the corner, clandestinely participating in a domestic moment in which the mother has put aside her mending (the open work box sits on the table) to read to her enraptured daughter. Significantly, none of these visual details corresponds to verbal details in Cook's accompanying poem; instead, the artist takes his cue from the speaker's memory of the draw of "A 'promised story'" (277).

OLD STORY BOOKS.

OLD Story Books! Old Story Books! we owe ye much, old friends,
Bright-colour'd threads in Memory's warp, of which Death holds the ends.
Who can forget ye! who can spurn the ministers of joy
That waited on the lisping girl and petticoated boy?
I know that ye could win *my* heart when every bribe or threat
Fail'd to allay my stamping rage, or break my sullen pet.
A "promised story" was enough—I turn'd, with eager smile,
To learn about the naughty "pig that would not mount the stile.'

277

Figure 4.6 John Gilbert, headpiece for "Old Story Books," in Eliza Cook, *Poems: Selected and Edited by the Author* (Routledge, 1861), 277.

 In this illustration, Gilbert creates an imagined scene of reading that allows him to connect simultaneously with a familiar genre in visual culture and with the collection's concerns with the domestic, the maternal, the past, and the pleasure and power of printed story.

Cook's hortatory poem celebrates popular print culture, with its chapbooks, woodcuts, folktales, and fairy tales. In so doing, Cook champions a common heritage of imaginative literature as well as the benefits of reading. The speaker of "Old Story Books" (277–79) recalls the visual displays of street peddlers and the childhood dilemma of whether to spend a precious penny on candy or one of the "'Story books,' upon a string, [that] appeared in brilliant row." The poem self-reflexively comments on the mass-produced and elegant product of industrialized consumer culture in which it appears: "Talk of your 'vellum, gold emboss'd,' 'morocco,' 'roan,' and 'calf,' / The blue and yellow wraps of old were prettier by half." This nostalgia for a past common culture is, however, balanced by the poem's celebration of an ongoing, and broadened, contemporary common culture. With references to Jenny Wren, Tom Thumb, Cinderella, Red Riding Hood, Jack (of beanstalk fame), Robin Hood, and Robinson Crusoe, Cook intermixes national folk culture with continental, and both with an eighteenth-century novel appropriated by popular broadsides and chapbooks. Print culture, the poem implies, has the power to "level up" those who acquire literacy skills, just as popular culture has the ability to transform elite literature into reading material for ordinary folk.

For Cook, as for many other working-class radicals of her generation, the nineteenth century's democracy of print offered the hope of a nation united by a common heritage working toward shared goals, a nation in which the distinctions of class had been erased. As Solveig Robinson has persuasively argued, Cook used her own position as a self-taught working-class woman to connect with "the people" with whom she identified—"agricultural and industrial laborers" ("Haymakers," 233–34). One of her means of connecting was by relaying stories of her childhood from the position of an international author who supported herself by her pen. Her personal life history provided an example of "the liberating effects of reading in particular and education in general" (241).

In one of her earliest poems, "A B C" (64–65), Cook recalls the labor involved in learning to read. The scene of reading that Gilbert pictures is one of instruction: a small girl "thumb[s]" her primer "beside some Mrs. Trimmer," who corrects her from her own book (fig. 4.7). As in "Old Story Books," with its contrasting choice between the immediate gratification of candy and the long-term pleasure of narrative, "A B C" initially characterizes learning the alphabet as "fun and freedom's earliest foe." Gilbert captures this tension in his implied

A B C.

OH! thou Alpha, Beta row,
Fun and freedom's earliest foe;
Shall I e'er forget the primer,
Thumb'd beside some Mrs. Trimmer,—
While mighty problem held me fast,
To know if Z were first or last?
And all Pandora had for me
Was emptied forth in A B C.

64

Figure 4.7 John Gilbert, headpiece for "A B C," in Eliza Cook, *Poems: Selected and Edited by the Author* (Routledge, 1861), 64.

contrast between the whispering girls on the back bench, who appear to be experiencing some limited fun and freedom, and their unhappy classmate, called up to read to the teacher. As the poetic narrative continues, however, and the speaker acquires literacy, the situation changes, and the new reader gains both pleasure and liberty for her pains:

> But when the giant feat was done,
> How nobly wide the field I'd won!
> Wit, Reason, Wisdom, all might be
> Enjoyed through simple A B C.
>
> ("A B C," 65)

In the course of these modest stanzas, reading opens a wide vista of possibility for personal advancement, with "Steps that lead to topmost height / Of worldly fame and human might." But the poetically arranged lines of type also offer the hope of collective advancement. Cook's politics are evident as her speaker emphasizes that it is through education that democracy may be achieved. Although they may be as lowly and common as the individual letters of the alphabet, her readers nevertheless have great power in an organized group. With characteristic humor, Cook expresses the utopian hope that, once universal literacy is achieved, class distinctions should have no more meaning than letters placed in specific sequences, which can be both earned and arbitrary:

> Ye really ought to be exempt
> From slighting taunt and cool contempt
> But drinking deep from learning's cup,
> We scorn the hand that fill'd it up.
> Be courteous, pedants—stay and thank
> Your servants of the Roman rank,
> For F.R.S. and LL.D.
> Can only spring from A B C.
>
> ("A B C," 65)

Some of the most powerful songs Cook selected for *Poems* are directed to the middle-class reader she knew would have the surplus guinea to spend on the gift book. "A Song for the Ragged Schools" (361–62), for instance, enjoins those who are affluent to improve the nation by working for the education of less privileged citizens: "To work, to work! Ye good and wise, / Let 'ragged' scholars grace your schools." Arguing that literacy brings knowledge, moral direction, and ambition to the poor, Cook also implies that poverty and ignorance breed crime and hopelessness. She makes this causal connection the explicit burden to her "Song of the Spirit of Poverty" (292–96). Written in common meter, the song is sung by "the beldame Queen" herself, "A Queen that the world knows well; / Whose portal of state is the workhouse gate; / And throne, the prison cell." As in "Song for the Ragged Schools," these verses are addressed to the middle-class readers who need to recognize the common humanity of the impoverished in their midst. Insisting that poor women are also members "of gentle womankind" and meant to be "Daughters of Beauty, . . . like ye," Cook uses direct address to her female reader to encourage empathy through comparison. "If I'd held your cheeks by as close a pinch," the Queen asks rhetorically, "Would that flourishing rose be found?" Gilbert's headpiece for "Song of the Spirit of Poverty" collaborates with Cook's verses to inspire horror and disgust for poverty's witchlike power to kill mothers and children and sap the strength of men in their prime (fig. 4.8). Taken together, picture and poem convey a position that readers of the *Illustrated London News* would recognize, particularly at Christmas, when the middle classes were accustomed to being enjoined to benevolent, but short-lived and apolitical, acts of kindness.

The splendid dress of the bibliographic format, however, is not entirely at ease with the politics of Cook's verses. For the *Saturday Review* critic, the divergence between the book's "get up" and its author constituted a failure to "pass": "We scarcely expected to find Miss Eliza Cook's *Poems* rank as a Gift Book. Our knowledge of this poetess—who, as we find from her portrait, has a somewhat androgynous aspect—was limited, and we had an indistinct vision of her only as the Sappho in ordinary to the *Weekly Dispatch*" (Dec. 1, 1860, 702). The language puts Cook in her place as a working-class woman who should have no pretensions to the middlebrow art form of the gift book, while also alluding to her assumed lack of appropriate heterosexual femininity in the references to her "androgynous" appearance and her work as "the Sappho in ordinary" for a radical paper.

While Johanna M. Smith has done much to recuperate Cook "as an unnamed lesbian" who used her *Journal* to open up a space for lesbian discourse, her own contemporaries used coded language to denigrate her "mannish" appearance and allude to her female friendships ("Textual Encounters," 59). The reviewer's attacks on Cook's gender, orientation, class, and politics must be seen in the context of what Laurel Brake names the *Saturday Review*'s "egregious and notorious misogyny" (*Print*, 91). The previous year, it had declared, "We do not want our women to be androgynous," in response to Bessie Parkes and Barbara Bodichon's essay "The Market for Educated Female Labour," published in the *English Woman's Journal* in 1859 (quoted in Schroeder, "Better Arguments,"

SONG OF THE SPIRIT OF POVERTY.

A song, a song, for the beldame Queen,
  A Queen that the world knows well;
Whose portal of state is the workhouse gate;
  And throne, the prison cell.

I have been crown'd in every land
  With nightshade steep'd in tears;
I've a dog-gnawn bone for my sceptre wand;
  Which the proudest mortal fears.

No gem I wear in my tangled hair,
  No golden vest I own;
No radiant glow tints cheek or brow;
  Yet say, who dares my frown?

Oh! I am Queen of a ghastly court,
  And tyrant sway I hold;
Baiting human hearts for my royal sport
  With the bloodhounds of Hunger and Cold.

293

Figure 4.8 John Gilbert, headpiece for "Song of the Spirit of Poverty," in Eliza Cook, *Poems: Selected and Edited by the Author* (Routledge, 1861), 293.

256). For the *Saturday Review*, middle-class women working for pay—including women supporting themselves by the pen—abandoned their natural femininity when they encroached upon masculine preserves.

## Adelaide Procter (1825–1864): From *Household Words* to Household Word

While Adelaide Procter shared with Eliza Cook an energetic commitment to social issues, particularly those related to feminist causes, as well as an enormous, transatlantic popularity as a poet, her social background could not have been more different. Procter was already a household word and associated with music—at least in middle-class homes—even before she published her most famous poem, "The Lost Chord," in 1860, which Arthur Sullivan made a musical hit the following decade (Gregory, *Life*, 3). When she was a child, her father's poem celebrating his elfin daughter, "Golden-Tressed Adelaide," was set to music and, according to Margaret Maison, "became a fashionable song, much in demand in Victorian drawing-rooms" ("Queen Victoria," 636). Writing under the pseudonym Barry Cornwall, Procter père was a romantic poet associated with the Cockney school of poetry whose popularity as "the prince of English songsters" was compared to that of Eliza Cook in an 1847 review of her work in the *Anglo-American* ("Cook," 343). Inevitably, reviews of Adelaide Procter also placed her in the context of her father's poetic fame and style. But while the Procters may have shared a reputation as popular poets with Cook, they were not "of the people." Far from being Cockney or working class, the Procter family was cultured and cosmopolitan. Adelaide grew up in a fashionable London home full of books and artwork (her father collected paintings, especially portraits), where her mother, a salon hostess, presided over literary and artistic gatherings of the period's eminent cultural producers (Gregory, *Life*, 174, 2–3). As her close friend, Bessie Rainer Parkes, wrote in her memoir in 1895, "Everybody of any literary pretension whatever seemed to flow in and out of the house. The Kembles, the Macreadys, the Rossettis, the Dickens, the Thackerays, never seemed to be exactly visitors, but to belong to the place" (quoted in Gregory, *Life*, 5).

Adelaide Procter spoke and read French, Italian, and German as well as English, and she traveled on the Continent (Dickens, introduction, n.p.). Her poetry draws on the folklore and legendary stories of Europe, the political life of the nation, and the social issues of the metropolis, rather than on personal autobiography. A devout Catholic and committed feminist, Procter expressed deep religious faith as well as an active concern for the vulnerable, particularly women and children, in her verses. Although one might expect that these ideologies would marginalize her impact on mainstream Victorian culture, the reverse was true. Procter enjoyed an enormous popularity. According to Maison, she was Queen Victoria's favorite poet; her devotional verses "became hymns in common use"; and her love poetry "inspired the courting, comforted the unrequited, and consoled the bereaved" ("Queen Victoria," 636).

Unlike Eliza Cook, Adelaide Procter did not rely on her pen for her living and seems to have had few domestic responsibilities in the upper-middle-class home she lived in all her life. Rather than taking advantage of the privilege she enjoyed, however, Procter worked tirelessly for the improvement of women's lives. An active member of the Langham Place circle of feminists, Procter was described by Jessie Boucherett as the "animating spirit" of the *English Woman's Journal* (quoted in Gregory, *Life,* 27). She also worked for the Society for Promoting the Employment of Women, published *A Chaplet of Verses* in support of a Catholic women's shelter, and edited the first anthology published by Emily Faithfull's Victoria Press, *The Victoria Regia,* as a practical means of employing women in the publishing industry (Gregory, *Life,* 26–28). In both poetry and prose, Procter used her pen not to make her own living but to improve the living conditions—physical, social, legal, spiritual, and intellectual—of other women. Didactic in tone and intent, her verses were written predominantly about, and for, women. For her critics, this was her great strength as well as her limitation. As Lucy Larcom, millworker-turned-writer, observed, Procter's "habit of conveying a lesson in a song would keep [her] outside the charmed circle of poets in the opinion of some fastidious critics," but Procter did not write for this restricted field of cultural producers. As a result, "hearts too lowly and too timid to approach the great shrines of genius bless her," and "her memory will be bedewed with the gratitude of thousands of women for the sisterly comfort she has unconsciously breathed through so many of her songs" ("Procter," 381, 382). From Queen Victoria to the millworkers of Massachusetts, Adelaide Anne Procter's poetry struck a responsive chord, not only in her lifetime but throughout the century.[17] As the critic for the *Living Age* summed up in 1899, "Writing for the mass of her sisters, her attitude towards life is that of the majority of women, touched by the light of the ideal; and the form in which she embodies her conceptions and thoughts is of less importance to her than that what she writes out of the fullness of her heart should reach the hearts of her audience" (129).

Like Eliza Cook, Adelaide Procter presents a fascinating combination of immense popularity and feminist politics. The reception of their gift-book editions, however, was markedly different. Procter's upper-middle-class status, literary lineage and credentials, modest and nonautobiographical verses, and early death combined to produce favorable reviews for the posthumously published gift-book edition of *Legends and Lyrics* in the Christmas season of 1865/66.[18] Always on the attack against the Langham Place circle of feminists and the *English Woman's Journal,* the *Saturday Review* nonetheless gave Procter qualified praise, balancing class against gender. While categorizing the illustrated *Legends and Lyrics* as verses by a second-rate (female) poet for second-rate (female) readers, the paper's critic proclaimed that "such a collection of little fugitive pieces—always pretty and graceful, and some of them betraying considerable powers"—seemed just "the right thing for a gift-book" and particularly apt for its audience (Dec. 16, 1865, 765). Asserting that there is a place for "good second-rate poems," the reviewer went on to locate it in a specifically female, middle-class readership: "[Y]oung ladies, after all, may get more which their mental powers can assimilate out of . . . Miss Procter than out of Tennyson and Shelley" (765).

The publisher, Bell and Daldy, marketed the lavishly produced collection of Procter's two series of *Legends and Lyrics* as a Christmas present for her middle-class sisters, who could now possess the complete works of their favorite poet in ornamental bindings and decorated pages. As a Christmas present for a young lady, the book's credentials were impeccable. Many of its poems were on Christmas themes, as they had originally appeared in the Christmas numbers of Dickens's *Household Words* or *All the Year Round;* most were more obviously inflected by Procter's Christian faith than her feminist convictions. The *Illustrated London News* approved "the prevailing tone of her mind, and . . . its tendency towards the contemplation of the most mysterious facts of spiritual consciousness, allied with the purest and loftiest strain of moral aspiration" (Jan. 6, 1866, 13). For its part, the *Athenaeum* declared, "The place of Adelaide Anne Procter is in the Golden Book of English poetesses" (Chorley, review, 799).

If Procter is a second-rate poet for second-rate readers, the gift-book edition of her verses, with twenty full-page wood engravings tipped in and textual ornaments and decorative initial letters scattered throughout its gilt-edged pages, nevertheless conferred cultural status and esteem. *Legends and Lyrics* was also a bibliographic monument enshrining the earthly remains of Adelaide Anne Procter after her death at the age of thirty-nine. As the *ILN* critic observed, the edition constituted "an interesting memorial of the amiable and accomplished lady whose premature death is sincerely deplored by the numerous circle of her private friends and a substantial addition to the sterling treasures of our poetical literature" (Jan. 6, 1866, 13). The personal nature of this bibliographic memorial was enhanced for Procter's thousands of readers by the addition of her frontispiece portrait in the form of "a very fine steel engraving, with a wonderful air of *vraisemblance*" (*Round Table,* review, 269). Signed in autograph facsimile "Yours very truly Adelaide A. Procter," the photograph presented itself to readers as a personal trace of the poet's life (fig. 4.9). Wearing a black lace mantilla and hoop earrings, with her abundant hair modestly brushed back, Procter gazes at the reader with an aura of saintly sorrow.

Charles Dickens, Procter's first editor and publisher, and a family friend, is given top billing with Procter on the title page and in countless reviews. As the *Athenaeum* noted, this paratextual feature, too, was "value added" to the gift book, for the "few pages by Mr. Dickens . . . will live in connexion with Adelaide Procter's poems, so long as any sympathy for her verses shall endure" (Chorley, review, 799). Indeed, the introductory pages provide a critical frame

Figure 4.9 Frontispiece portrait (steel engraving after a photograph) of Adelaide A. Procter in *Legends and Lyrics* (Bell and Daldy, 1866).

for Procter's collection. In his elegiac preface, Dickens all but raised Procter to sainthood in a poignant re-creation of her deathbed worthy of little Nell's. Subsequent reviews in the periodical press frequently quoted this movingly realized scene in full. Inevitably, Procter became remembered for her chaste and charitable life and her sentimental verses, rather than her feminist principles and activities. In this encomium for the poet whose poetry dominated both the regular and Christmas numbers of his *Household Words,*[19] Dickens laid to rest his caricature of Procter as women's-rights champion Belinda Bates and in its place erected the icon of saintly Adelaide: graceful, feminine, modest, cheerful, selfless, and ladylike.

Although printed in black and white rather than illuminated colors, there is a missal-like quality to the bibliographic format of *Legends and Lyrics* that reinforces the sanctity inscribed in Dickens's introduction. Rather than the usual layout of wood engraving and poem on the same printed page, the twenty wood engravings are all printed separately as full-page illustrations and are inserted to face their respective poems. The danger of incoherent book design inherent in this format is averted by graphical ornamentation on each textual page, with attention paid to the double-page opening whenever possible. Each poem begins with a decorated initial letter set within a ruled square that descends down through four lines of print, disrupting the left alignment of the first stanza. All poems are headed by rectilinear friezes, usually containing vegetative decoration only, but sometimes also incorporating miniaturized objects and figures. When they appear on the same textual page, poems are separated by a smaller, unframed, and purely vegetative frieze, but when a poem ends on its own page, its final stanza is usually punctuated and embellished by a pendant floral or vegetative emblem.

Typographic printers' devices rather than illustrations responding to a text, these ornamental flourishes recall the methods of hand illumination even while celebrating the possibilities of mechanical reproduction and corporate authorship. Although numerous and varied, the devices necessarily repeat over the 330 pages of text. These repetitions of modular units constitute a kind of graphical poetry, chiming throughout the volume and integrating it with the rhythms of nonverbal design. The textual devices also add a gravitas associated with the religious books of the fifteenth and sixteenth centuries, the models from early print culture that inspired Charles Whittingham Jr. at the Chiswick Press to amass his large stock of woodcut initials and devices. No wonder American poet and critic Edmund Clarence Stedman observed, "It is like telling our beads or reading our prayer book to turn over her pages" (quoted in Matthew, "Procter," 691).

 In printing Procter's *Legends and Lyrics* for Bell and Daldy, the Chiswick Press appears to have taken pains to select apt devices for the headpiece friezes and terminal emblems. Cherubs often appear in the decorative devices heading verses about children and angels; a pair of pipes is frequently central to the devices placed above poems featuring musical motifs;[20] and urns of various kinds adorn verses about death or lost hope. The precut graphic lines of the printer's devices interact in complicated ways with the printed lines of text. Their appearance at the head of the textual page signals the importance of the visual by requiring the formation of the letterpress to depend on the ornament's size and placement. The opening of the poetic contents, for example, uses an extra large headpiece and initial letter to announce the authority and dignity of the first page of Procter's verses, as distinct from the sixteen pages of front matter (fig. 4.10). As a result, the first stanza of "The Angel's Story" (1–7) does not begin until almost halfway down the page, verbal narrative ceding place to visual ornament.[21] The headpiece frieze and decorated initial chime with the verses. Narrating the Christmas Eve death of a middle-class child, the verses show him carried into heaven by an angel who in life had been an impoverished street urchin to whom the boy had given roses. The angelic youth motif is taken up in the graphic ornaments, which feature naked cherubs in both the headpiece and the initial letter. With its acanthus leaves, flowers, animals, urn, and angels, the initial headpiece presides over the page and volume like a carved headstone over a grave. Various elements of its natural and supernatural features are repeated throughout the subsequent pages in a variety of forms, as if the volume were a veritable cemetery of headstones marking buried hopes and lost loves.

A favorite device features a cherub in a shell that could be either a cradle or cockleshell boat, surrounded by decorative vines and leaves. This headpiece frieze embellishes several of Procter's verses about infants, including "Cradle Song for the Poor" (51) and "A New Mother" (222). Its most resonant textual placement, however, occurs in the double-page opening for "Home at Last" (174–75), where it faces the full-page illustration by W. T. C. Dobson (fig. 4.11).[22] One of Procter's many lugubrious verses half in love with easeful death, "Home at Last" is spoken in the voice of a mother to her child. The poem opens with the words "Child, do not fear" as the two embark for home on calm waters under a clear sky. By the second stanza, however, the child's apprehension is no longer a general fear of boats and water but the specific terror of capsizing in a storm, for the waves and wind have suddenly made their voyage perilous. Nonetheless, the mother remains confident, despite clear knowledge of their impending doom, that they will reach home safely. The third and final stanza concludes,

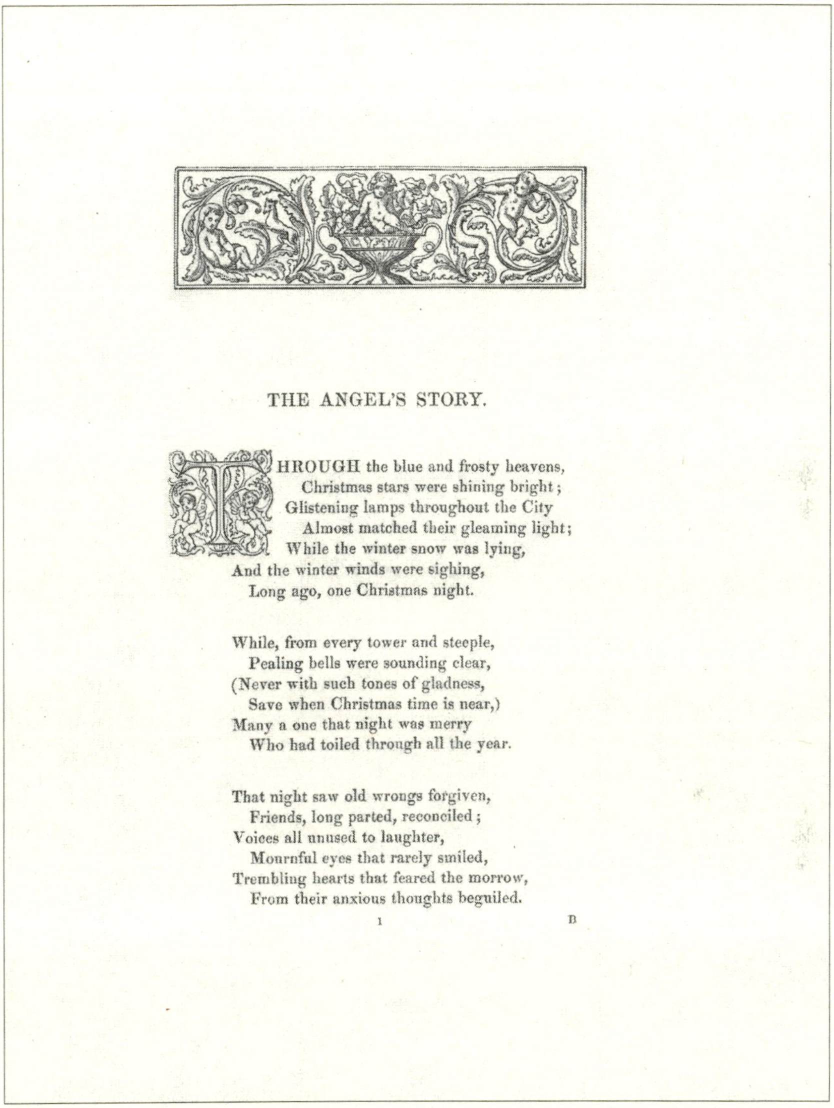

THE ANGEL'S STORY.

THROUGH the blue and frosty heavens,
 Christmas stars were shining bright;
Glistening lamps throughout the City
 Almost matched their gleaming light;
While the winter snow was lying,
And the winter winds were sighing,
 Long ago, one Christmas night.

While, from every tower and steeple,
 Pealing bells were sounding clear,
(Never with such tones of gladness,
 Save when Christmas time is near,)
Many a one that night was merry
 Who had toiled through all the year.

That night saw old wrongs forgiven,
 Friends, long parted, reconciled;
Voices all unused to laughter,
 Mournful eyes that rarely smiled,
Trembling hearts that feared the morrow,
 From their anxious thoughts beguiled.

1 B

Figure 4.10 Printer's devices for layout of "The Angel's Story," in Adelaide Procter, *Legends and Lyrics* (Bell and Daldy, 1866), 1.

  Be not afraid;
But give me thy hand, and see
 How the waves have made
  A cradle for thee.
Night is come, dear, and we shall rest;

## HOME AT LAST.

CHILD, do not fear;
We shall reach our home to-night,
For the sky is clear,
And the waters bright;
And the breezes have scarcely strength
To unfold that little cloud,
That like a shroud
Spreads out its fleecy length;
Then have no fear,
As we cleave our silver way
Through the waters clear.

Fear not, my child!
Though the waves are white and high,
And the storm blows wild
Through the gloomy sky;
On the edge of the western sea,
See that line of golden light,
Is the haven bright
Where home is awaiting thee;
Where, this peril past,
We shall rest from our stormy voyage
In peace at last.

Be not afraid;
But give me thy hand, and see
How the waves have made
A cradle for thee.

174

Figure 4.11 Double-page opening for "Home at Last," with a full-page facing illustration by W. T. C. Dobson, in Adelaide Procter, *Legends and Lyrics* (Bell and Daldy, 1866), 174.

HOME AT LAST.

So turn from the angry skies,
And close thine eyes,
And lay thy head on my breast:
Child, do not weep;
In the calm, cold, purple depths
There shall we sleep.

("Home at Last," 174–75)

The simple, direct language of the poem and the situation convey, with a Tractarian symbolism, the image of life as a troubled journey under the protection of a loving parental figure, with the promise of eternal "rest from our stormy voyage / In peace at last."[23] The verses also allude to the biblical story of Christ walking on the water, quelling the storm, and comforting the disciples with the words "Be not afraid"—the repeated opening for each of Procter's stanzas.[24] The clause thus associates divinity with the mother. Like her contemporary Christina Rossetti, Procter drew on the emblematic methodology of Tractarian poetics to convey spiritual truths in familiar domestic forms, often portraying maternal love as an earthly example of the divine love of God. As a devout Catholic, Procter also frequently incorporated the image of the Virgin Mary as a powerful source of feminine power and inspiration. In this particular instance, her illustrator, W. T. C. Dobson, realized both the literal and spiritual levels of Procter's verses by making visible the hidden allusions.

With a composition in the style of a devotional tract, the illustration reinforces the spiritual emblems of journey, home, and rest that the monologue evokes by depicting mother and son as biblical figures. In a small boat on a stormy sea, a Madonna-like mother holds her Child-Jesus-like son with one protective arm while pointing firmly toward the horizon where they will find their heavenly home. The mast and sail heave toward the upper left corner, in the direction of the headpiece frieze on the facing page, where the small cherub rocks safely in his miniaturized boat/cradle. In this context, the headpiece graphically performs the function of the traditional verbal motto of emblem literature, which precedes poem and picture and points to their jointly revealed spiritual theme. This double-page opening for *Legends and Lyrics* provides a rich bibliographic vehicle for Procter's simple message of faith and hope, but this material format may also push her message toward an exclusively religious interpretation.

Reading the poem in the context of *Household Words*,[25] where it was first published in April 1858, and against numerous verses with similar themes by Barry Cornwall, Gill Gregory identifies "Home at Last" as one of a group of poems Procter wrote on the "fallen woman" theme, always with a focus on absolute renewal rather than shame and punishment (*Life*, 165–69). Certainly the Victorian iconography of the "fallen woman," associated with death by drowning, resonates with the speaker's desire for a rest "in the calm . . . purple depths." Moreover, her illustrator, Dobson, seems to have deliberately connected "Home at Last" with the only other poem he illustrated for *Legends and Lyrics*, "Homeward Bound." Because Procter indisputably tackles the "woman caught in adultery" theme in this latter poem, the visual link effected by Dobson between "Homeward Bound" and "Home at Last" suggests that contemporary readers may well have read both poems as narratives of the fallen woman redeemed. The interpictoriality of Dobson's work within *Legends and Lyrics* works to encourage such a reading.

Dobson's distinctive outline style and mannered religious references make an immediate visual link between "Home at Last" (fig. 4.11) and "Homeward Bound" (fig. 4.12). Once again, Dobson's picture sanctifies the maternal with

Figure 4.12 W. T. C. Dobson, illustration for "Homeward Bound," in Adelaide Procter, *Legends and Lyrics* (Bell and Daldy, 1866), facing page 39.

the religious aura of the Madonna, but this time the religious iconography is explicitly attached to an (innocently) adulterous mother and her (apparently) illegitimate child. Procter's long narrative poem, "Homeward Bound" (34–40), which first appeared in the Christmas number of *Household Words* in 1856, anticipates Tennyson's *Enoch Arden* and Elizabeth Gaskell's *Sylvia's Lovers* in its narrative of a woman who remarries, wrongly believing her first husband to be dead (Gregory, *Life*, 228). Procter's poem is narrated by a sailor who, after being shipwrecked and captured by Moors, manages to escape after ten years and return home, only to find—like Enoch—that his child has died and his wife has married an old friend and borne him a son. It is this dramatic recognition scene that Dobson chose to illustrate. Framed by the open door and illuminated by the light within, the mother is positioned like the Madonna in religious paintings, with her cherubic infant naked on her knee. Beside her, the new husband rests his hand on her shoulder and reaches toward the babe like a protective Joseph. Standing outside in an attitude of grief, the stricken sailor clasps his hands over his eyes, unable to look through the casement window at the happy domestic scene.

In Procter's poem, the three people involved—husband, wife, and former husband—have a poignant recognition scene in which they embrace and weep together before the sailor leaves forever. As in *Enoch Arden*, the fact that the woman's relationship is legally bigamous, as she has two living husbands, is privately resolved with no blame accruing to her. Unlike Tennyson, however, Procter gives the unnamed woman full knowledge of her situation and thus makes her a participant in its resolution rather than a passive and unwitting recipient of male generosity.[26] As with many of the fully reclaimed "fallen" women who populate Procter's poems without shame or retribution, the mother in "Homeward Bound" is sanctified by her maternity rather than stained by her sexuality. Significantly, Dobson's illustration, with its iconography of the nativity scene, associates this "adulterous" woman with the Virgin Mary. And because the iconography of the Madonna visually links "Homeward Bound" with "Home at Last," their themes of fallen woman, heroic maternity, and heavenly hope also connect. Published for the same Christmas market as the gift-book edition of Tennyson's *Enoch Arden*, Procter's *Legends and Lyrics* offered women readers an alternative approach to issues concerning women inside and outside marital relationships.

Although she often celebrates the mother-child relationship, Procter is critical of marriage in many of her poems. In "Philip and Mildred," she shows the negative effects of feminine passivity (in contradiction of the prevailing ideology), while in "A Parting" she implies that self-sufficient spinsterhood may be preferable to marriage (Hickok, *Representations*, 126, 23–24). This outlook is evident in several poems she published in the feminist *English Woman's Journal*, including

"A Comforter" (275–78). Like "Home at Last," this poem is spoken by a mother to her child. In this instance, however, and despite the suggestive title, the verses are not an extended metaphor for Christian pilgrimage. Rather, they represent the long, confidential monologue of a middle-class mother to her young daughter, in the stolen moments before the nurse comes to put the child to bed and the mother returns to her guests. The silent, loving daughter is the "comforter" for a mother whose secret trouble is never revealed, though the implication is that an unhappy marriage is the reason that "Life is so hard to bear." The vague nature of the speaker's sorrow allows the woman reader to project her own unhappiness into the verses, while drawing common comfort from the assurance "That to help and to heal a sorrow, / Love and silence are always best." The silent daughter, Effie, represents the potential source of earthly comfort offered by daughters to mothers and also, perhaps, by women to women. This perspective is reinforced by the accompanying picture, which is one of two contributed to *Legends and Lyrics* by the volume's only female illustrator, M. E. Edwards (fig. 4.13).

Figure 4.13 Mary Ellen Edwards, illustration for "A Comforter," in Adelaide Procter, *Legends and Lyrics* (Bell and Daldy, 1866), facing page 275.

A popular and prolific magazine illustrator, Mary Ellen Edwards's work for *Good Words*, the *Argosy*, *Belgravia*, *Cassell's Magazine*, the *Churchman's Family Magazine*, the *Cornhill Magazine*, the *Illustrated Times*, the *Girl's Own Paper*, and *London Society*, as well as for children's books and periodicals, would have made her pictorial style very familiar to the middle-class readers of *Legends and Lyrics.*[27] Her visualization of "A Comforter" delineates a highly realized middle-class setting full of luxury and comfort. Unlike the scene of instruction and delight portrayed by Gilbert for Cook's "Old Story Books," in which the mother is shown taking a break from her mending to read to her child, Edwards's composition suggests the problems of leisure rather than literacy. Although books abound in this well-appointed room—there is a small stack on a chair and an open one thrown carelessly on the floor—they are not treated as treasures. "I am tired of trying to read, dear," the mother confides to little Effie. In this context, the intratextuality of Edwards's "A Comforter" portrays, not a scene of reading, but rather a scene in which books are domestic objects and cultural props no different than the fan that also lies, unused and uncared for, on the floor. While the open casement and vase of flowers on the sill seem to offer access to light and hope, the mother has turned listlessly away from the window toward her young daughter, whom she holds by the chin. Seated in an ornately carved high-backed chair, the mother appears to be weighted down by her voluminous skirts, which take up an inordinate amount of the picture plane. Taken together, picture and poem suggest much more than the intimacy and primacy of the mother-daughter bond. They also point toward the necessity for women to have purpose and employment in their lives, a perspective that Edwards apparently shared with her author. For Edwards, this had personal resonance: a working professional, she also trained her own daughters to work in the visual art field (Casteras and Peterson, *Struggle*, 58).

In a review in the American magazine *Round Table* (*Legends and Lyrics* was released concurrently by Bell and Daldy in London and Ticknor and Fields in Boston), Edwards's two illustrations were singled out for special admiration. Edwards's picture for "Expectation," the reviewer wrote, "is perhaps the finest of all. There is something weird and strange in it, quite beyond the poem it illustrates, which hardly rises above the commonplace" (269). Although not as weird and strange as Dante Gabriel Rossetti's illustration of the three sisters in "The Maids of Elfen-Mere" (see fig. 1.3), Edwards's fairy-tale illustration is both beautiful and haunting (fig. 4.14). Standing on a terrace by the sea as night approaches, the princesses embody various attitudes of expectation in keeping with Procter's verses. The accompanying poem, a lyric of five five-line stanzas, articulates different attitudes toward waiting and watching, emblematic of the faithful's

EXPECTATION.

Figure 4.14 Mary Ellen Edwards, illustration for "Expectation," in Adelaide Procter, *Legends and Lyrics* (Bell and Daldy, 1866), facing page 309.

expectation of Christ's second coming (*Legends and Lyrics*, 309–10). As Christina Rossetti does in many of her poems on this subject, Procter casts the faithful in feminine form, kin to the patient virgins of biblical story who wait through the night for the coming of the Bridegroom. In "Expectation," Princess May, "weary . . . of waiting and sighing," longs for the night to come because "Hope deferred makes the spirit sick." The biblical reference—"Hope deferred maketh the heart sick: but when the desire cometh, it is a tree of life" (Proverbs 13:12)—puts an apocalyptic cast on the coming night. In contrast to May, Princess Alice finds the day passing too quickly, fearing "the dark To-Morrow" and "The terrible hour I wait and dread!" Edwards depicts her seated on the wall, gazing longingly over the harbor to the town, reluctant to give up her hold on worldly life.

As is usual in fairy tales, the youngest princess, Gwendoline, has the most insight and models the ideal attitude. Kissing and comforting her sisters, she reminds the impatient May that "Expecting joy is a happy pain," and cheers on the reluctant Alice with the encouraging "Those who still dread, are not quite forsaken." Edwards depicts Princess Gwendoline leaning on her oldest sister's shoulder, with her eyes cast down. Her prayerful attitude and supportive words show her to be Procter's model Christian and feminine ideal. This poem, like many others in the collection, conveys a feminist as well as a devout message in its affirmation of spinsterhood. Although in fairy-tale form and interacting with scriptural parable, "Expectation" reinforces Procter's reiterated view that single women ought to work to support each other while awaiting the reward of faith, a theoretical position she seems to have put into daily practice. As Alice King wrote in her piece "Adelaide Procter" for the *Argosy*, Procter "wrote poetry that made its way with power and sweetness into English brains and hearts, but she did not give up her life to literature alone; she did other and noble work for her fellow men [*sic*]" (152).

## Jean Ingelow (1820–1897): "Queen of Modern Poetesses"

Writing for the *Continental Monthly* in 1864, shortly after Adelaide Procter's death and Jean Ingelow's publication of *Poems,* the American critic "L.D.P." observed that the two poets "have become 'household words' in our midst." Their poems "bring tears to the eyes of all who have really lived and sorrowed; and the more we read them, the more do they come home to us" ("Procter," 605). The writer's emphasis on readers' affective response is typical of the records of reception that print culture has bequeathed us. Like Cook and Procter, Ingelow wrote verses that connected to people in their everyday lives and resonated with their daily experiences and emotions. Like them, too, Ingelow wrote many lyrics that were later set to music and sung by people from all walks of life, but she particularly excelled at narrative poetry and ballads. The Victorians valued her long, dramatic verses for performances of the recited word, particularly at the end of the century, when ladies' elocution classes had become popular sites of poetic transmission and cultural enhancement.[28]

The *Woman's Herald* reported on one such event that took place in 1891 before "an audience who evidently warmly appreciated the pleasant hour thus spent with Jean Ingelow" (323). After a "deeply interesting sketch of the life of Jean Ingelow, which served as introduction to the recitations," the young ladies of the school performed various pieces, including the ever popular "Songs of Seven" (323). Ingelow's poetry, in this setting, is variously valued for its connection to a woman writer; its ability to move an audience; its capacity for dramatic performance; and—perhaps most of all—its ability to assist young ladies in acquiring the currency of cultural capital: literary knowledge and the cultivated skill evident in "the beauty of expression and the charm of intelligent elocution" (323). In his obituary notice for the *Times,* Sir John Skelton was unsure whether people at the fin de siècle still *read* Ingelow's poetry, which had reached the apex of its popularity in the sixties and seventies, but was certain that they continued to be familiar with her verses, including "Songs of Seven," "Divided," and especially "High Tide on the Coast of Lincolnshire." "These fine dramatic lines, with their haunting rhythm and refrain," he noted, "have long been a favourite with public reciters" ("Ingelow," 8).

It seems apt that Ingelow, who reached back into the oral tradition for her narrative poetry, dialect poems, and ballads, should have been esteemed in the new oral culture of popular recitation. But as Eliza Cook's "To My Readers" and "Old Story Books" remind us, ballads had long been part of popular print culture as well as oral tradition. With the woodcut chapbook giving way to the illustrated poem in the periodical and gift-book literature of the nineteenth century, Jean Ingelow's poems were as much at home in contemporary print culture as they were in popular performance. They were frequently to be found in the illustrated pages of *Good Words,* for example, where they were accompanied by pictures from the hands of some of the period's best artists, including John Millais, Arthur Boyd Houghton, Arthur Hughes, and George Pinwell.

A year after she brought out her initial collection in 1863 to enormous popular and critical success, Ingelow became the marquee contributor to a Dalziels' Fine Art Gift Book. In its review of *Home Thoughts and Home Scenes,* the *Illustrated London News* hailed Ingelow as the "queen of modern poetesses" (Dec. 21, 1864, 653). Meanwhile, her *Poems* went into multiple editions; in the first three months after the first edition, Ingelow earned over £327, and she continued to profit from her poetry throughout the century (Peters, *Ingelow,* 64). Capitalizing on a strong seller, Longmans followed up three years after the initial printing with a lavishly illustrated edition, produced under the auspices of the Dalziel brothers' engraving firm, with illustrations by Pinwell, North, Poynter, Houghton, Wolf, Small, and Thomas and Edward Dalziel. Her American publishers, Roberts Brothers, issued this gift-book edition simultaneously, but they had already published an illustrated *Songs of Seven* as a stand-alone poem for the previous Christmas season of 1865/66. This was a significant indication of Ingelow's enormous popularity, as few authors other than Tennyson (see chapter 5 discussion) could boast an audience willing to purchase a single long poem in book form, merely for the added beauty that binding, typography, and pictorial embellishment could bestow.[29] At five dollars a copy in cloth or eight dollars in morocco binding, this was a luxury item that only those with disposable income could afford—particularly in the difficult months after the Civil War.

*Songs of Seven* was considered an ideal gift book for a lady, as it was by a woman poet, writing irreproachably about the seven "seasons" in a woman's life, each a multiple of seven years—Exultation (7 × 1), Romance (7 × 2), Love (7 × 3), Maternity (7 × 4), Widowhood (7 × 5), Giving in Marriage (7 × 6), and Longing for Home (7 × 7)—evidently, a woman's life was over by the age of forty-nine. Each of the seven sections was adorned with a head and tailpiece vignette and a full-page illustration. Printed on one side only, all twenty-nine pages of type and engraving were enclosed in a red rectilinear frame, marked with cruciform devices in each corner. With a frontispiece engraving of the poet, an artistic floral-wreathed vignette on the page devoted to the epigraph, and a large illustration on the title page encapsulating all seven stages to come, the Roberts Brothers' *Songs of Seven* was hailed with great enthusiasm by the popular press. Among the religious magazines, the *Zion's Herald and Wesleyan Journal* gave *Songs of Seven* the stamp of evangelical approval, saying that "it will make a fine present for the holidays" (Dec. 20, 1865, 204), while the *Christian Examiner* indicated, "It would be difficult to find a book more attractive, both in appearance and contents" (Jan. 1866, 143). Contents and get-up were equally admired by more worldly publications. *Arthur's Home Magazine* called it the most "exquisitely beautiful" of the season's "elegant books," particularly recommending it as "a gift book for a lady of taste and cultivation" (Jan. 1866, 78). *Godey's Lady's Book and Magazine,* the most popular monthly magazine of the day, concurred: "The book is beautiful in appearance, being in every way adapted for a holiday gift, and will prove a particularly attractive ornament upon the drawing-room table. We recommend it to the attention of those who wish to remember their lady friends during the present holidays" (Jan. 1866, 94).

The following year, when Longmans and Roberts Brothers brought out the complete collection of Ingelow's *Poems* in Britain and the United States, with over ninety wood-engraved illustrations by the Dalziels' stable of artists, the transatlantic critics were united in their praise. Writing for the *Contemporary Review,* Henry Alford underscored Ingelow's deserved popularity, asserting, "Every one knows, or ought to know, Miss Ingelow's beautiful poems" ("Notice" [1866], 620). As did most reviewers, Alford ranked poetry and pictures high in the annals of art and industry, establishing the volume as "among the most beautiful of illustrated books, as the poems which are illustrated are among the choicest productions of our time" (620).[30] J. R. Wise, for the *Westminster Review,* agreed. "Everyone will rejoice to see the poems of Miss Ingelow in their new form," he enthused, noting that the gift-book edition "may be fairly placed on the same shelf with the many illustrated editions of Tennyson, to whom Miss Ingelow, in many of her characteristics, bears so striking a resemblance" ("Belles Lettres," 273–74). Ingelow's poetry had been compared with Tennyson's ever since the first publication of her *Poems;* even the laureate appreciated the similarity, saying, "Miss Ingelow, I do declare you do the trick better than I do" (quoted in Peters, *Ingelow,* 61). With the appearance of her *Poems* as an illustrated gift book, the comparisons extended to bibliographic format. The influential *Athenaeum* acknowledged that "it is agreeable to see, as we do here, how readily one artist interprets the meaning of another" and predicted that the illustrated *Poems* "will be a favourite with the public" (Doran, "Literary Table," 607).

But while the critic, John Doran, insisted that "the poems of Miss Ingelow cannot be read without profit as well as pleasure (607), the *Saturday Review,* as usual, found it difficult to see anything of substance in publications by women authors for women readers. Remarking on the "pre-Raffaelite manner" of some of the artists, the paper's comparison of Ingelow's illustrated *Poems* to "the famous illustrated Tennyson" implicitly undermined the stature of the laureate and his audience, for the reviewer slammed Ingelow as a "minor poet" and her readers as incapable of taking in anything substantive (Dec. 1, 1866, 684). This alignment of second-rate poet and reader, however, made the illustrated edition a perfect match for its purpose: "[A]s a drawing-room book, nothing could be more suitable; there is just that grace and soft pleasant sentiment, and precisely that length, in Miss Ingelow's poems, which suits them to a five-minute study. And," the reviewer went on, invoking the *ut pictura poesis* adage, "as are the poems, so are the pictures—graceful, slightly suggestive, and sufficiently varied" (684).

Connecting place of reading with the reader's gender and available leisure for study, the critic suggests that the illustrated edition of Ingelow's *Poems* is an ideal manifestation of the gift-book genre. The critic's attitude is clearly derogatory, but we may well consider the implications of introducing this kind of pictures and poetry into everyday life. While a "five-minute study" implies a cursory reading and superficial understanding of poetic and graphic lines that challenge neither intellect nor imagination, there are other ways of approaching such fleeting interactions with the printed page. As Michel de Certeau reminds us, "readers are travelers," an image he uses to suggest nomadic movement through exotic lands that the reading experience entails (*Practice*, 174). If, for instance, we consider that the owner of Ingelow's *Poems* might have possessed few books, and fewer still that combined poetry and pictures, we might adjust the critic's sketch of a singular five-minute scene of reading to renewed visits and repetitive scenes of reading. Repeated study, even in short increments, allows both the words and the images to impress themselves on the mind. Indeed, iterative study in fleeting moments encourages memorization, which could allow the reader "to store up a source of pleasure," as a woman's advice book of the period suggested (quoted in Flint, *Woman Reader*, 79). For middle-class women working within the home, memorized pieces of poetry could provide an imaginative pleasure palace of stimulation and repose, constituting a private mental retreat during the drudgery of daily tasks.[31]

In *The Woman Reader, 1837–1914*, Kate Flint summarizes several nineteenth-century advice manuals that encourage poetry reading for "second-rate readers" interested in self-cultivation. In *Maternal Counsels to a Daughter* (1855), for instance, Matilda Pullan emphasized that "[p]oetry, indeed, can be learnt in odd minutes,—from an open book while working, or whilst brushing the hair at night, or at many other periods that are too often wasted" (79). In *Thoughts on Self-Culture Addressed to Women* (1850), Maria Grey and Emily Shirreff promoted the practice of reading poetry as a means of training the imagination, believing that it "contained enough manifestations of strong emotion for a reader to be able to associate herself readily with its contents" (Flint, *Woman Reader*, 78). By the end of the nineteenth century, as we have seen, this private practice of memorization had become, after the impetus of the Board Schools with their emphasis on poetic recitation, the public art of elocution. But reading poetry also continued to be valued as a leisure pursuit for women. In 1891, E. A. Walker, in *Womanhood; or, Thoughts for Young Women*, recommended, among other suggestions for "thoughtful reading," *A Thousand and One Gems of Poetry* (Flint, *Woman Reader*, 115–16). This popular Christmas gift book, with over five hundred pages of poetic selections arranged by Charles Mackay and numerous illustrations by Millais, Gilbert, Tenniel, Birket Foster, and others, was still in print and selling strongly thirty years after it was published by Routledge in 1867[32]—the same Christmas market that saw Ingelow's illustrated *Poems* first issued.

If the illustrated collection in the private space of the family drawing room allowed repeated, if intermittent, engagements with the expressive elements of picture and poetry, it also facilitated this engagement through the expressiveness of the book itself as a physical object. Jerome McGann has written extensively about how "artists and writers gradually developed a new and extraordinarily sophisticated understanding of the expressive character of physical text" between about 1820 and 1930 (*Rossetti*, 82), but this formulation should be extended to acknowledge the contributions of engravers and printers. The Dalziels' involvement in Jean Ingelow's illustrated *Poems* exemplifies the development of the expressive potential of the iconic page. The Dalziels engraved and oversaw the entire artistic production of the collection, with Edward and Thomas contributing numerous original designs themselves. The Dalziels also printed the book at their Camden Press and are thus responsible for the layout of one of the most deliberate designs in their Fine Art Books series. Headed by a running title and page number underscored by a thin rule, the remainder of each page is devoted exclusively to poetic text and framed pictures, with none of the additional graphical embellishment found in Procter's *Legends and Lyrics*. In a variety of poetic forms and layouts and a range of illustrative styles, sizes, and frames, each page expresses the narrative and emotive power of the subject taken up by image and text.

The opening poem in Ingelow's illustrated collection, "Divided" (1–9), shows the Dalziels' skill at illustrating, engraving, printing, and designing books when they were at the peak of their craft (fig. 4.15). Ingelow's "Divided" presents a chronology of loss over eight sections that elaborate, in emotionally charged scenes, the gradual separation of the speaker and her childhood beloved. Section I opens with an idyllic scene of unity and possibility, as the children play together on the moors:

> An empty sky, a world of heather,
>     Purple of foxglove, yellow of broom;
> We two among them wading together,
>     Shaking out honey, treading perfume.
>
> ("Divided," 1)

By the end of this section, the snake appears to signal the end of Eden and the beginning of division. At a distance, the children catch the glimpse of the stream, "Green like a ribbon," that will insinuate itself between them. Section II begins with the children wading in the stream together, unaware that this first step will lead to their ultimate separation. In the next section, the two follow the

2 *Divided.*

Flusheth the rise with her purple favour,
Gloweth the cleft with her golden ring,
'Twixt the two brown butterflies waver
Lightly settle, and sleepily swing.

We two walk till the purple dieth
And short dry grass under foot is brown,
But one little streak at a distance lieth
Green like a ribbon to prank the down.

Figure 4.15 Thomas Dalziel, page layout with two engravings for "Divided," in Jean Ingelow, *Poems* (Longmans, Green, Reader and Dyer, 1867), 2.

stream's western descent, "Till one steps over the tiny strand," and they begin to "move apart," each unable to cross to the other's side. As the stream between them widens in Section IV, their parting seems inevitable:

> Then cries of pain, and arms outreaching—
> The beck grows wider and swift and deep;
> Passionate words as of one beseeching—
> The loud beck drowns them; we walk, and weep.
>
> ("Divided," 5)

After this midpoint in the poem, not only youth but also day have passed. In Section V, the two continue on their separate sides, "With the moon's own sadness in our faces, / Where joy is withered, blossom and bud." By the next section, the beck has become a river that "'plaineth of love's disloyalties," and the speaker confirms that the "two are walking apart for ever, / And wave their hands for a mute farewell." Together with the speaker, we lose sight of her beloved in Section VII, as the river flows toward the sea. The eighth and final section introduces an unexpected conclusion. Instead of the speaker blaming the beloved for forsaking her, she asserts,

> And yet I know past all doubting, truly—
>     A knowledge greater than grief can dim—
> I know, as he loved, he will love me duly—
>     Yea, better—e'en better than I love him.
>
> ("Divided," 9)

The beloved's superior love is cast in a new light in the final stanza, as the dividing river not only represents the barrier between the living and the dead but also offers a connecting link between the two:

> And as I walk by the vast calm river,
>     The awful river so dread to see,
> I say, "Thy breadth and thy depth for ever
>     Are bridged by his thoughts that cross to me."
>
> ("Divided," 9)

As in many Victorian poems, from Tennyson's "Crossing the Bar" to Procter's "Home at Last" and Ingelow's "Seven Times Seven: Longing for Home," "Divided" draws on the trope of death as an immense river or sea that must be crossed before reaching what Gerard Manley Hopkins eloquently called "Heaven-Haven."[33] In "Seven Times Seven" (197–200), Ingelow's female speaker mourns the loss of her husband, who "sailed to the heavenly shore," and expresses her wish to join him: "There is the home where my thoughts are sent, / The only home for me— / Ah me!" Thomas Dalziel's headpiece illustration for "Seven Times Seven: Longing for Home" (fig. 4.16) connects interpictorially with his sequence of designs for "Divided," effectively making a bridge between the two poems. A romantic night scene, the view of the sea by moonlight is sublime in its dwarfing of the small female figure standing on the shore under brooding cliffs. The illumination of the horizon faintly expresses the speaker's longing for home on the unseen shore. Illustration and layout also effectively dwarf the poetic text, casting an emotional shadow on the words that follow. The large, black picture dominates the page like a headstone, pushing down the poetic text and dividing the six-line first stanza in half.

SEVEN TIMES SEVEN. LONGING FOR HOME.

I.

A song of a boat:—
There was once a boat on a billow:
Lightly she rocked to her port remote,

Figure 4.16 Thomas Dalziel, illustration for "Seven Times Seven: Longing for Home," in Jean Ingelow, *Poems* (Longmans, Green, Reader and Dyer, 1867), 197.

The two final images Thomas Dalziel contributed for "Divided" similarly show a solitary woman on the shoreline, but with much different effect (fig. 4.17). Here, the final two quatrains of the poem are matched by two pictorial representations of the narrative and its emotional conclusion. In the rectilinear image that heads the page, a woman stands on the shore with her back to the sea. Hands clasped over her heart, and eyes looking downward to the lines of type below the picture frame, the woman appears to have deliberately turned from the sea to land—from the eternal to the human. This is confirmed in the roundel that punctuates the poem. In this final pictorial comment, Thomas Dalziel provides a telescopic glimpse into the woman's future. Far from "longing for home" as in "Seven Times Seven," this woman has chosen life. Walking away from the sea, engrossed in a book she is reading, the pictured woman of "Divided"

*Divided.* 9

VIII.

And yet I know past all doubting, truly—
A knowledge greater than grief can dim—
I know, as he loved, he will love me duly—
Yea, better—e'en better than I love him.

And as I walk by the vast calm river,
The awful river so dread to see,
I say, 'Thy breadth and thy depth for ever
Are bridged by his thoughts that cross to me.'

2

Figure 4.17 Thomas Dalziel, illustration and tailpiece for "Divided," in Jean Ingelow, *Poems* (Longmans, Green, Reader and Dyer, 1867), 9.

critiques her sister in "Seven Times Seven," who at age forty-nine has fulfilled her earthly function as wife and mother and can only wish for death.[34] Indeed, the miniature scene of reading Thomas Dalziel places at the end of "Divided" works intratextually to suggest that the thoughts that bridge the "awful river so dread to see" may be contained in a printed book such as Ingelow's own *Poems.*

Thomas Dalziel produced a total of eleven pictures for the eight sections of "Divided." In a range of different sizes and shapes, these small, framed pictures show the simultaneous maturation and separation of a small girl and boy. Inserted between stanzas as well as at the head and tail of sections, the illustrations create a textual page that works to enact the subject of the poem. Just as "the green ribbon" widens and divides boy from girl, man from woman, so too do the pictures separate stanza from stanza and divide the reader's attention between image and text. In the first section, for example, which represents the children occupying a Blakean unity before division, the textual page graphically expresses the impossibility of this imagined state of wholeness (see fig. 4.15). The two "cuts" literally carve their space out of the page between the lines of type, which are also formed through relief impression. Graphically and visually, the reader sees the page as a block of four black-and-white lines, followed by a small circle containing black-and-white lines, followed by another block of four black-and-white lines, followed by a large, divided (semi)circle of black-and-white lines. The repetition, alternation, and alteration effect a graphical comment on the arbitrary creation of meaning through lines of sequenced letters and images formed by ink and pressed into pages. Bearing silent witness to the mechanized world of print culture and the contemporary experience of reading, the divided page of "Divided" testifies to a fractured industrialized world in which humans experience daily life as repeated rupture mitigated by a nostalgic longing for wholeness.

In a largely admiring summation of Jean Ingelow's poetry for *Longman's Magazine* after her death, Andrew Lang acknowledged that hers was a poetry ineluctably part of large-scale cultural production (as Bourdieu describes it): "Her appeal, except on rare occasions, is less to poets or devotees of poetry than to the great mass of people" (Lang, "Ingelow," 237). In contrast, Lang ascribes Christina Rossetti's poetry to that written for the restricted field of other cultural producers: poets, critics, and educated "*raffinés.*" As a result, Ingelow "was as widely read as Miss Rossetti was little known. . . . [Ingelow's] success was the success which she would have desired; she added greatly to the sense of the beauty of life, among the mass who like beauty when brought to their doors, as it were, but who do not wander longingly and curiously after it through difficult ways" (Lang, "Ingelow," 238). Certainly Rossetti's collections of 1862 and 1866, even with the addition of Dante Gabriel Rossetti's illustrated frontispieces and title pages and elegantly designed bindings, and despite their affordable price of five shillings, never achieved a popular readership. The enormous nineteenth-century audience for Ingelow's poetry—in the United States alone, she is said to have sold two hundred thousand copies (Peters, *Ingelow*, 64)—bears up Mackenzie Bell's assessment of her for *The Poets and Poetry of the Century* (1893): "[T]he general reader, whatever the extent of his culture, could at least understand and enjoy its directness and its simplicity, together with its lovely descriptions of some of Nature's more familiar aspects" (in Miles, *Poets*, 386–87).

## Rating the Everyday

The popularity of the illustrated gift book in the age of mechanical reproduction may be accounted for, among other things, by its ability to offer pages expressive of modern life without the distractions that distinguished the periodical press, with its double columns of topical news, practical advice, social and political analysis, essays, and fiction abutting pictures and verses. Here, between the covers of beautifully bound books, readers could linger on, and return to, pictures that represented recognizable scenes and verses that expressed familiar thoughts, feelings, and experiences in accessible language, elevated by poetic rhythm and rhyme. The gift-book collections of popular poets such as Eliza Cook, Adelaide Procter, and Jean Ingelow, met a nineteenth-century need for multimedia expression at a time when visual culture was dominating social experience.

Enshrined in costly covers signaling the cultural value of their contents, and occupying a place in the family home dedicated to leisure and self-improvement, gift books connected private affect with public expression, everyday life with "high" culture. Their illustrated and ornamented pages, moreover, offered expressive and interactive reading experiences for an audience accustomed to navigating the crossing paths of image and text. But whereas the prestige of a guinea gift book may have elevated the poetic stature of Cook, Procter, and Ingelow in their own day, it had the opposite effect (as discussed in the next chapter) for Tennyson. Placed on the table with illustrated Ingelows, Cooks, and Procters, the illustrated Tennysons produced in the sixties began to acquire similar associations with "second-rate readers" and the mass appeal of visual culture.

# five

# Poet and Publishers

## *Tennyson and the Image*

> I today, Lord of myself and ways, the next
> A popular property . . .
>
> *Alfred Tennyson*[1]

Alfred Tennyson's antipathies toward illustration, the publishing "trade" (as opposed to the gentlemanly occupation of writing poetry), and celebrity culture are well known. Yet it is also true that he dominated and helped shape each of these image-making fields of nineteenth-century visual culture. Despite his dislike of both annuals and illustrated periodicals, he published a significant amount of original work in these popular forms, thereby extending his reputation and attracting new readers.[2] After 1850, in his prominent position as poet laureate, Tennyson became, in a sense, the "popular property" of the reading nation. The popularization of his poetry is manifested in the illustrations of his work by both amateurs and professionals, who used every technology of reproduction available: lithography, chromolithography, steel engraving, wood engraving, etching, and photography.

Throughout the sixties, as we have seen, Tennyson's poetry appeared in both illustrated collections (such as the 1857 edition of his *Poems*, discussed in chapter 2) and anthologies (such as Willmott's *Poets of the Nineteenth Century*, discussed in chapter 3).[3] This chapter examines how his popular narrative verse helped establish a new genre whose aesthetic and economic potentials were not fully realized until the fin-de-siècle fine-printing revival: the publication of a long poem embellished by a single artist and encased in covers specially designed for the contents.[4] The new, more elegant and unified format was immediately hailed by critics as an aesthetic advance in the gift-book genre. "Of late a somewhat better style of Christmas Books has been brought into the market," observed the *Saturday Review:* "A single author, or a single work of an author, is now usually published" (Dec. 5, 1863, 738).

By way of maximizing sales and readerships when Tennyson's popularity peaked in the 1860s, his publishers commissioned individual artists to design stand-alone editions of the laureate's most popular poems as Christmas gift books. As part of their image-marketing strategy (in which the laureate was complicit), publishers fronted his books with engraved photographs of the poet in his most Tennysonian poses. Indeed, the Tennyson image was so valuable that photographic portraits of the laureate—rather than, as one might have expected, his sovereign—were the first to be registered for copyright in England (in August 1862) (Ledbetter, *Tennyson*, 144). Tennyson was, indeed, as Kathryn Ledbetter claims, "the world's first media poet" in the sense of mass image appeal to a global audience connected by print (2). As a result of his embeddedness in nineteenth-century visual culture, Tennyson's poetry reached audiences from the "working men of England" to the royal family.[5]

The story of Tennyson and the image is an important chapter in Victorian publishing history and visual culture. It marks the convergence of restricted-field poetry with large-scale cultural production and shows how, as the power of the image gained ascendancy, the authority of the author over his work diminished. The annual release of illustrated editions of Tennyson's works along with other ornate Christmas gift books in publishers' lists, advertisements, shop windows, and drawing rooms effectively associated the laureate's image with consumer culture, domestic poetry, and a putatively female readership. Then, too, in every illustrated edition, Tennyson shared title-page billing, periodical reviewing, and reader influence with other creative artists, whose representations might not coincide with his own vision of his verses but were nevertheless permanently bound up with them. Furthermore, as his publishers planned formats, commissioned artists, and orchestrated marketing strategies, they, too, became part of the corporate authorship that produced the works of Tennyson.

From 1857, when Moxon brought out the illustrated *Poems*, to the end of Tennyson's career, the poet fought an ongoing battle for authoritative control of his work within the commercial world of Victorian publishing. His sequence of publisher moves—from Edward Moxon (1832–68) to Alexander Strahan (1869–73) to Henry S. King (1874–78) to Kegan Paul (1879–83) to Alexander Macmillan (1884–92)—was accompanied by an escalating legality in defining authorial versus publisher rights (discussed further below).[6] Even though Tennyson began to exert greater control over his works in his contracts, enabling him at last to call a halt to new illustrated editions, he was not able to check the reissuing of the popular illustrated volumes that were produced during the 1860s. Christmas after Christmas, gift books featuring the laureate's poetry were offered for sale; in any given year, a shopper could choose from a range of Tennyson titles, formats, and prices. The sale of illustrated Tennyson editions was such an assured market that one of Macmillan's first actions after Tennyson died in 1892 was to secure the woodblocks, stereotypes, and copyright for the illustrated *Poems* from Routledge and to republish it under the Macmillan imprimatur as a limited edition with the illustrations printed on Japanese paper.[7]

Twentieth- and twenty-first-century editors and publishers have typeset Tennyson's poems in scholarly editions printed on plain paper, embellished with paratextual footnotes rather than graphic decorations or pictorial images. Such valuable editions establish Tennyson's credentials as academia's most consecrated Victorian poet and authenticate his status within the field of restricted cultural production, but they come at a cost. In our intense focus on the poetic word, we lose an opportunity to touch and see the past—to get a sense of how these verses expressed their meanings in physical formats to nineteenth-century readers. Despite astute attention to the many contexts in which Tennyson's poetry was written and read, literary critics have only recently begun to analyze the material importance of illustrated editions of his work.[8]

The immensity of this oversight shows how committed we remain to a romantic ideology of poetry as the creative expression of individual genius—the disembodied voice and inspired breath of the poet. But breath cannot exist outside a living body, and bodies are always enmeshed in human social relationships. The work of many makers, a book is both a material object and an event whose passage through time and space is ongoing. The gift-book editions of Tennyson's poems give us insight into the changing conditions under which poetry was produced and received in an emergent mass market. While we cannot read with nineteenth-century eyes, the materiality of nineteenth-century paper, type, illustrations, graphic ornament, and binding can tell us a great deal about a work's readers. The historical record of letters, reviews, notices, advertisements, periodical publications, manuscripts, preliminary studies, proofs, trial books, and publishing ledgers also offers a rich archive of paratextual matter.

These documents allow us to examine illustrated editions as historical objects, opening up interpretation to the weight and heft of their material forms and cultural contexts. The production of a series of illustrated versions of Tennyson's popular poems as Christmas gift books bears very materially on their textual and social meanings as multimedia, worldly events in a society increasingly dominated by the image.

Tennyson's publisher, Edward Moxon, learned some important things about producing gift books for the contemporary market from the initial failure of the illustrated *Poems* of 1857 (as discussed in chapter 2). First, timing was crucial. To generate sufficient sales to offset costs, an illustrated volume of poetry must come out in the fall in time to be marketed aggressively as a Christmas gift book through periodical advertisements, notices, and reviews. Second, a broad middle-class audience was willing to pay up to a guinea, but not more, for a quality gift book at this season. Moxon learned these two critical facts when the illustrated *Poems*, which he had priced at 31 shillings sixpence, was remaindered, reissued at 21 shillings, and then sold so well for successive Christmas seasons that Routledge had printed a further ten thousand copies by decade's end. Third, Moxon understood that the mode of production had to be streamlined to ensure that the gift book was published on time and in a cost-effective way. After working with eight artists and five engravers on the illustrated *Poems*, and experiencing many delays and difficulties in consequence, Moxon switched to employing a single artist for Tennyson's gift books. The final insight was that issuing an illustrated reprint of a popular long poem encased in content-specific bindings was an effective marketing strategy capable of extending readerships and generating steady sales over many seasons. In the age of the image, one could, indeed, sell a book by its cover.

When Edward Moxon died a little more than a year after the publication of the illustrated *Poems*, he had already begun the move to gift-book editions of single long poems. Over the next decade, his publishing firm, lead by the aggressive James Bertrand Payne, embarked on this new strategy with exceptional vigor. Moxon's Christmas gift-book versions of *The Princess* (1860), *Enoch Arden* (1866), and individual poems from *Idylls of the King* (1866–68) followed the successful publication of some of Tennyson's most popular volumes. *Enoch Arden and Other Poems* (1864), for instance, had already sold sixty thousand copies (Hagen, *Tennyson*, 112) when Moxon brought out an illustrated version of the title poem for the following year's Christmas market. The successful sales of the illustrated *Enoch Arden* over successive Christmas seasons, like those for the illustrated *Princess* and *Idylls of the King*, underscores the power of the image to sell poetry. The Christmas shopper buying these books was not, strictly speaking, paying for the poet's words. He or she either had a copy of the poem already or could purchase the verses for a fraction of the gift book's cost.[9] Rather, the consumer was purchasing the book-as-object, a work whose cultural value was enhanced through the combination of the laureate's name and fame with pictorial images by well-known artists.

The production and reception of these illustrated editions eroded Tennyson's authorial autonomy, and he became embroiled in a decade of disputes with Moxon. When he moved his assets to Alexander Strahan, the poet did his best to stop any new illustrated editions and refused to accept the pictures by Arthur Hughes that Strahan had commissioned for *The Window* (1871). Undaunted, the publisher deployed the rejected images as an advertising come-on for the book by printing them in his periodical, *Good Words*. In this mass-circulated monthly, the poet's lyrics reached an even larger audience, while the publisher's power was reconfirmed. When Tennyson moved to H. S. King, he made a final attempt to assert control over the images associated with his poems. He himself proposed his last illustrated edition and selected the artist, his neighbor, Julia Margaret Cameron. Tennyson's proposal that the low-priced Cabinet Edition, targeted at "working men," be illustrated shows his recognition of the appeal of the image in mass culture while also suggesting his desire to author the whole book. As we shall see, however, the publisher curtailed not only the poet's but also his chosen artist's creative control over format and presentation.

Tennyson's selection of Julia Margaret Cameron as illustrator for the Cabinet Edition is in line with the poet's career pattern of tacit acceptance of women artists. This highlights an interesting gender dynamic in the production of illustrated editions of his work. Female illustrators apparently did not threaten Tennyson's sense of being the dominant author on a project in the way that male illustrators hired by Moxon seem to have. Although there is no doubt that Tennyson disliked illustrated books in general, his principal concerns were as tied up with power struggles with his publishers and anxieties about the image his books generated of him (he feared the taint of commercialism) as they were with the pictorial images themselves. Significantly, Tennyson does not seem to have had these concerns when women artists illustrated editions of his poems and brought them out with other publishers. The most well known of these is by Eleanor Vere Boyle (E.V.B.), who illustrated an edition of *The May Queen* for Sampson Low with Tennyson's blessing in 1861. Less known today is *The May Queen* published the same year by Day and Son, beautifully illuminated by a Mrs. W. H. Hartley and chromolithographed by W. R. Tymms. Day and Son also published an *Idylls of the King* illustrated by Amy Butts in 1862. Perhaps this exposure to the excellent work of Day and Son, who were lithographers to the queen, influenced the selection of this firm for Tennyson's own illuminated work, *A Welcome to Princess Alexandra* (1863), designed by Owen Jones, and published as a souvenir edition for the Christmas following the royal wedding.

Certainly Day and Son's color printing was superior to Kent's, who published *Three Gems in One Setting*, including Tennyson's "Poet's Song," with illustrations by Anne Lydia Bond and chromolithographed by David Brand in 1860.[10] Seven years later, Bond illustrated *The Miller's Daughter* (fig. 5.1) with seventeen engravings. This edition of the laureate's popular poem was distributed by Routledge and advertised in the publisher's "Illustrated Gift-Books Suitable for Drawing-Room Presents," listed in the Christmas catalog.[11] When Macmillan was negotiating the purchase of the woodblocks and stereotypes for the Moxon Tennyson in 1892, Routledge offered to sell Bond's steel plates as well.[12] Macmillan, however, was not interested in Bond's illustrated work, and her *Miller's Daughter* has—like an earlier *Miller's Daughter* published by H. Bohn (1857), the *Dora: A Poem* illustrated with lithographs by Paulet

Figure 5.1 Anne Lydia Bond, decorated title page for Alfred Tennyson, *The Miller's Daughter* (W. Kent, 1867). *Tennyson Research Centre, Lincolnshire County Council, United Kingdom.*

 Mildmay (Vernon, 1856), and the *Mariana* illustrated with etchings by Mary Montgomerie Lamb (Worthing, 1863)—largely disappeared from the view of all but bibliophiles and book collectors.

If their appearance on Victorian publishers' lists and in periodical reviews indicates that these forgotten books had a place on the drawing-room tables of their own day, why have we neglected them? As so often happens, scholars may have taken their cue from the poet. While the historical record details his ongoing assertion of rights with regard to illustrated editions got up by his own publishers, it is largely silent about these gift books illustrated by women artists for other imprints. Tennyson's letters and manuscripts have little to tell us about his views on these publications, even when "by permission of the author" is grandly announced on the title page (fig. 5.1). Perhaps the poet viewed some of these works in the category of fandom, as the burden that celebrity must bear. He may have recognized that his large audience of women readers, built up in illustrated annuals and periodicals, was accustomed to reading poetry in an image-rich environment and that some of these readers might wish to respond visually to his work. Tennyson seems to have been predisposed to view illustration as an appropriately feminine activity—a means by which women could reflect, and add grace to, the creative masculine word without challenging its authority or threatening the poet's dominance. Whatever the rationale for accepting these publications, what seems indisputable is that both the poet and his official publisher gained insight into the salability of an illustrated long poem from these women's work.

## Illuminating Women

The first illustrated edition of Tennyson was not, as is usually claimed, the *Poems* of 1857, but rather *Dora,* illustrated by Paulet Mildmay in spring 1856 in a large folio priced at twenty-five shillings. Printed in pale brown ink, the verses and simple line drawings were surrounded by decorative wreaths of oak leaves and acorns. The significance of Mildmay's *Dora,* like that of *The Miller's Daughter* (illustrated by an anonymous artist and published the following year), far exceeds the modesty of its artistry and reputation. These are not simply the first illustrated editions of Tennyson's poetry to be published; they also introduce what became the dominant publishing pattern for the laureate's gift books: the single narrative poem separated out for decorative treatment and issued as a stand-alone volume. And while they demonstrated the market for embellished single poems, they also pointed to a preferred subject matter: Tennyson's domestic idylls, focusing on female characters.

The most popular of Tennyson's contemporary characters is indisputably the eponymous heroine of *The May Queen.* A sentimental narrative detailing the seasonal sequence of the May Queen's spring crowning, autumn illness, and winter dying, the poem inspired enthusiastic visual responses on both sides of the Atlantic, in virtually every style and register. In 1857, Thomas Dalziel contributed a design for each of the three sections of the poem for Willmott's *Poets of the Nineteenth Century;* the same year, J. C. Horsley produced four illustrations for the poem for the Moxon Tennyson. As Julia Thomas reminds us, *The May Queen* was everywhere in Victorian visual culture, with fifteen paintings of the poem and multiple illustrated versions (*Pictorial,* 64).

Women artists were the first to bring out the poem in illustrated volume form. Two of these were beautiful works of illumination directed at upper-class audiences. Mrs. W. H. Hartley's illuminated edition of *The May Queen,* published in March 1861, was dedicated to Lady Georgiana Codrington, who was invested as a Lady, Royal Order of Victoria and Albert. The following decade, *The May Queen,* in illuminated borders designed by L. Summerbell, was published in a limited edition for eighty-five subscribers including Lord Bute and other dignitaries. Both books testify to the resurgence of illumination, calligraphy, and miniature painting as mid-nineteenth-century book arts inspired by the period's medieval revival (Bettley, *Art,* 15). The technological development of chromolithography permitted the delicate handwork to be mechanically reproduced in glowing colors and multiple copies.

In 1861, Eleanor Vere Boyle illustrated *The May Queen* with twenty-six half-page pictures and numerous textual decorations as a Christmas gift book brought out by Sampson Low. A slim octavo of forty gilt-edged pages, *The May Queen* is bound in cloth boards blind-stamped with a trellis of roses around a central cartouche containing the title and the names of author and artist traced in gold. Mimicking hand-drawn calligraphy, the gold letters are in a gothic font embellished with a tracery of leaves, vines, and mayflowers (fig. 5.2). This display of Tennyson's and Boyle's names represents a rare acknowledgment of the gift book's plural makers. With the exception of Gustave Doré, none of Tennyson's official illustrators shared the prestige of cover billing with the poet; instead, their contribution is acknowledged inside, on the title page.[13] The prominent coupling on the cover of *The May Queen* confirms that the edition has the poet's sanction while also recognizing the authorial role of the artist who conceived and produced it. When E.V.B., an admired illustrator of children and gardens, wrote to Tennyson in 1860 seeking permission to illustrate *The May Queen,* he replied, "I would rather you than any one else should do it." According to Hallam Tennyson, his father very much admired E.V.B.'s "drawings of children"

Figure 5.2 Cover design for Alfred Tennyson, *The May Queen*, illustrated by Eleanor Vere Boyle (Sampson Low, 1861).

(*Memoir*, 2:29–30), an appreciation shared by Ruskin. After the publication of E.V.B.'s *Child's Play* (1852) and *A Child Summer* (1853), Ruskin wrote to the artist with the following tribute: "I never saw anything in modern art approaching [your etchings]—except the finest thoughts of Millais and Hunt, and one or two of their almost unknown associates" (quoted in de Beaumont, "EVB," 14).

Ruskin's early association of E.V.B.'s graphic style with the Pre-Raphaelites is significant, because it predates the Pre-Raphaelites' first ventures into the book arts with *The Music Master* in 1855 and the Moxon Tennyson and *The Poets of the Nineteenth Century* in 1857. For their part, the Pre-Raphaelites recognized E.V.B. as one of their own. After the publication of her first two books, Millais invited Boyle to join the Etching Club, and Rossetti, after seeing her illustration in *Child's Play* for "the Nursery Rhyme on which 'S[aint] M[argaret's] Eve' is founded," decided to take "The Maids of Elfin Mere [*sic*]" as his subject for Allingham's *Music Master* instead of "Saint Margaret's Eve," as he had initially planned (*Correspondence*, 1:379). E.V.B. was undoubtedly influenced by Pre-Raphaelite painting, but it seems equally clear that her book art had some impact on Pre-Raphaelite illustration. Certainly her work strongly influenced the Pre-Raphaelite associate who became one of the period's finest illustrators: Arthur Hughes. Both his pictures for Christina Rossetti's *Sing-Song* (1872) and his format for Tennyson's *Enoch Arden* (1865) display indebtedness to E.V.B.'s *May Queen*.[14]

E.V.B. approached Tennyson's text with two styles: a bold, black-outline method for "true to nature" images of domestic scenes (like the Pre-Raphaelites, E.V.B. drew from life);[15] and a less defined line for symbolic images representing spiritual states or visions.[16] The two styles are connected by the natural motifs, predominantly flowers, that E.V.B. wove throughout her visual narrative. E.V.B.'s emblematic motifs give the octavo an integrated design from cover to cover not often seen in the period's gift books. In the title-page vignette, for example, a garland of roses embellishes the tree branches above the head of an infant May Queen, similarly crowned with roses and held in the protective embrace of a cherubic angel (fig. 5.3). Together, the childish heroine and her angelic companion suggest a spiritual state shadowed forth on earth by the forms of nature—an emblematic approach akin to Blake's. This symbolic vignette introduces a series of realistic engravings showing the adolescent May Queen in her domestic surroundings. As an emblematic reminder of the presence of the spiritual in the quotidian, either the rose wreath or some other flowers often appear in the scene. This prepares us for the textual decoration found near the end of part 2, "New Year's Eve," when the fading May Queen is reminding her mother that she will be with her after death (fig. 5.4). A stark line drawing of a

*THE*

MAY QUEEN

BY

ALFRED TENNYSON

POET LAUREATE.

ILLUSTRATED BY E. V. B.

LONDON:

SAMPSON LOW, SON & CO. 47, LUDGATE HILL.

MDCCCLXI.

Figure 5.3 Eleanor Vere Boyle, decorated title page for Alfred Tennyson, *The May Queen* (Sampson Low, 1861).

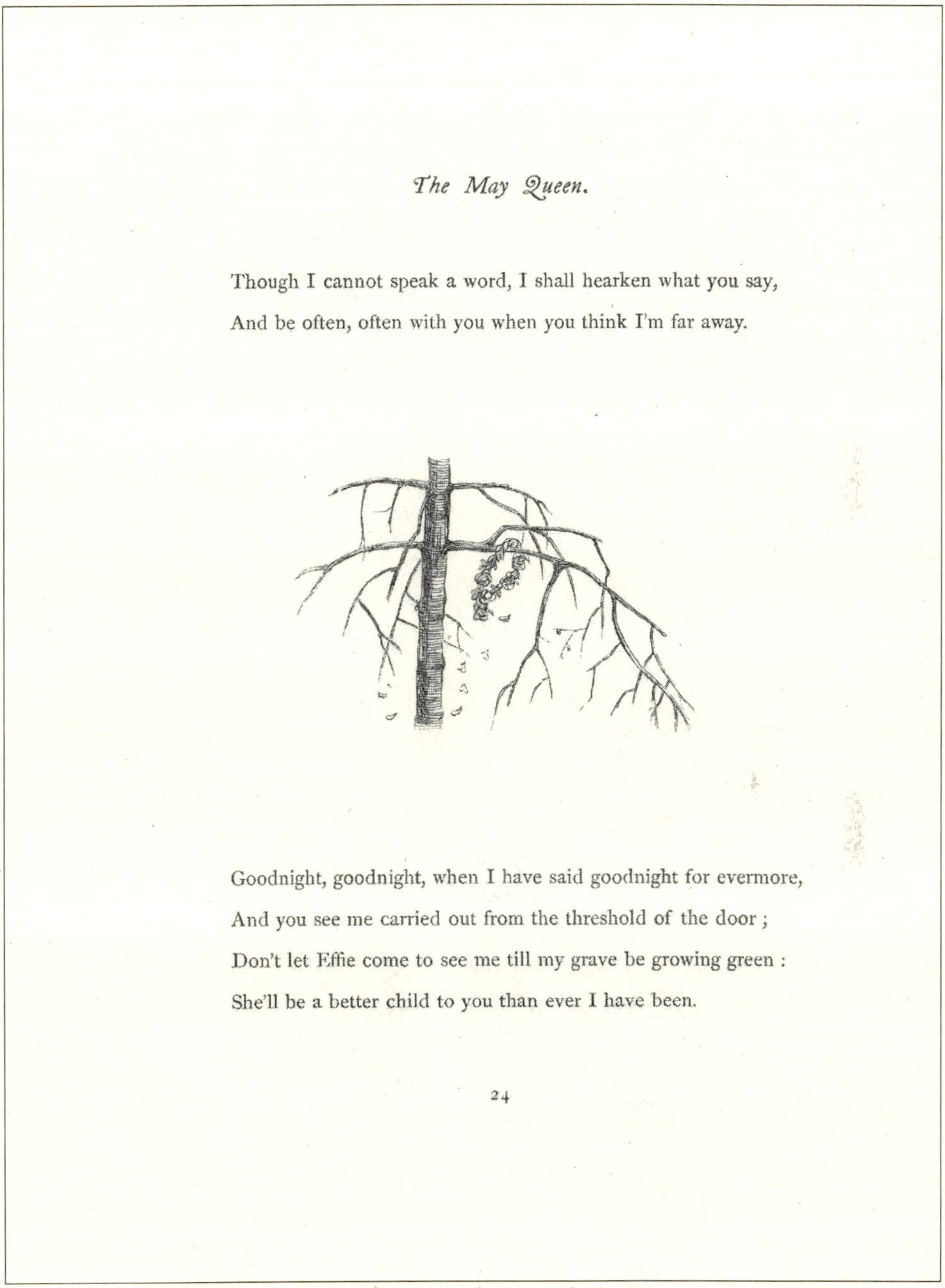

*The May Queen.*

Though I cannot speak a word, I shall hearken what you say,
And be often, often with you when you think I'm far away.

Goodnight, goodnight, when I have said goodnight for evermore,
And you see me carried out from the threshold of the door ;
Don't let Effie come to see me till my grave be growing green :
She'll be a better child to you than ever I have been.

24

Figure 5.4 Eleanor Vere Boyle, page decoration in Alfred Tennyson, *The May Queen* (Sampson Low, 1861), 24.

leafless tree with the abandoned crown of flowers hanging from its branches, the image evokes the ongoing effects of memory and the capacity of sensory objects to hold traces of the past in their scent and form.

The final engraving for the "New Year's Eve" section of the poem (fig. 5.5) is an emblematic representation of the death of the Old Year and the imminent departure of the May Queen. The shrouded spirit of death stands at the mouth of a cave, holding a rose branch of living flowers; behind him, the setting sun alludes to the closing of the May Queen's earthly day. Although the figure is frightening, the light on the side of the cave and the familiar roses illuminate the image with the religious hope that the girl's final earthly day may transform into a divine new day for her. The floral motif suggests a natural continuity between life and death and may even allude intertextually to Dante's use of the rose as a symbol for the divine in his *Paradise*.

*The May Queen.*

Goodnight, sweet mother : call me before the day is born.
All night I lie awake, but I fall asleep at morn ;
But I would see the sun rise upon the glad New-year,
So, if you're waking, call me, call me early, mother dear.

Figure 5.5 Eleanor Vere Boyle, tailpiece for "New Year's Eve," in Alfred Tennyson, *The May Queen* (Sampson Low, 1861), 26.

The engraving that concludes the book (fig. 5.6) reinforces this hope by repeating the emblems of rose and sun. The illustration depicts the May Queen stretched out like Sleeping Beauty, covered in roses, and dreaming serenely in the warm glow of a maternal, breastlike sun.[17] Of all of Tennyson's illustrators of *The May Queen,* only E.V.B. managed to capture the apocalyptic emotion of the final lines, which she achieved by moving to the symbolic register. The girl's last words to her mother—"To lie within the light of God, as I lie upon your breast— / For ever and for ever, all in a blessed home"—are interrupted by the placement of the engraving in the middle of the text. The typography and layout of the final page of *The May Queen* require the reader to pause, like the girl's immediate audience, before reaching the final lines: "And there to wait a little while till you and Effie come— / And the wicked cease from troubling, and the weary are at rest" (39).

*Conclusion.*

To lie within the light of God, as I lie upon your breast—
For ever and for ever, all in a blessed home—

And there to wait a little while till you and Effie come—
And the wicked cease from troubling, and the weary are at rest.

Figure 5.6 Eleanor Vere Boyle, illustration for "Conclusion," in Alfred Tennyson, *The May Queen* (Sampson Low, 1861), 39.

If Tennyson's dying village girl was everywhere in Victorian visual culture, the same can also be said for one of his expiring high-born maidens. Images of the Lady of Shalott were ubiquitous in painting and print; both the poem and the illustrations by William Holman Hunt and Dante Gabriel Rossetti for the Moxon Tennyson of 1857 caught the imagination of many subsequent artists.[18] Among these were Walter Crane, who secured himself a position (without paying the usual premium) in W. J. Linton's studio after showing the engraver his designs for the poem (Engen, *Dictionary*, 57), and Henry Peach Robinson, who created a photographic representation of Tennyson's ballad in 1861, using an experimental technique with two negatives (Gernsheim, *Photography*, 42). But it was an unknown female artist who first brought out a stand-alone edition of the poem. Published by Kent in 1859 and sold for ten shillings, this *Lady of Shalott* was illustrated anonymously, by "A Lady," as nameless as Tennyson's heroine. Like the *Idylls of the King* (1862) illustrated by Amy Butts—which similarly preceded the later Moxon edition by Doré—and the *Mariana* (1863) illustrated by Mary Montgomerie Lamb, this *Lady of Shalott* seems to have been the outcome of an amateur artist responding visually to a favorite poem. The existence of these books reminds us that, if illustration remained a largely masculine preserve in the professional world of the 1860s, there were nevertheless many women who used their pencils to illuminate their private reading. Publication—possibly at their own risk—allowed them to share their imaginative visions with other readers.

In 1863, Tennyson was an official collaborator on an illuminated edition of *A Welcome to Princess Alexandra*, brought out as a guinea gift book for Christmas. In March, the Prince of Wales had married the Danish princess with great public festivity and widespread enthusiasm for the bride. Tennyson's manuscript version of the poem arrived at Windsor on the day of the wedding, and the fact that it was published, without his authorization, in the *Times* the same day emphasizes the degree to which his office as laureate made him a public property. As Kathryn Ledbetter points out, "*The Times* publication of his poem served as a gift to readers of all classes, advertising the union of domestic love and national fervor" (*Tennyson*, 155). This ephemeral "gift to readers of all classes" became class- and gender-specific when the poem was materialized in an illustrated edition for the drawing-room tables of middle-class families.

Prepared as a souvenir edition, the lavish gift-poem was ready by the end of the year, and it, too, participated in the movement of the Tennyson image through Victorian visual culture. Embellished with gilt decorative devices and bound in red-and-white covers in honor of Denmark's colors, the gift-book edition of *A Welcome to Princess Alexandra* is presented in a title-page flourish "To her Royal Highness the Princess of Denmark"—thereby allowing the middle-class owner to possess a copy of the royal gift—"From the Poet Laureate / Owen Jones Illuminator / Day and Sons Lithographers to the Queen." Significantly, only the designer and publisher are named; Tennyson's personal name, like Alexandra's, is replaced by his royal office. This dodge allowed the poet to escape the taint of commercialism in this souvenir edition. The book is produced, the title page implies, by royal decree, or at least in fulfillment of the official obligations of the laureateship.

Reviewers saw this illuminated work as an obvious gift choice for women that Christmas season. While fearing that its sweetness might be too much even "for female natures to bear," the *Athenaeum* opined that nothing could be "more certain of the popularity of the boudoir than this publication"—"nor could the drawing-rooms wish for anything more charming" (Dec. 19, 1863, 842). As usual, the critic for the broad-based *Illustrated London News* was more effusive: "Pen and ink cannot express the princely gorgeousness with which Mr. Owen Jones has illuminated, the publishers have bound, and the score or so of simple but perfect lines in which Mr. Tennyson echoed the sentiments of welcome with which the (supposititious) 'sea-king's daughter from over the sea' was received by her adopted people." Effectively denying individual authorship to the laureate with this reference to his poetic "echo," the *ILN* insisted that the poet was but "the melodious mouthpiece" of the nation (Dec. 26, 1863, 663). As laureate, Tennyson was understood to be a representative voice of his readers' sentiments; as a "popular property," what mattered most was the material form in which these graceful expressions were preserved, presented, and displayed.

## *The Princess* (1860): A Marriage of Image and Text

While Tennyson welcomed Princess Alexandra with bibliographic flourish and glowing colors, his reception of his own *Princess*, got up in similar red-and-ivory covers, illustrated by Daniel Maclise, and published by Moxon as a Christmas gift book, was considerably less warm. In December 1859, twelve years and seven editions after the first publication of *The Princess*, Emily Tennyson recorded the arrival at Farringford of the illustrated edition whose complicated, prolonged, and treacherous birth had almost killed Tennyson's decades-long relationship with the House of Moxon the previous year.[19] "Beautifully got up," Emily conceded, "but the Illustrations we cannot admire" (*Journal*, 140).

The Tennysons' lack of enthusiasm may have had an aesthetic basis, but it was also informed by a lingering resentment against the publisher for bringing out an illustrated *Princess* in the first place. Indeed, relations with the House of Moxon first began to unravel over disputes about the illustrated editions of *Poems* and *The Princess*. When Edward Moxon died in the summer of 1858, the new management tried to claim nearly £9,000 from Tennyson for losses associated with the illustrated *Poems*. It was at this highly contentious moment that Tennyson learned of the publisher's plan to bring out a Christmas gift-book edition of *The Princess*, illustrated by Daniel Maclise. This occurred in late October, when proofs of twenty wood-engraved pictures arrived unexpectedly at Farringford. With no prior agreement about an illustrated *Princess*, Tennyson was incensed. After consulting with friends and seeking legal advice, Tennyson let the publishers know that he was ready to take his work to another firm unless both an apology and a new agreement were forthcoming.[20]

Tennyson's anger over the illustrated *Princess*, which almost caused a complete rupture with his publisher, can be characterized as a crisis of authority. On a textual and hermeneutic level, Maclise's illustrations challenged the poet's ability to direct the reader's interpretation through the power of his poetic voice. Culturally and commercially, the unauthorized packaging of his poetry as a Christmas gift book undermined Tennyson's ability to determine the material conditions in which his verses reached their public. His preference was always for moderate prices, unpretentious bindings, and clear typography set on good paper with ample margins (Hagen, *Tennyson*, 101). He particularly disliked the explicit commercialism of gift books. Unable to put a stop to the edition because the Moxon firm had already invested over £550 in payments to the artist and engravers, Tennyson insisted on a deferral until the following year.[21] Thus, the illustrated *Princess* appeared for Christmas of 1859 (though dated 1860), rather than for the 1858 season as the publishers had planned. When Tennyson received his copy in its gilt-stamped crimson bindings, he had the further shock of seeing that the six songs from *The Princess* had been embellished—no proofs of these vignettes had been sent to him—in addition to the twenty half-page illustrations he knew would accompany the fairy-tale narrative.[22]

In claiming that he had no knowledge that an illustrated edition of *The Princess* was in the works, Tennyson was being somewhat disingenuous. By his own admission, he had heard a rumor "that Maclise was in Italy or had been in Italy (I forget which) making drawings for an Illustrated edition having to the best of my belief never had a word with Moxon on the subject except that he once said in a casual manner, 'We must get Maclise to illustrate the Princess' to which I as casually answered 'Oh ho' and thought no more about it until the news of Maclise came" (*Letters*, 2:211). The historical record shows that the illustrated edition of *The Princess* had been in the works since 1854. Moxon seems to have contracted with the artist for a fully illustrated edition of *The Princess* when he gave Maclise the commission for the two "Morte d'Arthur" designs for *Poems.* Maclise worked on the two books, with their related medieval themes, concurrently. The Dalziel brothers' proofs book, which was made up at the time the engravings were done, shows that the engravers began cutting designs and pulling proofs for *Poems* and *The Princess* in winter 1856 as part of the same Moxon work order.[23]

Despite his selective memory, Tennyson was certainly told about Maclise's illustrations for the *Princess,* just as he was kept informed about the various artists' and engravers' work for *Poems.* In an undated letter written in the first half of 1856, Moxon speaks of the two illustrated projects in virtually the same breath. After regretting that "Millais' first illustration to the Miller's Daughter [for *Poems*] is certainly not good," Moxon goes on to say, "You will I think be pleased with Maclise's designs for The Princess. The whole (20) are ready, but two only have yet been engraved. In justice to him I must say that he has taken on an immense deal of pains with them."[24]

The publisher had every reason to expect that the poet would approve his choice of illustrator for *The Princess.* Tennyson and Maclise had met socially and shared a common friend in John Forster. Moreover, in both public stature and artistic interests, artist and poet were well suited. Primarily a history painter, Daniel Maclise was one of the most popular and prolific artists of the period, particularly admired for his medieval, romantic themes (Altick, *Paintings,* 5)—a perfect match, the publisher must have thought, for Tennyson's "Morte d'Arthur" and *The Princess.* In 1847, the same year that Tennyson first brought out *The Princess,* Maclise painted *The Spirit of Chivalry* for the House of Lords. Like Tennyson, Maclise turned to medieval subject matter to contrast present degeneracy with former greatness, while at the same time emphasizing the continuum of history as a way to reclaim the nobility and heroism of a chivalric age.

Daniel Maclise did indeed take "an immense deal of pains" with his illustrations for *The Princess,* the last book commission of his career and the one closest in style to his history paintings (National Portrait Gallery, *Maclise,* 105). Maclise prepared for his commission by reading and annotating the most recent (fifth) edition of *The Princess,* probably given to him by Moxon at the time of the commission.[25] The artist's marked-up copy, preserved in the Prints and Drawings Department of the Victoria and Albert Museum, offers a rare glimpse into how one of the period's foremost book illustrators approached a text. Maclise created a system of pencil notations to guide his representation of characters, scenes, and events, marking selected passages with vertical scores and occasionally underlining an important word or phrase or making a hasty marginal sketch. In his finished illustrations, he used two distinct pictorial styles to distinguish the fairy-tale narrative and the interspersed songs. In keeping with the romantic medieval setting of the former, he drew on his familiar "grand manner" (Buchanan-Brown, *Early Books,* 208), enclosing the twenty historical tableaux within rectilinear frames. For the songs that provide lyrical interludes for the narrative, he used a contemporary bourgeois realism, setting these six vignettes within rounded enclosures.

In addition to marking passages selected for illustration, Maclise also noted those that conveyed the mood, tone, or theme he wanted to capture. For example, Maclise highlighted the verses in part 2 that describe Lady Blanche, "Of faded form and haughtiest lineaments, / With all her Autumn tresses falsely brown," for pictorial use in part 4, where she makes her first appearance in an illustration—the image of the hateful crone among innocent maidens (fig. 5.7). This composition also incorporates details from passages Maclise marked in part 4. His notations highlight verses describing the Prince and Florian standing before the Princess, who is seated on her throne under a lamp, with "a single jewel on her brow." Other marked passages include those referring to the Princess's wet hair being combed by "a handmaid on each side" while "Eight daughters of the plough" stand guard behind. Maclise also marked lines about Psyche's child lying before the throne "Half-naked as if caught at once from bed," with Melissa weeping on her knees while her mother, Lady Blanche, delivers a tirade. His condensed composition draws on all these disparate details from the poem. Maclise arranges this scene like a tableau within a series of gothic arches and pillars reminiscent of the theatrical setting for *The Spirit of Chivalry,* which shows a similarly enthroned high-born maiden.

In Maclise's designs for *The Princess,* the medieval archway becomes a graphic trope that carries the past into the present and visually connects the medieval illustrations with the contemporary vignettes. For example, the design immediately following the half-page illustration of Princess Ida is a contemporary scene set within an arched frame (fig. 5.8). Four of the six vignettes illustrating the songs from *The Princess* are in similarly domed frames, thus repeating in the domestic Victorian scenes a visual motif from the gothic designs for the fairy tale.[26] Like the six lyrics interspersed between the narrative sections, which Tennyson added in the third (1850) edition, the contemporary vignettes appear to have been an afterthought to Maclise's original pictorial narrative. In his 1856 letter about Maclise's designs for *The Princess,* Moxon referred to only twenty illustrations, but two years later he paid the artist for twenty-six. It seems probable that Maclise initially produced the twenty half-page designs exclusively for the narrative sections, leaving the interspersed lyrics unillustrated. Whether Maclise later produced the six designs for the lyrics at the publisher's instigation or his own initiative is unclear, but it seems likely that he was prompted.

A MEDLEY. 97

W. THOMAS. Sc.

And chiefly you were born for something great,
In which I might your fellow-worker be,
When time should serve; and thus a noble scheme

o

Figure 5.7 Daniel Maclise, illustration for Alfred Tennyson, *The Princess* (Moxon, 1866), 97.

A MEDLEY. 31

As thro' the land at eve we went,
  And pluck'd the ripen'd ears,
We fell out, my wife and I,
O we fell out I know not why,
  And kiss'd again with tears.

For when we came where lies the child
  We lost in other years,
There above the little grave,
O there above the little grave,
  We kiss'd again with tears.

Figure 5.8 Daniel Maclise, vignette for Alfred Tennyson, *The Princess* (Moxon, 1866), 31.

The artist's ideas for these vignettes are recorded in the edition he used to plan his *Princess* designs: he drew each vignette directly on the page on which its accompanying lyric was printed. Unlike the hasty marginal sketches in the fairy-tale narrative, his drawings for the songs are not preliminary artist's notations. Rather, as is evident from the comparable engravings, these pencil drawings represent finished pictorial concepts, right down to the framing devices. For example, the vignette for the first lyric, sketched in pencil at the bottom of page 29 of Maclise's working copy (fig. 5.9), is identical (apart from being reversed) in its compositional details to the cut printed on page 31 of the illustrated *Princess* (fig. 5.8). Responding to the two-verse, ten-line lyric in which a male speaker describes a disagreement and subsequent reconciliation with his wife,[27] Maclise depicts a man embracing a woman. The nineteenth-century figures are positioned beside a small grave and set against a rural backdrop with fields and farm buildings in the distance. Their linked right hands hold a flower plucked from the burial mound. This tender scene is given an added sanctity by being positioned within an arched frame reminiscent of a church window. Through this opening the viewer becomes a privileged witness to a private domestic moment tinged with grief and love.

Figure 5.9 Daniel Maclise, pencil sketch in artist's working copy of *The Princess*. ©*V&A Images/Victoria and Albert Museum, London.*

Tennyson recorded his intense dislike of this engraving in his copy of the illustrated *Princess* with the single, emphatic word, "Wrong!" in the margin beside the first vignette (fig. 5.10).[28] His anger seems directed at both the representation itself and its typographical placement. By dividing the first verse from the second, the intervening cut effectively slices the poem in half, disrupting the balanced measures of its lyrical rhythms, both poetic and temporal. The poem poises inexplicable marital discord—"O we fell out I know not why"—against inexplicable human loss, represented by the early death of "the child / We lost in other years" (31). Incremental repetition and anaphora hold the poem's temporal movement fast to its single moment of assurance—"We kiss'd again with

A MEDLEY. 31

As thro' the land at eve we went,
And pluck'd the ripen'd ears,
We fell out, my wife and I,
O we fell out I know not why,
And kiss'd again with tears.

For when we came where lies the child
We lost in other years,
There above the little grave,
O there above the little grave,
We kiss'd again with tears.

Figure 5.10
Annotated page in Tennyson's hand in the poet's copy of *The Princess* (Moxon, 1866), 31. *Tennyson Research Centre, Lincolnshire County Council, United Kingdom.*

tears"—while locating that moment in a world of change and recurrence represented by diurnal and seasonal cycles. The interpolation of the vignette between these balanced verses effectively skews the lyrical exploration of time, change, and repetition:

As thro' the land at eve we went,
　　And pluck'd the ripen'd ears,
We fell out, my wife and I,
O we fell out I know not why,
　　And kiss'd again with tears.

For when we came where lies the child
　　We lost in other years,
There above the little grave,
O there above the little grave,
　　We kiss'd again with tears.

(*The Princess*, 31)

Tennyson's angry "Wrong!" may express the outrage of a poet who, fully understanding the role of typography and page design in conveying meaning, resented the disruption of lyrical pause with pictorial defacement.[29] Equally, the annotation could reflect his view that the composition itself was "wide of the text," despite the many details that conform to the song's representation of character, setting, and mood. Consistent with the lyric, the couple in the vignette are embracing over a child's grave in a rural evening scene; Maclise could not simultaneously have shown them plucking "the ripen'd ears." The problem highlighted by Tennyson's marginal notation, however, is not simply that of representing a temporal art with a spatial one; it is also one of interpretation. The difference between the poet's visualization and the artist's might be traced to their respective understandings of the lyric's landscape. For Maclise, the text's twilight autumn fields seem merely to provide a poignant rural setting. For Tennyson, they might well have symbolized the couple's advancing age as they approach their own deaths. In this case, of course, Maclise's young couple would be seen by the poet as completely and definitively wrong for his own image of the poem.

Given Tennyson's objection to this vignette, he must have found the publisher's decision to crop it for the binding's decorative design particularly offensive (fig. 5.11). Elaborately blind-stamped and blocked in a gold pattern, the red cloth bindings of *The Princess* surround a central sunk panel containing an embracing couple. As the only representational feature of the cover design, the delicate figures in the cream-colored cameo carry particular interpretive weight. Located

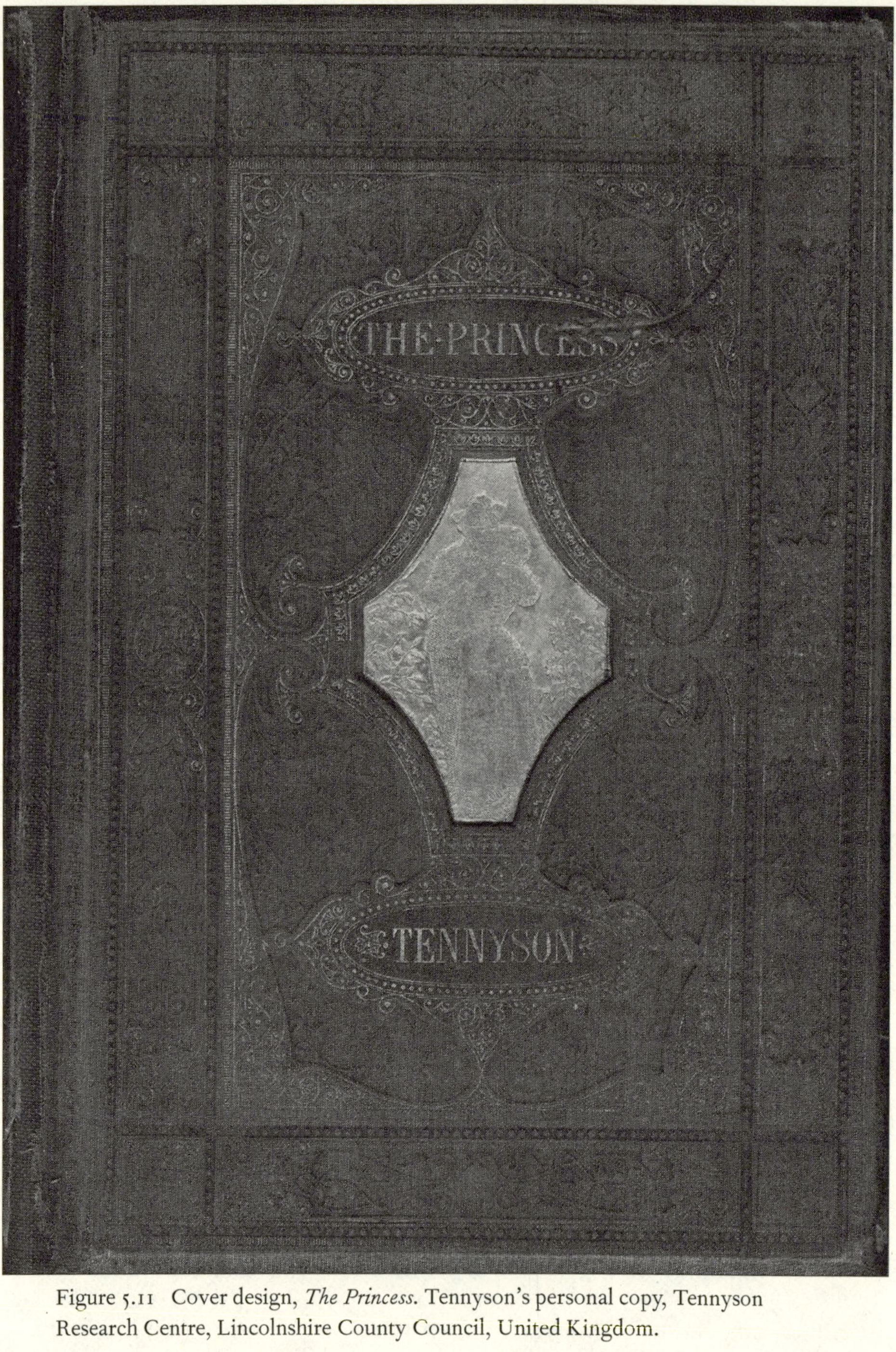


Figure 5.11 Cover design, *The Princess.* Tennyson's personal copy, Tennyson Research Centre, Lincolnshire County Council, United Kingdom.

between the lettering announcing title and author, the cropped close-up taken from the first vignette (fig. 5.8) introduces and comments on the work as a whole. The cut-and-paste constructs new associations for both the individual picture and the narrative poem. First, the cut-out literally severs the picture from its poetic context, as the cropping discards the grave of the original vignette along with the accompanying verses. Second, the paste-in creates a new context for the image by attaching the contemporary figures in the ivory cameo to the medieval princess, whose royal title, doubling as the book's title, is emblazoned in gilt letters above.

The gilt design of the onlay, encased within a decorative cartouche, functions like the locket containing Princess Ida's image, which the Prince wears next to his heart. Enclosing an object of desire both erotic and economic, the locket sets the seal on a contract established by kings of adjoining realms for the future marriage of their infant heirs. Centered on the cover of *The Princess,* the gilt miniature of the embracing couple foretells and celebrates the happy ending of the fairy tale in which the Prince marries the Princess. The positioning of the man bending over a clinging woman who looks up to him while he holds her hand aptly illustrates the closing lines of the medieval narrative:

> . . . Indeed I love thee: come,
> Yield thyself up: my hopes and thine are one:
> Accomplish thou my manhood and thyself;
> Lay thy sweet hands in mine and trust to me.
>
> (*The Princess,* 181)

Spoken in the voice of the Prince, the final lines seem retrospectively haunted by the lyric speaker of the first song, thanks to the associations inscribed on the front cover. The image moves the embracing couple from vignette to cover and from contemporary middle-class moment to imagined medieval past. In its effacing and overshadowing of the woman's features by the man's, the cover image replicates the narrative's focus on the Prince rather than the eponymous Princess, represented textually in the passage quoted above by Ida's silence—a sister silence to that of the first lyric's addressee, the speaker's wife. At the same time, the cover image retains its trace history of the marital discord for which it was designed, and thus proleptically troubles the narrative promise of the fairy tale's "happily ever after" ending. In this way, the cover announces the work's intention to resolve its interrogation of the woman question in favor of the patriarchy even while acknowledging that its tactic will be to evade the real issues.[30] In the physical features of *The Princess*'s cover, an age-old story about the structures of power and representation plays out in the interaction of lyric, narrative, and visual design.

In celebrating the conquest of the Princess by the Prince (that event to which the whole poetic creation moves), the poem reaffirms not only patriarchal hierarchies but also nationalistic ones based on the assumed superiority of Teutonic peoples—the very folk viewed by Victorians as the moral custodians of Christmas as a domestic festival (Connelly, *Christmas,* 11). The Prince comes from an unnamed northern country. His father, the king, seems the epitome of barbarity but also represents (like Sir Walter Vivian in the frame narrative) hearty northern strength and power. The Princess's father, who rules the southern kingdom, is represented as small, weak, and ineffectual, easily "master'd" by his daughter's poetic declamations on the theme of women's rights (23). Maclise's illustrations effectively realize the physical contrasts between the kings

A MEDLEY. 17

Now, while they spake, I saw my father's face
Grow long and troubled like a rising moon,
Inflamed with wrath: he started on his feet,

D

Figure 5.12 Daniel Maclise, illustration of the northern king for Alfred Tennyson, *The Princess* (Moxon 1866), 17.

and insinuate moral ones (figs. 5.12 and 5.13). The images illuminate what the poetic narrative does not wish to acknowledge, that is, that the union of this northern Prince and southern Princess *appears* to represent the harmonizing of the best in each "race" as in each gender, but in fact the medley remains unmixed: men are men and north is best. Moreover, the gendered geographies of north and south support the implicit masculine/feminine hierarchy not only in the embedded narrative of *The Princess* but also in its modern frame. The poem concludes with Sir Walter's oldest son praising "the narrow sea" that keeps the British Isles separate from their dangerous neighbor to the south. With its "[r]evolts, republics, revolutions," France is a country only too "[l]ike our wild Princess" for his Tory taste (182, 183).[31]

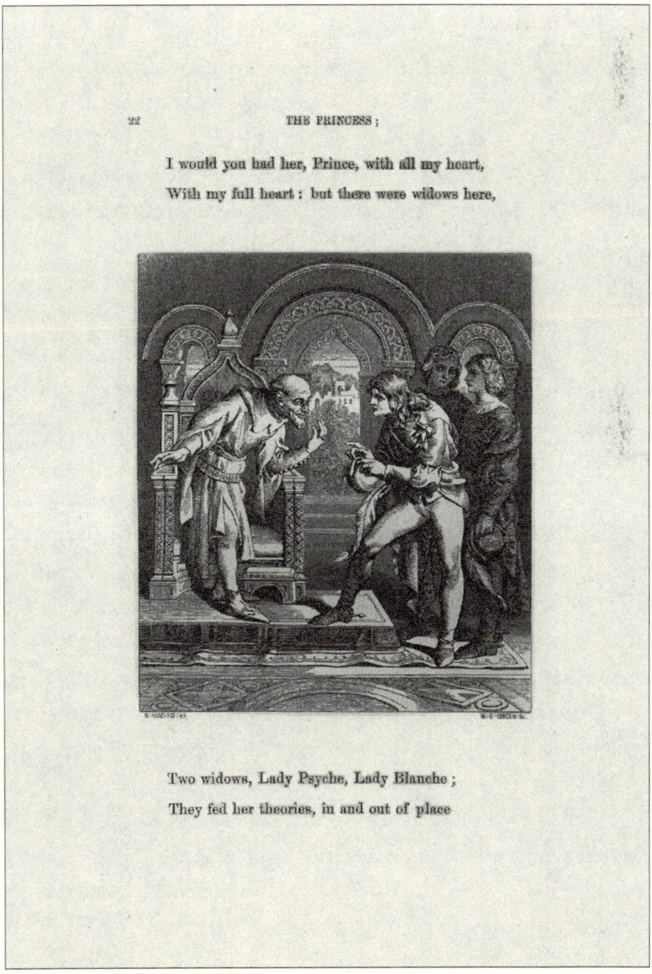

22 THE PRINCESS;

I would you had her, Prince, with all my heart,

With my full heart: but there were widows here,

Two widows, Lady Psyche, Lady Blanche;

They fed her theories, in and out of place

Figure 5.13 Daniel Maclise, illustration of the southern king for Alfred Tennyson, *The Princess* (Moxon, 1866), 22.

*The Princess*'s affirmation of such bourgeois British values as northern and masculine superiority was materially expressed in the work's publication as an illustrated gift book. Like *The Princess*'s characterizations of the northern and southern kings, the press drew on north/south gendered geographies, positioning a masculine and moral Britain against an effeminate and trifling France. While France, in the words of one reviewer, "celebrate[d] its Christmas . . . by sumptuous outlay in bronzes and jewels, and . . . bonbons and chocolate," the moral British gave respectable gifts of books; as "befits the solidity and strength of the manly English character," they were committed to spending "money in a way which shall do us credit" (*SR*, Dec. 19, 1857, 557–58).

In this context, the production of the illustrated *Princess* for the Christmas gift-book market seems as much a foregone conclusion as Princess Ida's marriage to the Prince. In presenting this gift, the giver could feel certain that he was laying out his money in an approved British way as a credit to himself and a tribute to his nation. A popular work by the poet laureate, illustrated by an artist presently engaged in painting frescoes celebrating national greatness on the walls of the Houses of Parliament,[32] *The Princess* could not fail to "be the Christmas favourite" in 1859 and for many Christmases to come (Bohn, "Gossip," 816). In its fairy-tale subject matter purporting to deal with the contemporary woman question but silencing feminist aspirations through the institution of marriage and the biological imperative of maternity, Tennyson's *Princess* was just the thing for ladies, who would also, no doubt, admire Daniel Maclise's romantic illustrations. Indeed, the destined female readers of this gift book could be schooled in their domestic responsibilities by perusing its contents, just as Princess Ida "lessons herself in the conventional woman's roles" by reading a book of poetry while nursing the Prince. As Herbert Tucker points out, the episode is remarkable "for its implication that a poetry anthology is the proper hornbook for Ida to spell her new self by" (*Doom*, 367). Notably, these ideological lessons come from an anthology, not from verses of Ida's own making. Indeed, this poignant scene of reading marks the moment in which the rebellious poet Ida disappears and the disciplined, domestic Ida emerges.

Just as the plot of the poem hinges on Ida's submission to a marriage contract established without her consent, so too does the publication history of the illustrated *Princess* revolve around Tennyson's ultimate yielding to a commissioned gift-book edition he did not approve. In terms of the power politics involved in this publication history, Tennyson's position as author is feminized: like Ida, he loses authority and autonomy through a forced relationship to a representing Other and becomes involved in an economic partnership not of his choosing.

### *Enoch Arden* (1866): Reproducibility and the Image

Victorian visual culture permeates Tennyson's tale of the simple fisherman who returns home after a long absence in which he has been shipwrecked on a desert island to find his wife married to his former rival. At every level, *Enoch Arden* is obsessed with the power of the visual and the status of originals versus copies. The reproduction of the poem as an illustrated picture book within sixteen months of its first publication manifests the text's engagement with Victorian material culture and its visual technologies. The illustrated *Enoch Arden* is not only a book *with* pictures (both metaphorical and literal) but also a book *about* pictures in a society increasingly concerned with reproducibility, substitution, ownership, and visual display.

Given the costs incurred in production, James Bertrand Payne, who managed the Moxon firm in the sixties, needed to market the illustrated edition aggressively. He did so by exploiting the visual culture of the image and the technologies and institutions that drove it. The publisher cultivated consumer desire for *Enoch Arden* as a Christmas gift book by capitalizing on the reproductive potential of the engraving process, the market appeal of pictures to a popular poem by the People's Poet, and the distribution system of the illustrated periodical. One of his first moves was to advertise the book in the *Shilling Magazine*, whose subtitle dubs it an illustrated *Miscellany of Literature, Social Science, Fiction, Poetry, Art, etc.* (Goldman, *Victorian Illustration*, 54). Shortly before the book appeared in the shops, Payne had a three-page extract of the poem, complete with "Three Illustrations to 'Enoch Arden,'" published in the periodical as a "preliminary exhibition of . . . Mr. Hughes's powerful rendering of the very crisis of the story" (*Shilling Magazine*, 434). This preview functioned as an enticement to consumers to purchase a well-known poem on the basis of its visualization by an appealing artist, the Pre-Raphaelite painter Arthur Hughes. As the introductory blurb to the selected illustrations emphasized, the reproduced pictorial sequence represented only "three out of many more, which the purchaser will find when the volume is published" (434). After publication, Payne secured a glowing critical review in the all-important *Athenaeum* (Pritchard, review, 894) and encouraged middlebrow interest by providing the *Illustrated London News* with one of Hughes's illustrations for use in their "Illustrated Books for Christmas" review essay. Thus Payne harnessed the power of the image to promote sales through the mass circulation potential of the periodical press.

After the record-breaking success of *Enoch Arden and Other Poems*, Tennyson seems to have been resigned to a separate illustrated edition of the title poem and offered little resistance when Payne proposed Arthur Hughes (1832–1915) as the artist. The poet's only stipulation was that he should see the artist's drawings before they were sent to the engraver. No doubt he wanted to ensure that the unpleasant surprises of *The Princess* would not be repeated. Perhaps, too, he hoped to have some influence on the artist. Hughes—who was to produce a binding design, twenty-one vignettes, and four full-page illustrations—readily agreed to show his work as it progressed. However, Hughes was not able to keep this promise. Payne gave the artist the *Enoch Arden* contract at the end of August and put great pressure on him to produce his drawings quickly so that the book could be published for Christmas. As Hughes explained apologetically in a letter to the poet dated October 18, 1865, "I had to set to work at once to produce my drawings to feed the engraver one or two at a time as I have been able" (Roberts, *Hughes,* 256). Thus, the demands of the publisher and the market schedule overrode the wishes of both poet and artist.[33]

Although he went on to become a well-known book illustrator (notably, for Christina Rossetti and George Macdonald), Arthur Hughes had not previously been responsible for an entire illustrated book when he received the *Enoch Arden* commission. His principal reputation at the time was based on such appealing paintings as *April Love* (1856), a sentimental study in purple and green of a young woman weeping in an ivy bower while her indifferent lover turns his back to her. Like many other paintings of the period, *April Love*'s meaning was reinforced by an explicit connection to poetry. In its first appearance at the Royal Academy, the painting was accompanied by verses about love's fragility from Tennyson's "Miller's Daughter."[34] Featured at numerous public exhibits, including the Art Treasures of the United Kingdom Exhibition in Manchester, *April Love* quickly became a well-known icon in Victorian visual culture. Engravings of this popular painting were made available as early as the December 1856 issue of the *National Magazine* (Roberts, *Hughes,* 134). At the same time that Hughes's paintings were becoming accessible to middle-class consumers through reproduction technologies, his graphic work was also being disseminated through the mass circulation of print. Hughes contributed to Allingham's *Music Master* (1855) and Willmott's *Poets of the Nineteenth Century* (1857), and his illustrations also appeared among the wood engravings of the *Cornhill, Good Words,* and the *Illustrated London News.*

In his approach to the Tennyson commission, Hughes took advantage of the photographic technology just beginning to be used as an aid to wood engraving. Hughes's *Enoch Arden* seems to have been one of the first major works to transfer an artist's original design onto the engraver's woodblock using photography.[35] Pioneered by the engraver Thomas Bolton, this process involved photographing the artist's pen-and-ink drawings and transferring the negatives to a sensitized woodblock. Perhaps Hughes originally opted for this innovative technology because he was planning to show his designs to the poet in advance. But the technology also had many other advantages for the artist. Photography allowed Hughes to work in a larger scale than the small woodblock, as the negatives could be reduced when they were transferred. He could also draw his images exactly as they were to appear instead of in reverse, because the negative would perform the mirroring process for him. By working on paper, Hughes could preserve the originals, which he could then use at the proofing stage to ensure fidelity.

The use of photographic technology was also advantageous to the publisher. The preservation of the original drawings meant that they could become part of the marketing mechanism used to promote interest in the illustrated *Enoch Arden* as an aesthetic commodity. In the winter season of 1866, just after the book's publication, the Dudley Gallery—"open to all comers," as the *Art Journal* reminded readers in its review—exhibited ten of Arthur Hughes's pen-and-ink illustrations for *Enoch Arden* (Hamerton, "General Exhibition," 71). It is important to remember that the drawings exhibited at the Dudley Gallery belonged to the publisher who commissioned them, not the artist who produced them. Their value to Moxon lay in their public connection to the printed book.

The technologically reproducible image was critical to Moxon's marketing plan. When Payne sent the review copy to the *Illustrated London News*, the newspaper promoted the illustrated *Enoch Arden* as one likely to "be eagerly caught up by those who are casting about for a suitable Christmas present" (Dec. 23, 1865, 608). Payne also sent the stereotype of one of Hughes's pictures—the courting scene of Enoch and Annie—for reproduction in the paper. Cognizant of the new mania for photographically illustrated books that season,[36] the reviewer drew particular attention to the new technology in his reference to "the engravings, which, we believe, have been executed from photographs made on the blocks, direct from the artist's designs" (608). As if this technological assistance in the reproduction process carried with it some of photography's documentary authority, the reviewer went on to ask, "Who does not recognize the pair of lovers, 'Enoch and Annie, sitting hand in hand,' as they were found one autumn evening by Philip Ray, when the young people had made up a nutting party among the hazels, and these two had strayed away from their merry companions to exchange their vows of mutual affection in the green hollow of the wood?" (608). The claims of recognition made here are precisely those typically advanced in favor of photography's power to bring the real world into domestic print culture. In the *Illustrated London News* review, photographic realism combines with the illustrator's art to confirm the authenticity of the reader's experience of poetic narrative. Significantly, as I develop at more length below, the reader/viewer is positioned (like the unseen Philip Ray) as a voyeur whose activity makes the scene seen.

A brief synopsis of the narrative will help establish how the technological, bibliographic, and linguistic codes work together in *Enoch Arden.*[37] As with all of Tennyson's domestic idylls, the poem narrates a series of pictures, or tableaux. The story opens with three children playing on the beach. Annie Lee, "the prettiest little damsel in the port," takes turns being wife to the orphan Enoch Arden, "a rough sailor's lad," and Philip Ray, the well-off "miller's only son" (3), but she clearly likes Enoch best. This little set piece prefigures the story to come in which Annie becomes wife to each man in turn while both are alive. Annie and Enoch grow up, marry, and have children. Later, when Enoch fails to return from a voyage to repair the family's failing fortunes by trading in the Orient, Annie gives way to Philip's persistent courtship and marries him, persuaded of Enoch's death by a dream she has of him sitting under a palm tree. She has been cruelly deceived, however. What Annie takes to be a picture of paradise turns out to be a vision of Enoch shipwrecked on a tropical island. The castaway is eventually rescued and returns to the village after many years, only to find "Philip, the slighted suitor of old times" in his place on the hearth, with Enoch's erstwhile wife and children gathered around him and Philip's "babe across his knees" (66). Although heartbroken, Enoch determines not to "shatter all the happiness of the hearth" (69) by identifying himself (and incidentally exposing Annie's bigamy and the baby's illegitimacy). He lives on in the village, where he remains strangely unrecognized, revealing his identity only on his deathbed to his landlady, Miriam Lane. His last words, "A sail! A sail! / I am saved," imply that the final rescue occurs only when he has crossed the bar. Despite the spiritual resonance of this imagery, however, the poem ends on a notoriously material note:

> So past the strong heroic soul away.
> And when they buried him the little port
> Had seldom seen a costlier funeral.
>
> (*Enoch Arden*, 81)

Like the conspicuously expensive funeral that has occasioned much criticism—from Victorian critics to contemporary ones—the purpose of the illustrated *Enoch Arden* was to be *seen.* The gift book's raison d'être lay precisely in its material value as a ritual object (a seasonal gift) meant for display. Consequently, the bibliographic format of the illustrated *Enoch Arden* is a critical point of entry for understanding the poem in the context of its readership. In his cover design, Hughes gives each of Annie's suitors his own side of the story, reifying the poem's tensions between the material and the immaterial as they are expressed in the moral question at the heart of the story's love triangle. In contemporary reviews of the poem, more than one critic complained that Tennyson had presented Annie's bigamy and infidelity without moral judgment and had been guilty, too, of insufficient discrimination: both Enoch and Philip are presented as good men worthy of a good woman's love. Arthur Hughes's decorated binding design, called by Eric de Maré "one of the best of Victorian book covers" (*Woodblock,* 130), brings these issues forward to the reader's attention before the first page is turned.

Representing Enoch's love on the front cover and Philip's on the back (figs. 5.14 and 5.15), the binding physically joins and equates their individual worth but simultaneously acknowledges their sequential relationship, allowing Enoch's story to take precedence. The two designs, stamped in gold on colored cloth boards, have a pleasing symmetry, but the changes in the symbolic details of the recto and verso initiate a comparison and intrude a judgment on this male contest to possess (and, literally, to cover) a feminine body. In Victorian bibliographic discourse, the gift book was doubly feminized, first as an object to be presented to women, and second in terms of the ornamental makeup that constituted its physical desirability. From its "robustly male-reader position," the *Saturday Review* consistently recognized that "the 'get-up of the book' feminises" it (Brake, *Print,* 165). As the magazine's critic observed, "a reviewer who wants to write about [gift books] has only to take down his Dibdin, and ring the changes on 'creamy' paper and 'velvetty expanse' of type and the other almost erotic phrases" that made the gift book, like the body of the sexualized woman, an object of desire (*SR,* Nov. 24, 1866, 653).

On the front cover, Hughes designed a decorative gilt border made up of a ship's cable and anchor chain with scallop shells holding the corners (fig. 5.14). Inside this border, intersecting diagonal lines create a net, with many fishes caught in its meshes. The design refers, of course, to Enoch's occupation as a fisherman as well as to his sea voyage to the East. But the iconographic details of the design suggest something more. Centered on the meshes, four circular medallions with ships' bells form a cruciform shape. A dangling, broken rope calls attention to the severance of the ties that bind Enoch and Annie. In the middle of this configuration, positioned over the title (which is also, of course, the hero's name), is a ship's anchor. Long a symbol of steadfastness, the anchor here may represent Enoch's faithfulness while at the same time ironically alluding to the infidelity of the woman who failed to wait for him because she misread

Figure 5.14 Arthur Hughes, front cover design for Alfred Tennyson, *Enoch Arden* (Moxon, 1866).

Figure 5.15 Arthur Hughes, back cover design for Alfred Tennyson, *Enoch Arden* (Moxon, 1866).

a spiritual sign. Thus the cover presents, in a very material way, the poem's concerns with seeing and interpretation as well as with ownership and possession.

The back cover design, representing Philip's side of the love triangle, repeats the general composition of the front cover while introducing new symbolic details that substitute harvest imagery for nautical (fig. 5.15). The outside border is formed by stalks of wheat, alluding to Philip's occupation as a miller. Inside the border, the diagonal lines form leafy stems rather than the meshes of a fishing net, suggesting something more fruitful and less destructive. Moreover, instead of fish trapped *behind* a net, butterflies soar *over* the leafy stems. They seem to represent freedom and beauty in the midst of fecundity and abundance, implying a positive judgment on Annie's choice of life over death, comfort over poverty, Philip over Enoch. The central details of the design complicate this positive interpretation, however. As on the front cover, a cruciform shape is created by four circular medallions containing bells; at the center, instead of an anchor, are the blades of a windmill. Once again, this central symbol seems to hold two possible meanings, one moral and one material, one applied to the man and one to the woman. If we associate the windmill with Philip, it appears to be an emblem of power and production commenting on his wealth and social stature. If we associate it with Annie, however, the turning blades seem to allude to her fickleness, her turning from Enoch to Philip.

Inside the decorated covers, the alternation of vignettes, headpieces, tailpieces, and full-page illustrations echoes the verses' patterns of repetition. As Patrick Scott observes, Hughes makes the most of the Enoch/Philip equation by using "similar compositions to bring out the parallelism of incident in Tennyson's poem; Philip, after he has seen Enoch and Annie in the wood and Enoch, after he sees Philip and Annie together in their home, are both shown prostrate with shock" (*Tennyson,* 19) (figs. 5.16 and 5.17). Each vignette records a hidden viewer's response to a private scene in which the participants are unaware that they are on display.

The first of these occurs after Philip sees "Enoch and Annie, sitting hand-in-hand" (7) in a hollow in the wood at the moment they plight their troth. Philip "read[s] his doom" in the lovers' "eyes and faces" and in their kiss (8) and slips away to grieve privately at his evident loss of the woman he loves (fig. 5.16). Significantly, his pain is protected from sight; he has "his dark hour unseen" (9). Similarly, when Enoch—"the dead man come to life"—sees "His wife his wife no more" (67) through the windows of Philip's house, he creeps out to the waste, where he falls prostrate, determined not to be seen or known by Annie and his family (fig. 5.17). Like Philip, he seems to be determined to protect Annie's happiness by giving way to the reigning rival. However, as Anne

8 ENOCH ARDEN.

His large gray eyes and weather-beaten face
All-kindled by a still and sacred fire,
That burn'd as on an altar. Philip look'd,
And in their eyes and faces read his doom;
Then, as their faces drew together, groan'd,
And slipt aside, and like a wounded life
Crept down into the hollows of the wood;

Figure 5.16 Arthur Hughes, illustration of Philip for Alfred Tennyson, *Enoch Arden* (Moxon, 1866), 8.

70 ENOCH ARDEN.

His fingers into the wet earth, and pray'd.

'Too hard to bear! why did they take me thence?
O God Almighty, blessed Saviour, Thou
That did'st uphold me on my lonely isle,
Uphold me, Father, in my loneliness

Figure 5.17 Arthur Hughes, illustration of Enoch for Alfred Tennyson, *Enoch Arden* (Moxon, 1866), 70.

Humpherys comments, Annie has no "dark hour unseen" ("Silence," 338). Rather, her private experiences and emotional responses remain largely untold but always—as the two scenes described here demonstrate—on public display, always available for voyeuristic consumption. The illustrations materialize the narrative's indifference to Annie except as a body to be owned and a text to be viewed, interpreted, and possessed.

Poems themselves are visual objects; their spatial display is part of their communication to readers. Humpherys astutely notes the resonance in the typographic gap between Enoch's last words, "I am saved," and the narrative's terse four-line conclusion describing his funeral. Humpherys comments that Enoch's putative heroism "is achieved through the denial of Annie's pain," which the poem "marks . . . with the silence of a blank space" (340). In the illustrated edition of *Enoch Arden*, the distribution of type on the page is a particularly important material signifier. By means of typography and layout, the 911 lines of verse are stretched to eighty-one printed pages, making the slim volume valuable for its quality of paper, type, illustrations, and binding rather than weightiness of contents. The poem's length is extended by wide margins, double-spaced lines, and generous blanks between verse paragraphs as well as by the introduction of the twenty-one vignettes and four full-page illustrations.

The visual experience of the poem on the page shapes the readings that *Enoch Arden* makes available. Typography and page design reinforce the text's thematics of repetition with difference by emphasizing the material and the realizable, particularly at moments in which sight contends with sound. The full-page illustrations, for instance, appear with only a single line islanded below the image, thus removing the poetic line temporarily from narrative progression by requiring it to serve simultaneously as a pictorial caption. Functioning as a visual double to Enoch's courting of Annie (fig. 5.18), the full-page illustration of Philip proposing to Annie many years later (fig. 5.19) replays the scene of youthful innocence and hope as one of tired experience. The caption at the bottom of the page—"Should still be living; well then—let me speak"—implies that the power of persuasion lies in the human voice (37). However, the sheer size of the image positioned over this line makes visible the text's argument that "things seen are mightier than things heard" (68), a view reinforced by Annie's refusal to accept Philip's proposal until she has a vision of Enoch's death. Significantly, Hughes's misty illustration of her dream of Enoch sitting under a palm tree is the next picture to appear in the sequence (44).[38] Annie's misreading of this dream underscores her lack of power throughout the narrative, a weakness described in the text and reified in the illustrations as her inability to see. In this regard, it is significant that in both courting scenes, Arthur Hughes makes

Figure 5.18 Arthur Hughes, illustration of Enoch and Annie for Alfred Tennyson, *Enoch Arden* (Moxon, 1866), 7.

Figure 5.19 Arthur Hughes, illustration of Philip and Annie for Alfred Tennyson, *Enoch Arden* (Moxon, 1866), 37.

Annie the object of the gaze who does not look herself; her eyes are always averted or downcast. In the first scene, she is the object of the gaze of Enoch, who holds her hand, and of Philip, who watches the couple unseen, as well as of the reader/viewer, who holds the book and contemplates the page. In the second scene, Philip looks at Annie while the reader/viewer takes in the pair's private moment for personal pleasure.

While the full-page illustration with a single line of text brings the narrative to a halt by focusing the reader's attention on the image, the inset pictures, framed by lines of text above and below, interrupt the reading experience in even more dramatic ways. The most significant of these scenes of typographic disruption occurs at the poem's climactic moment of personal and domestic crisis, occasioned by Enoch's shock at seeing that Annie is now Philip's wife (fig. 5.20). This crucial tableau is inserted between two pairs of separated blank-verse lines. Printed above the inset illustration are the following lines: "And him, that other, reigning in his place / Lord of his rights and of his children's love,—" (68). Printed below the inset picture, the following truncated lines appear:

> Then he, tho' Miriam Lane had told him all,
> Because things seen are mightier than things heard,—

The sentence hangs in the air, awaiting completion by the page turn: "Stagger'd and shook . . . " (69). The typographic isolation of "Because things seen are mightier than things heard" physically separates it from the clause on the recto to which it is syntactically and semantically attached, thus reinforcing the overpowering significance of this individual line in the illustrated version of the poem. As the inset picture that disrupts the narrative makes clear, the illustrated *Enoch Arden* is all *about* the power of things seen over things heard—the power of the visual and the material over the verbal and immaterial.

The puff piece promoting the gift book in the *Shilling Magazine* describes this scene as representing "Mr. Hughes's powerful rendering of the very crisis of the story" ("Three Illustrations," 434). This crisis does not occur when Enoch hears of Annie's remarriage from his landlady, Miriam Lane, but rather when he looks through the window of his family's new home to see them gathered around the hearth with "that other, reigning in his place." In other words, the crisis is brought on when the unseen, but understood, becomes a visualized tableau—a picture whose poignancy is articulated (as in photographic discourse) as repetition with loss, presence with absence. Enoch, the "original" father and "lord" of the wife and children, is shut out of the picture that copies his former experience, his status relegated to that of spectator. His presence as voyeur

And him, that other, reigning in his place,
Lord of his rights and of his children's love,—

Then he, tho' Miriam Lane had told him all,
Because things seen are mightier than things heard,

Figure 5.20 Arthur Hughes, illustration of the Ray family for Alfred Tennyson, *Enoch Arden* (Moxon, 1866), 68.

highlights his absence from the scene he used to inhabit. Meanwhile, the presence of "that other," Philip, seated in his place by the hearth and enjoying the pleasures of the family reconstituted as Rays rather than Ardens, marks Enoch's loss by repeating the familiar domestic configuration under new ownership.

As Gerhard Joseph suggests, the described scene is a "highly stylized group pose, reminiscent of the Victorian family tintype" that one might find in middle-class homes throughout the nation (*Tennyson*, 69). Joseph rightly remarks that Enoch reads the picture (framed by the window through which he is viewing, which serves in this case almost like a camera's scopic lens) from right to left of the hearth, which is "the picture's focal point" (69):

> And on the right hand of the hearth he saw
> Philip, the slighted suitor of old times,
> Stout, rosy, with his babe across his knees;
> And o'er her second father stoopt a girl,
> A later but a loftier Annie Lee,
> Fair-hair'd and tall, and from her lifted hand
> Dangled a length of ribbon and a ring
> To tempt the babe, who rear'd his creasy arms,
> Caught at and ever miss'd it, and they laugh'd:
> And on the left hand of the hearth he saw
> The mother glancing often toward her babe,
> But turning now and then to speak with him,
> Her son, who stood beside her tall and strong,
> And saying that which pleased him, for he smiled.
>
> (*Enoch Arden*, 66–67)

Tennyson's description is so specific, he is virtually giving stage directions to his prospective illustrator for the correct composition of this tableau, lending credence to Scott's thesis that the sequence of pictorial set-pieces in *Enoch Arden* was occasioned by Tennyson's expectation of a forthcoming illustrated edition (*Tennyson*, 19). In his visualization of this scene, Arthur Hughes is careful to conform to Tennyson's instructions, with one notable difference. Philip is seated on the right of the fire and Annie on the left—not for the reader/viewer but for Enoch, who must be imagined as an invisible presence on the other side of the darkened window. Hughes locates the viewer not where the poet places him, in the position of Enoch looking through the window at the family group seated before the fire, but in the position of the invisible hearth, so that all the poet's specifications as to right and left are reversed. The unseen hearth is not only the picture's focal point but also the place from which the viewer surveys the scene. The viewer thus occupies a privileged position, ideologically central to the representation of Victorian middle-class domestic values.

Since the viewer is also the owner of the scene in its bibliographic form, the picture's function is linked to Victorian commodity culture in important ways. As a spectacle of middle-class comfort, the picture produces and reflects a modern consumerism "characterized by the consumption of luxuries, either superfluous goods or sensuous pleasures" (Loeb, *Consuming Angels*, 4). The middle-class consumer who holds the book in her hand sees reflected in it a scene that confirms and validates her own middle-class aspirations. The room that provides the backdrop for this carefully arranged family group has paneled walls, curtained and diamond-paned windows, heavy furniture, a grandfather clock, and a harp—the latter an especially important marker of gentility as an effect of luxury and sensuous pleasure. The comfort of class is confirmed by the figures occupying this domestic space. The dresses worn by Annie and her daughter are made of richly patterned fabric. The father and the stepson, who frame and partially block the window that represents the unseen body of the impoverished Enoch, are stalwart and respectable in both attitude and attire.

The reader/viewer cannot see from the position of Enoch because the picture deliberately excludes his seeing position, making it only an imagined viewpoint on the periphery of a scene that stolidly celebrates middle-class materialism. Seen from the perspective of the domestic hearth, this room has no room for another father. Although it contains the same dramatic personae that occupied Enoch's original hearth—father, mother, daughter, son, baby—both infant and father are substitutes for former figures. Like a photograph, the picture that Enoch sees and the reader/viewer witnesses exists on the threshold of presence and absence, visibility and invisibility, record and change. Like a photograph, the picture substitutes material repetition for a lost and unrecoverable original experience.

The image that immediately follows (also reproduced in the *Shilling Magazine* advertisement) shows Enoch's response to this scene of domestic repetition that excludes by replacing him (fig. 5.17). Lying face down on the ground outside Philip's comfortable home, with the windmill that is the source of that prosperity located directly above Enoch's head, the homeless man digs his "fingers into the wet earth and pray[s]" for the strength never to reveal his presence to Annie and her family, because to do so would be to "shatter all the happiness of the hearth" (70, 69). Domesticity, as Bob Watts comments, "is an exclusionary force, defining itself against a marginalized construct of what is not family, not domestic" ("Slow Prudence," 501). Enoch represents the working class that must be marginalized in favor of the ascending middle class, represented by the wealthy Philip Ray (ibid., 501–2). The back cover design of the expensive gift edition, with its windmill blades, stalks of wheat, and free-flying butterflies positively representing Philip, literally closes the book with the affirmation that wealth is the material sign of moral worth.

Image, text, and book invite the reader to receive Enoch's self-silencing as an appropriate and heroic sacrifice, necessary to keep the home fires burning cheerfully without disrupting the material comforts of the domestic hearth. The logic of the visual/verbal sequence is to confirm the desires of a consumer society for which the acquisition and accumulation of commodities represented increased social status and cultural validation. At the same time, the beautifully bound book offered the consumer a powerful pleasure denied the eponymous hero: the pleasure of having, holding, and displaying an attractive and prized possession. Produced at the height of the golden age of illustration and the peak of the laureate's fame, the illustrated *Enoch Arden* comments on and participates in a material culture whose technologies and visual media repeatedly enacted the poem's central statement that "things seen are mightier than things heard."

## *The Window* (1871): Music, Image, Text

Tennyson's next major collaborative undertaking, *The Window; or, The Songs of the Wrens,* had the potential to become a truly remarkable gift book, combining the arts of poetry, painting, and music from first-rank Victorian artists. This composite of things seen and heard originated in an overture from a musical impresario to a publisher. In early October 1866, George Grove, editor of *Macmillan's Magazine,* secretary of the Crystal Palace, and a friend of both Tennyson's and Arthur Sullivan's, wrote Payne to propose that Tennyson write a song-cycle, or *Liederkreis,* a musical mode popular in Germany but unknown in England.[39] Helpfully sending the poet Heine's *Lieder* because they were "often used by the German musicians to set to music," and particularly invoking Schumann's settings of Songs I–VIII, Grove set the stage for what he hoped would be a historic collaboration (quoted in H. Tennyson, *Memoir,* 2:40).

Tennyson and Sullivan were to be the English Heine and Schumann, introducing a new musical form of linked songs narrating a romantic story. Scores and lyrics would be published in gift-book form for the Christmas market, bringing popular music and poetic prestige together. For added appeal, the volume was to be enhanced with twelve full-page illustrations by John Everett Millais, who was, like Grove, a friend of both Sullivan's and Tennyson's. As an illustrated album of songs for pianist and singer, the gift book would bring, Sullivan hoped, "the three sister Arts, poetry, painting, and music," into middle-class parlors (quoted in Stuart-Wortley, "Millais," 421). In turn, these domestic entertainments would reinforce the public's taste for the Crystal Palace afternoon concerts at Sydenham, where the young Sullivan was beginning to make his name (Jacobs, *Sullivan,* 1, 58). Finally, a gift book that brought together the united strengths of Tennyson, Millais, and Sullivan would also have significant celebrity appeal.

Payne immediately saw the commercial possibilities of the album as a Christmas book and encouraged the poet to receive Grove's proposal graciously. Surprisingly, Tennyson did so, inviting Grove and Sullivan to Farringford to discuss the collaboration within weeks of receiving the initial letter.[40] In the meantime, he read Heine's poetry to Emily and tried his hand at some lyrics.[41] Although not a man to be dictated to in subject or structure, Tennyson was receptive to Grove's hint that "[i]f the idea of the first song could be brought back again in the last it would help the composer very much, for nothing is so charming in music as to wind off a composition in that way" (quoted in H. Tennyson, *Memoir,* 2:40). Apparently intrigued by the possibilities of the cycle as a narrative composed of individual but linked lyrics, Tennyson did indeed help Sullivan as Grove suggested by arranging his twelve songs around the central motif of the window. This liminal space, both barrier and opening, symbolizes the threshold experience of courting as the lover woos his beloved through seasons of hope, uncertainty, promise, and fulfillment, mapped onto the months of the year.

At first, Tennyson contributed enthusiastically to the developing plans for the collaborative work. In the months leading up to Christmas 1866, Tennyson made several trips to Sullivan's house in Claverton Terrace, Pimlico, to discuss the project. Francis Byng, vicar of the church where Sullivan was then organist, recorded one such occasion: "I was present, by [Sullivan's] Invitation, at a Dinner when he, Tennyson and Millais dined together at his house. Tennyson read The Window—Song of the Wren—Millais gave his notions of the Illustrations suitable—Sullivan suggesting the Music—An unique pleasure and privilege—. . . . Poetry—Music and Art" (quoted in Young, *Sullivan,* 53).

Byng's pleasure and privilege were indeed unique, as the composite work combining poetry, music, and art failed to materialize. After his initial enthusiasm, Tennyson developed cold feet; by February 1867, he was already worrying, according to Sullivan, that the songs were "too light" and would "damage his reputation." Sullivan's prediction that "there will be a great difficulty in getting [the songs] from him" proved correct (Lawrence, *Sullivan,* 72), though the publisher appeared to have no inkling that his planned Christmas publication was in jeopardy. In August of that year, Payne wrote Sullivan to say that Tennyson had finished the lyrics. He then inquired how long Sullivan would need to compose the music and wondered whether Millais would have the twelve illustrations ready in time (Allen, *Sullivan,* 60).

Payne's optimism was ill founded. In actual fact, it was three long years before Sullivan received the songs, due in part to Tennyson's delaying tactics and in part to the poet's increasingly strained relationship with his publisher. In the meantime, Tennyson continued to test the effect of his unset lyrics, reading the songs at friendly gatherings and having them privately printed by Sir Ivor Guest at his Canford Press (H. Tennyson, *Memoir,* 2:44, 48). Then in January 1869 Tennyson left Moxon for Alexander Strahan, an event that had unexpected consequences for the publishing history of *The Window.* The following fall, Tennyson discovered that Payne had published, without his permission, the *Concordance to the Entire Works of Tennyson* and included the privately printed version of *The Window* in it—"another breach of trust on Mr. Payne's part," according to the increasingly irate Tennyson (quoted in E. Tennyson, *Letters,* 242n). A poorly printed facsimile edition of *The Window* appeared on the heels of the *Concordance,* and by the following spring, pirated American copies were selling in Glasgow bookshops.[42] Writing to Tennyson about an unauthorized copy he had obtained for thirty shillings, Frederick Locker advised his friend to "write a line to Sir Ivor Guest and to Millais and Sullivan. I think it is as well that [*The Window*] should now be published" (A. Tennyson, *Letters,* 2:535). When Sullivan and Strahan descended upon Tennyson in the fall of 1870 to urge publication, Tennyson reluctantly agreed (E. Tennyson, *Journal,* 312).

After four years it was too late, however, for the twelve songs to be illustrated by Millais. The artist wrote Sullivan to say that it was impossible for him to contribute to the gift book: "I am very sorry, . . . as of course I should have liked to have carried out the original idea. You must remember that I did keep the drawings for *months* before they were parted with. One line from him (Tennyson) at the time would have saved the trouble" (quoted in Sullivan and Flower, *Sullivan,* 84). The details of these drawings—their number and subjects—remain unclear. Sullivan could recall only one of Millais' original illustrations: "a lovely drawing of a girl at the window, birds flying around and 'vine and eglantine' trailing about it" (quoted in Stuart-Wortley, "Millais," 421).[43]

Unwilling to relinquish the commercial potential of a Christmas gift book combining music, image, and text, Strahan commissioned Arthur Hughes to illustrate the twelve songs. However, in another attempt to jettison the project—he had already tried to buy Sullivan out with an offer of £500—Tennyson declared that "no one but Millais shall illustrate" (*Letters,* 2:556; Young, *Sullivan,* 46). By that time, Hughes had already completed four pen-and-ink drawings for the work—these were considered by the artist and many subsequent critics to be among the best of his career. But the excellence of the artwork made no difference to the poet. Hughes explained to a friend, "The Tennyson subject fell through for some reasons I don't understand between the poet & publisher, and the poem is brought out without illustrations. . . . They seem to be using the four I had sent in in 'Good Words,' but as they were made a much larger size, they calmly take off about an inch and a half all round them to fit the magazine" (Roberts, *Hughes,* 261).[44]

Strahan published two songs with Sullivan's musical scores, Tennyson's lyrics, and Hughes's full-page illustrations as promotional pieces in the Christmas number of his periodical, *Good Words.* Footnotes identified them as from *The Window,* "just published by Strahan & Co," despite the fact that the illustrations were not, of course, in the book at all (Tennyson, "Mist," 113; and "Where," 32). In publishing Hughes's illustrations with these excerpts, Strahan was borrowing Payne's image-marketing technique for *Enoch Arden.* In an astute variation of Payne's method, Strahan did not display the crisis of the story, only the uncertainty leading up to it—a strategy no doubt calculated to generate curiosity about how the song sequence would unfold. Indeed, one of the images Strahan selected for *Good Words*—that for "And I may die but the grass will grow" (Tennyson, "Mist," 113) (fig. 5.21)—seems designed to encourage readers to imagine a tragic and sentimental end akin to that in *Enoch Arden.* Hughes's illustration for this song depicts the lover cast down upon the ground and refers interpictorially to his earlier illustration of the despairing Enoch Arden after seeing his wife married to another (see fig. 5.17).

Provoking curiosity is a good marketing strategy in the book trade. In the promotional piece in *Good Words,* as an enticement to purchase the gift book, Strahan deliberately left readers uncertain about how the love story of *The Window* would end. He effected this uncertainty by severing Hughes's illustration for Tennyson's "Sun comes, moon comes, time slips away"—the song in which the happy lovers set the wedding day (Tennyson, *Window,* No. X)—from the puff piece for *The Window* in *Good Words* (fig. 5.22). Rather than associating this image with Tennyson's lyrics and Sullivan's music, Strahan placed it 150 pages later in the magazine, accompanied by "The Dial," a mournful poem of lost love by F. W. Simmons. Despite this new association, its original context as an illustration made for *The Window* is clear. Hughes's principal visual motif, the sundial, aptly represents the theme of Tennyson's song, in which the lover pleads with the beloved to "fix a day" (Tennyson, *Window,* No. X). Like the lover, the sundial can measure only a day's worth of time, not a year's, a month's, or a week's. Although well suited to the song cycle and the pictorial narrative Hughes planned to accompany it, "The Dial" (as the picture was titled in *Good*

Figure 5.21 Arthur Hughes, "And I may die . . . ," illustration for Alfred Tennyson, "The Mist and the Rain," in *Good Words* 12 (1871): facing page 113.

*Words*) had little resonance with Simmons's accompanying poem in the periodical. This mismatch is a timely reminder that the magazine editor's role in layout, sequence, adjacency, and association could, and often did, insinuate visual/verbal relationships that were simply marriages of convenience. The hermeneutic relations of picture and poem are matters determined by destination rather than origin. They are in the hands of readers.[45]

Despite the publisher's efforts to promote *The Window*, the book was not a success, its failure to realize a harmonious union of the three sister arts spelled out for all to read in its disjunctive physical features. Every detail of paratextual matter expressed the work's brokenness. The gift book appeared with decorative devices

Figure 5.22 Arthur Hughes, "The Dial," in *Good Words* 12 (1871): 183.

but without the full-page illustrations that seemed to be promised by the puff piece in *Good Words.* The cover announced "Music by Arthur Sullivan" at the top of the decorative panel and "Songs by Alfred Tennyson" at the bottom, a listing that seemed to make the poet subservient to the musician. The title emblazoned in gilt between the collaborators' names—*The Window, or the Loves of the Wrens*—did not line up with the one printed in red on the title page—*The Window, or The Songs of the Wrens.* But whether assigned loves or songs, the wrens' role in the ensuing cycle remains opaque. All this confusion is reinforced by an ungracious preface by Tennyson drawing attention to his regret "that his four-year-old puppet should have to dance at all" to Sullivan's tune. The puppet image is a telling one, suggesting the poet's helplessness in the face of publisher string-pulling.

The ordering of the twelve songs suggests further rivalry between the two supposed collaborators. Perhaps to indicate priority of prestige, Tennyson's lyrics were published as separate poems on the verso of each double-page opening, facing the musical score, which also included the lyrics printed interlinearly. However, because Tennyson had continued to revise after the version sent to Sullivan, the words printed on the verso did not always agree with those printed under the score on the recto. The implied correction of the composer by the poet was highlighted by the presence of errata slips in the volume and by footnotes on the contents page. A note to "The Letter" indicated that "[t]he Music was composed to an earlier version of this song" (published in *Good Words* under the title "Where Is Another Sweet as My Sweet?").[46]

Although the poetic sequence is intact, the song cycle is disrupted. Undermining the use-value of the book for musical performance, only eleven of the twelve songs have musical settings. The missing melody and accompaniment are signaled on the contents page with the out-of-sequence number IXB, "Ay" ("Be merry, all birds to-day"), and a footnote stating, "This Song has not been set to Music." Sullivan appears to have used the privately printed Canford Press version of *The Window,* which did not include "Be merry, all birds, to-day," as his copy-text. Before going to press, Tennyson apparently substituted this poem for "Take My Love," a song not in the Strahan edition but included in the Canford trial book.[47] Because the composer did not have sufficient time to provide a setting for the new lyrics, a musical lacuna resulted. The cycle of songs was broken, leaving the narrative incomplete and the modulations unharmonious.[48]

Tennyson's anxiety that his reputation might be impaired by the publication of verses that were "nothing in themselves and only will become something when . . . set" to music proved well founded (*Letters,* 2:469). A Christmas Eve review of *The Window; or, The Songs of the Wren* [*sic*] voiced the following dismissive view of *The Window* in particular and gift-book editions in general:

"We almost hesitate at giving to our Poet Laureate a mere paragraph in our notice of Christmas Books, but after all, if our king of poets condescends to mingle among his subjects, he cannot fairly complain of unceremonious treatment" (*SR*, Dec. 24, 1870, 813).

Not surprisingly, *The Window* was the last in the series of Tennyson's single poems produced as sumptuous Christmas gift books. Conceived at the height of the sixties, *The Window* might have been a unique collaborative work by three of the period's principal artists in music, painting, and poetry. Instead, it was published in a final skirmish over publishing rights with Moxon and with Tennyson's grudging compliance with his promise to Sullivan and his obligations to Strahan. After the broken *Window* of 1871, the next time the "king of poets" chose to mingle with his subjects would be in an inexpensive "People's Edition," not a lavish gift book. And it would be in a venture in which he could assume as much authority and control as the conditions of corporate authorship in commercial publishing allowed.

### *Idylls of the King* and the Cabinet Edition: Two Directions for Poetry and Pictures

In late 1866, while Tennyson was drafting his songs for *The Window* and meeting with Millais and Sullivan to discuss ideas for the collaborative work, Moxon was working with French artist Gustave Doré on the first of four illustrated volumes of *Idylls of the King*. These lavish Christmas books, which came out between 1866 and 1868, represent the final works in the publisher's illustrated series of the laureate's poetry, launched in 1857 with *Poems*. Like Julia Margaret Cameron's later album of photographs, *Illustrations to Tennyson's "Idylls of the King"* (1875), the Doré *Idylls* aspires to the "fine art" pole in combining pictures and poetry. In contrast, the illustrated Cabinet Edition of Tennyson's *Works* aims squarely at the popular in both bibliographic format and the mixed indexical and iconic uses of the image. Whether for the upper- or lower-income band of the broad middle classes, however, the separate directions for poetry and pictures are displayed in the physical features of both works. What the Doré *Idylls* and the Cabinet Edition share is their modern deployment of the image as a marketing tool and a means of connecting a poet with a mass readership. Their use of various methods of mechanical reproduction—steel engraving, wood engraving, mechanical ruling, Woodbury mechanical process, autotype, and photography—also mark the wane of the wood-engraved book's dominance.

In the Christmas book reviews of 1865—the year *Enoch Arden* was published—the greatest excitement and interest were generated by a new species of gift book to hit the market: the volume illustrated by photographs. Emerging first in conjunction with the developing tourist industry and the travel literature it produced, the photographically illustrated book soon hitched its ascending star to the established tradition of the poetic gift book (Wood, *Shock*, 173, 185–95). The *Westminster Review*—never an enthusiastic proponent of the picture book—hailed Longfellow's *Hyperion*, illustrated with "twenty-four photographs taken in Switzerland, [in] the Tyrol, and on the Rhine," as "*the* Gift-book of the season," a volume that "deserve[s] the good word of those who give and receive a present for the drawing-room table" (331). The novelty of sun-pictures that combined the appeal of the real with the excitement of the technologically advanced and the geographically exotic provoked some excitement in the periodical press. Within two years, the *Saturday Review* used its annual Christmas book column to question whether the traditional genre with wood-engraved (or xylographic) illustrations might have played itself out. "If there is any marked characteristic of this year's literary gift-books," the *Review*'s critic observed, "it is the substitution of photography for xylography" (Dec. 15, 1866, 743).

Despite this enthusiasm for photographically illustrated books, the technology for reproducing photographs with letterpress would not be developed until the 1880s, when photorelief processes were introduced (Beegan, *Mass Image*, 75–77). Until the late 1860s, individual photographs had to be pasted onto separate pages, so photographically illustrated books were an expensive novelty available only in limited editions (C. Armstrong, *Scenes*, 423–24). Moreover, the wet collodion process used at this time resulted in considerable fading of photographic illustrations; as Helmut Gernsheim points out, "while the purchaser could judge the aesthetic value of . . . a photographically produced book, he had no means of proving its durability" (*Photography*, 259). In 1869, Walter B. Woodbury perfected a method of mechanically producing large-scale reproductions of photographs that could not be distinguished from those taken from the original negative (*New York Times*, "Photographic"). Considerably less expensive than the carbon print method of reproducing photographs for books that Joseph Swan had developed in 1864, the Woodbury Mechanical Process had a significant impact on image reproduction in print culture. Although Woodbury types could not be printed directly onto the page and had to be mounted separately, the mechanized process made them relatively inexpensive and fast, and they were used in book illustration from about 1875 (Gernsheim, *Photography*, 263–64). From this moment to the end of the century, the mass production of pictures and text would be increasingly dominated by photomechanical processes. However, as Gerry Beegan's work has shown, even at the fin de siècle, the mass image was influenced by the aesthetic of the wood engraving and was similarly produced by a combination of manual and mechanized processes. By this time, according to Beegan, Victorian visual culture had witnessed an ongoing "dialogue between photography and engraving for half a century" (*Mass Image*, 8).

Photography's presence is ubiquitous during the period dominated by the wood-engraved gift book. To start with, artists used photography as a means of recording their drawings on the woodblock before the engravers effaced them through cutting. Later, engravers began to use photography to transfer the artist's design from paper onto a sensitized woodblock, thus leaving the original artwork intact. Publishers also realized that they could extend the variety of formats, prices, and markets by exploiting photography's reproduction potential and cultural appeal. When Moxon advertised the folio edition of the Tennyson-Doré *Elaine* in December 1866, priced at a guinea, the publisher simultaneously offered the work with "Photographs from the Original Drawings in lieu of Engravings, price Two Guineas." Clearly directed at the emerging bourgeois collectors' market, this version of the newly released *Elaine* was joined by "A few impressions of the Plates, Proofs before Letters," which Moxon offered for five guineas.[49] At such prices, both the photographs and the proofs were aimed at members of the upper middle class with surplus income and a desire to amass and display cultural objects enhanced by the aura of restricted production—even while those objects were simultaneously part of mass culture.

In contrast, the Cabinet Edition—or, as the poet referred to it, the "workingmen's edition"—of the *Works of Tennyson* was directed at the lower end of the market, with each of the ten small volumes issued as a monthly part and priced at two shillings sixpence. Yet it, too, made the most of photography's capacity for image-making in all senses of the word. The size and name of the edition were branded by the popular "cabinet" photographs that had replaced the smaller cartes de visite as "the poor man's picture gallery" in 1867 (Gernsheim, *Photography*, 201–2). To capitalize on this branding, the publisher issued each volume in the Cabinet Edition with an image of an actual cabinet-sized photograph. To do this cost-effectively, however, the photograph had to be mediated by an additional mechanical process. For example, the frontispiece to volume 1 used the Woodbury Mechanical Process to translate John Mayall's photograph of Tennyson into an image that would be reproducible in an initial print run of 12,000 (fig. 5.23).[50] In effect, this put the laureate's personal calling card into the humble reader's domestic space, a move that simultaneously took advantage of emerging celebrity culture and confirmed that the laureate belonged to the people.[51] Some frontispieces to other volumes similarly capitalized on the appeal to human interest by fronting the poetry with reproduced images from

Figure 5.23 Photograph of Alfred Tennyson by Messrs. Mayall and Collins, printed by the Woodbury Mechanical Process, frontispiece to *The Works of Alfred Tennyson*, vol. 1, *Early Poems*, Cabinet Edition (King, 1874).

the poet's personal life. These photographic frontispieces included images of the marble bust made of Tennyson by Thomas Woolner (reproduced by Autotype); his garden at Swainston; a fragment of manuscript; Arthur Henry Hallam in profile, reading a book; and so on. Although mediated by the machinery of mass reproduction, these images nonetheless retain some of photography's intimate association and indexical function. Their purpose is not so much decorative or aesthetic as referential, grounding the disembodied words of the poet in traces of his body and lived experience and giving the reader a sense of presence.

Other frontispieces in the *Works* aim at being more iconic. In these images, the photograph has been treated as if it were a drawing—an artistic design that could be cut on the wood and reproduced in relief. This was not the way Julia Margaret Cameron imagined her artistic photographs would be used when Tennyson called on her to ask if she would illustrate his *Idylls* for the Cabinet Edition. Her self-reported response—"Now *you know* Alfred that *I* know that it is immortality to me to be bound up with you" (quoted in Ford, *Cameron,* 71)—suggests the lofty heights she hoped her art and fame might reach when connected with the laureate's. Although Cameron had, by that time, exhibited and sold some of her photographs, her work was known principally to a small group of other artists and makers: the famous people (including Browning, Carlyle, Darwin, and Longfellow) she photographed when they visited Freshwater (Ford, *Cameron,* 40, 49). Cameron had experimented with illustrating scenes from literature by posing friends, family, servants, and neighbors in costumed and highly theatrical tableaux vivants, then taking innumerable photographs of them until she was satisfied with the result. When Tennyson invited her to illustrate his *Idylls,* she had already made photographic illustrations for his *Enoch Arden* and "The Gardener's Daughter," as well as for Coventry Patmore's *Angel in the House,* all of which Tennyson would have known. Perhaps the staged "living pictures," presented with the documentary reportage of the camera, seemed to him to offer mimesis rather than interpretation, grounding his Arthuriad in "the real."[52] Or perhaps he viewed these photographed scenes, with their costumes, staging, and dramatic poses, as a form of captured, objectified theater. In any case, Tennyson's attitude anticipates Henry James's openness to the use of photographs in his works, despite his dislike of graphic illustration. Like James, Tennyson seems to have viewed photographs as "images always confessing themselves mere optical symbols or echoes, expressions of no particular thing in the text, but only the type or idea of this thing or that thing."[53]

Cameron, in contrast, saw her photographs as a form of visual poetry and thus an apt artistic companion to the laureate's verses (Groth, *Victorian*

*Photography,* 161). She also welcomed the opportunity to achieve mass circulation for her work and reach a broad public. But she failed to take into account the material constraints of the codex form, perhaps because she was unaware of the publisher's intended format for the Cabinet Edition. Henry S. King's plan limited the illustrative contents to a frontispiece for each of the ten volumes and did not extend to additional pictures for the three devoted to the *Idylls of the King* (volumes 5–7). However, Cameron set to work photographing twelve scenes from Tennyson's entire Arthuriad (as it existed in 1874). King selected only two of these, *Elaine* and *Arthur,* as illustrative frontispieces; he also chose an image that Cameron had produced for *Maud.*[54] Significantly, as Helen Groth points out, in each case King chose close-up shots, rather than tableaux vivants, so that the visual motif of the portrait continued across the volumes (*Victorian Photography,* 153). In addition to reducing the number and kind of Cameron's images, moreover, the publisher also reduced her large photographs to cabinet size to accommodate the duodecimo format. The final indignity was that the publisher commissioned engraver Tom Lewin to translate the fuzzy edges of Cameron's soft-focus tonal portraits into the bold black and white of linear wood engravings (fig. 5.24).

In this form, the reproduced image was both affordable and legible to the consumers most likely to purchase it, working-class and artisanal readers whose visual-verbal literacy had been developed by the illustrated periodical press. For this mass audience, wood-engraved pictures constituted a familiar graphic language for imaginative illustrations, just as the reproduced photographs of Tennyson's carte-de-visite portrait, garden, and bust represented the newest technological means of representing contemporary lives, places, and objects.[55] The publishers' genius in the People's Edition was the deft combination of celebrity photographs associated with the poet's personal life and a handful of newly produced wood engravings for the laureate's popular *Idylls of the King,* based on photographs by a lady counted among his intimate friends.[56] Another canny calculation on King's part must have been that, by using Cameron's photographs, he could save himself the cost of paying an artist to illustrate. Neither Cameron nor Tennyson seems to have expected the publisher to reimburse the photographer for her work.

In preparing her twelve large photographs, Cameron gave little thought to either bibliographic format or intended readership. Instead, she anticipated that her work would vie with and outclass Gustave Doré's wildly successful folio illustrations for the *Idylls.* As Cameron emphasized in a letter to her friend Sir Edward Ryan,

Figure 5.24 Julia Margaret Cameron, "Elaine," wood engraving after a photographic study, frontispiece to *The Works of Alfred Tennyson*, vol. 6, *Idylls of the King*, Cabinet Edition (King, 1874).

> I do it for friendship not that I would not gladly have consented to profit if profit had been offered. Doré got a fortune for his *drawn* fancy Illustrations for these Idylls—Now one of my large photographs, take one for instance illustrating Elaine who is May Prinsep (now Hitchens) at her very best would excite more sensation and interest than all the drawings of Doré—and therefore I am producing a volume of these large photographs to illustrate the Idylls, 12 in number all differing (with portrait of Alfred Tennyson) in a handsome half morocco volume priced six guineas—I could not make it under for it to pay at all. (quoted in Lukitsh, "Cameron," 249)

While Cameron was correct in asserting that Doré was well paid for *Idylls of the King*—Moxon admitted to paying the artist an astronomical £6000 for his thirty-seven illustrations (*Doré*, 16)—she was less astute in calculating the finances of her own audience. At six guineas, her *Illustrations to "Idylls of the King"* was affordable only to a tiny niche market. Moreover, although Henry S. King agreed to publish the *Illustrations* in folio, he did so at Cameron's expense (Olsen, *From Life*, 232) and put neither energy nor money into promotion. Judging by the style of writing and the inside knowledge of production, it even seems likely that the only two notices in the press were written by Cameron herself.

Cameron's *Illustrations*, with her handwritten and underlined excerpts selected from the *Idylls*, does not appear, as she had fondly hoped, as "a beautiful Xmas gift book or Wedding gift book" (quoted in Lukitsh, "Cameron," 249) but rather as a new-media, and expensive, version of the illustrated folios produced by earlier lady amateurs such as Amy Butts and Paulet Mildmay. The underscored words and phrases also provide, like those in Maclise's working copy of *The Princess*, insight into her approach to the text as an illustrator. As is clear from the alignment of text and image, each underlined passage constituted a stage direction, suggesting props, costumes, surroundings, poses, and expressions to the photographer.[57] Thus, it comes as no surprise that Cameron's selected texts illustrate her photographs, rather than the other way around, as Carol Armstrong (following Roland Barthes in *Image Music Text*) observes (*Scenes*, 365).

Armstrong is, however, off the mark in her suggestion that Cameron's album is akin "to books illustrated with wood engravings and other hand-originated mechanical reproductions" (362). Each photograph is mounted separately on heavy paper within a single rule, then followed by the selected passage from the poem in a facsimile of Cameron's handwriting. This mixture of mechanical and hand processes bears little resemblance to the relief-printing of letterpress type and wood-engraved pictures, which resulted in a unified page with balanced weights of ink and an integration of text and image. While the theatrical tableaux may remind us of some of Maclise's compositions for *The Princess*, and the close-up portraits of women may recall some of the Pre-Raphaelite images for *Poems,* Cameron's *Illustrations* is much more akin to the folio editions with steel engravings after Doré than it is to the wood-engraved book that was characteristic of the 1860s. Indeed, its closest comparator, after the folios of Butts and Mildmay, is to *The Doré Gift Book of Illustrations to Tennyson's "Idylls of the King."* Like Cameron's *Illustrations,* the *Doré Gift Book* was a folio of pictures rather than an illustrated book. Seeking to recirculate Doré's illustrations for the *Idylls* but no longer able to reprint the poems, because Tennyson had gone to another publisher, Moxon published, in 1878, a large folio of Doré's pictures, accompanied by titles and brief quotations. In this publication, the Tennyson name is evoked merely as a brand, and his verses become mere captions to another artist's work. His poetic *Idylls* become literal idylls, pictures presenting scenes and incidents. Not only the poet but also his poetry becomes detached from the work.

Nowhere is the detachment of the author from his work within the visual culture of the sixties gift book more evident than in the publication history of the illustrated *Idylls of the King.* From the moment these popular gift books first appeared on the market, the *Idylls* belonged as much to Doré as they did to Tennyson. When Moxon published *Elaine* in 1866, the first of Doré's four illustrated *Idylls,* the artist had no less than "seven of the most sumptuous and expensive volumes" advertised in Cassell's list of Christmas gift books. As the *Saturday Review* critic observed, with some justice, "This year, at any rate, may be pronounced to be the Doré year" (Nov. 24, 1866, 653). The French artist was, quite simply, the most admired of contemporary illustrators; when he undertook a work—always a Western classic—reviewers could not seem to keep the word *monument* or *monumental* out of their reviews. Cassell, his usual London publisher, promoted Doré's books by attaching the artist's name to the titles he illustrated, and demoting that of the author: it was *Doré's Milton's "Paradise Lost"; Doré's Dante's "Inferno"; Doré's Bible,* and so on.[58] For Moxon to secure Doré for the gift-book editions of Tennyson's *Idylls* was therefore quite a coup, and it made good advertising copy:

---

On December 1st, 1866, will be published, in imperial 4to. with paper and type *made expressly for the Work,* and in elegant cloth, price 21*s*.

**E L A I N E.**

By ALFRED TENNYSON.

**ILLUSTRATED BY GUSTAVE DORÉ.**

---

 As if the typographic code were not enough to indicate the relative importance of contributors, the advertisement goes on to quote the artist (but not the poet). In addition to two gracefully worded quotations in French, the ad includes Doré's (translated) hope that the work would "be a Monument to Mr. Tennyson and to his own powers." Here the monumentalizing honor is heightened by the dignity of black-letter font. To make this gift book especially coveted by collectors, the publisher stressed two unique aspects of the Doré *Elaine:* that these illustrations constituted the artist's first designs for steel (rather than wood) engraving; and, as an emphatic honor to the British laureate, that these were Doré's first illustrations for a living poet.[59]

In typographic lettering, white space, display, and quotation, the advertisement's physical features expressed Moxon's intentions for this series of gift books. At every level, Moxon marketed Doré as coauthor of the *Idylls.* As the *Saturday Review* critic wrote, commenting on the unusual formulation of the title, "*Elaine—Tennyson—Doré* (Moxon)": "As we understand it, it means that in this magnificent volume . . . we have the poet and his artist ranked on an equal pedestal" (Dec. 8, 1866, 717). The critic went on to suggest that the purchaser of *Elaine* would gain "two masterpieces" in the arts of poetry and pictures, by two of the greatest artists of the day (717). Significantly, the critic also recognized the publisher's authoring role: "Mr. Moxon is to be congratulated on having produced the most ambitious and ornate work of the day; and the Laureate has in this volume received those honours of typography and general sumptuousness which have hitherto been reserved for the fixed stars of poetry. This edition of *Elaine* is like erecting a statue to a hero in his lifetime" (717).

Perhaps the most iconic of Doré's illustrations for *Elaine* is the image of her corpse in its barge, propelled by the dumb servitor (fig. 5.25). A ghostly moon in the sky above the castle illuminates the maiden's face, bright hair, white dress, and lily flower. Both romantic and sublime, the image captures the hushed tone and stately progress of the poet's descriptive lines, despite the fact that the embankment and architecture do not seem to be part of Tennyson's Arthurian landscape. As many critics observed—especially by the time *Enid,* the final illustrated *Idyll,* had been published—Doré placed the stories in a medieval European setting rather than an ancient British one. This is not surprising, as the artist did not read English and relied on a translation when he composed his designs (Hagen, *Tennyson,* 113). As a visual translation of a verbal one, his work is, therefore, at a third remove from Tennyson's poetry. According to an indignant Ruskin, the linguistic barrier also marked severe national, aesthetic, and moral differences: "Those *Elaine* illustrations are just as impure as anything else that Doré has done; but they are also vapid, and without any one merit whatever in

Figure 5.25 Gustave Doré, "Elaine," for Alfred Tennyson, *Idylls of the King*, vol. 1, *Elaine* (Moxon, 1866).

 point of art" ("Time," 401). Ruskin took it as "a sign of what is going on in the midst of us, that our great English poet should have suffered his work to be thus contaminated" (401).

Ruskin's angry reaction to Doré's illustration of Tennyson's *Idylls* highlights the critic's increasing anxiety about the ways in which popular visual culture was encroaching on the preserves of fine art and poetry as the sixties drew to a close. To him, Doré's illustrations represented the industrialized factory's approach to art. Following mechanized grids to produce tonal facsimiles of Doré's brushed artwork (James, *English Book Illustration*, 49), the artist's army of engravers were merely cogs in the machine of mass production, churning out illustrated book after illustrated book. Both the factory-style mode of reproduction and the tonal image it produced mark the move away from hand-drawn pictures and manual engraving toward the photographic processes that would dominate the fin de siècle. Unlike the linear black-and-white of the typical wood-engraved illustration, the tonal engraving shares a similar graphic language with the photograph. As Gerry Beegan notes, this paved the way for the later acceptance of the halftone in print culture: the engraver W. J. Linton "had foreseen in 1879 that by moving from linear interpretation to tonal facsimile, wood engraving would eventually be replaced by methods that were more tonal, photographic, and mimetic" (Beegan, *Mass Image*, 68). Both the Doré *Idylls* and the Cabinet Edition of Tennyson's *Works* mark a transition from the wood-engraved gift books that characterize the sixties toward new forms of mass-produced book art that emerged with the halftone print. In their own ways, they also represent important landmarks in the history of authorship and reading.

Although the Cabinet Edition is far removed from the sixties gift book in format, presentation, and purpose, it did participate in the ongoing elevation of the image in print culture, the corporate practices of nineteenth-century publishing, and the concomitant detachment of the author. In this publication of pictures and poetry for "the working men of England," the reading laborer was given visual images of a restricted world he could not enter, reproduced in a mechanized language emblematic of his industrialized, urban life. But the author, too, was mechanized, with photographic mementos of his personal life mass-produced to sell his poetry.

The story of Tennyson and the image traces the poet's increasing distance from his own authorship as a result of the mechanization and professionalization of the publishing industry. Although he fought with Kegan Paul, King's manager, over the frontispiece photographs of his portrait, home, and manuscript, he was forced to give way when Paul reminded him "that illustrations could hardly 'be considered other than a publishers' question'" (Hagen, *Tennyson*, 140).

Tennyson's only recourse, the next time he signed a contract—which, as it happened, was in 1879 with Kegan Paul, who had gone into business for himself—was to assert his authorial control in legal language that restricted the publisher from initiating any new illustrated editions or "distasteful" advertising copy without the poet's express permission.[60] After the Cabinet Edition, there were no more new illustrated editions in Tennyson's lifetime.

Distinct as they are in reproductive technologies, image-making processes, formats, prices, and audiences, Tennyson's *Idylls of the King* of 1866–68 and Cabinet Edition of 1874–75 mark the end of an era for the illustrated gift book. They also demarcate two directions for illustrated books for the remainder of the century: the expensive edition for collectors and the cheap series for a mass audience. In the 1870s, experimentation in illustration, layout, typography, and binding moved largely into the realm of juvenile publishing, where designers found new ways of capitalizing on the book's expressive forms and capturing consumer markets. Poetry and pictures for adults degenerated into recycled offerings of recombined "gems" and images, or reprints of the most popular illustrated anthologies, such as *The Poets of the Nineteenth Century.* Not until the fine-printing revival of the fin de siècle did designers begin to realize, in a remarkable series of books designed specifically for the poetry they housed, the expressive possibilities inherent in the codex form.

# Coda

## *Poems and Pictures in the Modern Age*

In the first week of December 1874, the *Athenaeum* remarked upon an apparent decrease in Christmas books for review: "Our table is less heavily loaded than is usually the case in December with the glittering trifles of the season, but doubtless an avalanche is impending of resplendent volumes, gold and green and blue without, hot-pressed and highly illustrated within" (Dec. 5, 1874, 756). Whether or not the expected "avalanche" of books descended that December, the nature of the "glittering trifles of the season" was evidently changing in format. Christmas book reviews, publishers' records, and the material evidence of the books themselves show that by the mid 1870s, the ornamental quarto of poems with original pictures was being displaced. Illustrated poetry was churned out in popular libraries, reprints, and cheap editions; not until the fin de siècle did publishers reimagine the book of poems and pictures with first-edition appeal for the aesthetic collector. Meanwhile, a new type of Christmas gift book emerged. Directed principally at a juvenile audience, it substituted works of fantasy for poetry and replaced black-and-white wood engravings with lavish color plates printed in the new three-color process.

Just as the early Victorian annuals looked old-fashioned by the 1850s, so too the gift books of the sixties began to seem a little out of step with the times in the last quarter of the nineteenth century. The hybrid form combining poetry by national authors and pictures by acclaimed living artists, so innovative in 1855, had become a standardized commodity by 1875. Rather than commissioning new illustrations for a freshly conceived anthology, collection, or single poem—as had the Dalziels for *The Poets of the Nineteenth Century* (1857), Bell and Daldy for

Adelaide Procter's *Legends and Lyrics* (1866), and Moxon for Tennyson's *Enoch Arden* (1866)—publishers simply reprinted their best sellers. These tended to be edited anthologies: for example, R. A. Willmott's *Poets of the Nineteenth Century* and *English Sacred Poetry* and Charles Mackay's *Home Affections Pourtrayed by the Poets* and *A Thousand and One Gems of Poetry.* By the 1880s, the low costs of printing from existing electroplates, coupled with large print runs, allowed publishers to offer these anthologies at the low price of three shillings sixpence (Haass, "Victorian Poetry," 56)—a far cry from the guinea gift book. Published in bulk and brought out annually at affordable prices, the illustrated book of poetry extended its circulation among common readers in popular culture but lost its prestige value. Disconnected from producers of current art, the work no longer mediated restricted and large-scale cultural production, manual and mechanical means of reproduction, and art and commerce. The poetic gift book became, literally and culturally, a stereotyped cliché of the sixties.

Nowhere is the gift book's dissociation from contemporary creators of art and poetry more evident than in the putatively "new" Christmas volumes brought out in the 1870s. Always risk-averse, publishers increasingly took advantage of the gift book's modular form and recycled poems and pictures from old stock in different combinations, tricked out in new bindings. In the *Athenaeum* of December 1874, for instance, two such cannibalized offerings were reviewed: *Picture Poesies* and *Happy Day Stories for the Young* (Dulcken). Both provide insight into the declining state of the Dalziel Fine Art Gift Book that had been the most characteristic publication of the period.

*Picture Poesies* is essentially a mishmash reprint of two earlier anthologies: *A Round of Days* (the Dalziel Fine Art Gift Book for 1866) and the following year's *Wayside Posies,* edited by Robert Buchanan (the last of the Dalziel Fine Art Gift Books) (Goldman, *Victorian Illustration,* 328, 333). Within a review chiefly devoted to gift books for children, *Picture Poesies* is presented as a lesser accomplishment, subordinate to these leading works of the season and infantilized in association with them. Also infantilized by association are the intended recipients of *Picture Poesies,* the adult women readers whom the critic identifies as children "of larger growth" (*Athenaeum,* Dec. 5, 1874, 756). The critic's lukewarm commendation of a few of the pictures—recycled works by Walker, Pinwell, Stanfield, Mulready, Wolf, and others—as being "charmingly executed," together with his unequivocal condemnation of the verses as "trash, sentimental or dull" (756), indicates what the future held for the sixties book. An object for the collector and bibliophile interested in wood-engraved pictures and decorative bindings, the gift book became an incidental container for "charmingly executed" sixties illustration. The poetry was merely the disposable occasion for the work; it consequently faded from critical view as literary "trash" not worthy

of reading, let alone analysis.

This disposability is inherent in the gift book's modular format; the book's capacity for recombination permitted publishers to redirect old contents to new audiences. H. W. Dulcken's *Happy Day Stories for the Young* shows how illustrations from sixties gift books could be reassigned to take advantage of the burgeoning field of juvenile publishing. This collection of stories for children was a piece of commercial ekphrasis designed for the increasingly child-centered focus of Christmas gift-giving. Admitting that all the illustrations had been taken from Arthur Boyd Houghton's images of "child life" for *Home Thoughts and Home Scenes* (1865), the preface claims that "the favourable appreciation accorded by the Public . . . has induced the Publishers to re-issue the pictures, as illustrating a collection of stories for children; and it is hoped that they will prove no less welcome in this their second than they proved in their first appearance" (n.p.). This mystification of the market covers up the true facts of the case: *Home Thoughts and Home Scenes* was never a big seller and received mixed reviews on its first appearance for Christmas 1865. However, the poetry received shorter shrift than Houghton's illustrations, which were universally praised by critics (as discussed in chapter 3). This being the case, the pictures of "child life" might still be made to pay if they accompanied a collection of short stories, as occasional literature of this kind generally sold well in the Christmas season. The Dalziels hired a jobbing editor, H. W. Dulcken, to write short stories (each one only a couple of pages in length) for thirty of Houghton's pictures.[1]

The substitution of Dulcken's stories for the original verses by Jean Ingelow, Dora Greenwell, Dinah Craik, and other female contributors to *Home Thoughts* marks an important shift in the gift-book trade, from production and marketing strategies that targeted women to production and marketing strategies that targeted children. But the reception of *Happy Days* also signals a shift in aesthetic taste informed by changing technological processes. While the *Athenaeum* reviewer praised Dulcken's stories as "simple and pleasing, with a carefully concealed moral," he panned Houghton's recycled pictures as "essentially commonplace, not to say dull" (Dec. 5, 1874, 756). Houghton's black-and-white images of bourgeois domestic life were, indeed, commonplace and dull compared to the colorful works of fantastic illustration by Walter Crane, which represented the aesthetic ideal of decorative art at the time. Also published by Routledge, Crane's works were, the *Athenaeum* critic claimed, "charmingly brilliant specimens of what is right in chromatic book decoration of high artistic order" (756). The two singled out for top billing in this review, *Goody Two Shoes' Picture Book* and *The Marquis of Carabas's Picture Book*, demarcate the new directions for gift-book publishing that emerged in the 1870s, with important implications for the history of nineteenth-century authorship, reading, and publishing.

In the new, color-plated gift books for children, the traditional literature of folktale, fairy tale, legend, and nursery rhyme displaced the contemporary writer. This move allowed publishers to take firm control of lucrative annual offerings in an age in which authors were becoming increasingly professionalized and concerned about intellectual property rights. Under these simplified conditions of corporate authorship, format and design were the chief selling features. Publishers produced books in modular units available in different versions, allowing for the diversification of sales and the promotion of new consumer practices of collecting. *Goody Two Shoes* and *The Marquis of Carabas*, for instance, each contained four tales;[2] these were also available individually for a shilling apiece. As an added enticement to purchase, the covers for the individual issues served as advertisements for the series and as collecting come-ons, each one "adorned with an excellent and beautifully-coloured design" (*Athenaeum*, Dec. 5, 1874, 756). Rather than two books with decorated covers, a consumer had the option of buying eight.

The small format and low price of Routledge's "Toy Books" created a new market for children's books; Crane's designs, startlingly original and new, form an important link between the book art of the sixties and that of the fin de siècle (McLean, *Victorian*, 137).[3] The Routledge Toy Books series schooled the consumer as a collector of art in commodified form. Both adult purchaser and child recipient were promised access to aesthetic cultural capital. "The volumes," the *Athenaeum* critic asserted, "are likely to develope [*sic*] good taste when it is dormant and to correct vagaries, however vulgar" (Dec. 5, 1874, 756). The rhetoric of aesthetic education and cultural currency associated with a gift book like the Moxon Tennyson of 1857, connected with the up-and-coming Pre-Raphaelite art then on view at exhibitions in Manchester and London, was transferred, in the 1870s, to the gift book of color plates for children. An entire generation of late-Victorian children had their tastes formed in the pages of these new gift books. They became the aesthetic consumers of the 1890s, willing to purchase a slim first edition by a contemporary poet, impeccably designed by a Bodley Head book artist, for their own select library: for example, E. Nesbit's *Pomander of Verse* (1895), designed by Laurence Housman, or Oscar Wilde's *Sphinx* (1894), designed by Charles Ricketts.

The ornamental "quarto poets" began to look a little dated and uncultivated, if not downright "vulgar," in the aesthetic drawing rooms of the 1870s. In 1912, Joseph Shaylor suggested that the sixties Christmas book met its demise "because drawing-rooms ceased to contain tables capable of holding such tomes, and, as a result, there was no place for them" (*Fascination*, 55). Certainly the rise of the aesthetic movement, with which Crane's decorative art was associated, had an impact on notions of what constituted "good taste" in fashionable middle-class homes. But other social, economic, and technological factors also played their part.

Social historians have noted that the 1870s and 1880s mark a definitive cultural transition to a modern life marked by mass media and leisure (S. Mitchell, *Daily Life*, 11; L. K. Hughes, "1870," 35). Critical turning points include the Education Act of 1870, which established government-funded, compulsory education; the second Reform Bill of 1867, which extended democracy by doubling the electorate; and the Married Woman's Property Acts of 1870 and 1882, which, along with the establishment of Girton College in 1869 and Newnham College in 1871, substantially increased rights and opportunities for women.

The intensified public demand for female franchise also dates from 1870, when Lydia Becker established the *Women's Suffrage Journal* (L. K. Hughes, "1870," 36–39). While the feminist "New Woman" was not a recognized subject until the fin de siècle, middle-class women were increasingly asserting and implementing their rights to person, property, and employment. If the drawing-room décor of the 1870s could no longer accommodate tables capable of displaying the quarto poets, this may also mark a change in the woman reader who had, for decades, been associated with the gift book's winning combination of ornamental appeal and irreproachable moral character.

With the disappearance of the guinea gift book, what was poetry's place in the emerging modern world of mass print media and leisure? Rather than building books for display on central tables, publishers brought out illustrated libraries of standard authors, to be lined up in uniform bindings on shelves. As a middlebrow aesthetic object mediating the fields of restricted and mass cultural production, the poetic gift book had retained some prestige value: its display on the drawing-room table signaled both its artistic credentials and its owner's claim to cultivation. The library series, in contrast, belonged entirely to the field of large-scale cultural production. In shifting books from table displays to shelves, the library series asserted that its owner was an educated citizen, schooled in a common national literature. The shift also indicates a mass-market generalization of audience: rather than targeting women specifically, these works addressed themselves to a global middle-class readership, the standardized bindings and format working to unify male and female subjects alike. Notable among these libraries is the Illustrated Popular Poets series introduced by Moxon after Tennyson decamped for Strahan. Brought out annually for Christmas sales between 1870 and 1880, Moxon's Popular Poets was edited by William Michael Rossetti, who provided a critical introduction to each volume. Although decorated with textual ornaments and illustrated with wood-engraved pictures (generally about eight) from Moxon's stock, these works were intensively text-focused. Printed on thin paper, sometimes in double columns, the verses in each collection occupied a compendious four hundred pages, or even more—all for three shillings sixpence per volume.

Moxon's advertisement for the series took as its motto Matthew Arnold's claim "The power of English literature is in its poets." The ad asserted that this cultural capital was recognized worldwide by English-speaking people: "The press and the public, alike in Great Britain and her Colonies, and in the United States, unite in their testimony to the immense superiority of Messrs. Moxon's Popular Poets over any other similar collections, published by any other house." The self-aggrandizing advertisement also implied that the publishing industry's control over intellectual property made English poets the common "property" of all owners of this definitive series: "Their possession of the Copyright works of Coleridge, Hood, Keats, Shelley, Wordsworth, and other great National Poets, places this series above rivalry."[4] A publisher of national poets since 1830, Moxon found lucrative ways to place his stock in the 1870s by connecting his press to a consecrated poetic canon unifying English-speaking peoples around the world.

Absent from Moxon's Popular Poets series was, of course, the reigning "People's Poet," whose intellectual property was no longer in the publisher's purview and thus stood outside the canon constructed by this library. But Tennyson was also engaged in bringing out a popular series of his own, the Cabinet Edition of 1874–75. Bound in crimson cloth, the ten tiny volumes, each priced at two shillings sixpence, were published as a workingman's library, thereby extending the popular reach of his collected poetry. This series, as the last illustrated edition to be published with the poet's authorization, represents Tennyson's concession to popular publishing for a mass audience (as discussed in chapter 5). But its material form also constitutes a bibliographic argument against the illustrated editions of his poetry that his former publisher, Moxon, had published throughout the sixties. Indeed, the Cabinet Edition seems deliberately designed to remove the poet and his works from the stigma of "drawing-room books" aimed at a female audience.[5] The Cabinet Edition's format and pricing boldly reclaimed Tennyson's popular publishing for a masculine audience: working men engaged in the public sphere, not middle-class women cloistered in drawing rooms. The books were made portable enough to fit into a masculine pocket and attractive enough to sit in a row on a modest bookcase.[6]

In the 1870s, as Tennyson maintained his popularity but began to lose ground in critical acclaim, it seemed all too evident that Moxon's lavish gift-book editions, from the illustrated *Poems* of 1857 to the Doré *Idylls* of 1866–68, may have had a deleterious effect on the poet's standing in the field of restricted cultural production. Reposing in quarto on the drawing-room table, lined up in a star-formation with gift-book editions of verses by Eliza Cook, Jean Ingelow, or Adelaide Procter and anthologies such as *Home Thoughts and Home Scenes,* Tennyson's poetry was made the property of women readers. Just as the ornamental covers, creamy pages, and decorative illustrations were identified with the female bodies these books were made for, so too was the poet's association with the feminine materially confirmed.

It is telling that when the tide of critical opinion began to turn against Tennyson, Alfred Austin dismissed the poet's work by naming it "the poetry of the drawing-room" ("Tennyson," 305). The condemnation begs the question: where does poetry belong in the modern age? The various formats for standard works suggested that popular poetry belonged on bookshelves or in pockets, confirming the importance of readers over authors in the age of mass cultural production. But what about the work of living poets who aspired, not to popularity, but to critical acclaim? Austin's dismissive "poetry of the drawing-room" denigrated Tennyson's claim to canonical status precisely by associating his work with readers—and, most damning of all, women readers in domestic space. Such poetry did not belong to the field of restricted cultural production; it was made not for other cultural producers but for a nonproducing, feminine audience. The reaction to this "poetry of the drawing-room" asserted that, in the modern age, accredited poetry by living writers belonged to other cultural producers; its proper habitus was the academy and the private library.

Austin's 1870 critique of Tennyson condemned the poet in terms that became codified with the rise of modernism in the twentieth century. Looking back on the Victorian age with scorn, the modernists reasserted poetry's place in the restricted field of cultural production. A rarified literary form, modernist poetry would meet its educated readership on expansive pages of severe typography, whose only ornamentation was the odd Greek epigraph or authorial footnote. In bibliographic format as much as poetic form, modernism distanced itself from its Victorian forebears and assigned poetry a new position in the world. The poetic gift book fell from critical view.

As Johanna Drucker observes, "Work suited to parlor or sitting room may be deemed worthy of sociological or cultural historical attention, but art, in the modern era, is supposed to live up to the avant-garde agenda" ("*Petit Journal,*" 138–39). In this study of a neglected middlebrow artifact, I have aimed to demonstrate the significance of "drawing-room books" as both material objects and historical events. For Victorian middle-class readers, particularly the female audience for whom these works were made, illustrated gift books offered access to intellectual, affective, and artistic conceptualizations of what it meant to be human in an increasingly industrialized world. Their ornamented covers enshrined verses of the kind that newspapers and magazines had popularized and made meaningful. Their printed pages, scored with wood-engraved cuts that retained traces of the engraver's hands and the artist's lines, connected the mass-produced book with unique works of art, blurring, for a brief span of years, the categories of restricted and large-scale cultural production. A significant product of print culture in an increasingly visual age, the illustrated gift book detached the poet from the work and authorized readers as poets of their own acts of reading.

As the inheritors of this rich cultural legacy of poetic/pictorial expression and practice, we are privileged to touch and see the material past when we encounter the Christmas gift books of the sixties. The expressive pages of the poetic gift book offer new ways of looking at the place of poetry in the high Victorian period—of resituating Tennyson's works within female-coded processes of production and reception, and understanding the connections between periodical and volume publication in bringing women poets such as Eliza Cook, Adelaide Procter, and Jean Ingelow to a transatlantic readership. A hybrid multimedia form mediating "high" and popular art, the gift book's corporate authorship and feminine readership intervene in literary history to challenge romantic notions of individual creators and consecrated canons. With a weightiness that cannot be ignored, the ornamental quarto asserts the significance of poetry and pictures in everyday Victorian life and consumer culture.

# Notes

## Introduction: Poetry, Pictures, and Popular Publishing

1. *Anglo-American*, "Eliza Cook's Poetry," July 31, 1847, 343.

2. In my assessment of the relative roles of authors and readers in a commercialized publishing industry, I am indebted to Michel Foucault's notion of the "author-function" as an ideological and discursive principle in our culture, inseparable from the commodification of literature (see Foucault, "What Is an Author?" in *The Book History Reader*), and to Roland Barthes's insight that the death of the author and the rise of the reader make the text's destination more important than its origin (see Barthes, "Death of the Author" in the same anthology).

3. So far as I am aware, Marcel Proust was the first to describe the "the writer's work . . . [as] merely a kind of optical instrument" (*Time Regained*, 283).

4. Gleeson White, Forrest Reid, Percy Muir, Ruari McLean, Gordon Ray, Simon Houfe, and Paul Goldman have established the boundaries and characteristics of the "golden age of illustration," or the "sixties"; this study could not have been written without their archival and critical work. Although boundary dates for this period vary, there is general agreement that the sixties begin about 1855 or 1857 and end around 1870 or 1875. I have taken the most generous parameters, 1855–75, for my study, but most of my examples fall between 1857 and 1870.

5. See Tara Moore's comprehensive survey of Christmas books, their genres, and formats in *Victorian Christmas in Print*.

6. The derogatory term *furniture book* is ubiquitous in the period's critical reviews, but see especially *Fraser's Magazine*, "Furniture Books," January 1859.

7. Alexis Weedon's table showing the demand for English literature indicates that the sales of books priced at a guinea rose from negligible in the years before 1856 (i.e., prior to the emergence of the wood-engraved gift book) to about 5 percent of the market in 1866 (at the height of the "golden age") (*Victorian Publishing*, 106). Not all of these, of course, would have been books of poetry, and it is also worth noting that some gift books were priced between ten and fifteen shillings.

8. Throughout this study, I use the plural term *middle classes* to indicate the diversity of this group. Following Sally Mitchell's formulation in *Daily Life in Victorian England*, I have considered the broad middle classes as including that segment of the population who neither performed manual labor nor belonged by birth to the elite and whose annual income was between £300 and £800.

9. In "The Culture Industry: Enlightenment as Mass Deception," Max Horkheimer and Theodor Adorno's argument about the culture industry's standardized formats

provides some insight into the ideological work of poetic gift books, but it does not adequately take into account the possibility of reader agency. In contrast, Michel de Certeau's *Practice of Everyday Life* provides an alternative, less determinist, model for approaching the poetic gift book and situating it in the daily practices of readers. In my analysis, I try to balance my recognition of the institutional and ideological power of the culture industry and its ability to construct or interpellate (in Althusser's terms) subjects with an understanding of readers as "poets of their own acts" (de Certeau, *Practice*, xviii).

10. In *The Victorian Parlour*, Thad Logan suggests that the terms *parlor* and *drawing room* are virtually interchangeable (xv); like her, I have used them as such, though I generally prefer the term *drawing room* to *parlor*, as the latter seems more American to me. In this general preference, I follow Judith Flanders's usage in *The Victorian House*.

11. In its short print life of four monthly numbers, *The Germ* went through two subtitles: *Thoughts Towards Nature in Poetry, Literature and Art* and *Art and Poetry: Being Thoughts Towards Nature Conducted Principally by Artists*. See title pages in the facsimile edition of *The Germ*, edited by Andrea Rose.

## Chapter 1: Reading the Christmas Gift Book

1. *Athenaeum*, October 31, 1857, 1359.

2. First published by James Burns in 1846, *Poems and Pictures* was reissued by Sampson Low in 1860; I am working with the new edition of 1860, although I refer to the first edition in this section.

3. For excellent analyses of the parity of word and image in the *Illustrated London News* (*ILN*), see Sinnema, *Dynamics of the Pictured Page*, and Curtis, *Visual Words*.

4. Patricia Anderson's *Printed Image and the Transformation of Popular Culture, 1790–1860* and Brian Maidment's *Reading Popular Prints, 1790–1870* provide significant historical and critical contexts for this development. I am also indebted to Geoffrey Wakeman's *Victorian Book Illustrations* and Philip James's *English Book Illustration, 1800–1900*.

5. Thus, a woodcut is not the same as a wood engraving, even though Victorians typically referred to engravings as "cuts." See James, *English Book Illustration*, 18.

6. As Simon Eliot has shown in "Some Trends in British Book Production, 1800–1919," publishers' production schedules changed in the second half of the nineteenth century to focus on a Christmas sales season. Similarly, Lee Erickson notes that poetry sales centered on Christmas gift books ("Market," 350).

7. Eric de Maré notes that, in some cases, artists drew directly on the woodblock, then had this drawing photographed and transferred to a *second* woodblock. This practice can be examined today in the Victoria and Albert Museum's collection of blocks with drawings by, for example, Millais (de Maré, *Victorian Woodblock Illustrators*, 51).

8. For a fascinating account of the kinds of commentary and critique that Millais and Rossetti detailed for engravers on their corrected proofs, see Marsh, "Hoping You Will Not."

9. As Paul Goldman explains, the electrotype process, invented in 1839, replaced the old stereotype system with the more durable electrotypes. In contrast to stereotypes (which were made from plaster molds), electrotypes (made from metal) allowed finer

duplication of details; when well printed, these impressions may be almost indistinguishable from those pulled from the woodblock. Goldman, *John Everett Millais,* 15; see also Wakeman, *Victorian Book Illustrations,* 74.

10. As Raymond Williams explains in his entry "Art" in *Keywords,* the distinction between artists (painters and sculptors) and artisans (engravers) became consolidated in the nineteenth century, but it began in the eighteenth century with the exclusion of engravers from the Royal Academy (41). The radical engraver W. J. Linton continually railed against this denigration (de Maré, *Victorian Woodblock Illustrators,* 67).

11. For Christina Rossetti's active involvement in the illustration process of *Goblin Market and Other Poems* (Macmillan, 1862), *The Prince's Progress and Other Poems* (Macmillan, 1866), and *Sing-Song: A Nursery Rhyme Book* (Routledge, 1872), see Kooistra, *Christina Rossetti and Illustration.* Of these works, only *Sing-Song* could be considered a Christmas gift book, both because of the timing of its release (November 1871) and because of its ornamental covers. Although Macmillan intended to bring out *Goblin Market* and the *Prince's Progress* for the Christmas market, delays in the preparation of illustrations prevented him from doing so, and both works were issued in the spring. In "A Regular Illustrated Book," Timothy Boyd provides a detailed publishing history of the illustrated edition of *The Music Master,* noting that a similar delay in preparing the illustrations resulted in Allingham's book coming out in spring 1855 rather than for the Christmas market, as the poet and his publisher had planned.

12. See, for example, John Harvey, *Victorian Novelists and Their Illustrators;* Michael Hancher, *The Tenniel Illustrations to the 'Alice' Books;* Robert Patten, "Serial Illustration and Storytelling in *David Copperfield*"; and David Skilton, "The Relation between Illustration and Text in the Victorian Novel." For an insightful analysis of novelists and their illustrators in relation to print culture and its technologies, see Brian Maidment's seminal *Reading Popular Prints 1790–1870.*

13. The critical practice of examining images separate from their texts was initiated by the first critic to write on the illustrators of the sixties—Gleeson White, whose *English Illustration: "The Sixties"* was published in 1897—and continues to this day in books such as Gregory Suriano's *British Pre-Raphaelite Illustrators* and Julia Thomas's *Database of Mid-Victorian Wood-Engraved Illustration.* Paul Goldman *(Victorian Illustrated Books)* was one of the first critics to call for readings of sixties books that took into account relationships of image, text, and bibliographic context.

14. Benjamin's examples for the new political mass art for which the criterion of "authenticity" no longer obtains are, of course, photography and film. I am arguing for the wood-engraved gift book as a transitional and hybrid mass art that emerged in the mid-nineteenth century, when mechanical reproduction still involved manual mediation.

15. For insightful analyses of poetry and pictures in the illustrated press, see Hughes, "*Wellesley*" and "Inventing Poetry and Pictorialism"; Sinnema, *Dynamics of the Pictured Page;* and Maidment, *Reading Popular Prints.*

16. In *Early Victorian Illustrated Books,* John Buchanan-Brown offers a detailed genealogy of the development of the illustrated book in Britain between 1820 and 1860, demonstrating the importance of continental influences from France and Germany on

format, style, and technologies and providing an account of the rise of the wood-engraved book that characterized the 1860s.

17. I want to acknowledge my appropriation and redeployment of Virginia McKendry's connection of the *ILN* to "the invention of tradition" with respect to the monarchy in "The *Illustrated London News* and the Invention of Tradition."

18. See Peter Sinnema's analysis of the Christmas special from the *ILN* of December 21, 1850, and his conclusion about "the identification of Englishness with the 'authentic' celebration of Christmas" (*Dynamics*, 110–11); Mark Connelly also discusses the *ILN*'s role in constructing the celebration of Christmas as central to Englishness (*Christmas: A Social History*, 11). See also Tara Moore's informative chapter in *Victorian Christmas in Print* on how *Punch* and other periodicals educated consumers in British Christmas-keeping. For a useful overview of the historical development of Christmas in England, see Bowler, *World Encyclopedia of Christmas*.

19. See *George Routledge and Sons' Wholesale Catalogue of New and Popular Works for 1867–1869* under "Illustrated Present or Gift Books," Routledge Archive, University College Library Special Collections, London (hereafter cited as Routledge Archive).

20. In *Illustration*, J. Hillis Miller established an early guide to the analysis of illustrated texts when he insisted that "all works of art bring something new into the world rather than reflecting something already there" and emphasized "the necessity of vigilant and detailed rhetorical reading of works of art in any medium in order to identify what is different in each" (151). However, this methodology still implies a comparative model. In *Picture Theory*, W. J. T. Mitchell calls for a "revived iconology" that goes "beyond the comparative study of verbal and visual art" to consider their "mutually critical encounter with the discourse of ideology" (24–25); he further asserts, in *What Do Pictures Want?* that "all media are mixed media" (215). Robert Patten similarly argues for an end of mimetic criticism—comparing one art to another—in favor of reading the interaction of image and text as "complexly reciprocal" ("Serial Illustration," 91–92). In "The Centrality of Literary Illustration in Victorian Visual Culture," David Skilton calls for "an analysis of meaning production in the act of reading [illustrated texts] as bimodal works of art" (n.p.).

## Chapter 2: The Moxon Tennyson, Pre-Raphaelite Art, and Victorian Visual Culture

1. Letter of William Allingham to John Everett Millais regarding his illustrations for *The Music Master*, urging him to "be our better Hogarth" by illustrating high-quality books (Millais, *Life and Letters*, 1:257–58).

2. Hallam's reference is to the illustrated second edition of Robert Montgomery's *Oxford: A Poem*, with engravings by Joseph Skelton (and "notes including a biographical summary of eminent characters connected with the University"). Both the first and the second edition were published in 1831, and the book was still in print (in expanded form) in 1843 (sixth edition).

3. For a variety of approaches to early nineteenth-century visual culture, see John Buchanan-Brown, *Early Victorian Illustrated Books: Britain, France, and Germany*,

*1820–1860;* Jonathan Crary, *Techniques of the Observer: On Vision and Modernity in the Nineteenth Century;* Kate Flint, *The Victorians and the Visual Imagination;* Terence Hoagwood and Kathryn Ledbetter, *"Colour'd Shadows": Contexts in Publishing, Printing and Reading Nineteenth-Century British Women Writers;* Brian Maidment, *Reading Popular Prints, 1790–1870;* Sophie Thomas, *Romanticism and Visuality: Fragments, History, Spectacle;* and Gillen D'Arcy Wood, *The Shock of the Real: Romanticism and Visual Culture, 1790–1860.*

4. See Merriam, *Edward Moxon.*

5. In *Victorian and Modern Poetics,* Carol T. Christ shows the continuities between Tennyson's use of landscape to objectify a personality or consciousness, and Eliot's formulation and practice of the "objective correlative" (85–89).

6. The phrase is George Somes Layard's, in his *Tennyson and his Pre-Raphaelite Illustrators: A Book about a Book* (8).

7. Memorandum of an agreement with Alfred Tennyson 25 January 1849, draft manuscript, Tennyson Research Centre, Lincolnshire County Council, United Kingdom (hereafter cited as TRC). The amendments to the printed contract concerning the illustrations are written in Moxon's hand. The drafted contract is unsigned, but there is a stroke through Moxon's note that the publisher is responsible for directing the mode of "illustrating," and the verso is embellished with Tennyson's doodles, so clearly the poet at least read the proposal.

8. For the connection between the illustrated Keats and the Moxon Tennyson, see "A Statement of Facts Respecting the Illustrated Edition of My Poems" in *Letters of Alfred Tennyson,* 2:210. As a companion book to the illustrated Keats, Tennyson's *Poems* was initially to include George Scharf as one of the illustrators, "with a few gems from the antique" (letter to Tennyson from Moxon dated February 27, 1854, TRC letter #7869).

9. In an undated letter to Emily Tennyson, Moxon claimed to have spent "upwards of £1500" for the designs and engraving (TRC letter #7886). According to William Vaughan, Moxon paid £1,375 for the artists' designs, £540 for engraving, and £500 for printing and production ("Incongruous Disciples," 149). I have not been able to verify the costs Vaughan cites for printing and production. The figures provided by June Steffensen Hagen in *Tennyson and His Publishers* are not entirely reliable, as she confuses the costs of the illustrated edition of *Poems* with those for the illustrated *Princess* (see chapter 5).

10. William Holman Hunt told George Somes Layard that Tennyson may have recommended Maclise as well as Millais (Layard, *Tennyson,* 5n). In a letter to Tennyson dated February 27, 1854, Moxon wrote that as soon as Landseer, Mulready, Creswick, Millais, and Scharf had selected their subjects, he would call on Stanfield, Maclise, Horsley, and Frost for their choices. Whether Landseer, Scharf, and Frost declined to participate or whether the publisher and/or poet decided not to go forward with these artists after Rossetti and Hunt became involved is unclear. See TRC letter #7869. Moxon invited Rossetti in January 1855 (D. G. Rossetti, *Correspondence,* 2:7).

11. In March 1855, Dante Gabriel Rossetti wrote to William Allingham to say that, on hearing of Ruskin's praise of Elizabeth Siddall's designs (she had composed

illustrations for "The Lady of Shalott," "The Passing of Arthur," "St. Cecilia," and "Lady Clare"), the Tennysons "wish[ed] her exceedingly to join in the illustrated edition." According to Rossetti, "Mrs. T. wrote immediately to Moxon about it, declaring that she had rather pay for Miss S.'s designs herself than not have them in the book." I have not been able to locate either Emily's letter or Moxon's immediate response to this proposal, but I suspect that Siddall's lack of reputation as an exhibiting painter may have made the publisher less than enthusiastic. Rossetti himself acknowledged "the difficulty of wood-drawing" for Siddall as a novice artist (*Correspondence,* 2:26n3).

12. See McGann, *Dante Gabriel Rossetti.*

13. See Hagen, *Tennyson and His Publishers,* 106–9. Some of her details are inaccurate. Routledge bought up the remainders and brought out the illustrated edition as a Christmas gift book in late autumn of 1858 (this edition was forward-dated 1859). Tennyson's contract and the Routledge Christmas sales catalogs are in the Routledge Archive; see "New Illustrated Present Books" for 1858. See also Frank Lushington's letter at Christmas of that year: "I see the Illustrated Edition appearing as a guinea Xmas book in Routledge's advertisements" (TRC letter #3910).

14. Jean Hagstrum provides a good summary of the classical tradition from Plato to Horace in *The Sister Arts,* 3–36. Richard Altick, in *Paintings from Books,* provides a comprehensive examination of the tradition's development and demise in the nineteenth century. See also Henryk Markiewicz's historical summary, *"Ut Pictura Poesis";* and Paola Spinozzi's essay, "Interarts and Illustration," situating illustration specifically within this historical tradition.

15. See John Ruskin's *Ariadne Florentina* and commentary on it by Richard Altick in *Paintings from Books,* 200; and by J. Hillis Miller in *Illustration,* 75–79.

16. Michel de Certeau describes reading "as a form of the *bricolage*"; through a process of reusing and recombining, readers become inventive "poets of their own acts" (*Practice,* 174, xviii).

17. See Harris, "Pre-Raphaelites"; Vaughan, "Incongruous Disciples"; and Stein, "Pre-Raphaelite Tennyson." Stein is particularly insightful on the differences not only between the two groups but also among individual members. While I recognize the importance of these individual distinctions, my purpose here is to paint the larger differences in broad strokes to keep my focus on the material page and the relationships it proposes, rather than to become involved in comparative inter-art analyses.

18. Unless otherwise indicated, all references to Tennyson's illustrated *Poems* are taken from the 1859 edition.

19. In her compelling study *Poetry and the Pre-Raphaelite Arts,* Elizabeth K. Helsinger identifies "three of the most influential Pre-Raphaelite strategies for renewing poetry: acts of *attention,* explored as a mode of perception demanded by poetry and the arts . . . ; an emphasis on textual and historical patterns created through *repetition;* and *translation,* not only across languages and cultures but also across media" (2).

20. I am, of course, speaking of an effect on the reader rather than an intended design. The poetic text of the Moxon Tennyson was set up from the tenth edition of 1855, and the artists were given free rein to select their subjects.

21. Among the Pre-Raphaelite paintings featuring female figures extant in 1857 we must include Rossetti's *Girlhood of Mary Virgin* (1848–49) and *Ecce Ancilla Domini!* (1849–50); Millais' *Mariana* (1851), *Ophelia* (1851–52), *The Bridesmaid* (1851), *The Blind Girl* (1856), and *Autumn Leaves* (1856); and Hunt's *Hireling Shepherd* (1851–52) and *Awakening Conscience* (1853–54).

22. For Millais' illustration of fiction, see Skilton, "Centrality of Literary Illustration"; and Goldman, *John Everett Millais.*

23. For Rossetti's use of this twinning approach in his paired frontispiece and title page for his sister Christina's *Goblin Market and Other Poems* and *The Prince's Progress and Other Poems,* see Kooistra, *Christina Rossetti and Illustration.*

24. Ruskin is using the term *vignette* generically here, to indicate an engraving printed directly on the page rather than as a separate plate.

25. Macleod is particularly interested in middle-class collectors and patrons, but she also discusses the new community of beholders in more general terms, noting that it included over 600,000 workers (*Art,* 107).

26. According to Rodney Engen, Edward Dalziel "was the leading light in the firm of wood engravers, printers and publishers known as the Dalziel Brothers" and the one "who took the role of the draughtsman illustrator most seriously" (*Dictionary,* 64).

27. *Varley and Robinson's Guide for the Stranger in Manchester,* printed for the use of the exhibition's cultural tourists, highlights the Free Library in its walking tour: "Of all the institutions Manchester possesses (and there is a plenitude of them, charitable, literary, and scientific), she cannot boast of a greater [one] than this. [The Free Library] was built from the joint subscriptions of merchants, tradesmen, and artisans, and is a lasting memorial to the munificence of the men of Manchester—that class unscrupulously and unjustly libelled mercenary and sordid" (9). Richard Altick notes that 22,000 workers contributed to the Manchester Library fund in 1852, and he supplies a table of users recorded in its two branches in 1857–58; the largest category is "artisans and mechanics," followed by "Entirely unsubscribed (i.e., women and children)" (*Reader,* 227, 236).

28. For an extended analysis of this connection between the middle classes and collecting modern British painting, see Macleod, *Art.*

29. See D. G. Rossetti, *Correspondence,* 2:181n1.

30. Among the fin-de-siècle illustrators influenced by Pre-Raphaelite illustrations, we must include Charles Ricketts, Laurence Housman, and Aubrey Beardsley.

## Chapter 3: The Dalziel Brothers' Fine Art Book and the Mass Production of Culture

1. Ruskin, "Cestus of Aglaia," 155. Ruskin qualified this remark by arguing that the wood engraving of the time operated in "false conditions" by attempting to achieve the fine engraving that is possible in steel, rather than accepting the limitations of wood.

2. Gérard Genette distinguishes these categories as the *peritext*—the elements that surround and support the text proper (such as title pages, prefaces, illustrations, and the like)—and the *epitext*—the elements that comment on the text in the public sphere,

"distanced" elements that exist either with the help of media or "under cover" (for instance, in private correspondence) (*Paratexts,* 5).

3. For details of the publication and distribution of affordable editions of the standard poets for working-class readers, see St. Clair, *Reading Nation;* see also Klancher, *Making of English Reading Audiences.*

4. St. Clair identifies the "old canon" poets as Butler, Chaucer, Collins, Cowper, Dryden, Falconer, Gay, Goldsmith, Gray, Milton, Pope, Shakespeare, Spenser, Thomson, and Young and demonstrates the integral connection between intellectual property and canonization (*Reading Nation,* 128).

5. See especially part 1, "Media History: The Serial and the Book," in Brake, *Print in Transition,* 3–83.

6. Nineteenth-century commentators, including the Dalziels, refer to this series variously as the Dalziel Fine Art Books, the Dalziel Gift Books, and the Dalziel Fine Art Gift Books.

7. British mathematician and inventor Charles Babbage (1792–1871) designed an analytical engine to perform mathematical calculations to twenty decimals, but given his necessary dependence on mechanical, rather than electronic, devices, this prototype of the computer was never built in his lifetime.

8. As a result of Linda K. Hughes's pioneering research on poetry in the periodical press, an index of poetry in *Wellesley* periodicals has been initiated. See Hughes, "*Wellesley,*" note 56.

9. These titles are selected from volume 1 of *Good Words,* which was published in 1860.

10. See Anderson, "Illustration," 136; see also Srebrnik, *Alexander Strahan,* 64. According to Srebrnik, "in the course of 1864, if Strahan's own advertisements are to be believed, *Good Words* achieved an average circulation of a staggering 160,000 monthly, outselling not only the *Cornhill* but every other monthly magazine in the English-speaking world" (64).

11. "The Mother and the Angel, by a Railway Surfaceman," illustrated by Arthur Hughes, *Good Words* 12 (1871): 647–48; "Out among the Wild-Flowers, by a Police Constable," illustrated by F. Walker, *Good Words* 3 (1862): 657–59; "Some Verses Written by a Working Man for the Children to Sing at an Anniversary Meeting in Hertfordshire," illustrated by J. D. Watson, *Good Words* 3 (1862): 433–34; "Go and Come," by "D.," illustrated by William Holman Hunt, *Good Words* 3 (1862): 31–32; "O the lark is singing in the sky," by R.B.R., illustrated by J. E. Millais, *Good Words* 5 (1864): 65; "A Scene for a Study," by Jean Ingelow, illustrated by J. E. Millais, *Good Words* 5 (1864): 160; "True or False?" by Adelaide A. Procter, illustrated by A. B. Houghton, *Good Words* 3 (1862): 721–22; "The Victim," by Alfred Tennyson, illustrated by A. B. Houghton, *Good Words* 9 (1868): 17–18; and "My Treasure," by R.M., illustrated by A. B. Houghton, *Good Words* 3 (1862): 503–4.

12. Rodney Engen's multiple entries on the Dalziel brothers in his *Dictionary of Victorian Wood Engravers* provide a fund of information on each member of the family as well as on the firm itself.

13. Routledge and Warne later split into separate companies.

14. Lee Erickson estimates that "in 1851 there were about 250,000 readers in Britain who might buy a poetry book. Later, in 1900, there appear to [have] be[en] about 1,000,000 of them" ("Market," 350).

15. For example, Christina Rossetti's *Goblin Market and Other Poems* (1862), illustrated with a frontispiece and title-page vignette by her brother Dante Gabriel, was priced at five shillings.

16. The Dalziels likely paid Willmott £100 to edit *The Poets of the Nineteenth Century;* this is the amount recorded in the ledger in the Routledge Archive (f160), itemizing the costs of *English Sacred Poetry* (the companion volume to *Poets*), which Willmott edited for them in 1861.

17. Like all gift books, *The Poets of the Nineteenth Century* was available in variant bindings, in colors to match every décor.

18. The title of Coleridge's poem is "Love"; Genevieve is the poem's heroine.

19. William E. Buckler notes that the usual payment for illustrations in *Once a Week* was two guineas per half-page illustration, although prestigious illustrators such as Tenniel and Millais were usually paid five pounds, and sometimes as much as eight pounds, for their contributions ("*Once a Week*," 938).

20. Mary Elizabeth Leighton and Lisa Surridge have established a useful taxonomy of narrative functions performed by illustrations in serial fiction: proleptic, analeptic, repetitive, iterative, extradiegetic, and interpictorial ("Plot Thickens," 67). As my "Prisoner of Chillon" example suggests, some of these functions are equally applicable to narrative poetry.

21. In "Domestic and Idyllic," Linda Peterson provides a useful summary and analysis of the appetite for domestic poetry in the nineteenth century.

22. This method of hiring a writer to "write up" a series of pictures was also, famously, the origin of *Pickwick Papers.* However, Dickens ultimately turned around the relationship of artist and author so that instead of the author supplying a narrative to accompany the pictures, the pictures illustrated his narrative text.

23. Foster's biographer Frank Lewis recounts a rumor that "Foster, under instructions from the publisher he was then working for, [had] actually started work on Tennyson's poems when differences arose and Tennyson declined to allow [the] work to proceed" (*Foster,* 15). Foster and Tennyson knew each other personally, with Foster visiting Farringford on at least one occasion (15).

24. In his preface to *Pictures of English Landscape,* Tom Taylor draws attention to the "rarity" factor for the book: "The Designs should have the more interest for the public as they are the last works for Wood Engraving likely to be produced by the artist" (n.p.). In 1860, Foster was elected as a member of the Society of Painters in Water Colours and thereafter devoted his time to painting.

25. Tom Taylor was an art critic for the *Times* and a contributor to *Punch,* of which he subsequently became editor. Laura Taylor wrote two poems for *Pictures of English Landscape* and contributed subsequently to *Home Thoughts and Home Scenes.*

26. Linda K. Hughes provides an insightful analysis of this editorial practice in "Inventing Poetry and Pictorialism."

27. Both quotations are taken from the "Opinions of the Press," extracts published with the advertisement for *Home Thoughts and Home Scenes* at the back of the Dalziels' Fine Art Gift Book for 1866, *A Round of Days*.

28. The difficulty of bibliographic citation for *Home Thoughts and Home Scenes* underscores its corporate authorship. The book could be listed by the first-named, star author, citing "Jean Ingelow et al.," or by the featured artist, Arthur Boyd Houghton. Because the Dalziel brothers are the ones who conceived the book, it could equally be cited under "Dalziel," perhaps with an editorial accreditation. To group these Dalziel books together bibliographically, as in the text discussion in this chapter, I have opted to reference the book under the series title: Dalziel Fine Arts Books. All references are to Routledge's 1868 reprint.

29. See, for example, "True or False?" illustrating a poem by Adelaide Procter (*Good Words* 3 [1862]: 721–22); "My Treasure," illustrating a poem by "R.M." (*Good Words* 3 [1862]: 503–4); and "Childhood," illustrating an anonymous poem (*Good Words* 4 [1863]: 636–37). These illustrations are considered by some to be among Houghton's best work.

30. The 35 poems were supplied as follows: Dora Greenwell, 10; Jennett Humphreys, 9; Dinah Mulock, 5; Laura Taylor, 4; Amelia Edwards, 3; Jean Ingelow, 2; Mrs. Norton, 1; and "Anon.," 1.

31. This comment is from the *Morning Post* and was taken from the "Opinions of the Press," extracts published with the advertisement for *Home Thoughts and Home Scenes* at the back of the Dalziels' Fine Art Gift Book for 1866, *A Round of Days*.

32. I examine Eliza Cook's poetry in detail in chapter 4.

33. Terence Hoagwood and Kathryn Ledbetter's work on British women writers in the context of the illustrated gift-book tradition establishes a critical foundation for my analysis in chapter 4 and for future work in this area. See Hoagwood and Ledbetter, *Colour'd Shadows*.

34. I discuss Ingelow's popularity in detail in chapter 4.

35. Dalziel Fine Art Book's prefatory "Advertisement" to *Home Thoughts and Home Scenes*, n.p.

36. Dalziel Fine Art Book's prefatory "Advertisement" to *A Round of Days*, n.p.

## Chapter 4: Second-Rate Poets for Second-Rate Readers

1. *Anglo-American*, "Eliza Cook's Poetry," July 31, 1847, 342.

2. Lucy Larcom (1824–93) was one of the Lowell mill girls who published the *Offering* as part of a workers' self-improvement society and went on to a literary career. See Buck, *Women's Literature A–Z*. The *Lowell Offering* published an energetic and entertaining parody of Cook's "Old Arm Chair" in 1842. Entitled "The Dentist's Arm-Chair: A Parody," the poem was contributed by "Quizziana" with the hope that it could be as "appreciated for its truthfulness, as the original has been for its beauty and pathos" (64).

3. The audience of *Eliza Cook's Journal* has been the topic of some debate. See Johanna M. Smith's "Textual Encounters in *Eliza Cook's Journal*," which argues that the

*Journal* expresses a "dual address" to "the people" and to their "self-appointed champions" of the middle classes (51).

4. In his unpaginated introduction to Procter's posthumously published *Legends and Lyrics,* Charles Dickens told the story of how the poet had submitted to his *Household Words* pseudonymously so that the editor might accept her work on its own merit, rather than as a favor to a family friend. After he took an early proof of the Christmas number of 1854 to the Procter home and encouraged Adelaide to read the featured poem by "Miss Berwick," however, Adelaide revealed her authorship and henceforth published under her own name.

5. Jan Marsh, unpublished typescript on Portfolio Society, cited with the permission of the author.

6. See Peters, *Ingelow,* 22, 54.

7. For a detailed analysis of the role of poetry in everyday Victorian life as evidenced in its prominence in large-circulation newspapers, see Houston, "Newspaper Poems."

8. In an essay in her *Journal* in 1854, Cook wrote optimistically, "The leveling of this day is all of the *leveling-up* character," noting that "[t]he mass too is advancing with education and knowledge, and they too must gradually become leveled up" (quoted in Robinson, "Of 'Haymakers,'" 229).

9. The illustrated *Poems* came out in late autumn 1860 for the Christmas market but was forward-dated 1861.

10. "Eliza Cook. 5s vol. 1859 and Illustrated Quarto 1860," entry in the Routledge Contract Book, vol. 1, A–H, 1853–73, in the Routledge Archive.

11. Ibid.

12. These details are taken from the Publication Book, vol. 3, 1858–81 and the Contract Book, vol. 1, A–H, 1853–73, Routledge Archive.

13. Eliza Cook had a masculine appearance, enhanced by a masculine style of dressing her hair and her person. At twenty, Cook's attachment to the daughter of a Kent landowner prompted some gossip in the press. She was romantically attached to the American actress Charlotte Cushman (later the partner of Mathilda Hayes), to whom she addressed some love poetry and dedicated early work. See Smith, "Textual Encounters," 59; and Shattock, *Oxford Guide,* 116.

14. Unless otherwise indicated, all references are to Eliza Cook, *Poems: Selected and Edited by the Author* (1861).

15. In this regard, it is interesting to note that Dora Greenwell published "The Babes in the Wood: A Lover's Dream," illustrated by J. D. Watson, a few months after Cook's illustrated *Poems,* with its prefatory poem, came out.

16. A visual equivalent of the textual practice of verbal allusion or quotation known as intertextuality, *interpictoriality* incorporates visual allusions or quotations from other pictures into an illustration or other composition. See Thomas, "Reflections on Illustration."

17. Margaret Maison observes that sales of Procter's poetry soared after her death in 1864 and continued to be high for the next quarter of a century (i.e., 1864–89) ("Queen Victoria," 636).

18. Bell and Daldy published Procter's first volume of *Legends and Lyrics* in 1858 and the second in 1861. The two series were combined after Procter's death in the illustrated edition of 1866, which was brought out for Christmas 1865.

19. According to Gill Gregory, Procter was Dickens's most frequently published poet in *Household Words,* with her poems accounting for about a sixth of the total. Frequently, hers was the only poem in the Christmas supplement (*Life,* 2–3).

20. As is characteristic of Victorian women's poetry, musical metaphors predominate in Procter's verses, leading Isobel Armstrong to assert that Procter "virtually typifies the woman poet's interests at this time" in her groundbreaking chapter on expressive poetics. See "'A Music of Thine Own': Women's Poetry—An Expressive Tradition?" in Armstrong, *Victorian Poetry,* 318–77; quotation on 336.

21. Unless otherwise indicated, all references to Procter's poetry are from the illustrated edition of *Legends and Lyrics* (1866).

22. Dobson is not a regular illustrator of either gift books or magazines, and I have not been able to locate much information about this artist, including gender. I refer to Dobson as male simply because book artists of this period were almost all men.

23. Gill Gregory has elaborated a persuasive argument for Adelaide Procter's Tractarian poetics in "Adelaide Procter." See also her biography of Procter, *The Life and Work of Adelaide Procter,* for a useful comparison of Procter's work to John Keble's.

24. Matthew 14:24–27.

25. "Home at Last" first appeared in *Household Words* under the title "Home and Rest" (Gregory, *Life,* 165).

26. See chapter 5 for an analysis of *Enoch Arden,* first published in 1864 and issued as an illustrated gift book at the end of 1865 (but forward-dated 1866). Patrick Scott notes that Elizabeth Gaskell's contribution to the Christmas number of *Household Words* in 1856 was "the story of *Enoch Arden* as 'The Manchester Marriage'" (*Tennyson's "Enoch Arden,"* 5). It seems more accurate to say that Gaskell was telling the story of Procter's "Homeward Bound," which Dickens had published in his magazine earlier that year. Although Tennyson had a copy of the first edition of *Legends and Lyrics* (1858) in his library, Hallam Tennyson denied that his father had any knowledge of the poem when he wrote *Enoch Arden* (Scott, *Tennyson's "Enoch Arden,"* 32n41).

27. Despite her prolific output, not much is known about M. E. Edwards. See Sutherland, *Stanford Companion,* 208; see also Reid, *Illustrators of the Eighteen Sixties;* and Casteras and Peterson, *Struggle for Fame.*

28. For a detailed discussion of this performative practice, see Robson, "Standing on the Burning Deck."

29. The illustrated *Songs of Seven* was only published in the United States. Roberts Brothers employed British artist John North as the principal illustrator, with the Dalziels as the engravers, but some of the work was apparently done by American artist Hammatt Billings (*Round Table,* December 16, 1865, 242).

30. In the same volume of *Contemporary Review,* Alford panned Christina Rossetti's *Prince's Progress and Other Poems,* saying, "Many of the pieces in this book are only fit for children" ("Recent Poetry," 503).

31. Although neither Victorian nor British, my mother, a first-generation Canadian for whom English was a second language, memorized masses of nineteenth-century poetry to relieve the tedium of her job at a canning factory when she was a teenager.

32. In 1897, *Thousand and One Gems* reached its twenty-third edition.

33. Gerard Manley Hopkins, "Heaven-Haven," in *The Poems of Gerard Manley Hopkins*, ed. W. H. Gardner and N. H. MacKenzie, 4th ed. (Oxford: Oxford University Press, 1984), 19.

34. "Seven Times Seven: Longing for Home" uses the trope of the "empty nest" to describe the female speaker's loss of purpose after her children are gone (200); as far as I have been able to ascertain, this is an early use of the metaphor that was frequently attached to middle-aged women in the following century.

## Chapter 5: Poet and Publishers

1. From an unpublished fragment in Christopher Ricks's *Selected Edition* of Tennyson's poems (161–63).

2. Kathryn Ledbetter's *Tennyson and Victorian Periodicals* persuasively connects the spread of Tennyson's transatlantic reputation to his publication in periodicals and provides a useful "Selection of Publications by Periodical Name" (appendix A) as well as "A Select Listing of Tennyson Poems in American Literary Annuals" (appendix C).

3. Because there was no international copyright agreement in the nineteenth century, American publishers could, and did, pirate Tennyson's work (although Ticknor and Fields was his official American publisher). The numerous illustrated anthologies, collections, and single-poem volumes of Tennyson's poems published in the United States are a subject unto themselves; this chapter focuses on the official publications of his British publishers.

4. In the 1890s, long poems designed and illustrated by a single artist-designer became a characteristic feature of belles-lettres lists. See, for example, Charles Ricketts's design for Oscar Wilde's *Sphinx*, Laurence Housman's design for Christina Rossetti's *Goblin Market*, Aubrey Beardsley's design for Alexander Pope's *Rape of the Lock*, and William Morris's design for Tennyson's *Maud: A Monodrama*.

5. Tennyson used the term *working men* to describe the audience for the "People's Edition," or Cabinet Edition, of 1874.

6. For an account of these various moves, see Hagen, *Tennyson*. Hagen includes Tennyson's 1879 contract with Kegan Paul in an appendix.

7. See Macmillan's letter to Routledge dated November 10, 1892, in the Routledge Archive (vol. 5, 1873–99, L–Z). Macmillan brought out his edition of the illustrated *Poems* in 1897, perhaps as a special gift edition to mark the Jubilee.

8. See, for example, Ledbetter, *Tennyson;* and Hoagwood and Ledbetter, *Colour'd Shadows*. Patrick Scott's biblio-critical essay on the production and reception of *Enoch Arden* and its various illustrated editions remains the fullest treatment accorded to any single illustrated poem by Tennyson.

9. Tennyson's unillustrated collections usually sold for about five shillings—less than one-fourth of the cost of the typical guinea gift book.

10. *Three Gems in One Setting* also included "Field Flowers" by Thomas Campbell and "The Pilgrim Fathers" by Felicia Hemans. In her review essay for *Blackwood's* in 1861, Margaret Oliphant wrote, "[T]he best that can be said of [this book] is, that it is sweetly pretty, and may be appreciated in quarters where art is unknown" ("Merry Christmas," 11).

11. The *George Routledge and Sons Wholesale Christmas Catalogue of Illustrated Works and Juvenile Books* (1868) may be found in the Routledge Archive.

12. Letter from Macmillan to Routledge dated November 18, 1892, Routledge Archive.

13. "Illustrated by Maclise" was, however, printed on the spine of *The Princess* for Moxon's 1860 edition.

14. All references to this work are from Alfred Tennyson, *The May Queen,* illustrated by E.V.B. (Sampson Low, 1861).

15. As her model for the heroine of *The May Queen,* E.V.B. used her beloved daughter, Alice, who died within the decade from consumption (de Beaumont, "EVB," 16, 19).

16. For an excellent reading of E.V.B. as an illustrator for *The May Queen,* see Thomas, *Pictorial Victorians,* 64–76.

17. Arthur Hughes's composition for "Baby lies so fast asleep" in Christina Rossetti's *Sing-Song: A Nursery Rhyme Book* seems to have been inspired by this illustration by E.V.B. (see page 127 in the Dover edition).

18. According to Christine Poulson, "Between 1850 and 1915 at least 54 works of art were based" on Tennyson's Lady of Shalott; this number does not include book illustration ("Death and the Maiden," 173). See also Lottes, *"Lady of Shalott";* and Nelson, "Tennyson."

19. Alfred Tennyson, *The Princess,* illustrated by Daniel Maclise (London: Edward Moxon, 1860). The book was forward-dated in conformity with Victorian publishing practice. Unless otherwise noted, I cite the 1866 reprint of this edition.

20. See "A Statement of Facts Respecting The Illustrated Edition [*sic*] of My Poems," A. Tennyson, *Letters,* 2:210–11. The editors of Tennyson's *Letters* have "Edition" in singular form; however, in the "Statement of Facts" recorded in the holograph manuscript in the TRC, "Editions" is plural in the header. This is confirmed in the body of the "Statement" itself, which devotes equal space to discussing the illustrated edition of the *Poems* and the illustrated edition of *The Princess.* In other words, the "Statement" dealt with two editions, not one: the illustrated *Poems* and the illustrated *Princess.* See also the letter from Charles Weld to Tennyson dated October 27, 1858, in which the Moxon firm's financial claims against the poet are elaborated (TRC letter #2419).

21. The payments to Maclise and the engravers (Williams, the Dalziels, Green, and Thomas) are recorded on an account statement located in the TRC. Hagen inaccurately connects this statement to the payments Moxon made for the illustrated *Poems* of 1857 (*Tennyson,* 106).

22. There were no proofs for Maclise's vignettes included with the twenty half-page medieval designs sent to Tennyson in October 1859 with the preliminary proofs for the edition. See "The Princess Illus ed. 1860. Proofs of pp 1–32," Cat. No. 4239 P183, TRC.

23. The proof for Maclise's design for the northern king is dated February 6, 1856. The Dalziels added the pencil note, "NOT Moxon Tennyson. The Princess 1860, p. 17," beside the proof as well as the information that it was later recut for the book by W. Thomas (Dalziel Brothers' Proofs Book for 1856, Dalziel Collection, Department of Prints and Drawings, British Museum, London). In the published copy of the illustrated *Princess,* the engraving is signed by W. Thomas, who cut the design after Maclise altered it, perhaps in response to Tennyson's request. In the Dalziels' Proofs Book, the composition is similar to the published engraving, but the figures have slightly different postures, facial features, and headgear, and the design lacks many details. The recutting seems to have occurred late in the process. In the trial book with some pasted-in proofs of engravings in the TRC (Cat. No. 4239 P183), there is a blank space on page 17 where the picture is to be placed, with the words "cut not yet finished" written in hand.

24. Letter from Edward Moxon to Emily Tennyson (1856?), TRC letter #7882.

25. Maclise's personal copy of *The Princess,* with the artist's notations and pencil drawings, is located in the Victoria and Albert Museum's Department of Prints and Drawings. It is the 1853 (fifth) edition of *The Princess* and contains Moxon's List of Books dated February 1854. In a letter to Tennyson dated February 27, 1854, in which he writes of prospective artists for the illustrated *Poems,* Moxon indicates his intention to call on Maclise (TRC letter #7869). It seems likely that this initial meeting with the artist also resulted in a commission for *The Princess* and that the publisher supplied the illustrator with the most recent edition of the work at that time.

26. Twelve of the twenty half-page illustrations for the medieval tale feature gothic archways in their compositions.

27. The lyric comprises two verses of five lines each, divided by a space between, in both Maclise's working copy (1853 edition) and the illustrated edition of 1859. In the reprint of *The Princess* in *Tennyson: A Selected Edition,* edited by Christopher Ricks (219–330), the lyric is printed in a single block of fourteen lines (239). The additional verses are inserted at lines six through nine and constitute a generalized reflection on the temporal moment the lyric celebrates. Tennyson included these lines when he added the songs in the 1850 edition of *The Princess,* but he discarded them in every subsequent edition between 1851 and 1861 (see Ricks's editorial notes on page 239 and pages 531–32). All references to this lyric are from the illustrated edition of 1866.

28. Author's copy of the first illustrated edition of *The Princess,* with twenty-six designs on the wood by Daniel Maclise, in TRC.

29. His subsequent reinsertion of lines six through nine between the two verses, closing up all the white space between them, may have been intended to make defacing the lyric with future pictorial colonizing impossible.

30. Critics have long deplored the inadequate treatment of the subject of women's rights in *The Princess.* See, for example, Christopher Ricks, who reckons that the problems with *The Princess* stem "from its innumerable evasions" (*Tennyson,* 189); W. David Shaw, who acknowledges that the poem "both defends and makes fun of Victorian feminism" (*Alfred Lord Tennyson,* 17); Marjorie Stone, who remarks on the poem's ideological conservatism, despite its apparent gender reversal ("Genre Subversion"); and

Herbert F. Tucker, who calls it a "textbook Victorian compromise" that avoids taking a position on the contemporary gender issue it addresses (*Doom*, 351).

31. Tennyson's note to the poem indicates that these lines, which were added in the edition of 1850—i.e., the same edition to which the women's intervening songs were added—were "[w]ritten just after the disturbances in France, February 1848, when Louis Philippe was compelled to abdicate" (*Tennyson: A Selected Edition*, 328).

32. Maclise began work on *The Meeting of Wellington and Blücher* for the new House of Parliament in 1860; three years later, he painted *The Death of Nelson* for the same national institution (National Portrait Gallery, *Daniel Maclise*, 17, 107). These large public works consumed all his energy in his last years, which likely explains why *The Princess* was his last illustration commission.

33. Tennyson later objected to two of Hughes's illustrations (the antelopes on the desert island and the "calling of the sea" vignette) but seemed otherwise satisfied with the book as a whole. See A. Tennyson, *Letters*, 2:413, 423, 456; Woolner, *Thomas Woolner*, 267; and Roberts, *Hughes*, 256.

34. The Royal Academy catalog for 1856 printed the following verses from Tennyson's "Miller's Daughter" in its entry for *April Love:*

> Love is hurt with jar and fret,
> Love is made a vague regret;
> Eyes with idle tears are wet,
> Idle habit links us yet.
> What is love? For we forget:
> Ah, no! no!
>
> (Roberts, *Hughes*, 134)

35. The first successful use of photography onto a woodblock was Thomas Bolton's engraving of a Flaxman relief sculpture in Catherine Winkworth's *Lyra Germanica* of 1861 (Suriano, *British Pre-Raphaelite Illustrators*, 26). Nevertheless, *Enoch Arden* was the first book in England to use the photographic process for a whole series of specially commissioned illustrations, a novelty highlighted in contemporary reviews (White, *English Illustration*, 127).

36. In the book reviews for Christmas 1865, the year the illustrated *Enoch Arden* was published, the greatest excitement and interest were generated by a new species of gift book to hit the market: the volume illustrated by photographs.

37. Unless otherwise indicated, all references to the illustrated *Enoch Arden* are from the 1866 edition.

38. Hughes seems to have taken some inspiration for this misty representation of the supernatural from E.V.B.'s illustrations for *The May Queen*.

39. George Grove (1820–1900) was also the founder-editor of the *Dictionary of Music and Musicians*.

40. See Grove's letter in A. Tennyson, *Letters*, 2:444.

41. Emily's journal records Tennyson reading Heine's songs to her on October 9, 1866, and refers to "his 'Song of the Wrens' which he has written for Sullivan" on

October 16, noting the completion of the cycle on October 21, about the time of Grove and Sullivan's visit to Farringford. See E. Tennyson, *Journal*.

42. See A. Tennyson, *Letters*, 2:535; and Jennings, *Lord Tennyson, 1809–1892*, 118–20.

43. Gregory Suriano lists *A Reverie* as a steel engraving published on page xiv in the 1878 *Magazine of Art*, reprinted from *Leslie's Musical Annual* (*British Pre-Raphaelite Illustrators*, 318). Arthur Jacobs claims that it was published in *Cassell's Family Magazine* of 1875 (*Sullivan*, 59). The only place I have been able to locate it is in *The Life and Letters of Sir John Everett Millais* (edited by John Guille Millais), where it is identified as "used in Leslie's 'Little Songs,' but originally drawn for a joint work by Millais, Sullivan and Tennyson" (423). *Little Songs*, however, was published in 1865, a year before Millais began collaborating with Sullivan and Tennyson on *The Window*.

44. With regard to critical evaluation of this work, see the artist's letter to Agnes Hale-White, dated March 23, 1913, referring to "one of my best pen and ink drawings . . . a large one made for Tennyson's 'Song of the Wrens'" (Roberts, *Hughes*, 261). See also White, *English Illustration*, 171; Reid, *Illustrators of the Eighteen Sixties*, 84, 87; McInnis, "Allegorizing," 76; and Goldman, *Victorian Illustration*, 53–54.

45. For an interpretation of Hughes's picture in relation to Simmons's verses, see McInnis, "Allegorizing," 76. Strahan published Hughes's fourth illustration for *The Window* at an even further remove, in the April 1872 issue of *Sunday Magazine* (Roberts, *Hughes*, 261).

46. J. R. Wise notes that the interlinear lyrics for Song VI (The Letter) follow the Canford Manor Folio, "whilst the words as given in the letter-press are the revised version" (*Bibliography*, 1:186–87).

47. Emily refers to "Take My Love" as a new song in May 1867 (H. Tennyson, *Memoir*, 2:44).

48. The extant song cycle moves from E minor in IX, "Two little hands that meet," to D major in X, "Sun comes, moon comes." According to Kim Chow Morris, a colleague of mine from the music program at Ryerson University, this is a virtually unheard-of modulation in Romantic music. Sullivan likely set (or intended to set) the missing song in G major. As the relative major for E minor and a perfect fifth below D major, a setting in G major would have effected a harmonious transition and established the positive and joyous turn in the musical cycle.

49. From Moxon's advertisement for "The Christmas Gift Book, 1866," in *Athenaeum*, no. 2040 (December 1, 1866): 729.

50. June Steffensen Hagen gives 12,000 as the initial print run for *Works* (*Tennyson and His Publishers*, 138), but the Cabinet Edition subsequently went into multiple reprintings and editions.

51. For an excellent analysis of the photographic frontispiece in the Cabinet Edition and of H. S. King's deployment of the portrait photograph as a means of popularizing the poet through celebrity images, see Groth, *Victorian Photography*.

52. See Marylu Hill's captivating article, "Shadowing Sense at War with Soul," which she begins with an anecdote confessing her momentary childhood belief, on first seeing Cameron's photographs of the *Idylls*, that Arthur and company might have been real after all, and then goes on to develop a sophisticated argument about

the ways in which these pictures play with the oscillations of life, death, past, present, reality, and illusion.



53. The quotation is taken from Henry James's preface to *The Golden Bowl* in *The Novels and Tales of Henry James,* a reprint of the "New York" edition, vol. 23 (New York, 1971), xi; quoted in Miller, *Illustration,* 70.

54. For volume 5, which included the first three *Idylls,* King reproduced Woolner's bust of Tennyson as the frontispiece, rather than selecting one of Cameron's photographs for *The Coming of Arthur, Gareth and Lynette,* or *Geraint and Enid.*

55. Wood-engraved pictures continued to dominate the periodical press until the 1890s.

56. Henry S. King and Charles Kegan Paul were both involved in publishing the Cabinet Edition. Paul was King's manager but went into business for himself on King's death, taking over much of King's original business (including Tennyson).

57. For alternative readings of the relationship between text, underlining, and image, see C. Armstrong, *Scenes in a Library;* and Groth, *Victorian Photography.*

58. Advertisement for "Cassell's Illustrated Volumes and Christmas and New-Year Gift-Books" in the *Saturday Review* 22, no. 579 (December 1, 1866): 692.

59. From Moxon's advertisement for *Elaine* in the *Athenaeum,* no. 2040 (December 1, 1866): 729.

60. See Hagen, *Tennyson,* appendix 2, Deed of Agreement.

## Coda: Poems and Pictures in the Modern Age

1. H. W. Dulcken edited the popular standard works in the Dalziel Illustrated Edition series published by Ward and Lock (Dalziel and Dalziel, *Record,* 226).

2. Routledge's *Goody Two Shoes' Picture Book* included "Goody Two Shoes," "Beauty and the Beast," "The Frog Prince," and "An Alphabet of Old Friends," with twenty-four illustrations. *The Marquis of Carabas's Picture Book* was similarly illustrated and included "Puss in Boots," "Old Mother Hubbard," "Valentine and Orson," and "The Absurd A.B.C."

3. Walter Crane (1845–1915) began his artistic career in W. J. Linton's engraving firm, where he learned to draw on the woodblock. Crane was a book artist, not an easel painter; in this respect, he anticipated the book designers of the 1890s.

4. Taken from an advertisement in the Moxon Popular Poets edition of *Byron's Poetical Works.*

5. Like the derogatory term *furniture books,*" the designation *drawing-room books* is frequently used by critics to describe poetic gift books. See, for example, Oliphant, "Picture-Books," 316.

6. The duodecimo format of Tennyson's Cabinet Edition, designed to fit easily into a masculine pocket, contrasted significantly with the quarto format of Moxon's Popular Poets series, which the *Saturday Review* critic complained could only be made for people who do not "want to carry [a poet] with them—a volume at a time—in their pocket" (December 24, 1870, 814).

# Bibliography


Alcott, Louisa May. "Glimpses of Eminent Persons: Jean Ingelow." *Independent,* November 1, 1866, 1.

Alford, Henry. Notice of Books. *Contemporary Review* 3 (December 1866): 602–24.

———. Notice of Books VI—Poetry, Fiction, and Essay. *Contemporary Review* 7 (February 1868): 303–6.

———. Recent Poetry. *Contemporary Review* 3 (December 1866): 502–4.

Allen, R., in collaboration with Gale R. D'Luhy. *Sir Arthur Sullivan: Composer and Personage.* New York: Pierpont Morgan Library, 1975.

Allingham, William. *The Music Master, a Love Story, and Two Series of Day and Night Songs, with Nine Woodcuts.* Routledge, 1855. Facsimile, New York: Legacy Press/Arno Press, 1967.

Althusser, Louis. "Ideology and Ideological State Apparatuses (Notes Towards an Investigation)." In *Media and Cultural Studies: Keyworks,* edited by Meenakshi Gigi Durham and Douglas M. Kellner, 79–87. Oxford, UK: Blackwell, 2006.

Altick, Richard D. *The English Common Reader: A Social History of the Mass Reading Public, 1800–1900.* Chicago: University of Chicago Press, 1967.

———. *Paintings from Books: Art and Literature in Britain, 1750–1900.* Columbus: Ohio State University Press, 1985.

Anderson, Patricia. "Illustration." In *Victorian Periodicals and Victorian Society,* edited by J. Donn Vann and Rosemary T. VanArsdel, 127–42. Toronto: University of Toronto Press, 1994.

———. *The Printed Image and the Transformation of Popular Culture, 1790–1860.* Oxford, UK: Clarendon Press, 1991.

*Anglo-American.* "Eliza Cook's Poetry." July 31, 1847, 342–43.

Anonymous. "Childhood." Illustrated by Arthur Boyd Houghton. *Good Words* 4 (1863): 636–37.

———. *Some Recollections of Jean Ingelow and Her Early Friends.* Port Washington, NY: Kennikat, 1972.

Armstrong, Carol. *Scenes in a Library: Reading the Photograph in the Book, 1843–1875.* Cambridge, MA: MIT Press, 1998.

Armstrong, Isobel. *Victorian Poetry: Poetry, Poetics, and Politics.* London: Routledge, 1993.

*Arthur's Home Magazine.* Review of *Songs of Seven,* by Jean Ingelow. January 1866, 78.

*Art Journal.* Review of *Poems,* by Alfred Tennyson, published by E. Moxon. 31 (July 1857): 231.

*Athenaeum.* Christmas Gift-Books. November 8, 1856, 1364–65.

———. Our Weekly Gossip. October 31, 1857, 1359–60.

———. Fine Arts: Gift-Books. November 22, 1862, 666.

———. Fine Arts: Gift-Books. December 19, 1863, 842–43.

———. Fine Arts: Illustrated Books. November 26, 1864, 712–13.

———. Fine Arts: Illustrated Books. December 23, 1865, 894.

———. Fine Arts: Gift-Books. December 5, 1874, 756–57.

*Atlanta Constitution*. "Well-Known Poetess Not Dead, as Reported—Some Facts about Her Life." January 8, 1873, 2.

Austin, Alfred. "'Mr. Tennyson,' *The Poetry of the Period*." 1870. In *Tennyson: The Critical Heritage*, edited by John D. Jump, 294–311. London: Routledge and Kegan Paul, 1967.

Barthes, Roland. "The Death of the Author." In *The Book History Reader*, edited by David Finkelstein and Alistair McCleery, 221–24. New York: Routledge, 2002.

———. *Image Music Text*. Translated by Stephen Heath. London: Fontana, 1977.

Beegan, Gerry. *The Mass Image: A Social History of Photomechanical Reproduction in Victorian London*. Houndmills, UK: Palgrave Macmillan, 2007.

Benjamin, Walter. "The Work of Art in the Age of Mechanical Reproduction (1936)." In *The Nineteenth-Century Visual Culture Reader*, edited by Vanessa R. Schwartz and Jeannene M. Przyblyski, 63–70. London: Routledge, 2004.

Bettley, James, ed. *The Art of the Book: From Medieval Manuscript to Graphic Novel*. London: V and A, 2001.

Bogue, David. *Christmas with the Poets: A Collection of Songs, Carols, and Descriptive Verses, Relating to the Festival of Christmas, from the Anglo-Norman Period to the Present Time*. Illustrated by Myles Birket Foster. Henry Vizetelly, printer and engraver. London: David Bogue, 1851.

Bohn, Henry G. Our Weekly Gossip. *Athenaeum*, December 17, 1859, 815–17.

Bornstein, George. *Palimpsest: Editorial Theory in the Humanities*, edited by George Bornstein and Ralph G. Williams. Ann Arbor: University of Michigan Press, 1996.

Bourdieu, Pierre. "Introduction: The Aristocracy of Culture." In *Media and Cultural Studies: Keyworks*, edited by Meenakshi Gigi Durham and Douglas M. Kellner, 322–27. Oxford, UK: Blackwell, 2006.

———. "The Market of Symbolic Goods." In *The Critical Tradition: Classic Texts and Contemporary Trends*, edited by David H. Richter, 1232–53. 2nd ed. Boston: Bedford Books, 1998.

Bowler, Gerry. *The World Encyclopedia of Christmas*. Toronto: McClelland and Stewart, 2000.

Boyd, Timothy W. "'A Regular Illustrated Book': William Allingham and His Pre-Raphaelite Friends Make *The Music Master*, 1854–55." *Publishing History* 37 (1995): 17–49.

Bradbury and Evans. *Catalogue of the Art Treasures of the United Kingdom Collected at Manchester in 1857*. London: Bradbury and Evans, 1857.

———. *A Handbook to the Gallery of British Paintings in the Art Treasures Exhibition, Being a Reprint of Critical Notices Originally Published in "The Manchester Guardian."* London: Bradbury and Evans, 1857.

———. *A Handbook to the Water Colours, Drawings, and Engravings in the Art Treasures Exhibition, Being a Reprint of Critical Notices Originally Published in "The Manchester Guardian."* London: Bradbury and Evans, 1857.

———. *Supplemental Catalogue. Drawings and Sketches of Old Masters, Engravings, Photographs*. London: Bradbury and Evans, 1857.

Brake, Laurel. *Print in Transition, 1850–1910: Studies in Media and Book History*. London: Palgrave, 2000.

Buchanan, Robert, ed. *Wayside Posies: Original Poems of the Country Life*. Dalziel Fine Art Gift Book. London: Routledge, 1867.

Buchanan-Brown, John. *Early Victorian Illustrated Books: Britain, France and Germany, 1820–1860*. London: British Library, 2005.

Buck, Claire, ed. *Women's Literature A–Z*. London: Bloomsbury, 1992.

Buckler, William E. "*Once a Week* under Samuel Lucas, 1859–65." *PMLA* 7, no. 67 (1952): 924–41.

Burne-Jones, Georgiana. *Memorials of Edward Burne-Jones*. 2 vols. New York: Macmillan, 1904.

Burns, James. *Poems and Pictures: A Collection of Ballads, Songs, and Other Poems, Illustrated by English Artists*. London: James Burns, 1846.

Byron, George Gordon, Lord. *Byron's Poetical Works*. Edited by W. M. Rossetti; illustrated by Thomas Seccombe. Moxon's Popular Poets. London: Moxon, 1880.

Cameron, Julia Margaret. *Illustrations to Tennyson's "Idylls of the King" and Other Poems*. 2 vols. London: Henry S. King, 1875.

Carroll, Lewis. *The Annotated Alice: "Alice's Adventures in Wonderland" and "Through the Looking Glass."* Illustrated by John Tenniel; edited by Martin Gardiner. New York: Bramhall House, 1960.

Cassell, John. *John Cassell's Art Treasures Exhibition: Containing Engravings of the Principal Masterpieces of the English, Dutch, Flemish, French, and German Schools, with Biographical Sketches of the Painters, and Critical Notices of Their Production*. London: W. Kent, 1858.

Casteras, Susan P., ed. *Pocket Cathedrals: Pre-Raphaelite Book Illustration*. New Haven, CT: Yale Center for British Art, 1991.

Casteras, Susan P., and Linda H. Peterson. *The Struggle for Fame: Victorian Women Artists and Authors*. New Haven, CT: Yale Center for British Art, 1994.

*Catholic World*. "The Poems of Adelaide Anne Procter." 2 (1866): 837–43.

Chapman, Alison. "'A Poet Never Sees a Ghost': Photography and Trance in Tennyson's *Enoch Arden* and Julia Margaret Cameron's Photography." *Victorian Poetry* 41, no. 1 (2003): 47–71.

Chorley, Henry Fothergill. Review of *Legends and Lyrics*, by Adelaide Anne Procter. *Athenaeum*, December 9, 1865, 799.

Christ, Carol T. *Victorian and Modern Poetics*. Chicago: University of Chicago Press, 1986.

*Christian Examiner*. Review of *Songs of Seven*, by Jean Ingelow. January 1866, 143.

Colclough, Stephen. "Readers: Books and Biography." In *A Companion to the History of the Book*, edited by Simon Eliot and Jonathan Rose; 50–62. Oxford, UK: Blackwell, 2007.

Cole, William. "Literal Art? A New Look at Doré's Illustrations for Dante's Inferno." *Word and Image* 10, no. 2 (1994): 95–106.

Connelly, Mark. *Christmas: A Social History*. London: I. B. Tauris, 1999.

Cook, Eliza. *Eliza Cook's Poetical Works*. 1859 one-volume edition. Reprint, London: Routledge, Warne and Routledge, 1862.

———. *Jottings from My Journal*. London: Routledge, 1860.

———. *Poems: Selected and Edited by the Author*. Illustrated by John Gilbert, J. Wolf, H. Weir, J. D. Watson, et al.; engraved by the Brothers Dalziel. London: Routledge, 1861.

———. "A Word to My Readers." *Eliza Cook's Journal* 1 (1849): 1–3.

Craik, Dinah Mulock. "A Woman's Thoughts about Women (1858)." In *Christina Rossetti: Maude; Dinah Mulock Craik: On Sisterhoods; and A Woman's Thoughts about Women*, edited by Elaine Showalter, 59–216. New York: New York University Press, 1995.

Crane, Walter. *The Decorative Illustration of Books (1896)*. London: Studio Editions, 1994.

Crary, Jonathan. *Techniques of the Observer: On Vision and Modernity in the Nineteenth Century*. Cambridge, MA: MIT Press, 1990.

Curtis, Gerard. *Visual Words: Art and the Material Book in Victorian England*. Aldershot, UK: Ashgate, 2002.

Dalby, Richard. *The Golden Age of Children's Book Illustration*. New York: Gallery Books, 1991.

Dalziel, Edward, and George Dalziel. *The Brothers Dalziel: A Record of Fifty Years' Work in Conjunction with Many of the Most Distinguished Artists of the Period 1840–1890*. London: Methuen, 1901. Facsimile, London: B. T. Batsford, 1978.

Dalziel Fine Art Books. *Birket Foster's Pictures of English Landscape, with Picture in Words by Tom Taylor*. London: Routledge, 1862.

———. *English Sacred Poetry of the Sixteenth, Seventeenth, Eighteenth, and Nineteenth Centuries*, edited by R. A. Willmott. London: Routledge, 1862.

———. *Home Thoughts and Home Scenes in Original Poems and Pictures*. 1865. London: Routledge, 1868.

———. *Picture Poesies*. Illustrated. London: Routledge, 1874.

———. *The Poets of the Nineteenth Century, Illustrated with One Hundred Engravings Drawn by Eminent Artists, and Engraved by the Brothers Dalziel*, edited by R. A. Willmott. 3rd ed. London: Routledge, 1858.

———. *A Round of Days Described in Original Poems by Some of Our Most Celebrated Poets and in Pictures by Eminent Artists, Engraved by the Brothers Dalziel*. London: Routledge, 1866.

———. *Wayside Posies: Original Poems of the Country Life*, edited by R. Buchanan. London: Routledge, 1867.

Darton, F. J. Harvey. *Children's Books in England: Five Centuries of Social Life*. 3rd ed. Revised by Brian Alderson. London: British Library and Oak Knoll Press, 1999.

de Beaumont, Robin. "EVB (the Hon. Mrs. Eleanor Vere Boyle): An Account of Her Life and a Bibliography." *IBIS* 2 (2002): 8–35.

de Certeau, Michel. *The Practice of Everyday Life*. Translated by Steven Rendall. Berkeley: University of California Press, 1988.

de Maré, Eric Samuel. *The Victorian Woodblock Illustrators*. London: Gordon Fraser, 1980.

Dickens, Charles. Introduction to *Legends and Lyrics*, by Adelaide Anne Procter. London: Bell and Daldy, 1866.

Doran, John. Our Literary Table. *Athenaeum*, November 10, 1866, 607–8.

Drucker, Johanna. "*Le Petit Journal des Refusées:* A Graphical Reading." In "Victorian Poetry and the Book Arts," edited by Lorraine Janzen Kooistra, special issue, *Victorian Poetry* 48, no. 1 (2010): 137–69.

Drucker, Johanna, and Emily McVarish. *Graphic Design: A Critical Guide*. Upper Saddle River, NJ: Pearson–Prentice Hall, 2009.

Dulcken, H. W. *Happy Day Stories for the Young*. Illustrated by A. B. Houghton. London: George Routledge, 1875.

*Eclectic Magazine of Foreign Literature, Science and Art*. "Eliza Cook: With a Portrait." March 1855, 430.

Eliot, Simon. "Some Trends in British Book Production, 1800–1919." In *Literature in the Marketplace: Nineteenth-Century British Publishing and Reading Practices*, edited by John O. Jordan and Robert L. Patten, 19–43. Cambridge: Cambridge University Press, 1995.

Eliot, Simon, and Jonathan Rose, ed. *A Companion to the History of the Book*. Oxford, UK: Blackwell, 2007.

Eliot, T. S. *The Sacred Wood: Essays on Poetry and Criticism*. 1920. London: Methuen, 1976.

Engen, Rodney. *Dictionary of Victorian Wood Engravers*. Cambridge, UK: Chadwyck-Healey, 1985.

Erickson, Lee. "The Market." In *A Companion to Victorian Poetry*, edited by Alison Chapman, Richard Cronin, and Antony H. Harrison, 345–60. Oxford, UK: Blackwell, 2002.

Feldman, Paula R., ed. *The Keepsake for 1829*. Peterborough, ON: Broadview, 2006.

Flanders, Judith. *The Victorian House: Domestic Life from Childbirth to Deathbed*. New York: HarperCollins, 2003.

Flint, Kate. *The Victorians and the Visual Imagination*. Cambridge: Cambridge University Press, 2000.

———. *The Woman Reader, 1837–1914*. 1993. Reprint, Oxford, UK: Clarendon, 2002.

Ford, Colin. *Julia Margaret Cameron: 19th Century Photographer of Genius*. London: National Portrait Gallery, 2003.

Foster, Myles Birket. *Birket Foster's Pictures of English Landscape, with Picture in Words by Tom Taylor*. London: Routledge, 1862.

———. "Christmas Eve—The Cottager's Return from Market." *Illustrated London News*, December 22, 1855, 720.

Foucault, Michel. "What Is an Author?" In *The Book History Reader*, edited by David Finkelstein and Alistair McCleery, 225–30. London: Routledge, 2002.

Frankel, Nicholas. "Aubrey Beardsley 'Embroiders' the Literary Text." In *The Victorian Illustrated Book*, edited by Richard Maxwell, 259–96. Victorian Literature and Culture. Charlottesville: University Press of Virginia, 2002.

———. *Oscar Wilde's Decorated Books*. Ann Arbor: University of Michigan Press, 2000.

*Fraser's Magazine*. "Furniture Books." 59, no. 349 (January 1859): 95–102.

Fredeman, William E. "'Woodman, Spare That Block': The Published, Unpublished and Projected Illustrations and Book Designs of Dante Gabriel Rossetti." *Journal of Pre-Raphaelite Studies*, n.s., 5 (Spring 1996): 7–41.

Genette, Gérard. *Paratexts: Thresholds of Interpretation*. Translated by Richard Macksey. Cambridge: Cambridge University Press, 1997.

Gernsheim, Helmut. *The Rise of Photography, 1850–1880: The Age of Collodion*. London: Thames and Hudson, 1988.

Gleadle, Kathryn. *British Women in the Nineteenth Century*. Basingstoke, UK: Palgrave, 2001.

———. *The Early Feminists: Radical Unitarians and the Emergence of the Women's Rights Movement, 1831–51*. New York: St. Martin's Press, 1995.

*Godey's Lady's Book*. Review of *Songs of Seven*, by Jean Ingelow. January 1866, 94.

Golden, Catherine J., ed. *Book Illustrated: Text, Image, and Culture, 1770–1930*. New Castle, DE: Oak Knoll, 2000.

Goldman, Paul. *John Everett Millais: Illustrator and Narrator*. Aldershot, UK: Lund Humphries, 2004.

———. *Victorian Illustrated Books, 1850–1870*. London: British Museum Press, 1994.

———. *Victorian Illustration: The Pre-Raphaelites, the Idyllic School and the High Victorians*. Aldershot, UK: Scolar Press, 1996.

Graves, Charles L. *Life and Letters of Alexander Macmillan*. London: Macmillan, 1910.

Gray, Donald. "Macaulay's *Lays of Ancient Rome* and the Publication of Nineteenth-Century British Poetry." In *Victorian Literature and Society: Essays Presented to Richard D. Altick*, edited by James R. Kincaid and Albert J. Kuhn, 74–93. Athens: Ohio University Press, 1985.

Greenhalgh, Paul. "The Art and Industry of Mammon: International Exhibitions, 1851–1901." In *The Victorian Vision: Inventing New Britain*, edited by John M. Mackenzie, 265–79. London: V and A Publications, 2001.

Greenwell, Dora. "The Babes in the Wood: A Lover's Dream; by the Author of 'The Patience of Hope.'" Illustrated by J. D. Watson. *Good Words* 2 (1861): 120–21.

———. "My Life, and What Shall I Do with It?" *North British Review* 36, no. 71 (1862): 62–88.

Gregory, Gill. "Adelaide Procter: A Poetics of Reserve and Passion." In *Women's Poetry, Late Romantic to Late Victorian: Gender and Genre, 1830–1900*, edited by Isobel Armstrong and Virginia Blain, 355–72. Houndmills, UK: Macmillan, 1999.

———. *The Life and Work of Adelaide Procter: Poetry, Feminism and Fathers*. Aldershot, UK: Ashgate, 1998.

Groth, Helen. *Victorian Photography and Literary Nostalgia*. Oxford: Oxford University Press, 2003.

Haass, Sabine. "Victorian Poetry Anthologies: Their Role and Success in the Nineteenth-Century Book Market." *Publishing History* 17 (1985): 51–64.

Hagen, June Steffensen. *Tennyson and His Publishers*. London: Macmillan, 1979.

Hagstrum, Jean H. *The Sister Arts: The Tradition of Literary Pictorialism and English Poetry from Dryden to Gray*. Chicago: University of Chicago Press, 1987.

Hall, Samuel Carter, ed. *The Book of British Ballads*, vol. 1. 2 vols. London: Jeremiah How, 1842.

Hallam, Arthur Henry. "On Some of the Characteristics of Modern Poetry and on the Lyrical Poems of Alfred Tennyson." 1831. In *Broadview Anthology of Victorian Poetry and Poetic Theory*, edited by Thomas Collins and Vivienne J. Rundle, 1190–1205. Peterborough, ON: Broadview, 1999.

Hamerton, Philip. "General Exhibition of Water-Colour Drawings, Dudley Gallery." *Art Journal* 28 (1866): 71.

Hamilton, Susan. *Frances Power Cobbe and Victorian Feminism*. London: Palgrave Macmillan, 2006.

Hancher, Michael. *The Tenniel Illustrations to the "Alice" Books*. Columbus: Ohio State University Press, 1985.

Harris, Jack T. "The Pre-Raphaelites and the Moxon Tennyson." *Pre-Raphaelite Review* 3, no. 2 (1983): 26–37.

Harvey, John. *Victorian Novelists and Their Illustrators*. New York: New York University Press, 1971.

Helsinger, Elizabeth K. *Poetry and the Pre-Raphaelite Arts: Dante Gabriel Rossetti and William Morris*. New Haven, CT: Yale University Press, 2008.

Heywood, John. *A Peep at the Pictures; or, A Catalogue of the Principal Objects of Attraction in the Manchester Art Treasures Exhibition, with Biographical Notices of the Painters, Ancient and Modern, and a Ground Plan of the Building*. Manchester: John Heywood; London: W. Kent; Liverpool: W. Gilling, 1857.

Hibbert, Christopher. *The "Illustrated London News": Social History of Victorian Britain*. London: Angus and Robertson, 1975.

Hickok, Kathleen. *Representations of Women: Nineteenth-Century British Women's Poetry*. Westport, CT: Greenwood Press, 1984.

Hill, Marylu. "'Shadowing Sense at War with Soul': Julia Margaret Cameron's Photographic Illustrations of Tennyson's *Idylls of the King*." *Victorian Poetry* 40, no. 4 (2002): 445–62.

Hoagwood, Terence, and Kathryn Ledbetter. *Colour'd Shadows: Contexts in Publishing, Printing and Reading Nineteenth-Century British Women Writers*. London: Palgrave Macmillan, 2005.

Hodnett, Edward. *Five Centuries of English Book Illustration*. Aldershot, UK: Scolar Press, 1988.

———. *Image and Text: Studies in the Illustration of English Literature*. London: Scolar Press, 1982.

Hogarth, Paul. *Arthur Boyd Houghton*. London: Gordon Fraser, 1981.

Horkheimer, Max, and Theodor W. Adorno. "The Culture Industry: Enlightenment as Mass Deception." In *Media and Cultural Studies: Keyworks*, edited by Meenakshi Gigi Durham and Douglas M. Kellner, 41–72. Oxford, UK: Blackwell, 2006.

Houfe, Simon. *The Dictionary of British Book Illustrators and Caricaturists, 1800–1914, with Introductory Chapters on the Rise and Progress of the Art*. Woodbridge, UK: Antique Collectors' Club, 1978.

———. *Fin de Siècle: The Illustrators of the Nineties*. London: Barrie and Jenkins, 1992.

Houghton, Walter E., ed. *The Wellesley Index to Victorian Periodicals, 1824–1900*, vol. 1. Toronto: University of Toronto Press, 1966.

Housman, Laurence. *Arthur Boyd Houghton: A Selection from His Work in Black and White, Printed for the Most Part from Original Wood-Blocks*. London: Kegan Paul, Trench, and Trübner, 1896.

Houston, Natalie M. "Anthologies and the Making of the Canon." In *A Companion to Victorian Poetry*, edited by Alison Chapman, Richard Cronin, and Antony H. Harrison, 361–77. Oxford, UK: Blackwell, 2002.

———. "Newspaper Poems: Material Texts in the Public Sphere." *Victorian Studies* 50, no. 2 (2008): 233–42.

Hueffer, Ford M. *Ford Madox Brown: A Record of His Life and Work*. London: Longmans, Green, 1896.

Hughes, Arthur. "And I May Die but the Grass Will Grow." *Good Words* 12 (1871): 113.

———. "The Dial." *Good Words* 12 (1871): 183.

———. "Go, Little Letter, Apace, Apace." *Good Words* 12 (1871): 35.

Hughes, Linda K. "1870." In *A Companion to Victorian Literature and Culture*, edited by Herbert F. Tucker, 35–50. Oxford, UK: Blackwell, 1999.

———. "Inventing Poetry and Pictorialism in *Once a Week:* A Magazine of Visual Effects." In "Victorian Poetry and the Book Arts," edited by Lorraine Janzen Kooistra, special issue, *Victorian Poetry* 48, no. 1 (Spring 2010): 41–72.

———. "What the *Wellesley Index* Left Out: Why Poetry Matters to Periodical Studies." *Victorian Periodicals Review* 40, no. 2 (2007): 91–125.

Huish, Marcus B. *Birket Foster: His Life and Work*. London: Art Journal, 1890.

Humpherys, Anne. "*Enoch Arden*, The Fatal Return, and the Silence of Annie." *Victorian Poetry* 30, no. 3–4 (1992): 331–42.

Hunt, William Holman. *Pre-Raphaelitism and the Pre-Raphaelite Brotherhood*. 2nd ed. 2 vols. London: Chapman and Hall, 1913.

*Illustrated London News*. Illustrated Gift Books. January 10, 1857, 10.

———. Illustrated Books for Christmas. November 10, 1860, 434.

———. Current Literature. December 26, 1863, 663.

———. Christmas Books. December 21, 1864, 653.

———. Illustrated Books for Christmas. December 23, 1865, 608.

———. Illustrated Books for Christmas. January 6, 1866, 13.

———. Illustrated Gift-Books for Christmas. December 15, 1866, 582–83.

Ingelow, Jean. *Poems*. Illustrated. London: Longmans, Green, Reader and Dyer, 1867.

———. *Songs of Seven*. Illustrated. Boston: Roberts Brothers, 1866.

Jacobs, Arthur. *Arthur Sullivan: A Victorian Musician*. 2nd ed. Aldershot, UK: Scolar, 1992.

James, Philip. *English Book Illustration, 1800–1900*. London: King Penguin, 1947.

Jennings, Henry J. *Lord Tennyson, 1809–1892: A Biographical Sketch*. London: Chatto and Windus, 1892.

Johnston, Judith E. "Eliza Cook's *Journal* (1848–1854)." In *Dictionary of Nineteenth-Century Journalism*, edited by Laurel Brake and Marysa Demoor. Ghent, Belgium: Academic Press, 2009. Also available online through The Nineteenth Century Index, ProQuest LLC.

Joseph, Gerhard. "Commodifying Tennyson: The Historical Transformation of 'Brand Loyalty.'" *Victorian Poetry* 34, no. 2 (1996): 133–47.

———. *Tennyson and the Text: The Weaver's Shuttle*. Cambridge: Cambridge University Press, 1992.

King, Alice. "Adelaide Procter." *Argosy* 30 (1880): 149–53.

Klancher, Jon P. *The Making of English Reading Audiences, 1790–1832*. Madison: University of Wisconsin Press, 1987.

Kooistra, Lorraine Janzen. *Christina Rossetti and Illustration: A Publishing History*. Athens: Ohio University Press, 2002.

———. *"The Germ."* In *Dictionary of Nineteenth-Century Journalism*, edited by Laurel Brake and Marysa Demoor. Ghent, Belgium: Academic Press, 2009. Also available online through The Nineteenth Century Index, ProQuest LLC.

Lang, Andrew. "Miss Ingelow's Poems." *Longman's Magazine* (July 1898): 236–49. Available at *Periodicals Archive Online*, http://opao.chadwyck.com.innopac.lib.ryerson.ca.

Larcom, Lucy. "Adelaide Anne Procter's Poems." *Arthur's Home Magazine* (June 1866): 379–83.

———. "Jean Ingelow." *Arthur's Home Magazine* (February 1867): 98–101.

Law, Graham, and David Haldane Lawrence. "The *Weekly Dispatch*." In *Dictionary of Nineteenth-Century Journalism*, edited by Laurel Brake and Marysa Demoor. Ghent, Belgium: Academic Press, 2009. Also available online through The Nineteenth Century Index, ProQuest LLC.

Lawrence, Arthur. *Sir Arthur Sullivan: Life Story, Letters, and Reminiscences (1899)*. New York: Duffield, 1907.

Layard, George Somes. *Tennyson and His Pre-Raphaelite Illustrators: A Book about a Book*. London: Elliot Stock, 1894.

L.D.P. "Adelaide A. Procter and Jean Ingelow." *Continental Monthly* (May 1864): 605–7.

Ledbetter, Kathryn. "Protesting Success: Tennyson's 'Indecent Exposure' in the Periodicals." *Victorian Poetry* 43, no. 1 (2005): 53–73.

———. *Tennyson and Victorian Periodicals: Commodities in Context*. Aldershot, UK: Ashgate, 2007.

Leighton, Mary Elizabeth, and Lisa Surridge. "The Plot Thickens: Toward a Narratological Analysis of Illustrated Serial Fiction in the 1860s." *Victorian Studies* 51, no. 1 (2009): 65–101.

Leith, Ian. *Delmotte's Crystal Palace: A Victorian Pleasure Dome Revealed*. Swindown: English Heritage, 2005.

Lewis, Frank. *Myles Birket Foster, 1825–1899*. Leigh-on-Sea, UK: Tithe House, 1973.

Life, Allan R. "The Art of Not 'Going Halfway': Rossetti's Illustration for 'the Maids of Elfen-Mere.'" *Victorian Poetry* 20, no. 3–4 (1982): 65–87.

Lightman, Bernard. *Victorian Popularizers of Science: Designing Nature for New Audiences*. Chicago: University of Chicago Press, 2007.

Lightman, Bernard, and Ann B. Shteir, ed. *Figuring It Out: Science, Gender, and Visual Culture*. Hanover, NH: University Press of New England, 2006.

*Living Age*. Review of *Home Thoughts and Home Scenes in Original Poems and Pictures*, December 24, 1864, 660–61.

———. "Some Women Poets." April 8, 1899, 123–33.

Lloyd, Amy. "*Good Words* (1860–1911)." In *Dictionary of Nineteenth-Century Journalism*, edited by Laurel Brake and Marysa Demoor. Ghent, Belgium: Academic Press, 2009. Also available online through The Nineteenth Century Index, ProQuest LLC.

Loeb, Lori Anne. *Consuming Angels: Advertising and Victorian Women*. New York: Oxford University Press, 1994.

Logan, Thad. *The Victorian Parlour: A Cultural Study*. Cambridge: Cambridge University Press, 2001.

*London Review and Weekly Journal of Politics, Literature, Art, and Society*. Christmas Books. 20 (November 17, 1860): 471–72.

Longfellow, Henry Wadsworth. *The Poetical Works of H. W. Longfellow*. Illustrated by John Gilbert; engraved by the Brothers Dalziel. London: George Routledge, 1856.

Lottes, Wolfgang. "*The Lady of Shalott:* Tennyson's Poem and Some Victorian Illustrations." In *Word and Visual Imagination: Studies in the Interaction of English Literature and the Visual Arts*, edited by Peter M. Daly, Karl Josef Höltgen, and Wolfgang Lottes, 269–302. Nurnberg: Universitaäts Bibliothek, 1988.

Lukitsh, Joanne. "Julia Margaret Cameron's Photographic Illustrations to Alfred Tennyson's *The Idylls of the King*." In *Arthurian Women: A Casebook*, edited by Thelma S. Fenster, 247–62. New York: Garland, 1996.

Macherey, Pierre. *A Theory of Literary Production*. Translated by Geoffrey Wall. London: Routledge and Kegan Paul, 1978.

Mackay, Charles, ed. *The Home Affections Pourtrayed by the Poets*. Illustrated. London: George Routledge, 1858.

———. *A Thousand and One Gems of English Poetry*. Illustrated. London: Routledge, 1867.

Macleod, Diane Sachko. *Art and the Victorian Middle Class: Money and the Making of Cultural Identity*. Cambridge: Cambridge University Press, 1996.

Maidment, Brian E. *Reading Popular Prints, 1790–1870*. 2nd ed. Manchester: Manchester University Press, 2001.

Maison, Margaret. "Queen Victoria's Favourite Poet." *Listener*, April 29, 1965, 636–37.

Markiewicz, Henryk. "*Ut Pictura Poesis* . . . A History of the Topos and the Problem." *New Literary History* 18, no. 3 (1987): 535–58.

Marsh, Jan. "'Hoping You Will Not Think Me Too Fastidious': Pre-Raphaelite Artists and the Moxon Tennyson." *Journal of Pre-Raphaelite and Aesthetic Studies* 2, no. 1 (1989): 11–17.

———. *Pre-Raphaelite Sisterhood*. London: Quartet Books, 1992.

Matthew, Russell. "Adelaide Procter." *Irish Monthly* 5 (1877): 691–704.

Maxwell, Richard, ed. *The Victorian Illustrated Book*. Charlottesville: University Press of Virginia, 2002.

Mazzeno, Laurence W. *Alfred Tennyson: The Critical Heritage*. New York: Camden House, 2004.

McGann, Jerome J. *Dante Gabriel Rossetti and the Game That Must Be Lost*. New Haven, CT: Yale University Press, 2000.

———. "Literature by Design since 1790." In "Victorian Poetry and the Book Arts," edited by Lorraine Janzen Kooistra, special issue, *Victorian Poetry* 48, no. 1 (2010): 11–40.

———. *The Textual Condition*. Princeton: Princeton University Press, 1991.

McInnis, Maurie. "Allegorizing on Their Own Hooks: The Book Illustrations of Dante Gabriel Rossetti and Arthur Hughes." In *Pocket Cathedrals: Pre-Raphaelite Book Illustration*, edited by Susan P. Casteras, 67–77. New Haven, CT: Yale Center for British Art, 1991.

McKendry, Virginia. "The *Illustrated London News* and the Invention of Tradition." *Victorian Periodicals Review* 27, no. 1 (1994): 1–24.

McKenzie, D. F. *Bibliography and the Sociology of Texts*. Cambridge: Cambridge University Press, 1999.

McLean, Ruari. *Victorian Book Design and Colour Printing*. 2nd ed. London: Faber and Faber, 1972.

Meredith, George. Belles Lettres and Art. *Westminster Review* 68 (October 1857): 585–604.

Merriam, Harold G. *Edward Moxon: Publisher of Poets*. New York: Columbia University Press, 1939.

Miles, Alfred H., ed. *The Poets and Poetry of the Century*, vol. 8. London: Hutchison, 1893.

Millais, John Everett. *The Life and Letters of Sir John Everett Millais*. Edited by John Guille Millais. 2 vols. London: Methuen, 1899.

Miller, J. Hillis. *Illustration*. Essays in Art and Culture. Cambridge: Harvard University Press, 1992.

Mitchell, Sally. *Daily Life in Victorian England*. 2nd ed. Westport, CT: Greenwood, 2009.

Mitchell, W. J. T. *Blake's Composite Art: A Study of the Illuminated Poetry*. Princeton: Princeton University Press, 1978.

———. *Picture Theory: Essays on Verbal and Visual Representation*. Chicago: University of Chicago Press, 1994.

———. *What Do Pictures Want? The Lives and Loves of Images*. Chicago: University of Chicago Press, 2005.

Moore, Tara. *Victorian Christmas in Print*. New York: Palgrave Macmillan, 2009.

Morris, Hazel. *Hand, Head and Heart: Samuel Carter Hall and the Art Journal*. Wilby, Norwich: Michael Russell, 2002.

Morris, William. *The Ideal Book: Three Essays on Books and Printing by William Morris*. Edited with introduction by Richard Mathews. Tampa: University of Tampa Press, 2007.

Moxon. *The Doré Gift Book of Illustrations to Tennyson's "Idylls of the King."* London: E. Moxon, 1878.

Muir, Percy. *English Children's Books, 1600–1900*. London: B. T. Batsford, 1954.

———. *Victorian Illustrated Books*. London: B. T. Batsford, 1971.

Mumby, Frank. *The House of Routledge, 1834–1934*. London: George Routledge and Sons, 1934.

National Portrait Gallery. *Daniel Maclise, 1806–1870*. London: National Portrait Gallery, 1972.

Nelson, Claudia. "Growing Up: Childhood." In *A Companion to Victorian Literature and Culture*, edited by Herbert F. Tucker, 69–81. Oxford, UK: Blackwell, 1999.

Nelson, Elizabeth. "Tennyson and the Ladies of Shalott." In *Ladies of Shalott: A Victorian Masterpiece and Its Contents*, exhibition by the Department of Art, Brown University, 4–16. Providence, RI: Department of Art, Brown University, 1985.

Nesbit, E. *A Pomander of Verse*. London: John Lane at the Bodley Head, 1895.

Nestor, Pauline A. "A New Departure in Women's Publishing: The *Englishwoman's Journal* and the *Victoria Magazine*." *Victorian Periodicals Review* 15, no. 3 (1982): 93–106.

*New York Times*. "Photographic Printing by Mechanical Agency." February 15, 1869.

Nissenbaum, Stephen. *The Battle for Christmas: A Cultural History of America's Most Cherished Holiday*. New York: Vintage Books, 1996.

Nodelman, Perry, ed. *Touchstones: Reflections on the Best in Children's Literature*. Vol. 3, *Picture Books*. West Lafayette, IN: Children's Literature Association, 1989.

Oliphant, Margaret. "A Merry Christmas!" *Blackwood's Edinburgh Magazine* 89 (January 1861): 106–14.

———. "Picture-Books." *Blackwood's Edinburgh Magazine* 81 (March 1857): 309–18.

Olsen, Victoria C. *From Life: Julia Margaret Cameron and Victorian Photography*. New York: Palgrave Macmillan, 2003.

Pater, Walter. *The Renaissance*. 1873. Introduction by Arthur Symons. New York: Modern Library, n.d.

Patten, Robert L. "Serial Illustration and Storytelling in *David Copperfield*." In *The Victorian Illustrated Book*, edited by Richard Maxwell, 91–128. Charlottesville: University Press of Virginia, 2002.

Peters, Maureen. *Jean Ingelow: Victorian Poetess*. Totowa, NJ: Rowman and Littlefield, 1972.

Peterson, Linda H. "Domestic and Idyllic." In *A Companion to Victorian Poetry*, edited by Alison Chapman, Richard Cronin, and Antony H. Harrison, 42–58. Oxford, UK: Blackwell, 2002.

Pope, Alexander. *The Rape of the Lock*. Illustrated by Aubrey Beardsley. London: Leonard Smithers, 1896.

Poulson, Christine. "Death and the Maiden: The Lady of Shalott and the Pre-Raphaelites." In *Re-Framing the Pre-Raphaelites*, edited by Ellen Harding, 173–94. Aldershot, UK: Scolar, 1996.

Prettejohn, Elizabeth. *The Art of the Pre-Raphaelites*. Princeton: Princeton University Press, 2000.

Procter, Adelaide Anne. *Legends and Lyrics*. Introduction by Charles Dickens. Illustrated. London: Bell and Daldy, 1866.

———. "True or False." Illustrated by Arthur Boyd Houghton. *Good Words* 3 (1862): 721–22.

Proust, Marcel. *Time Regained*. Translated by Andreas Mayor. London: Chatto and Windus, 1970.

Quizziana. "The Dentist's Arm-Chair: A Parody." *Lowell Offering* (December 1842): 64–65.

Ray, Gordon N. *The Illustrator and the Book in England from 1790 to 1914*. New York: Oxford University Press, 1976.

Reid, Forrest. *Illustrators of the Eighteen Sixties: An Illustrated Survey of the Work of 58 British Artists*. London: Faber and Faber, 1928. Reprint, New York: Dover, 1975.

Reynolds, Graham. Foreword to *The Brothers Dalziel: A Record of Fifty Years' Work in Conjunction with Many of the Most Distinguished Artists of the Period 1840–1890*. London: B. T. Batsford, 1978 [1901].

Reynolds, Jan. *Birket Foster*. London: B. T. Batsford, 1984.

*Reynolds's Miscellany of Romance, General Literature, Science, and Art*. "Lady Blessington, Miss Eliza Cook, and the Hon. Mrs. Norton." February 13, 1847, 233.

Ricks, Christopher. *Tennyson*. Masters of World Literature Series. New York: Collier Books, 1972.

———, ed. *Tennyson: A Selected Edition*. Berkeley: University of California Press, 1989.

R.M. "My Treasure." Illustrated by Arthur Boyd Houghton. *Good Words* 3 (1862): 503–4.

Roberts, Leonard. *Arthur Hughes: His Life and Works; A Catalogue Raisonné*. Introduction by Stephen Wildman. Woodbridge, UK: Antique Collectors' Club, 1997.

Robinson, Solveig C. "Of 'Haymakers' and 'City Artisans': The Chartist Poetics of Eliza Cook's Songs of Labor." *Victorian Poetry* 39, no. 2 (2001): 229–53.

Robson, Catherine. "Standing on the Burning Deck: Poetry, Performance, History." *PMLA* 120, no. 1 (2005): 148–62.

Rogers, Samuel. *Italy: A Poem*. Illustrated. London: Moxon, 1830.

———. *Poems*. Illustrated edition. 2 vols. London: Cadell and Moxon, 1834.

Rose, Andrea, ed. *"The Germ": The Literary Magazine of the Pre-Raphaelites*. Oxford, UK: Ashmolean Museum, 1992.

Rossetti, Christina. *The Complete Poems of Christina Rossetti*. Edited by R. W. Crump. 3 vols. Baton Rouge: Louisiana State University Press, 1979–90.

———. *Goblin Market*. Illustrated by Laurence Housman. London: Macmillan, 1893.

———. *Goblin Market and Other Poems*. Illustrated by Dante Gabriel Rossetti. London: Macmillan, 1862.

———. *The Prince's Progress and Other Poems*. Illustrated by Dante Gabriel Rossetti. London: Macmillan, 1866.

———. *Sing-Song: A Nursery Rhyme Book*. 1872. Illustrated by Arthur Hughes. New York: Dover, 1968.

Rossetti, Dante Gabriel. *The Collected Works of Dante Gabriel Rossetti*. Edited by William Michael Rossetti. London: Ellis, 1886.

———. *The Correspondence of Dante Gabriel Rossetti*. Edited by William E. Fredeman. 8 vols. Woodbridge, Suffolk: D. S. Brewer, 2002.

*Round Table*. December 16, 1865, 242–43.

———. Review of *Legends and Lyrics*, by Adelaide Anne Procter. December 30, 1865, 269.

Routledge Toy Books. *Goody Two Shoes' Picture Book*. Illustrated by Walter Crane. London: Routledge, 1875.

———. *The Marquis of Carabas's Picture Book*. Illustrated by Walter Crane. London: Routledge, 1875.

Ruskin, John. *Ariadne Florentina: Six Lectures on Wood and Metal Engraving*. 1872. London: George Allen, 1910.

———. "The Cestus of Aglaia (1865, 1866)." In *The Works of John Ruskin*, vol. 19, edited by E. T. Cook and Alexander Wedderburn, 41–159. Library Edition. London: George Allen, 1905.

———. *The Elements of Drawing*. London: Smith, Elder, and Co., 1857. Introduction by Lawrence Campbell. Unabridged reprint, New York: Dover, 1971.

———. "Time and Tide, by Weare and Tyne: Twenty-Five Letters to a Working Man of Sunderland on the Laws of Work." In *The Works of John Ruskin*, vol. 17, edited by E. T. Cook and Alexander Wedderburn, 294–482. London: George Allen, 1905.

Russell, Matthew. "Adelaide Procter." *Irish Monthly* 5 (1877): 691–704.

Sampson Low. *Poems and Pictures: A Collection of Ballads, Songs, and Other Poems, Illustrated by English Artists*. New edition. London: Sampson Low, 1860.

*Saturday Review*. Books for Presents. December 6, 1856, 714–15.

———. Christmas Books and Christmas Boxes. December 19, 1857, 557–58.

———. Christmas Books. December 18, 1858, 613–14.

———. Christmas Books. December 17, 1859, 744–45.

———. Christmas Books—Second Notice. December 31, 1859, 817–18.

———. Christmas Books—I. December 1, 1860, 701–2.

———. Christmas Books. December 7, 1861, 590–91.

———. Christmas Books. December 13, 1862, 721–23.

———. Christmas Books, No. I. December 5, 1863, 738–39.

———. Christmas Books, No. II. December 12, 1863, 766–67.
———. Christmas Books and Gift Books, No. 1. December 2, 1865, 711–12.
———. Christmas Books and Gift-Books, No. 2. December 16, 1865, 765–66.
———. Christmas Books—No. I. November 24, 1866, 653–54.
———. Christmas Books—No. II. December 1, 1866, 684.
———. Christmas Books—No. III. December 8, 1866, 716–17.
———. Christmas Books—No. IV. December 15, 1866, 743–44.
———. Christmas Books—I. December 3, 1870, 726–27.
———. Christmas Books IV. December 24, 1870, 813–14.
———. Christmas Books III. December 12, 1874, 776–78.
———. Review of the *Illustrated Edition of Tennyson* (London: Moxon, 1857). June 27, 1857, 601–2.

Schroeder, Janice. "'Better Arguments': *The English Woman's Journal* and the Game of Public Opinion." *Victorian Periodicals Review* 35, no. 3 (2002): 243–71.

Scott, P. G. *Tennyson's "Enoch Arden": A Victorian Best-Seller.* Lincoln: Tennyson Society, 1970.

Shattock, Joanne, ed. *The Oxford Guide to British Women Writers.* Oxford: Oxford University Press, 1994.

Shaw, W. David. *Alfred Lord Tennyson: The Poet in the Age of Theory.* Twayne's English Authors Series. New York: Twayne, 1996.

Shaylor, Joseph. *The Fascination of Books, with Other Papers on Books and Bookselling.* New York: G. P. Putnam, 1912.

*Shilling Magazine.* "Three Illustrations to 'Enoch Arden' by Mr. Arthur Hughes." 8 (1865): 434–36.

Simmons, F. W. "The Dial." *Good Words* 12 (1871): 183–84.

Sinnema, Peter W. *Dynamics of the Pictured Page: Representing the Nation in the "Illustrated London News."* Aldershot, UK: Ashgate, 1998.

Skelton, Sir John. "Jean Ingelow." *Times* (London), July 21, 1897, 8.

Skilton, David. "The Centrality of Literary Illustration in Victorian Visual Culture: The Example of Millais and Trollope from 1860 to 1864." *Journal of Illustration Studies* 1 (December 2007). http://www.jois.cardiff.ac.uk/articles.php?article=30.

———. "The Relation between Illustration and Text in the Victorian Novel." In *Word and Visual Imagination: Studies in the Interaction of English Literature and the Visual Arts,* edited by Karl Josef Höltgen and Peter M. Daly, 303–25. Nurnberg: University of Nurnberg, 1988.

Smith, Johanna M. "Textual Encounters in *Eliza Cook's Journal:* Class, Gender, and Sexuality." In *Encounters in the Victorian Press: Editors, Authors, Readers,* edited by Laurel Brake and Julie F. Codell, 50–65. Houndmills, UK: Palgrave Macmillan, 2005.

Smith, Tennyson Longfellow. *Poems Inspired by Certain Pictures at the Art Treasures Exhibition, Manchester.* Manchester: unknown publisher, [1857].

Spinozzi, Paola. "Interarts and Illustration: Some Historical Antecedents, Theoretical Issues, and Methodological Orientations." *Journal of Illustration Studies* 1 (December 2007). http://www.jois.cf.ac.uk/articles.php?article=43.

Srebrnik, Patricia Thomas. *Alexander Strahan: Victorian Publisher.* Ann Arbor: University of Michigan Press, 1986.

St. Clair, William. *The Reading Nation in the Victorian Period.* Cambridge: Cambridge University Press, 2007.

Stein, Richard L. "The Pre-Raphaelite Tennyson." *Victorian Studies* 24, no. 3 (Spring 1981): 278–301.

Stewart, Garrett. *The Look of Reading: Book, Painting, Text*. Chicago: University of Chicago Press, 2006.

Stone, Marjorie. "Genre Subversion and Gender Inversion: *The Princess* and *Aurora Leigh*." *Victorian Poetry* 25, no. 2 (1987): 101–27.

Strachey, Lytton. *Eminent Victorians*. 1918. Reprint, San Diego, CA: Harvest/HBJ, n.d.

Stuart-Wortley, Mrs. Charles. "Millais' Love of Music, by His Daughter." In *The Life and Letters of Sir John Everett Millais*, edited by John Guille Millais, 2:417–23. New York: Frederick A. Stokes, 1899.

Sullivan, Herbert, and Newman Flower. *Sir Arthur Sullivan: His Life, Letters and Diaries*. New York: George H. Doran, 1927.

Suriano, Gregory R. *The British Pre-Raphaelite Illustrators: A History of Their Published Prints*. New Castle, DE: Oak Knoll Press, 2005.

Sutherland, John, ed. *Stanford Companion to Victorian Fiction*. Stanford: Stanford University Press, 1990.

Taylor, John Russell. *The Art Nouveau Book in Britain*. London: Methuen, 1966.

Taylor, Tom. Preface to *Birket Foster's Pictures of English Landscape, with Picture in Words by Tom Taylor*. London: Routledge, 1862.

Tennyson, Alfred. *Dora: A Poem*. Illustrated by Mrs. Paulet Mildmay. London: Vernon, 1856.

———. *Enoch Arden*. Illustrated by Arthur Hughes. London: Edward Moxon, 1866.

———. *Idylls of the King*. Illustrated by Amy Butts. London: Day and Son, 1862.

———. *Idylls of the King*. Illustrated by Gustave Doré. London: Moxon, 1866–68.

———. *The Lady of Shalott*. Illustrated by "A Lady." London: Kent, 1859.

———. *The Letters of Alfred Tennyson*. Edited by Cecil Y. Lang and Edgar F. Shannon. 3 vols. Cambridge, MA: Belknap Press (vols. 1 and 2); Oxford, UK: Clarendon Press (vol. 3), 1981–90.

———. *Mariana*. Illustrated by Mary Montgomerie Lamb. London: Worthing, 1863.

———. *Maud, a Monodrama*. London: Kelmscott Press, 1893.

———. *The May Queen*. Illustrated by E.V.B. [Eleanor Vere Boyle]. London: Sampson Low, 1861.

———. *The May Queen*. Illuminated by Mrs. W. H. Hartley. London: Day and Son, 1861.

———. *The May Queen*. Illuminated by L. Summerbell. London: George Berridge, 1870.

———. *The Miller's Daughter*. Illustrated. London: H. Bohn, 1857.

———. *The Miller's Daughter*. Illustrated by A. L. Bond. London: W. Kent, 1867.

———. "The Mist and the Rain, the Mist and the Rain." *Good Words* 12 (1871): 113–15.

———. *Poems*. 2 vols. 5th ed. London: Moxon, 1848.

———. *Poems*. Illustrated. 1857. 2nd ed. London: Moxon, 1859.

———. *Poems, Chiefly Lyrical*. London: Moxon, 1830.

———. "The Poet's Song." In *Three Gems in One Setting*. Illustrated by Anne Lydia Bond. London: Kent, 1860.

———. *The Princess*. Illustrated. London: Dickinson, 1850.

———. *The Princess: A Medley*. 1860. Illustrated by Daniel Maclise. London: Edward Moxon, 1866.

———. *Some Poems of Alfred Lord Tennyson*. Preface by Joseph Pennell (Treating of the Illustrations of the Sixties); introduction by W. Holman Hunt. London: Freemantle, 1901.

———. *Tennyson: A Selected Edition*. Edited by Christopher Ricks. Berkeley: University of California Press, 1989.

———. *A Welcome to Princess Alexandra*. Illuminated by Owen Jones. London: Day and Son, 1863.

———. "Where Is Another Sweet as My Sweet?" *Good Words* 12 (1871): 32–33.

———. "The Window; or, The Song [*sic*] of the Wrens." In *The Poems of Tennyson*, edited by Christopher Ricks, 2:697–704. 2nd ed. New York: Longman, 1987.

———. *The Window; or, The Songs of the Wrens*. Music by Arthur Sullivan. London: Strahan, 1871.

———. *The Works of Alfred Tennyson*. Engravings after Julia Margaret Cameron. Cabinet Edition. 10 vols. London: H. S. King, 1874–75.

Tennyson, Emily. *Lady Tennyson's Journal*. Edited by James O. Hoge. Charlottesville: University Press of Virginia, 1981.

———. *The Letters of Emily Lady Tennyson*. Edited by James O. Hoge. University Park: Pennsylvania State University Press, 1974.

Tennyson, Hallam. *Alfred, Lord Tennyson: A Memoir by His Son*. 2 vols. London: Macmillan, 1897.

Thomas, Julia, ed. *The Database of Mid-Victorian Wood-Engraved Illustration*. http://www.dmvi.cf.ac.uk.

———. *Pictorial Victorians: The Inscription of Values in Word and Image*. Athens: Ohio University Press, 2004.

———. "Reflections on Illustration: *The Database of Mid-Victorian Wood-Engraved Illustration (DMVI)*." *Journal of Illustration Studies* 1 (December 2007). http://www.jois.cardiff.ac.uk/articles.php?article=37.

Thomas, Sophie. *Romanticism and Visuality: Fragments, History, Spectacle*. New York: Routledge, 2008.

*Tinsley's Magazine*. "Criticisms on Contemporaries: The Rossettis—Part II." 5 (1869): 142–51.

Tucker, Herbert F. "Literal Illustration in Victorian Print." In *The Victorian Illustrated Book*, edited by Richard Maxwell, 163–208. Charlottesville: University Press of Virginia, 2002.

———. *Tennyson and the Doom of Romanticism*. Cambridge, MA: Harvard University Press, 1988.

*Valley Farmer* (St. Louis). "Jean Ingelow." August 1864, 252–53.

*Varley and Robinson's Guide for the Stranger in Manchester: Art Treasures' Exhibition*. Manchester, UK: T. Digham, 1857.

Vaughan, William. "Incongruous Disciples: The Pre-Raphaelites and the Moxon Tennyson." In *Imagination on a Long Rein: English Literature Illustrated*, edited by Joachim Möller, 148–60. Marburg, Germany: Jonas, 1988.

Veblen, Thorstein. *Theory of the Leisure Class*. Reprint of 1899 Macmillan edition, New York: Kelley, 1965.

Waagen, Dr. *A Walk through the Art-Treasures Exhibition at Manchester, under the Guidance of Dr. Waagen, Author of "Treasures of Art in Great Britain," a Companion to the Official Catalogue*. London: John Murray and W. H. Smith, 1857.

Wakeman, Geoffrey. *Victorian Book Illustrations: The Technical Revolution*. Newton Abbot, Devon: David and Charles, 1973.

Watts, Bob. "'Slow Prudence': Tennyson's Taming of the Working Class." *Victorian Poetry* 37, no. 4 (1999): 493–505.

Weedon, Alexis. *Victorian Publishing: The Economics of Book Production for a Mass Market, 1836–1916*. Aldershot, UK: Ashgate, 2003.

*Westminster Review*. Belles-Lettres. 83 (January 1865): 320–38.

White, Gleeson. *English Illustration: "The Sixties": 1855–1870*. 1897. Reprint, Bath: Kingsmead Reprints, 1970.

Wilde, Oscar. *The Sphinx*. Illustrated by Charles Ricketts. London: Elkin Mathews and John Lane, 1894.

Williams, Raymond. *Culture and Society, 1780–1950*. Harmondsworth, UK: Penguin, 1963.

———. *Keywords: A Vocabulary of Culture and Society*. London: Fontana, 1976.

Willmott, Robert Aris, ed. *English Sacred Poetry of the Sixteenth, Seventeenth, Eighteenth, and Nineteenth Centuries*. Dalziel Fine Art Gift Book. London: Routledge, 1862.

———. *The Poets of the Nineteenth Century, Illustrated with One Hundred Engravings Drawn by Eminent Artists, and Engraved by the Brothers Dalziel*. Dalziel Fine Art Gift Book. 3rd ed. London: Routledge, 1858.

Wise, J. R. Belles Lettres. *Westminster Review* 87 (1867): 257–74.

———. *A Bibliography of the Writings of Alfred, Lord Tennyson*. 1908. 2 vols. Facsimile, London: Dawsons of Pall Mall, 1967.

*Woman's Herald*. "'An Hour with Jean Ingelow': At the Chaffe Noble School of Expression." 125 (March 14, 1891): 323.

Wood, Gillen D'Arcy. *The Shock of the Real: Romanticism and Visual Culture, 1760–1860*. New York: Palgrave, 2001.

Woolner, Amy. *Thomas Woolner, R. A., Sculptor and Poet: His Life in Letters*. New York: E. P. Dutton, 1917.

Young, Percy M. *Sir Arthur Sullivan*. London: J. M. Dent, 1971.

*Zion's Herald and Wesleyan Journal*. Review of *Songs of Seven*, by Jean Ingelow. December 20, 1865, 204.

# Index

The letter *n* following a page number refers to a note; the letter *f* following a page number refers to a figure.